RICHARD HALLIBURTON

Richard Halliburton.

RICHARD HALLIBURTON

His Story of His Life's Adventure

*As told in Letters
to his Mother and Father*

THE BOBBS-MERRILL COMPANY
Publishers
INDIANAPOLIS   *NEW YORK*

Copyright, 1940, by The Bobbs-Merrill Company

Printed in the United States of America

FIRST EDITION

PRINTED AND BOUND BY
BRAUNWORTH & CO., INC.
BUILDERS OF BOOKS
BRIDGEPORT, CONN.

CONTENTS

LIST OF ILLUSTRATIONS

vii

PUBLISHER'S NOTE

DURING the last twenty-two of his nearly forty years, Richard Halliburton wrote over a thousand letters to his mother and father. If they were printed in full they would fill several volumes the size of this. Their very number evidences an extraordinary devotion, and each individual letter enforces this with words of affection and understanding.

His travels carried him over much of the world. He was almost constantly in motion. Wherever he might be, he was intent to tell, as soon as possible, all that he had done and seen, and to pour out his impressions, his thoughts, his plans, to the two persons whom he regarded as partners in all his adventures, collaborators in all he wrote. "I try to tell you everything I do, almost to what I have for breakfast every morning."

So complete, so intimate, so revealing are they that, in a unique sense, these letters constitute an autobiography.

Richard Halliburton sailed from Hongkong on March 5, 1939, in the *Sea Dragon*. The passenger liner *President Coolidge* received a radio message on March twenty-fourth, giving the boat's position and reporting a storm. Nothing more was heard. The long, slow weeks dragged by, and at last hope held against hope had to be abandoned when the Navy Department reported that the U.S.S. *Astoria* with her four naval planes had searched a territory, starting from the craft's last radioed position, of 152,000 square miles. No trace of the *Sea Dragon* was found. Sometime later the author's father and mother were persuaded to consider the publication of the letters. The selection was edited and arranged by the publishers as a chronological narrative. The principle followed in choice and arrangement was to present those things that would disclose the man and tell with unity and continuity the story of Richard Halliburton's life. All else, as far as might be feasible, all that might interfere with progressive development and totality of effect, would be excluded.

For the reader's ease in going forward through a career of action and adventure, the words of salutation and conclusion are generally omitted, and just the date and place of writing given in bracketed italics. It is to be understood that these letters are addressed to both parents. On the rare occasions when Richard wrote to one and not to both, the salutation is printed. Included as belonging to the story are two letters to Princeton roommates, a letter or two to his publishers and his syndicated articles about the *Sea Dragon,* which he thought of as letters home.

Sometimes, especially when he was on lecture tours, the details of his movements, the schedules of arrival and departure were of interest only at the moment. In such cases, a sequence of letters is summarized, as far as possible in his own words, with only enough of these details as are needed to convey a sense of his activity. The repetitions inevitable to letters are omitted. Omitted also, because of the rigid limitations of space, are references to various relatives and to many, many acquaintances. Those who are not mentioned will understand that this implies no lack of his regard.

At times only a sentence or two may be taken from a letter; but the reader is to realize that the complete original is imbued with the same heartiness of filial love as when a letter is printed in full, and this is as true of letters at the end of his life as when he first left home for college.

The letters were written with no thought of publication, all with a pen, in a characteristic swift, terse style, too fast for concern about paragraphing, the words cascading over one another, and many of them abbreviated. All numbers were written as numerals. While the effect of this style is preserved, some concessions (for the reader's convenience) have been made to the conventions of the printed page.

Though his name is already a legend of adventure, it would be a great mistake to think of Richard Halliburton merely as a man of action. His life, as these pages disclose, was singularly the embodiment of a philosophy and a purpose that took form early and steadily controlled and determined his remarkable industry.

His cultivation, refinement, fastidiousness and his interest in travel are easily accounted for in his heredity and boyhood environment. It may be that his fervent imagination, his wild desire for adventure, his thirst for the romantic and the remote, are a long throwback to Scottish ancestors. For him all experience was an arch wherethrough gleamed an untraveled world whose margin faded forever when he moved. Some Samarkand always lay over the horizon. He longed always to see, and to make others see, the far-flung marvels of nature and man's spectacular achievements.

He was born at the advent of the new century. His manhood spanned the brief interval between the two World Wars. He is a spokesman for the youth of a generation isolated by these wars. In his own story are preserved the beauty that inspired his appreciation, always superlative and always genuine; the illusions he proudly cherished; the history that to him was not dead past but filled with eternal heroes. The map over which he wove the web of his travels is rapidly changing. Armed forces may destroy much that he found so various, so beautiful, so new. But romance and rapture, the capacity for wonder and admiration will remain wherever there are young unregimented hearts. To such hearts and for them Richard Halliburton will continue to speak.

CHAPTER I

A BOY'S WORLD

TOWARD the close of the nineteenth century, a young man and a young woman were married at the Methodist Church in Brownsville, Tennessee, a quiet, pastoral community. Wesley Halliburton came from a Scotch ancestry who, down the line, had loved the soil and lived close to it. He had been graduated at Vanderbilt University as a civil engineer in 1891, but soon chafed under the confinement of office work with a bridge company in Pennsylvania, preferring the activities of an outdoor life. Nelle Nance traced her ancestry back to French Huguenots on her father's side, and to Scotch soldiers and adventurers on her mother's. She was a graduate of the Cincinnati College of Music and was engaged in teaching music.

In the first half of the first month of the new century—January ninth to be exact—a son was born to them, whom after much debate they named Richard.

When he was still a very little boy, they moved to Memphis, Tennessee, and they have lived there ever since. A friend of the family, Mary G. Hutchison, mistress of a day school, early developed an unusual interest in Richard. He had no living grandparents. She did not think that was quite fair and declared that she meant to play the role of grandmother to him. She is the "Ammudder" who appears throughout his letters.

Another son was born three years after Richard. Strong and active, Wesley, Jr., had every prospect in life that his elder brother enjoyed.

Richard was prepared to enter the Memphis University School for Boys. He made a good record in scholastic work but took little interest in sports. He preferred romping with his dog "Teddy" and riding his pony "Roxy" through all the suburbs of Memphis, to baseball or football or track. Wesley, Jr., on the other hand, carried his mitt buckled to his belt and was fond of outdoor games.

In the summer time, Richard would visit the Thomas twins, Woodleif and Atha, in Brownsville.

1

Brownsville, Tenn.—July 18, 1912

My darling Mudder:—

I guess you think me negligant for not writing sooner but I haven't written to anyone. My two weeks are almost gone and I feel as though I had just arrived, time has flown so. The Twins and I are working hard to get enough money for them to come to Memphis on. We now have $10 but want $14. We sell apples and iron and milk. We get up early every morning and gather apples and then sell them. The other day a hornet bit me, and I thought it was a snake. We sleep in a tent in the back yard. We have electric lights and dogs in the tent. We have gone to few parties and have had so much to do. Although it is severe work I am having a better and more enjoyable time than I have had privious summers, when we had nothing to do better than read. Before we boared each other when together for too long a time, but this summer we enjoy each other's company more and more as our work increases and my visit lengthens.

We went out to Aunt Minnie's yesterday to see Wesley and spent the day. This morning we got up early and cooked our breakfast out in the woods.

There are a lot more things I wanted to tell you which I have forgotten just now, one of the things I just remembered is that Sunday we went to a "Sanctified Niger Baptism." We nearly split our sides laughing. One woman went into histerics.
                                                                  Sonny.

Later that summer, the family went to Tate Springs in East Tennessee for a vacation. From there he writes Miss Hutchison:

Aug. 13, 1912

Dear Ammudder:—

If you only knew how bad I want to see you! And just to think, I won't see you for another six weeks. I will write to you often and you, of course, will write to me and that will patch things up.

My sore throat is gone and I'm better than I've been since last year. I'm learning to play real golf. It's splendid all except the balls which are a great bother—because you loose them and spend three-fourths of your time hunting for them—I lost three this afternoon and they were each a 75c ball—only I bought the three for 25 cents. My first

Fifty miles north of Memphis is Brownsville, Tennessee, where, on January 9, 1900, Richard was born in an old red-brick house.

Richard was five years old and his younger brother Wesley two when this picture was taken with their mother.

experience at golf was simply hitting the ball and then looking for it. I play a great deal of tennis and enjoy that most of all. Two other boys and I took a six mile tramp through the mountains and got lost (that is why it was six miles). Immediatly after we got back we played half a dozen games of box-ball. We then went around the golf course two times. I then ate my dinner and immediatly after went around two more times (each round being a mile). We stopped to watch a fox chase and set out like little fools and tried to keep up with the hounds—after running a mile we come back home and played four sets of tennis until it got so dark we couldn't see the ball. We came in just in time to dress and get my supper, and now I will dance until 11 o'clock. Do you suppose that is enough exersise for one day? My program is on that order—and is what is making me feel so good.

Before we came here and were at "Sister's," Daddy and I had some very long walks and saw the whole country. We generally made an all day trip of it. One day we walked 25 miles, and got dinner at some mountaineer's house way up in the big mountains. It was fun.

We are all very comfortable. Mother and Wes are well and happy and I want you to be the same way.

Lovingly,

Sonny.

"Sister" in this letter was his Aunt Susie. Later he refers to her as "Auntie" and to her daughter Hafford (who married Dr. D. D. Stetson in New York) as "Haff."

The following year the family again went to Tate Springs for two weeks and then to Asheville for a month that offered unlimited adventures to the small boy.

Asheville, N. C.
Battery Park Hotel
Thursday, Aug. 21, 1913

Dear Ammudder:—

I am about to freeze to death—how are you in N. Y.? Ashville is as cold as ice.

We left Tate Sunday morning and oh I did hate to leave. Daddy and I fought and scrapped against leaving but Mother would come up here. I was having a grand time and would have been satisfied to have stayed there the rest of the summer.

The trip from Morristown to Ashville is simply marvalous. The track runs along the French Broad river all the way and the scenery was the best I have seen yet. We also had ice-cream on the train.

This hotel is perfectly enormous but very old. The grounds are perfectly beautiful but the building is very ugly. It is situated up on a hill right in the middle of town. This hotel has about 750 guests and there is not a single boy my size. I suppose boys my age are a rarity. I think I will go to a museum. Tuesday we had a long drive out through "Biltmore," Vandibuilts beautiful summer home. There are about 20 square miles of the most perfect and beautiful park I have ever seen.

Wednesday, Daddy and I joined the Ashville Country Club in order to play golf. Wed. evening we went to Grove Park Inn for dinner—the finest hotel resort in the world. It is simply wonderful. I can't describe it as I can't express it. It is simply a wonderful, beautiful building. Daddy and I play two rounds of golf every morning.

I found a little girl—Cornelia McMurry—over here who had danced with me at Tate and who had preceded us. She and I are the only ones in the hotel who know how to do the Hesatation Walse so we simply delight in showing off. My little pardner went home today so all I have to dance with is grown women. Wes and I are buisy so we are all having a good time. I want to go home for one day only—just to see Teddy.

Think about me because I think about you so, so much. I love you all the time and nothing, *nothing* shall ever stop it. Your own little boy

Sonny.

The active summer season waned and, with it, his spirits and his spelling.

Asheville, N. C.—Sept. 6, 1913

Dear Ammudder:—

I suppose you are at home now and I realy bet you were glad to get there. Daddy left Thursday. We carried on like he was dying and not only leaving. I am awful lonely without him. Yesterday I simply had to do something so I got out and started walking all by myself. It was 6:30 P.M. I got started and went clear to the top of Sun-set mountain about four miles. I took my time so by the time I got to the top it was near 8:00 o'clock and all I could see of Asheville was the thousands of lights. It was a beautiful sight, if it had ended there, but to think that I had to climb down that mountain in the dark wasn't very appitizying. I came down the short way—by a steep mountain trail. I ran down all the way and my feet all doubled down in the toe of my shoes. So when I got back to the hotel, at 9:00 all the skin was off my toes and I couldn't dance—it nearly killed me.

I have been takeing calamel for two days and my stomach is all off. Please excuse the specymine of brillant spelling, but it is only an example of how I feel. Daddy stopped at Chattoggaanna—you know, the place where Lookout mountain is. I feel to bad to try right hard to spell it.

Now that the vacation is about over, I want to get back to school awful bad—MAYBE! I want to get back home, but I would as soon as go without two meals as to get back to geomatry and Cicero.

I can't get enthusaskestic over this letter so will not boar you any more. Heaps of love.

Sonny.

There is a gap in the letters till August, 1915. While Richard continued at school, he began taking violin lessons and enjoyed them greatly. In January, 1915, because he had developed a fast beating heart, he was removed from school and put to bed. In April his mother took him to Battle Creek, Michigan, to be under the care of the Sanitarium doctors. There he met a Mr. Johnson from St. Paul, who became so attached to the lad that he invited him to be his guest on a camp hunt in the "big woods" of Wisconsin.

Teal Lake Forest Home,
Hayward, Wisconsin—Wednesday, Aug., 1915

Dear Dad:—

We are leaving today for home. The trip here has been somewhat of a disappointment to me. The country and woods are not attractive as I expected and the mosquitoes spoil what ever one tries to do. However, I am very glad I had this chance of seeing this country. Day before yesterday we had a trip up the river, and after supper Mr. J. and I paddled down again in search of deer. We saw five in one place and he shot one but it escaped into the swamp. As we were 40 miles from a railroad it was quite wild so, inside of one mile on the river, we saw seven deer, six beaver, six or eight muskrats, an otter, one black bear, about twenty porcupines and a flock of wild ducks. Just off the bank we could hear the wild cats screaming and the wolves howling. As soon as I get back I shall write you a letter about school, etc., but haven't time now.

St. Paul—Saturday, Aug. 1915

Dear Dad:—

We came all the way home on Thursday. It was one of the most pleasant days I ever spent. The country after leaving the "pine forest" was farm land, growing the most wonderful crops I ever saw. The farmers were all haying and every field was busy with men and mowers. We averaged 24 miles per hour the whole trip. This doesn't sound so extraordinary, but to *average* that in a touring car is some going. Just to give our ride a final touch the moon came up and we rode 50 miles in the moonlight. I'm awful glad to get back—I had a good time up there, but ten times better time here. This lake is much more beautiful than anything we saw—I'm not so crazy about being slouchy. Still the fact that the place was so very wild made the experience worth while.

Mrs. Johnson is very lovely to me. She sings and plays and dances. They have everything to make life pleasant—the lake is the greatest factor. Mr. J. and I go bathing—notice I said *bathing* not *swimming*—twice a day, before breakfast and before supper. I take about a dozen strokes and get out. I realize how strenuous dancing can be. During the evening I never dance more than half the dances— always skipping one or two. I watch my heart—it accelerates but very little—some, of course. Does that sound as if I "disregarded my physical affliction and put pleasure first"? I can see a big change in my heart now and a year ago. It never says "Be careful I am pounding myself to pieces." It's because I don't give it a chance.

Now about school. I have not been idle over this subject at the

San. I have talked to boys from Culver and Lawrenceville. The L. boys love their school. I will be near New York surrounded by friends. I have my heart set on Princeton—50 L. boys go into Princeton every year. About Worcester or Phillips Academy I know very little—they are not Princeton prep schools. It's 3:00 A.M. so I better go to bed—good night—

R.

Lawrenceville won over Culver Military Academy and with it also, of course, Princeton. For the year 1916-1917 Richard was elected editor-in-chief of the *Lawrence* board, publishers of the school paper. During the year of his editorship the *Lawrence* grew to be recognized, not only by the school faculty, but even by the Board of Trustees, as a vital and useful factor in school life. In June, 1917, he was selected to write the words and music for the class Ode, sung on graduation day:

"Great builder of God-fearing men,
  Great advocate of noble life,
We leave thee now, true sons to be
  Throughout this time of strife;
To fight the wrong, the right to free,
  Trust us till we come back to thee;
Lawrenceville, Lawrenceville,
  Trust us till we come back to thee.

"Restraining gates are opened wide,
  Ten thousand paths lead from this door,
God made us men to face the world,
  Whatever lies before.
If fight we must beyond the sea,
  Trust us till we come back to thee;
America, America,
  Trust us till we come back to thee."

It was at Lawrenceville that Richard met Irvine O. Hockaday ("Mike"), Edward L. Keyes, III ("Larry"), John Henry Leh ("Heinie"), James Penfield Seiberling ("Shorty") and Channing Sweet ("Chan"), who are mentioned frequently in his letters.

As Richard passed on to Princeton, Wesley, Jr., followed him into Lawrenceville from the same Memphis University School for Boys. They were happy to be only six miles apart. That November Wesley developed heart trouble and he was brought back home, to live less than five weeks. Richard was back for the Christmas holidays and was at Wesley's bedside when he died. The following letter was the first he wrote after he returned to Princeton. Later ones, until October, 1918, are missing.

Princeton—January 9, 1918

Dear Mother:—

I've thought of nothing else but my last week at home. I try to think of something else, but it's no use. I've tried to read, but I forget to read. Esther [Thompson] seemed heartbroken when I told her about Wes and we talked of little else, but seeing her helped a lot. She is so bright and cheerful, I could not stay sad long with her. She is without doubt the prettiest girl I ever saw.

I know just how lonesome and sad you are—I know it is much worse now than before I left. I never in my life hated absence from home as I do now. Someway the longer time elapses from New Year's dawn, the more terrible and unjust it seems. I know I did not comprehend that Wesley was *gone, actually,* but the more I think about it the more realistic it grows, and I, too, have that "sinking" feeling. But tomorrow, as you say, I can get to work and will have to think of other things, while you will have only reminders and recollections. We feel as if we could never smile again, but we must—we owe it to Wesley. He does not want us to seclude ourselves and exclude everything but him. I'm miles away in body but, like Wes, in spirit I, too, am with you in the sitting room, upstairs. I feel that what is left of our family is more of a unit than ever. Dad has suffered just as we have, and has felt that he must keep a strong hand to steer his boat in all this stormy time. I hope, if *I* ever have any children, I shall be as good a father as he is. I feel at times that I love nothing else but you and Dad, but there is, after all, a big place in my heart for Ammudder and Aunt Susie. They are not just friends, but something more that I cannot name. I suppose they have just a little of the same kind of motherly affection that you have and this makes them different.

During the summer, Princeton opened a training camp which Richard joined. By fall, the students had to decide which branch of Uncle Sam's fighting forces they would enter. Richard preferred the Navy, as it would take him places. But this made an unhappy situation for him.

[*Princeton—Saturday night, October 5, 1918.*] About last Tuesday, Colonel Pierson of the Army made the announcement that all the non-coms in the Army department would be sent to an O. T. C. the tenth of this month, and 30 new ones every succeeding month. If I had joined the Army instead of the Navy I would be packing up for a camp and have my leather putts all picked out. It was the last straw when I heard that. All my friends are in the Army and they bombarded me with delightful stories of commissions.

I didn't sleep a wink that night worrying over the situation. On top of that there was an announcement made by Professor Eisenhart that only those men twenty or above could take the naval courses—Ordnance and Gunnery, Navigation, Seamanship, etc.—which meant that I could not begin with the twenty-year-olds. I had to get around that—so I gave my age as twenty and am in all the classes I want. I have enough sense to know that it's mostly the practical training that is going to make me an officer, so I intend just about living in the observatory with the sextant and compass. I still have not been sworn in—which means no uniform. We are too inactive here, too much leisure time, not enough drill. I think I'll write the Admiral as much.

I am desperately lonesome with my pals gone—one can make new friends, but not new pals. I've been a "mess hound" for four days. What a vile job. In other words, I am a waiter in the commons, and it's perfect bedlam. My old black sweater is caked with butter and fish and soup and molasses. Each "hound" has to wait on ten people and unless one crashes through and gets his table set up before the hungry sailors get in, there's Hell to pay. So it's a fight to get in ahead and I'm pretty good at that. Carrying the dishes and food on to the table makes one hungry in spite of seeing the dago cooks flop slices of meat from the stoves into the dishes with their hands. I'll have to get used to all this, of course.

I have permission to be free in the morning. I guess we'll go to church. Some way when one is feeling unhappy, music and singing have a good influence. I hope to be able to see Mrs. Robinson* in the afternoon. She is so wonderfully sweet—never too broken-hearted to mend your own breaks, and never too sad to listen and sympathize and cheer the sadness of others. The older I get the more sadness there seems to be in the world. Maybe it's just because my emotions have become unusually sensitive in the last year or two. There seems to be something in turmoil inside me all the time. I intend to keep myself in control until the war is over and my education, and *then* I'm going to *bust loose* and let my restless, discontented spirit run its

---

* Mrs. Robinson was the wife of Professor Robinson of Lawrenceville, the master of the house where Richard lived during his first year at that school.

The strong family resemblance between Richard and Wesley is evident in
this portrait. They were respectively eleven and eight at the time.

When Wesley was twelve he posed for this picture which was proudly sent
to his brother Richard, then away at school in Lawrenceville.

course. The idea of leading a monotonous confined respectable life is horrible to me. Someday the fires inside are going to break out and I'll push my working table out the window and just be a wild man. I've got in the habit of running instead of walking. Something keeps saying *faster, faster*—move! It isn't nerves. I sleep like a log. I feel wonderful all the time. I try so hard to concentrate when I work—and all I get for my trouble

Unfortunately the remainder of this letter is lost. And the beginning of the next is mislaid. Or what follows may be a continuation next day, with a missing page or two:

It looks, Dad, as if you are going to have your "college man" after all. Wall Street is betting the war will be over in four months. The paper this morning says Germany and Austria both are asking for an Armistice. I'm not in the Navy yet, and I'm tired of waiting to be sworn in—maybe tomorrow! I will be an apprentice seaman and draw $32 a month—*when* I draw it. I'm not incurring any bills to be paid with my salary. In spite of all my gloom last night we are told here that if we pass the exams we will be sent (as *planned*) to an O. T. C.—four more months and I'll have what I want. Gosh, then 'spose the war ends. I don't want to be tied up.

No, Dad, I'm not such a gloom as I pretend to be. I could be more cheerful, I guess. I'll try.

Must stop and drop down to L'ville. I'm off mess duty after tonight. On account of the "flu" I'm walking today to keep off the cars.

[*Princeton—Sunday, November 10, 1918.*] We left in an auto for Atlantic City Thursday morning at seven and made the 110 miles in three and a half hours. It was quite cold, but we were buried under sweaters and rather enjoyed its being cold. We went straight out on one of the long piers and worked with sextants for two hours. It was *very* satisfactory as we had a chance to put into practice the pages of theory we had been studying. It was a clear, bright day and we could easily find the horizon.

About three we were freed—got a room at a hotel and made for the Boardwalk. It was the best day in the world to be there, as peace was reported in the paper and everybody simply went wild—over *us*. Someway a sailor seems to get more attention than a soldier. Anyway, we were bombarded with hurrahs and questions and acclamations of every sort. Everybody shouted "you did it" until we began to believe we had, really. We were showered with smokes and candy; were not allowed to pay for anything. As we went in to supper at the hotel, everybody rose and cheered and one table sent ours a big bouquet, and another a flag.

My friend Bill Brooks was with me. We strolled along the Boardwalk listening to all the dance music and hilarity going on in the restaurants. We decided to take advantage of our popularity and stop the first two girls we saw. We had not gone far when we spied two and asked them if they would mind walking with two lonesome sailors. They were very nice looking, and rather startled, but we didn't budge an inch. Later they told us that, but for the uniform and the day, they would have been insulted. We walked a while longer, then went for a ride in rolling chairs to one of the liveliest restaurants. It surely was a wild place. The denial of the peace report had not reached them yet, and everybody was celebrating. Uniform or no uniform, everybody was drinking and dancing. We ordered ginger ale and sandwiches, and had a very good time on that. Both the girls could dance very well. We stayed and danced till one, took them home (by foot) and went back to our room.

We had to be back at the pier at 9:30 next morning. We worked all morning—taking the very important noon observation, which gives the longitude. I missed my location by one mile which is quite good. We found our car at 2:30 and started for home, stopping in Trenton for supper. From there we dropped by Helen's [Pendergast]. We got home about 8:00. It was surely a glorious ride, no dust, good roads, bracing, keen air that makes you feel energetic and enthusiastic. I tried to make up some of my missed work but I was far too sleepy.

[*Later—Monday night.*] Peace is declared *again*. The report came about eight o'clock this morning. I am very happy way down deep—and the first thing I thought was, "Oh, how I want to be home!" We had a celebration this afternoon. I wrote the Admiral a personal letter this noon. I knew we were to have the Parade—which I thought would be entirely unsatisfying to the emotion caused by the good news. I thought we should have some sort of divine service to end the celebration, and a prayer of thanksgiving and acknowledgment seemed to me much more appropriate than a wild dance along the street, and the singing of "America" in the chapel more significant than wild shouts of passing merriment. I took the letter to the Admiral personally—and whether or not I was the cause, anyway the entire personnel of all the units in Princeton, 3000 men, were drawn up on the parade grounds before a minister who read from the Bible, and a priest who prayed. We had a long parade down Nassau Street afterward.

I shall let circumstances decide whether I stick to it till I am commissioned, or whether I shall try to get back to civilian life. The church bells and whistles have played all day. Some chimes in a church not far off are butchering the "Marseillais" on too few bells. It's going to be hard sledding to go on studying war when you see and hear nothing but peace.

When I was at L'ville last Saturday I looked in Wes's room again—first time since almost a year ago. It hurt almost as much as it did the last time. Thanksgiving will have little meaning to us hereafter. It is the anniversary of his first week of illness.

It's tantalizing to hear you speak about the duck shooting, Dad. Now and then I see isolated pairs of ducks headed for the coast. I guess the ducks rather enjoy the war, as the sportsmen have other things to shoot at.

What a memorable day this is—peace and relief from almost unbearable worries and horror! We are safe. It has not struck us— thank God.

After the Armistice excitement, inactivity almost to stagnation followed. Princeton played football in New York on the twenty-sixth and this gave the boys a fine opportunity to put training camps in the background and have a bit of fun. About a thousand went. On Tuesday the twenty-ninth Richard writes that he and three other boys planned a party in New York and had a glorious vacation for two days. "It's nice to be able to wash your face and be in evening dress again." To make up for the neglect of scholastic work he says, "From now on till end of term I'm going to institute a reign of terror with my books and get well on top so as to be prepared for anything." Helen has another "steady" in one "Chas." Richard writes: "Helen will be my guest at the prom—Score 1 for me! Helen and I are invited to a friend's home in Philadelphia Sunday—Score 2 for me! Chas. forgot Helen's birthday; I didn't. I gave her a twenty-five-cent fern. Score 3 for me! However, I think Chas. and Helen are already engaged—which doesn't bother me!" The letter closes with "The unit is all agog with wild rumors. Today we hear it's to be disbanded tomorrow. The sooner we are sworn out, the better. Everyone has lost interest in war preparation, and the determination and enthusiasm have given place to discontent and indifference—I guess I'm not dif-ferent from others."

Letters from November 29, 1918, to March 10, 1919, are missing. During this period the *Daily Princetonian* board held a contest for one new member. There were eight candidates. Quantity, quality and fitness of the news furnished were to determine the choice. Richard threw himself into the competition and won.

[*Princeton—Monday night, March 10, 1919.*] Just by force of contrast it seems to me as if I've been working terribly hard since the *Prince* contest, but don't seem to have accomplished much. I began last Monday on my English essay. Believing in originality at the sacrifice of almost all else, I couldn't get interested in the stupid subjects offered, so I tried to do something I was sure nobody else had ever tried—a burlesque on *Antony and Cleopatra* written in iambic pentameter, the same meter as Shakespeare. It's in play form—four acts. I think it's rather funny in spots—gosh, I worked hard enough on it, especially the poetry part, getting the lines to run smooth. I hope the Prof. will accept it, as Mr. Harper did my "Delirium Tremens" one.

Tomorrow I have to start on a 4000-word History essay. I've become very interested in the character of Napoleon III and the history of France in his reign. In fact, I've been devouring books about him. Someone has said—and well said—that a man's education is in proportion to his knowledge of Paris, and France, and French. The more I learn, in any direction, the stronger I am convinced that it is true.

The prom comes Friday. I asked Esther. Helen is coming up with my rival Charley.

The club elections come soon. For some reason I've taken the responsibility of my crowd onto my shoulders. I'm going to get us into the best club on Prospect Street or bust. I'm just bursting with schemes—and I'm sorry because I worry over it. Sometimes, I ardently wish I were one of the phlegmatic kind of students that stick to their books regularly and don't strain over anything and are too insensitive to worry over lack of position or influence. Often they leave college with a better mental capacity to handle life and business. But I would soon grow so dissatisfied living that way I'd be miserable. I go dashing around expending all my energy on things that count for nothing after I leave Princeton. What good is it going to do me if I do make the club I'm after and have to lose interest in my books and too much sleep? Is the *Prince* board with its grinding demands worth while? It's a question. Do you think, Dad, your Founder's medal is worth your bad stomach?

Day before yesterday my History Prof. asked me to stay after class. Being on the *Prince,* I was criticising the lax way in which work was extracted from the students. I suggested a daily test in his own class. Next day he *did* give a quiz. I had not reached the topic asked about in my lesson and had to hand in a blank paper except for "I can't be expected to preach and practice both."

Yesterday afternoon I could not stand my room any longer with· the sun so bright outside—jumped on my bicycle and went to Lawrenceville, had supper with Mr. Henry* and came back about nine o'clock. It was a clear, cool night—bright moon and stars. How I enjoyed the trip back! I'm going to repeat it—often. Shorty borrows my bike and furnishes the tires. He gets them free from Goodyear. He recently won the basketball managership. Russell is working hard for the same job for swimming, and Mike for track, and Heinie for the crew. Our crowd is all *doing* something. Larry is doing all the athletics for the bunch, Shorty the acting and debating, and I the writing—and we will all get *somewhere someday.*

---

* A teacher at Lawrenceville.

[*Princeton—Wednesday, April 16, 1919.*] Oh, but there's lots I have to tell you. First—about Cap and Gown. There were two cliques—sixteen of us and five of the other crowd—and some members of the two on unfriendly terms. The club wanted some of both cliques, but we wanted all or none and stuck together. It came to taking the sixteen of us or the five of them; C. and G. took the sixteen and with the objecting minority out of the way, we signed up next day. We had our banquet last night and I was never so happy. Princeton life is really opening up. The clubs cement the friendships one has made during his first two years, and coming not until a fellow is almost a Junior, the influence cannot harm.

Soon I start in on the *Prince* and "make up" twice a week till commencement. It's hard work, but great training. My report was not so good as might have been—all of which considering the *Prince* contest was fair enough.

Dad, I guess I'll have to admit I do feel my book work is somewhat of a "grind" to me. I never have loved to study but was too wise not to. If I let myself do what my emotions and instincts let me do, I wouldn't crack a book—except to read. I'd sit up all night reading history and English. I'd sleep all morning and walk or golf or tennis all afternoon—take my meals when I was hungry and above all *forget* my ambitions and duties. But instead of that I make my better sense prevail and do things with some system.

I realize the danger of being too esthetic, Dad, and I'll steer clear of too much of it. I would be very happy if I could get to the heart of the esthetic things I like without missing any of the really practical ways and means of living.

I've had the best of everything. Let's hope I have profited by it. I think if I work this summer I would prefer the paper; it will do me more good than anything else. Really what would appeal to me most of all would be to don a red flannel shirt and chop logs.

[*Princeton—May 8, 1919.*] The man who wrote *How to Live on Twenty-four Hours a Day* never came to Princeton in the spring. He would have found it couldn't be done. I could use 48 hours a day and have something still left undone—writing home "frinstance." In one of your late letters, Dad, you said while at Vanderbilt on the spring days you wanted to lie down under the trees and do nothing but breathe. That's hard for me to understand, for spring has the opposite effect on me. Every afternoon for two weeks now, I've gone to the gym about 4:30, put on my track clothes and jog-trotted for an hour or so along the lake or canal. The glorious, sunny air makes one want to dance along. I never enjoyed anything more—sometimes alone—sometimes not.

The *Prince* is a real pleasure—whereas I dreaded it before I took hold. I'm through by one o'clock—two nights the week. Things hum in the office. It's the only activity in college that has a business-like air about it. I've begun to think "Editor-in-Chief" of course, but I'm quite sure I don't want it. I know too much about it. The three men that run the paper are so many slaves. I'd rather be editor of one of the less important magazines.

We are up to our necks in Ethics, and I find I'm a perfect example of an Epicurean—or rather would like to be. Don't decide whether that is well or not until you really understand what an Epicurean is. He's not the contented pig, as I always thought.

[*Tuesday, May 13, 1919.*] I s'pose you're wondering where your child is wandering tonight. First of all he is obeying your orders about running—mostly because he's so busy he has not had time. However, I assure you both I've quite forgotten I have a heart (I can hear you saying, "I should say so—he writes us once a month"). I am as healthy as a bunch of Johnson grass in a cotton field, and no doubt cause as much trouble to my cultivators.

Oh, before I forget it—I was elected to the Editorial Board of the *Princeton Pictorial Magazine* (called *Pic* for short)—am sending two copies. I'm not terribly puffed up over the honor, but it helps to fill up the "what I've done" space under my picture in the yearbook and gives me another bangle to put on my watch chain. I don't see what's to keep me from becoming editor—I'm in the right club 'n everything. I've had a week's rest from the *Prince* and took advantage of it to get busy on an English essay. That always takes me a week as I strain a point to make them good. This one's a story—three stories in a row—the main one about a man condemned to death for a crime— murder—on circumstantial evidence. The real murderer goes to confess to save the innocent man, but is run down by the condemned man's wife in her automobile, just as he is entering the City Hall to see the judge. The wrong man gets electrocuted—too bad, but it makes a story.

Mother, I broke my promise about New York. I went up Saturday to see the Princeton Triangle show give its New York performance at the Waldorf. Russell—or rather the Hopkinsons in general—gave a bang-up party. We had a wonderful dinner party—twenty at the table. We were all carted down in their half a dozen automobiles and had the best and biggest box in the auditorium. The show was wonderful—knowing all the cast always adds—Shorty was the best in it. The dancing after lasted till two. We all had the time of our lives.

I've got to typewrite 2000 words or so before I get to bed and it's eleven o'clock now.

CHAPTER II

It BECOMES evident that a new Patrick Henry, different in some notable respects from the prototype, had arisen. Impatience at restraint had been smouldering within Richard until it was "liberty or death" for him. Doubtless his understanding parents would have saved him much mental unhappiness had he unburdened himself and pleaded for his "liberty"—but liberty he must have, and he proceeded in a calculating and determined way to achieve it.

[*New Orleans—Monday, July 18, 1919.*] Don't be alarmed at anything. Everything is as it should be. I'm very happy and very well and really *am* in New Orleans or rather was when this was written. You see, I didn't go to Brownsville at all, but took the 12:05 to New Orleans Thursday night. I'd been planning to go all summer, so it was no sudden move on my part. I'm going to Europe, leaving Tuesday night.

It's hard for me to realize how surprised you are, for it's such a long-planned and anticipated trip for me that it all seems matter-of-fact. I don't know when I'll be back and I'm not going to say. It may be the last of September and it may be January first. I know I was cruel to slip off as I did, but I knew too well that if I mentioned my plan and you did not agree you would argue me out of it. I would have continued to lead my restless, useless, unhappy existence the rest of the summer. If you remember, I wrote you in November how restless I was. I've never mentioned it since, for I don't understand it and can't explain what I don't understand. All I know is I'm infinitely happy at the prospect of my trip. This unrestrained feeling is what I crave. I'm going where I have an inspiration to go and when I get ready. The $15 Dad gave me I spent on my ticket and Pullman. I drew $65 out of the bank—which over-draws my account $15. I'll leave here with $45—and get $80 a month or $54 for the three weeks of the trip. That will land me in Europe with $95 or so.

19

I'm not acting under any sudden, silly impulse—nor am I running away from anything except my old self. It is not because I am unhappy and dissatisfied with you. Surely a boy never had a more comfortable and ideal home life than I have. It's not that. You would not be alarmed if I had gone west, to Montana or Canada, and were away from you for three months or so. This is not different, except that my plan is far more interesting, engrossing and *active*—active, that's the word. Please forgive me for slipping off; I considered everything and decided this was the best way. Don't come here to tell me good-by. I may have gone. It would weaken my resolution. It would make it hard for all of us. You would want to see my quarters and learn my duties. They may be unpleasant, and that would make you all the more uneasy. They may be very pleasant. I will not know until tonight.

Since I had to be in New Orleans these days, I decided I might as well see the place and begin my adventure *here*. I have "done" it—every nook and corner. With my guidebook and map I've explored here and there and have enjoyed it immensely. Saturday I walked out to Lake Pontchartrain and had a glorious swim. Last night I went to the end of St. Charles Street and back. I've hung around the French market and Jackson Square, spent a morning in the Cabildo and was well paid for my trouble. I think N. O. is the most attractive city I ever saw. I like the homes set high up off the ground—with broad steps—the one-story pillars and the gables—all brick covered with glistening white stucco—the pillars of iron, painted white. Everything is dazzling white and with the green palms and shrubs close about the house—well, I think they are the most striking and aristocratic-looking homes I ever saw.

His letter promptly produced this telegram:

7/19/19.

RICHARD HALLIBURTON

    COSMOPOLITAN HOTEL, NEW ORLEANS.

    GO TO IT AND MAY YOU HAVE A BULLY TIME. A LITTLE SURPRISED YES. DON'T FAIL TO WRITE US. FOR GODS SAKE TAKE CARE OF YOURSELF, BUT GET THIS TRIP OUT OF YOUR SYSTEM. WISHING YOU BON VOYAGE. DAD.

New Orleans—Wednesday, July 19, 1919

My own dear Mother:—

Well, I'm still in this hemisphere, and will be when you get this letter. Dad's wire was a big relief for I knew then that you know what I was up to and where I am. I've had nothing but obstacles and hard luck to overcome since I arrived here, but I'm not the least discouraged nor the least regretful that I undertook this thing. Also I joined the union and became a violent (?) I. W. W., paid down my $5 and the magic charm has worked. My card is No. 582. I could have gone on 50 boats to 50 different places—to Porto Rico, Mexico, etc., etc., but that's not my plan. I'm going to Europe.

Just for fun, I attended a meeting of the union here late this afternoon to decide what to do with several union men who had committed the unpardonable sin of working during the strike. We decided to fine them $10 and bounce them from our benevolent midst if they refused to pay. I hang around with my golf pants on and shirt collar turned in, sleeves rolled up and my straw hat hung on the back of my head. I look tough enough—trouble is I *do* speak English which is a serious disadvantage.

Last night I put on my walking shoes and had a ten-mile hike out Canal Street and back—just to be in trim for the other side.

New Orleans—July 19, 1919

Dear Mudder:—

Dad's letter just received breaks my heart. All the time I thought you were down in Montgomery enjoying a pleasant visit, you were at home worrying yourself to death about me. If only Atha had not come to Memphis till later. It makes me shudder to think about the days and nights of anxiety you went through on account of my—well, it wasn't thoughtlessness, because I figured that my letter would meet you when you got back.

When you think, Mother dear, that I *had* to go—that I owed it to myself to follow this overpowering obsession, and *then* consider how I went, you should be reconciled just a little. I would have gone last summer but for the war. My freshman year I was so restless, I had to fight myself to keep up an outward appearance of contentment. I said that I had to hold on till summer, then I could go. The summer army camp blocked all plans as did my navy enlistment. I came very near going in January but the fact that Europe was so inhospitable at the time, and that it was my last chance at the *Prince,* and that it was a wonderful chance to get through all my required courses at Princeton, and get founded in general, all this made me grit my teeth. And I was not sorry I had stayed—until May, when all that I had stayed for had been accomplished.

I got so mentally depressed and restless and then morbid that I'd find myself in tears—I don't know now exactly what over. I had home and parents who loved me and whom I loved devotedly. My marks were good, I felt physically all right, and so I thought of nothing but summer, summer when there would be no war and I could go at last. I was never sad in the thought of going. But it did hurt deep when I thought of our separation, and after you left me at the station Thursday night, I watched you from the steps till you were out of sight—and I've never had so heavy a heart since the day Wesley died. I did not even shake Dad's hand to say good-by—there were tears in my eyes when I left the house. There were tears, too, when I kissed you good-by, Mother, but I held them back till you had rolled away.

I have not really run off—I've simply gone on a trip where I have to work my way, and it's going to be the most glorious trip anybody ever had.

Now, Mother, please try to realize that I've only done the right thing in the wrong way. Try to forget those four anxious days—to forgive me for being responsible.

[*New Orleans—Thursday, July 20, 1919.*] This has been the most unusual day I ever spent. My chance came with the *Octorara,* 3000 tons, licensed May, 1919, wooden, American, route to Hull, England, and back to New Orleans via New York. The paint is hardly dry on it, it's so new. But it's small—about 300 feet long and purely a freighter. The entire crew is but twenty men. I've signed up as an Ordinary Seaman and I'm satisfied and glad I have. I've gone on duty. She is being loaded with lumber. I've got a bottle of oil and three bars of soap and a bottle of iodine. I'll write every day till we sail and tell you all I do. Dad, *of course* I'm going to finish my two years at Princeton. Ten to one I will finish right with my class. I work eight hours and no more—didn't dare overwork for fear of being damned by my union. I left the hotel at six this morning and carted my bag out to the ship, reported to the mate and was put to work at once.

I was told to get the paint brushes ready. I found exactly thirty-eight hard as nails with caked paint, but a big bucket of coal oil and a bucket of hot water and Gold Dust and scrubbing brush and five hours' work and all the brushes looked like new. There are six sailors—four A. B.'s and two Ordinary. The other Ord. beside myself is a young fellow from Houston, Texas, Allen Longbridge, in his Sophomore year at Rice Institute. He's twenty and has never been to sea before. He's quite cultivated and will make a very pleasant companion, especially as the other four seamen are the proverbial sea-going type—hard as nails but as good as gold. They are all in their twenties and a jolly bunch. All six of us have the same room—three double-tiered bunks. We are right "aft"—and get full benefit of a heavy sea. I thought it was a little boat but when you look into its great empty bowels where the freight is packed, it seems monstrous. They've been packing in lumber for three days and haven't more than covered the floor of the hull.

For breakfast we had oranges, oatmeal, boiled potatoes, bacon, fried eggs, coffee and ice water, but also condensed milk and a number of flies. The flies will leave as soon as we get to sea. We had a huge menu for dinner—three times too much. The overpowering amount of food takes my appetite. The four A. B.'s clean every dish, though, and never get enough. The sun is blazing on the river and this morning I mixed paint, and moved the row boat by ropes as needed, this afternoon. We quit at five. Allen and I came in town after supper, went to the movies and are spending the night at a Catholic Service Club. We get a clean bed and shower for twenty-five cents. We are going to sleep here until we sail as the ship is very hot and unscreened to the mosquitoes.

[*New Orleans—Friday, July 21, 1919.*] I've been busy as a bee today—washed and scraped the unsatisfactory paint off the Captain's floor this morning and helped load stores this afternoon until eight.

The latter was lots of fun. We put a boxcar load of food on our ship—four weeks' supply for 25 or 30 men. It put me to thinking what the Army Supply to France must have meant where there were 2,000,000 to feed—that would make 80,000 carloads of food required for three weeks' supply, and over a million men were in France a year. I can't comprehend the amounts. We have a great variety of food all stored snugly away—hams and jellies and jams and pickles and delicacies as well as canned spinach and canned everything else, including roast beef. The Captain said we must prepare to sail Tuesday. He's an old seadog but a gentleman and we are going to get along in great shape.

[*Monday night, August 5, 1919.*] It's been steady work for eight hours a day, but I enjoyed it immensely and never felt better. I make the best longshoreman you ever saw, and can handle a two-wheel truck like a nigger. I got paid again today—$10 for four days' work, one of which was Sunday when I didn't go near the boat. Allen and I are buying a kodak, so I can bring back pictures of my trip and show you your son as he emerges from packing flour sacks in a bath of perspiration with nothing on but a pair of pants. I clean up every evening in a self-washed white shirt, and shave, and I assure you no one ever suspects I'm a seaman.

[*New Orleans—Wednesday, August 7, 1919.*] Our steam is up— our boat is loaded until it's almost sunk out of sight. The decks are piled six feet in lumber. I feel just about as excited as if I were going for a ride on a freight train. I'm perfectly equipped for my, as Dad says, "personally conducted tour."

It would seem that the delays and false starts of the *Octorara* would dissipate anyone's enthusiasm. Richard arrived in New Orleans July fourteenth. His boat did not sail till August eighth, and then anchored almost in sight of New Orleans for three days on account of imperfect machinery. Headed for the Bahamas, the *Octorara* developed new engine troubles which made it necessary to turn up the coast to Norfolk for repairs. At last they were off on August twenty-seventh, when they should have been in Hull.

This he wrote to his Princeton roommate, John Henry Leh:

Norfolk—Wednesday, August, 1919

Heinie old man:—

Don't blame this paper on me. [It was a delicate pink.] I borrowed it from the Captain—it belongs to his wife. I'm writing you first tonight because you scoffed the most at my proposed trip to Europe, you old devil. Well, I can say pipe down now, for I'm well on the way—1800 miles on the way in fact. I'm writing from Norfolk, Va., where my ship has stopped for repairs and coal. From here we go to the Azores Islands and then to Hull, England. I won't reach Hull much before September tenth and I guess I won't be coming home till the start of the second term at Princeton. I'll use my Summer Camp credits for the first term. I meant to write you long ago, Dutchman, but thought I'd wait till there was something to write about.

After I left Princeton, I went straight home and loafed and played golf and snaked until July fifteenth, when I had my plans made to go to New Orleans for a ship. The darned shipping strike came then, and I waited till the 23rd. My parents would have disapproved of the action I was taking, so I left one night "for a visit up state" and landed in New Orleans. The fellow I said I was going to visit appeared in Memphis the next day and said he hadn't seen me. My family went wild—write-up and picture in the paper—"foul play feared," etc. I got a job as soon as the strike was over, joined the seamen's union and cry "down with the damned capitalists, down with everything." I picked out the ship because it was sailing soonest and was new. It's a very small tub—250 feet long—loaded with lumber. I worked two weeks lifting sugar barrels and sacks of bacon, etc., nearly died the first few days, but caught on after a while and can swing as wicked a steel truck as any nigger stevedore on the wharf. The trip through the Gulf of Mexico and around Florida was great. Our chief amusement was feeding the sharks. They would come from out of sight and snatch food off the water in a twinkle. As a seaman my duties were mostly painting, polishing, etc. I get $80 a month clear and no chance much to spend it. Here in port I'm night watchman every other night and all day off—horribly hard work.

I am keen to learn how the rest of the bunch fared this summer and if their plans worked as well as mine. I'll miss you fellows next fall, but once I'm across I'm going to make it worth while. I plan to work south from Hull to London and then to Belgium and see all the war remains I can. I hope to reach Paris early in October. I may attend the Sorbonne University there three months or may go on south into Italy and Austria and Greece. I want to walk most of the way. I wish I had you along for company; still I guess you would balk at any distance greater than Princeton to Lawrenceville. This ship has a good bunch of seamen on board—two other Americans and four Norwegians who are always saying they "were yust out of Yale" meaning just out of jail—which I'm sure Roy Holden would appreciate.

This is one of the biggest ports of call in the world—Hampton Roads. From the crow's-nest I can count 187 ships anchored around us, and we are in a stone's throw of the Atlantic Battle Fleet. Our ship is so small the slightest bit of rough weather makes her stand on her head, but I've managed to keep my lunch when the old salts were losing theirs. Are you still working at the store and are you still single? Next time you osculate with Dot, say, "That's for Dick." I haven't spoken to a girl since I left Memphis except two I picked up to dance with in N. O.

I'm practicing daily saying, "Bon jour, Mademoiselle, voulez-vous promenader avec moi?"—which means, of course, in English, "Lady, do you take in washing?" However, as I got rosin in my hair and had it all clipped off to get rid of the stuff, they'll give me one look and say, "No, I ain't washin' no more." I wonder if Mike and Chan got their trip, and Larry and Russ. How many times have you written my darling Mary? I'll have to watch you. I wonder if Helen's *"gotten"* married in my absence. Please apologize to Dot about the dance I cut with her. I wouldn't have done it for anything on purpose. Recite this poem to her for me. It ought to help me out with her.

> Heinie's girl wears silks and satins.
> My girl wears calico.
> Heinie's girl is tall and slender.
> My girl is fat and low.

The responsibilities of an editor-in-chief weigh heavily on Richard at
Lawrenceville.

Four of the five inseparables—Mike, Shorty, Dick and Larry—at the end
of their first year in Princeton, the summer of 1918.

Heinie Leh, the fifth, separated from the
four inseparables, and his wife Dot.

Heinie's girl is fast and wicked.
My girl is peeure and good.
Would I change for Heinie's girl?
You know damn well I would.

I'll write some of the other fellows now. I may see you, Heinie, in October—and I may never see you again.

[*Norfolk—August 27, 1919.*] I have to write fast for the pilot boat may be along any minute and collect the last mail before we sail. Steam is up at last. All my dissatisfaction and restlessness have gone with the approach of sailing. I surely picked the wrong boat, for I could have crossed just as quickly with Columbus on his *Santa Maria*. It will be two full months from the time I boarded this ship to the time I get to Hull. I counted on two weeks.

[*At Sea—Saturday, September 6, 1919.*] This has been the most glorious day I ever spent—our approach to the Azores. All the happiness of our twelve days at sea, all my impressions and sensations, have been dwarfed by the wonder of the things I've seen today. This noon the mate beckoned us to look ahead. Allen and I saw a queer gray cloud resting on the horizon. I said, "I believe that's a mountain." About four o'clock the mountain was distinct, rising miles into the clouds. As the sun sank and the rays struck the side of the slope, Allen and I would cry like two kids, "Look, a house!" or a church or a lighthouse. We got closer and closer—oh, what a *glorious* sight—the mountain crowned with clouds, dotted with innumerable white specks, the surf roaring on the huge cliffs, as big as Gibraltar's, and sheer rock-sides topped with trees, a white sail here and there, and the air of untamed wildness and grandeur in everything. We were feasting so on this view no one noticed the towering pinnacle beyond, another island rising even higher.

We rounded a promontory and all at once the most beautiful sight on earth, I'm sure, stood before us. It was the harbor of Horta. Myriads of lights, fireflies they seemed, flying about the big clusters of glistening white buildings, piled in terraces on top of one another, any way, every way right up the mountain side. Above, the most star-filled sky I ever saw; and the moon flicked the waves before us and made the bay and beach sparkle and glisten. I can hardly wait to see it in the morning.

When I got my fill of the harbor I came down to write you so that I may have a letter ready to mail when I go ashore tomorrow. I feel that my sea trip is near the end—we've "crossed." We've had always a strong, steady wind that caused great swells, but they were slow and regular and the heavy rolling at night made the ship a cradle that rocked us to sleep. Every night after supper Allen and I came out on deck and plopped down on a great coil of rope to watch the sun and sea go down. We discussed, or rather argued—we argue everything—literature and philosophy and geography and the stage—Allen is about as well informed as I. About eight we got our buckets of water, washed ourselves, and then our clothes, crawled in bed to read a chapter or two in a book, and then to sleep until seven-thirty next morning. We have plowed along at a snail's pace with disabled engines at six knots an hour all the way. Tomorrow I'm going to drink fresh milk ashore till I can't waddle and bring my suitcase back full of fresh fruit which I crave more than anything. Even so, I'm safe and well as a young ox.

While Richard had traveled about his homeland, from New York to California, this was his first experience with the ocean and ships and foreign shores, and he greeted it with boundless enthusiasm. Many of the following letters were endlessly long, for he takes on the attitude of being the discoverer of the things he sees and wants to report everything about these unknown lands.

[*Hull—Te Deum Laudamus—Monday, September 22, 1919.*] I saw the mail come aboard tonight, and my hands trembled with excitement and suspense as I grabbed for my share of it—two letters from Mother and two from Dad, one from Ammudder and one from Heinie Leh. If I had not become so hard-boiled on this boat, I'm sure I would have wept hard and long after I'd finished reading them. I can't explain the feeling I had tonight—so homesick I want to throw up everything and come back to you at once—yet, at the same time, inspired even more to go on and finish what I've started.

I wrote you from Horta harbor, the picture of which I'll never forget. The day of departure we were constantly in sight of some one of those rugged islands with the roaring breakers at their feet, and tree-covered giant rocks behind. We were up in time to watch the approach to Ponta Delgada on the clearest, warmest morning, and I was never so well able to appreciate Browning's little song, "The year's at the spring—and day's at the morn." A swarm of native venders clambered on board with canary birds, lace work, bottles of wine, and baskets of fruit. I blew myself to the fruit.

We didn't wait for supper in order to get ashore. Our ferry was a funny little boat with one oar, set astern, and worked as a fish uses his tail. Allen and I didn't know which way to go first, each way seemed so inviting. We followed the nearest street and found it well paved with little cobblestones and beautiful mosaic sidewalks—inlays of white and black stones. Houses, all of a type I think very beautiful—walls perfectly unbroken except by the second-story balcony of iron grating, and such colors—green, lavender, pink, every color imaginable, and all packed close together into a solid wall, with semi-tropic vegetation here and there. Every other house had a wineshop on the ground floor. The six days we were there I never saw a drop of drinking water—don't believe the natives ever heard of it.

We prowled up one street and down another looking very rudely at everything and everybody. Everybody walks and drives in the street. We saw lots of barefooted old hags, and burros and goat-driven wagons. All the vehicles seemed to have two wheels only with the driver bouncing up and down and making a loud his-s-s which could be heard a block and served as a whip for his animal and a klaxon for all pedestrians.

On a later night we passed along a particularly slum-like street. The children romped in that street in hundreds. It wasn't long before we were recognized as Americans and a howl of "mune" (money) went up. We were followed in swarms, and there was not one of them over seven years old. Foolishly I threw one a penny. That was my Waterloo. They became so many wolves after us two sheep. They followed us in diminishing numbers for half a mile, sounding like a flock of cawing blackbirds in a thicket. Finally when all our pennies had been expended, Allen gave each of them one of his 100-for-5 cents Azores cigarettes and they went back inhaling like steam engines and seemingly well addicted to the weed—the girls as well as the boys. I'll never forget the sight of these infants strutting along with their cigarettes and flicking away the ashes with their chubby fingers.

One day out from Ponta, we hit a sure-enough storm. I had wished for one—I *got* it. We rolled and pitched and it seemed our fo'castle would go so far down it would never right itself. It got worse as night came on and I enjoyed it immensely until I went to bed. I was lying on my bunk (an upper one) reading when I heard a violent slap, a roar, and the force of the ocean dashed through the portholes and knocked me over the rail of my bunk onto the prostrate form of a seasick sailor below. I was never so surprised in my life—it all happened so quickly. My bed and I were drenched, the room was flooded. I had to laugh at my startled friend who was so rudely snapped out of his agony by a young Niagara of very cold water accompanied by 140 lbs. of me, all at once on his neck. I was soon sick enough to die. I greatly enjoyed the liberty of next day as the waves were running so high we didn't dare work on deck. We made exactly fifteen miles that twenty-four hours. All the way to the Channel the sea was uncomfortably rough, and it took us ten days instead of seven to make it here.

When Saturday morning I woke up we were not rocking—it was sunny once more and there right out my port was Beachy Head, the great glistening chalk cliff on the English coast. What a wonderful first view of England, and what an interesting day! Ships by the swarm, little ones, big ones, going and coming in streams. That day the bosun raved because I stopped doing everything to look—how hard I looked! The minute we got into the North Sea we began to stand on end again, and the thermometer dropped a mile. Cold? I had on three pairs of pants and my four shirts, but the knife-like wind found me dressed in gauze. Late this afternoon we fought the snow and wind twenty miles up the Humber River, and after frantic efforts of being towed and pushed through a maze of shipping and locks and canals so narrow we almost had to grease the ship to get by, we've docked.

When I get back I'm going to sail into history and books of travel with a new zest and purpose, and when I come again I'll be ready. I know only enough now to know that I have everything to learn about Europe. Its geography is at my finger tips, but not its history and literature.

[*Lichfield—September 28, 1919.*] Even though I am half starved I'm already an Anglomaniac, and a raving one at that, and I've been here only a week. I liked the first glimpse of it, Beachy Head, so glistening and commanding, and then I liked the Channel, and I was delighted with Hull and my enthusiasm has grown with every hour.

Everything on wheels in this country is on a strike; not a railroad car, freight or passenger, has moved for three days. There is no food, no milk, nothing, being transported. I got all my information just tonight sitting in the smoking room here at Lichfield when a distinguished looking civilian and I began to converse as we stood side by side before the fire. Later a British Army officer looked in and said, "Oh! therr you arrrr, General. I think we can go to supper now." And I found out just a minute ago that my friend was General Allenby, deliverer of Jerusalem, and one of the heroes of the war. In the dining room everyone was all eyes, and if I'd been a minute sooner I might have suggested to the General that we go to supper together and continue our conversation. You'll have to admit *that* was bad luck. Well I hope next time I meet General Haig or Admiral Beatty I'll know it.

Oh, well, let's go back to Hull. I saw the Captain of the *Octorara* and said the shipboard in N. O. had assured me we were making only a two-months' trip and I'd made my plans accordingly; that we had been *so* delayed I felt I was justified in asking that I might be freed to follow my plans made in N. O. It worked beautifully. I got my extra $25 and was taken to the Consul. I found he was a Yale man, and so I emphasized my college connection and he did everything I suggested.

Well, once free of the ship I went to see the movies to celebrate— Charlie Chaplin—nothing but American films in this country. I passed a side entrance to the theater on my way to the front and found a bunch of gamins four to eight years old bubbling with excitement over seeing Charlie. I took about half a dozen in with me for a shilling or so and they were delighted beyond measure. One of the four-year-olds insisted upon sitting on his benefactor's lap so I could read him the leaders. Charlie in *Sunnyside* was not half so amusing to me as those kids who almost fell out of their seats.

Thursday noon I was off for Manchester for no other reason than that I preferred central England to eastern. I got there about six. It has not one virtue except the hundreds of mills which spin our cotton.

 Oh, let me tell you before I forget it—I grew a dandy mustachio on the ship. It was quite creditable but was taking on the Chinese mandarin aspect, so I began to clip the edges, till I had only a Charlie Chaplin mustache left which was so funny looking I cut it all off and bought me a walking stick as a substitute proof that I am a grown man.

Now get out the atlas, Mother and Dad, and turn to England. I bought a wonderful detail map and it enables me to know where I am to within a few hundred yards. From Manchester I went to *Macclesfield,* twenty miles, getting there about eight o'clock—wonderful farm country, small *green,* green fields checkered with low stone fences, cattle every place and very few crops except hay, but the beauty of these fields, and scattered trees and hills and church spires! The churches, built in 1200, 1250, 1300, and still being used every Sunday, and vying with one another on Sabbath mornings to see which can out-sound its neighbor with its chimes until the melody reaches from one corner of England to another.

Macclesfield to *Leek* along the most beautiful road in the world I know—lakes, hills, forests and fields, each of which looks like a sixteenth-century Dutch painting. Leek to *Ashbourne* where I stopped at the Inn with *"Built in 1619"* over the door—exactly 300 years old—and I suppose the feather bed I slept in was not much younger.

Through *Uttoxeter* I came yesterday to *Lichfield,* through more ever-changing scenery, along the Dove River, a tourist center even to Englishmen. I decided to rest today. My feet were tired and I wanted to write you and I *did* want really to see this wonderful little town. I spent the morning in Dr. Samuel Johnson's birthplace and home, pouring over his relics. I've always been an admirer of his and have been well schooled in his life so I could appreciate it all. The afternoon I spent in the Cathedral, the most beautiful building I ever saw, begun in 1150 and so old it seems all melted together. And tomorrow morning I'm off for *Kenilworth,* you know what's there better than I. I've avoided Birmingham like poison, you see, after Manchester.

I'm so well and happy, never so fit and pepful. I walk just enough—30 miles or so a day, the happy medium. My bag's checked to London.

[*Stratford—October 2, 1919.*] I've had the best time the last two days, since I wrote you at Lichfield. The walk to Tamworth was made very early in the morning, from seven to nine, and I enjoyed it so much I shall get that early a start every day in the future. Tamworth castle is just the happy mean between Kenilworth and Warwick. The "battlements in tufted trees" make it romantic enough, not to mention the wonderful carvings, woodwork, etc. There is a dark and dank dungeon, and there are cold little bedrooms in the tower from which you can see for miles over these beautiful English landscapes. *Marmion* mentions this castle.

I walked on at noon to Kenilworth, reaching there after dark, and having come another thirty-two miles from Lichfield. Next morning I went straight to the castle, and what a wonderful morning I had! Misty rain kept all other visitors away so I had the guide all to myself—a marvelous guide! He had pictures and charts in stacks which we studied carefully before we began the rounds that I might get a good picture in my mind of what the castle was in all its glory—and I got it wonderfully. So before we started I saw what wasn't there at all. As we went slowly along, the guide gushed torrents of description and history, and whenever he slowed up I had a leading question ready which would crank him up again.

He gave me the history of England—the details of the history of the castle—the Pageant Leicester gave to Elizabeth. The man was an encyclopedia of Kenilworth knowledge and a student of it. He stood where Robsart stood and quoted Scott—and then Elizabeth with all the gestures—and then we moved down the marble steps and saw before us the lake and its boat pageant. There was the garden where Robsart and Elizabeth had their first meeting; here was described a wonderful tapestry that hung where only the sky hangs now; here was the room that Leicester ransacked all Europe to furnish; here were the kitchens where the common soldiers were fed, and there were the beautiful carved stone apartments of Elizabeth and of Leicester; the moats and drawbridges; there was the spot where Shakespeare stood as a boy of eleven to watch the entertainment, and here it was that Tennyson's son told my guide that Tennyson stood when he composed the lines, "The splendour falls on castle walls"—and on and on, incident after incident, history, customs, quotations. The man was a genius in his line and I have never been so highly entertained. I went at ten, I left at three. We had both forgotten all about lunch. I lived in 1560 during those hours, not 1919.

I hurried on to Warwick and was not quite so well guided. I was allowed to see only half a dozen rooms or so on one side of the building, but they were very beautiful and historical, and when one considers that they have been untouched since 1675 they appear the more remarkable. Of course, I enjoyed the pictures most—the dozen or so Vandykes and Rubens—and the view of the Avon out the Great Hall window with the old broken bridge and waterwheel. It was after five and as I had nine miles to go to make Stratford, I had to hustle.

Shakespeare's birthplace got me first, of course, and I spent an hour or more racking the guides with questions. Most interesting were the signatures on the walls of Byron, Scott, Dickens, Thackeray and lots of others. I met an Australian soldier, on furlough, and we did the town together, which made it most pleasant. The church, Trinity, got us next. We were there hours and found a guide who was as voluble as the one at Kenilworth. We examined every inch of the place to a great flow of description, and I took two rolls of films. Our guide gave us every privilege in the church and let us *stand* on Shakespeare's grave and take a picture of the inscription—

"Good friend, for Jesus' sake forbeare," etc.

We next went to the tower of the Memorial Theatre and got that

famous view of Trinity tower across the Avon, the view seen everywhere in pictures. We walked out to Anne Hathaway's cottage but
didn't go in, and in the late afternoon took a punt and paddled up the
river a mile or two—very, very beautiful. We went to the movies last
night—and rather ruined the mood I was in—sort of sublime to
ridiculous contrast.

This morning I'm going on my way to Oxford—two days' trip.
These cool sunny days are delightful for such a tour as mine. I gave
myself a week to get to London and I'm taking nearer two—thank
goodness.

[*Oxford—October 4, 1919.*] Two more jumps and I'll land in
London, for I'm in Oxford tonight. What a glorious city, such as
America can never have with all her millions.

All my bad luck at the beginning of my trip has turned to good,
lately, for today at nine o'clock a man came along and asked if I
wanted a guide. Indeed I did. We parted at 6 P.M. I know Oxford
from stem to stern after the most pleasant and instructive day I've
had yet. But I must admit I've seen so much and heard so much my
brain is in an Oxonian jumble—maybe this letter will help to disentangle it.

In his efforts to disentangle his brain from the Oxonian jumble he
wrote a letter of interminable length. In the architecture of the
Gothic buildings he finds "every door and window and cloister and
arch of my college." He is again reminded of Princeton—"What did
I see in the Quad at Corpus Christi but a sundial, an exact copy of
which Princeton has in McCosh Court? It did look home sure
enough." He meets the shade of Dr. Johnson at Pembroke College:
"I saw the original portrait, his desk, his rooms—a tiny, cold bedroom, and a dingy little sitting room still in use." He covers a
good deal of ground when he says, "Yes, All Souls Chapel is the most
beautiful room in the world, and the Library comes second only to
the Chapel." The letter goes on:

I've been thinking all day, "Well, would you like to come here for
a college course?" and I've been unable to decide. The place inspires

and yet suffocates me. If I were an Englishman going to live in England I would have but one ambition—to get a degree from here. But for an American who will have had four years at Princeton and who is not going to take up any special line that demands great research work, I think Oxford a waste of time. Still, I may change my mind next week.

The walk yesterday from Stratford to Oxford was the best day's walk yet—the most beautiful up and down hill country, the most glowing October sun, and the ripest roadside blackberries which cost me at least an hour.

I can see my breath in this room so I'm going to bed before I get too cold.

[*London—October 10, 1919.*] The day I left Oxford was a bright Sunday and I started walking early on the longer road to London. I believe I enjoyed that walk most of all—the road led over high hills and through deep, dark valleys, and for ten miles in the late afternoon right along the bank of the Thames and past hundreds of estates in the river valley.

It was nearly night when I reached London and I had to find a boarding house. I saw that my beloved *Cyrano de Bergerac* was being played here—so I went that very night. It was even better on the stage than on paper, uproariously funny. Next day I spent in the National Gallery and at the Tate. I saw the original of "The Avenue" by Hobbema, a picture which has hung over my desk for four years. That night I went to the Russian Ballet. What music—100-piece orchestra—and what color and wonderful dancing! So agile and graceful and powerful, it's hard to believe they are human. *Prince Igor* had such wild music and wild dancing I *had* to see it again last night.

Yesterday it was again clear and cold and with my walking stick I felt that anything but walking would be too slow. I skipped down to the Victoria Embankment, and sailed down the Embankment with my cap on one ear and passed everything on wheels. The sub *Deutschland* that came to Baltimore in 1916 was tied up along the Embankment—I got a good look and a picture. I reached St. Paul's and spent some three hours inside. I *cannot* appreciate Wren's buildings. The exterior of St. P. is beautiful enough, but all the gilt and gaudiness inside rub me the wrong way. The entire church inside is not worth the tiny jewel chapel at All Souls College in Oxford. *But* St. Paul's *dome* is a miracle of architecture. I climbed until I got up into a little cupola immediately below the big gilt cross on top the dome. The view was so magnificent that I stayed until the door man in the gallery below came laboring up the ladder to see if I'd jumped out the opening. Well, I came down and sailed across London Bridge so I could be on the other side and able to come back across the Tower Bridge, which put me right at the Tower, where I spent the rest of the afternoon. The crown jewels interested me most, but if I had not had a fair knowledge of English history the Tower trip, all in all, would have been rather stupid. So far, I believe, Kenilworth, Oxford and St. Paul's *dome* have been the best adventures yet. I did enjoy Westminster, though.

Tomorrow I'm going to Paris—by airplane; at least I might if I am not overcome by my better judgment. London to Paris by air, what, Mother and Dad, could be more romantic and satisfactory? I may change my mind tomorrow, for my Palm Beach suit looks— well, if I were at home—oh, but I'm not at home and don't give a rip how I look. My flannel shirt and woolens and raincoat will keep me as warm as I want to be. My cap and army shoes are the acme of comfort and I've walked 225 miles in Ammudder's wool socks and there's no hole *yet,* and they've withstood some hard scrubbing, too.

I've had enough of London—just "one jammed thing after another"—I *never* saw such traffic jams and so many people. I go miles in every direction and the crowds never seem to thin out. I *am* getting hungry—tea and marmalade and ham and eggs, margarine and usually "out of eggs." The menu would hide the side of a house and all they have to serve is tea and no sugar and margarined toast. Tell Laura* I think of her three times a day—and fruit is worth its weight in platinum. If I forgot to say I'm terribly well, "leaving the table hungry" keeps one well. Oh, well—I'll go for more blasted tea and then to the ballet.

They'll be using a winch and pulley to get this letter aboard if I don't stop.

---

* Laura was the Halliburton's cook.

[*Hotel Vendôme, Paris—October 15, 1919.*] So this *is* Paris! My soul won over my better judgment. I left London at 2:30 and reached Paris at 5:00—275 miles—by air. But you see I'm still alive to tell the tale, and now I can weep because there are no more thrills to conquer.

That night before leaving London I went again to the Russian Ballet and enjoyed it more than ever. *Les Sylphides, Petrouska* and *Cleopatra* were the ballets that night. I forgot all about my air journey during those three artistic hours.

I was up early next morning and attended to everything and was at the Piccadilly Hotel at 10:30. None of the four in my car had ever been on a long air trip before and were all somewhat excited. Our plane was rolled out—a huge one—a Handley-Page, with two great Liberty motor engines. It carried twelve passengers beside the pilot. I asked if fur coat, goggles and helmet could be furnished and found they could. I asked if I could have the outside seat—the very *front* one. "Yes." I was given a heavy sheepskin coat, helmet and goggles which I put on over my raincoat. We were all stamping with impatience and cold. It was 2:30 when we rumbled over the ground to the opposite corner of the field to get started, turned around and, with a roar that was deafening, raced across the bumpy ground for 200 yards, and then took to the air. The first sensation I had was "wrap up." We turned straight into the cold wind at 100 miles an hour, and the wind was forced into every opening. I strapped the helmet tight as wax over my ears. My cab protected my body from the wind—only my head extending above the shield. By the time I got my clothes adjusted and looked over the edge we were right over the Thames and all London was stretched out before us—St. Paul's and the Tower I could make out. We kept climbing higher and higher until by the time we reached the coast we were 8000 feet up. The Channel was streaming with tiny specks—ships—and looked very narrow for we could see miles inland both in France and England. It was clear enough to make out the rolling bottom of the Channel—here were hills and there valleys. I can easily see what a menace to subs a plane might be.

At the French coast we began to come down to about 2000 feet. On up the Seine, never changing speed. The sun was getting low. During the first hour my nose and cheeks got so cold and felt so funny I was sure they were frozen, especially since they wouldn't wiggle. Also, in my cramped position, my legs began to go to sleep. So I began to squirm and beat my hands and jiggle my legs till I grew warm again, and my nose melted and actually got warm, too. There was Amiens, and the cathedral, and as far as one could see were trenches, zigzagging every place. They were the last line of British trenches in March, 1918, when the Germans nearly broke through and were within twelve miles of Amiens. The soil is chalky, so the trenches made white streaks in the brown fields. Then it began to rain—oh, how it rained! The drops felt like pin pricks. Then the driver lost his bearings in the semi-dark and had to circle the Eiffel Tower to find them again. The landing field is some three miles outside the city wall. We made a beautiful landing. One gets the real flying feeling where I sat—may as well go by train as sit all closed in. I'm very happy I did it and I'm going to have a plane myself some day.

That night, my first night in Paris, I went to bed at 8:30 and slept thirteen hours. I guess the trip tired me, after all. Next day was Sunday, but you'd never know it—all the shops were open and traffic clogged the streets as usual. Paris is terribly crowded, almost as much as London, but everything is motorized here, like New York. I started walking—across the Place Vendôme—past the Opera House— of course I had a good map and knew where I was going—and some way or other around to the Champs-Elysées. What a beautiful street! It makes a vista that dwarfs all other cities. The man that planned this part of Paris had a divine imagination.

Yesterday I walked twenty miles, I suppose—visited Notre Dame and the Ile de Cité—on across the river to the Panthéon, which was closed—the Sorbonne—Jardin du Luxembourg—down Montparnasse Boulevard to the park facing the Invalides. I got into the Auto Show for a few minutes.

I've seen a lot of Paris and am having plenty of trouble with the language but guess I won't starve.

[*Hotel Vendôme—Wednesday.*] I've been working. I've studied French some twelve months in classes and I scarcely know how to ask for a glass of water or a postage stamp. I've found a first-class school—strictly private lessons. I'll go to a French boarding house where I can live reasonably and never hear a word of English. I'll have to speak French and think French. It's the only way to get it. And I've got to be able to talk with my hands before I return to Princeton. That would take but about three hours a day of my time. I propose to use as much time studying *piano*. If I can concentrate on those two things—and exercise—I can accomplish much by January fifteenth. I must speak French because I'll use it all my life, for when I die there will have been few better traveled men than I.

I do not see much of France if I stay here—but there's next summer, and the next, and years to come. This morning I wrote to Helen, and this afternoon I spent in the Louvre. I put in four hours and got a snap of Venus di Milo when she wasn't looking. Which reminds me, I haven't seen Rodin's *Thinker*—must do it.

[*Written in Paris, mailed at Lille—Saturday, October 18, 1919.*] Your cabled money reached me this morning. I deposited 1800 francs in the banking department of the American Express and at once began to prepare for my trip north. My shoes needed half-soling—the walk from Hull to London had quite an effect on the soles, and in the devastated country I'm going through, I'll need heavy shoes. I wanted a big-scale map of the battle area. I walked the streets an hour, going into every bookshop I saw. They had huge maps of France, but never heard of "une carte du territoire de la guerre." Then I had an inspiration—Brentano's! Sure enough there it was, a map of northern France printed in New York by the *Times*. I've made one other purchase—a new pair of heavy socks—the pair I've worn and washed and worn have given up the ghost at last.

It was such a glorious, snappy day I couldn't *think* of *riding* to Versailles, so I walked it—and raised dust on the way. The policeman could not understand that I wanted to get my directions to go "à pied"—he kept telling me what tramways to take. It was just a nice three hours' walk. I had a good guide and we spent another four hours in the building. The Hall of Mirrors where the Treaty was signed has been all cleared away but the table. I'm sure I'd have gone mad living with all that gilt and glitter around me. The fountains were not playing that day, but the grounds were beautiful

enough without that. Coming back I got off the car at the city gate
and walked home—it's such a waste of eyes to ride in Paris.

I'm getting on fine with français and the short week I've been
here I've gained confidence enough to ask any way for what I want.
When I get in a French lodging out of this English-ridden part of
town it will come fast.

[*Back in Paris, very safe—October 28, 1919.*] This is going to be a
ponderous letter. I think I'll start backward. I got back to Paris
Sunday afternoon about five with the one thought of food. I went to
the Vendôme for the night to my room, had the first bath in a week
and went to bed at 7:30. And yesterday I went to about eight tailor
shops looking for a suit. Paris may be heaven for women shoppers,
but it's the opposite for a man. These ready-made suits are every color
that *isn't* dark and affect a style that makes one all bosom and hips

 like this. Really that's a good picture. I finally
got a motley very dark gray. Then came the real
Battle of the Marne. "Jack, of New York" would
not, could not, understand why I refused *all* his
picture book "bosom and hips" styles. Finally I gave him my own
coat and told him to copy it, and if there was one measurement one-
tenth of an inch different I wouldn't take the suit.

I needed a walk after a round with him and hurried to the Sorbonne where I had a very satisfactory interview. They said the
Alliance Française had anything and everything I could wish. So
I bade the Sorbonne good-by—and sadly—it's such a dignified, inspiring place. The Alliance Française offered me every grade of
class—and I was placed in one elementary but well above beginners—
two hours six days the week.

Then for a lodging. Well, at last when I was very weary and
discouraged, I *found* it. The apartment faces the "Jardin Luxembourg," in the midst of academic Paris. The owner is a Professor of
Chemistry at the Sorbonne. His wife is a very motherly sort of
woman and has three children. There are three other Sorbonne
professors as boarders, and it's close to my school. I was rewarded
indeed for my persistence.

This morning I got up "and went to school." The class has nine—

and a splendid teacher. The pupils are all about my speed. But I've got a front bench so I can miss nothing. We had two hours this morning. This class is only incidental to my *real* class in the afternoon—one hour private lesson. I'm going to take 50 such lessons. They are mostly conversation. I talk and use what I learn in the morning. The husband of my landlady-to-be wishes to exchange lessons with me. We may alternate nights. He speaks enough English to get along but wishes perfection. So, you see, I'm throwing myself into this with a vim. I'm through tearing around, for a while, and am going to grind.

Among the students in my morning class are two girls—one from Chicago and one from New Orleans. They are about the sizes of Mutt and Jeff, but very sociable and fun to talk to, and Mutt says she can dance. So next Saturday night with my new suit, we'll go to one of the million dance places here. Well, voila!

Well, I mailed you a letter from Lille, written in Paris. To Amiens the country was normal. The work of the Germans in 1914 before the Marne has disappeared. But at Albert, where the British finally stopped the greatest German drive in March, 1918, I got a visual blow all at once. What dreadful desolation—a wall here and there, cleared streets, and then bricks and mortar and more bricks on every hand! A corner of the utterly destroyed Somme country, in which the Boche killed every blade of grass before he retreated. Someway it didn't look earthly. Dead water, gray, dead tree trunks, dead shambles all overgrown with dead weeds, dead hopes, dead, dead—that's the only word to describe what one could see.

The Germans never reached the center of Arras, but the railroad station was being rebuilt. Of course, such an important rail center was a target for Hun guns, and as Arras all during the war was situated with the line on three sides, you can imagine what happened to it. Farther on I saw batches of fat German prisoners, and the few other humans were Chinese laborers.

And then Lille, the biggest city held by the Huns in France. The station has been put back, but in the square opposite and every block around—more shambles, big, beautiful stone columns half buried in bricks and timbers. Poor Lille! The day I got there it was celebrating its first anniversary of liberation. It was Sunday and the buildings were decked with flags and the streets with people. I stopped an English Captain to ask about the destroyed buildings. "All done by Allied airmen," he said. "Lille was one of the very biggest transportation centers the Germans had and the station and railroads caught it." Lille would have starved but for the American Red Cross—it almost did anyway—especially just after the German evacuation, when every bridge leading into the city was blown up to prevent the Allied advance. So for ten days there was literally no food in the city, and it was during those days that Paris obliterated the great statue of Lille in the Place de la Concorde with expensive flowers and served champagne banquets in Lille's honor, when Lille had not even a crust of bread. But that's typically French.

The situation is the same still. Paris has money to burn—and burns it. The more outrageous the price, the bigger the fight to purchase. The agents at the automobile show were swamped and sold all available stock in two days. Jewels, gowns, luxuries for Paris, but not one cent for the brave starving farmer who has returned and is sticking to a space of earth that reels in shell holes and is impassable with barbed wire, living in a cave or dugout and trying to clear his fields and begin to level them and to build a more substantial dwelling from the blasted stones of his former home. They have realized "what we wish done we must do ourselves."

The ruling question is, "Where is the Germany indemnity we have been promised? Where are the machines and stock, and motors and *capital* we were to have received from Germany? The Huns have stolen, and destroyed what they could not steal, and now that France is victorious our possessions are not returned, nor are we given any assistance to obtain more." No wonder the country is still dead after a year of "freedom." It's not given a chance to come to life—but it *is* coming in spite of the *devil* himself. With nothing but their two hands those people will reconstruct their homes. For when there is such a spirit prevailing—why, I saw a mother and father and four little children, each with a heavy iron wire-cutter, laboriously clearing the fields of the barb—when there's *that* spirit, nothing else is really necessary. But I'm writing what I should save for the end.

Monday morning I left Lille and tramped south toward Lens.

The fields along the road to Seclin were in cultivation—no houses left, but the crops were there. At Seclin the entire aristocratic section of the town had been dynamited house by house by the Hun officers who had occupied such comfortable quarters. The Lille-Lens road has a big sign "Kronprinz Strasse"—no doubt it's left there just for ridicule.

Along toward noon I approached Lens and entered the Hindenburg line. I suppose there was more desperate fighting around Lens and more British and Canadian lives were lost there than at any other spot on the front. Lens is France's Pittsburgh. The one thing that distinguished the German and Allied lines always was the fact that the German was concrete flanked by steel pillboxes and concrete dugouts which are still intact, so strong they were, and the Allied lines had no protection, or very little.

Lens is simply the greatest ruin the world ever saw. A city the size of Memphis. Standing at the center where the "Grand Place" used to be, one can look for two miles in all directions and see nothing, almost, but a sea of bricks and wreckage. Not *one* house, not one *wall,* was left standing. The highway from Lille to Arras has been cleared and patched, but all other streets were obliterated. This wreckage was leveled and then churned by the guns and then bombed from above and trench dug only to have the trenches bombarded.

Here and there is a frame shack and in several places an entire row of houses built from the bricks of the old. On a miraculously preserved gate post only half shot away, I saw a big red sign: "Grand Bal, City of Lens—Place de la Guerre—Octobre 22." I stared at that sign. A grand ball in such a desert! "City of Lens" was pathetic, too.

Then on to Vimy and its famous ridge, just as the evening wave shadows enveloped everything again. I stood on the edge of the great crater, a mile long, 125 feet deep, 600 feet wide—something I'd longed to see ever since the report of it stirred the world. The acres of closely packed graves told the story.

It was black night and I had some six or seven miles to go to Arras, so I hailed a French lorry and the driver promptly drove off the road into a deep water-filled hole and the water killed his engine. He got awfully peeved because I wouldn't get out in water up to my neck and crank while he held the brakes to keep the machine from rolling deeper into the hole. I couldn't take his place, as we tried to change once and in doing so slid in some three feet deeper. Understand, we had no light and it was the darkest, foggiest night you ever saw. He yelled French at me which I couldn't understand, and I English at him which he couldn't. I crawled on top the canvas top and waited till he got tired of holding the brake and let her go. It didn't go much deeper—but left me seated on a little white, but dry, island. An ambulance (English) came along and heard our cries and found a long plank on which we climbed to the ridge. The ambulance took me to Arras.

But my troubles had only begun. Not a room for $1000—but I found two Tommies and they took me to their barracks and fixed me up, for nothing. I had dinner, though, in a hotel, where the dining room was once all mirror covered. A Hun shell had landed in the room—and you ought to see those mirrors. About every other house in Arras is standing.

Then on to Bapaume. I'm sure I've read the name "Bapaume" 500 times in the papers. It was fought over in the battles and prayed for at home, as if it had been Paris itself, whereas it's a tiny village— some 500 people once—but it had a big moral effect when captured or lost, and it took England a year to advance the ten miles to Bapaume from her 1915 front. The Bapaume advance cost England nearly 1,000,000 dead, wounded and prisoners—only to lose every foot of it and as much again in March, 1918. Well, Bap. is only thirteen miles from Arras, but I spent twelve hours getting there and walked some thirty miles. I met a Tommy on the road who suggested that he take me to the Hindenburg line close by.

This country, which once was a checkerboard of fields, with numerous houses and trees, fences and ditches, has all been scrambled into one desert, with nothing to stop the big plow for miles and miles. I got to the pile of bricks called "Bapaume" about six—dark—and went to the one *estaminet* for lodging. I got supper there, then was escorted to the *salle de coucher,* and was given the one cot—in the iron room—half of an empty cylinder, like this. I slept on the springs

 with two blankets on top, so that I froze from beneath and my teeth chattered so all night they kept me awake.

Next morning I was up early and off for Cambrai. Along that road one saw a patch of plowed ground here and there and a cow or so and mine holes 100 feet deep. You can imagine what walking was like.

I must stop here, and continue in our next. I've so much to tell, I can't put it all in one letter.

[*Paris—Monday, November 3, 1919.*] How I've ground my teeth over a news item in the *Herald* (Paris Edition)! The Germans have successfully sidestepped the Allies, not only in refusing to return the property they stole but now in having the brazenness to send a committee to London (*not* to Paris, please note) to grovel and plead that the 150,000 milch cows which they admit they stole from North France, they be allowed to retain in opposition to the Peace Treaty— because if they return them all the *German children will starve.* Did I see one *drop* of fresh milk from Lille to Rheims? I did not. I saw not over ten cows the entire trip. The condition of the children is so pitiful it racks one to look at them. Have they tasted milk since 1914—some of them since they were born? They have not! And now the Germans come whining and beg that they be allowed to keep these poor babies in this same state for years longer. What an insult! I cannot see why the English did not mob the delegates. If I handled it I'd make them not only return animal for animal, but two for one, for justice's sake. You see I'm still full of my trip north. I'll always be full of it—the impressions and indignations are there to stay.

Well, I'm working night and day now. I believe this new home I'm in dropped from Heaven for my special needs. It's a delight. The Professor, the landlord, is a typical teacher, impractical, unbusinesslike, untidy, but a real student and awfully learned. At night from eight to ten we exchange lessons. I'm not of very much use to him, but he is invaluable to me. The landlady is very kind and corrects my many mistakes and helps me in a hundred ways. The three boys—aged ten, six, four—are unusually bright children and we have a half-hour or so after lunch looking at their school books, and I manage to be interesting and learn a lot from them. I can *almost* keep up with the table conversation already.

How I enjoy the two-hour Cosmopolitan class. Miss Mutt and I have a jolly time together, and as we are a bit keener than the other pupils, rather dominate the class. I called on her Saturday afternoon and we had a long walk in the snow and found some real American ice-cream, which we attacked at once.

I've about given up any idea of music. My nights are taken up in study. In fact, I have from four to six open and nothing else. I'm trying so hard to get my French *moving*. Once I can get *into* the conversations, the victory is won.

I'll finish my trip hastily. I left you at Cambrai, didn't I? The road to Saint-Quentin led straight through the middle of the Hindenburg line. St. Q. is a shell, just like all the rest. I got there after dark, but found a shamble called "hotel" and had a very good meal in the only undemolished room in the building. The one room contained kitchen, dining room, office, etc. Next day I spent the morning roaming around. Here, too, all the old and beautiful public buildings were scrapped. The big cathedral, built on the top of the biggest hill for miles, and very white, still stood—no roof, no steeples, no interior, just four punctured walls.

I planned to take the train to Laon so as to rest a day before the Chemin des Dames, but I found the trains very unsatisfactory and decided I could walk it quicker—which I did. It took me four hours to get out of sight of the St. Q. cathedral, only to spend the next four trying to reach the quite visible cathedral at Laon. Laon was far enough behind the lines to escape, although it was alive with Germans and a concentration point for them. I had to pass through the forest of St. Gobain between La Fère and Laon. Not to have seen any trees from Lille and all at once to meet this deep forest, aflame with autumn colors, was startling.

I had a heavy day ahead, so I took a truck to the end of the Chemin des Dames I wished to begin at. What a day! The Chemin des Dames and both sides of it for some six or eight miles make the Somme battlefield look like a flower garden. The C. des D. area was too sterile and hilly for cultivation before the war, so it has been *utterly* abandoned since. I expected a great highway. I found an uncertain path, with a few cobblestones here and there of the remains of the former pavement. This area has not been touched—tanks, guns, equipment, thousands of shells—just as it was in November a year ago. Trenches still camouflaged, but one huge crater after another, all big-gun craters, so that following the serpentine path was very difficult. On the tip top of the highest point are the remains of Fort Malmaison, the greatest French effort in the way of fortifications, excavated into the very bowels of the earth, room after room, passage after passage, all surrounded with stone walls and arches eight feet thick. The outside only was wrecked. The passages were 60 feet underground. But it all fell in April, 1918, to the surprise German attack and is now a heap of ruins also, but so interesting I lingered almost two hours exploring that utterly desolate place. Then I went on down the trail for some six miles, when all of a sudden the most violent explosion 200 yards ahead all but knocked me off my feet and showered me with dirt and stones. In a moment I realized it was a depot explosion I'd run into. All the unused shells are gathered and exploded—for safety—in some such forlorn place as I was in. Lucky I was no closer.

A mile farther on and the path simply disappeared and only barbed wire in heaps, and shell holes, confronted me, so I gave it up and retraced my steps a few hundred yards to where a path led down the side of the hill, but my map gave no roads or directions whatsoever. I got completely befuddled and lost—it was nine o'clock, three hours of darkness—before I finally straggled onto the Rheims highway. I saw not one human being from five to nine o'clock to ask my way and not a light to indicate where one might live. On the highway I ran into an *estaminet* or wine tavern, where I was given supper and a bed on the floor.

On to Rheims next day. Poor Rheims! It was a beautiful white stone city, once, and the houses that have had the destroyed parts replaced and then the old stones cleaned to equal the new are little gems of buildings. It is not so bad as Lens—nothing could be—but next to Lens it has suffered most (except Verdun, I suppose). The cathedral! Well, I don't see how it stands. Many of the flying buttresses and outer walls seem to hang by a hair. All the beautiful carvings, in which R. was the richest cathedral in Europe, is gone. The statues—if they still exist—are shapeless hunks of stone. All the stone tracery and lace-work are battered into gnarled nothings. But the foundations, the *supports,* of the building still stand. The roof is gone. All the windows and window facings are gone. The inside is a grass-grown heap of blasted stones ten feet deep.

[*Paris—November 20, 1919.*] I've had a new adventure since I wrote last—in a hospital. Oh, but I'm out—was only in four days with a bad cold and sore throat. I went to an American doctor right away as I had a little fever and a very sore swallower. He said just go to bed and gargle this, etc.

Sometimes I feel I'm making no progress at all with the language. The worst part about French, real modern French, is that after you have the nouns and verbs and think you are quite ready to say anything, you find that no one understands you because they use the words in an entirely different way from English. We may know "Que—what," "est—is," "la—the," "date—date," and we say, "Presto, I can say 'What is the date—que est la date?' " But that means nothing at all. "What is the date?" is "le combien sommes nous?" ("the how much are we?"). But I'll get there some day if I have to come to France every summer for 40 years.

Dad, you'll be glad to hear my "soul" says for me to be home by February first, although, if I were on the move, it might say different. I'm not recklessly happy here, as I was until I got back from the north. I'm here now just to work and am as restless as ever. I wonder if I'll be restless in Heaven and want to "move on." Oh, I just thought of something—my morals and wicked Paris. The only reason I've not mentioned it before is honestly because it never occurred to me. All the stories about Paris are the products of an evil and wild imagination. The "battle of the boulevards" has entirely failed to materialize. I've not been spoken to on the streets *once*—so I guess I'll live through it. Yesterday Miss Mutt and I had a walk in the rain to our "American" ice-cream parlor.

No, Dad, my experience has not been a "frolic"—altogether; I took it too seriously. It wasn't *Europe* I was after. Mars would have served the purpose. Just some place where I could take the lid off and boil over—with hopes of simmering down. I've simmered a lot but not so much as I hoped to. If I don't go to bed soon it will be time to get up.

[*Paris—November 29, 1919.*] Two fat letters from Princeton, one from Larry and one from Heinie, make me eager to be back in New Jersey. I'll stack my friends there against anybody's. I'm doing all I can to keep in touch with them, but as I find it terribly hard to live on 24 hours a day as it is, my correspondence with them is scanty. With the $5 you sent me I saw *Romeo and Juliet* and never enjoyed anything more. Of course, the opera house is gorgeous beyond description, and the opera itself was artistic and glorious. I'm going to a Gluck concert next week with Madame and Monsieur Lebrettre with whom I live.

Yes, Dad, I *have* gone to the bat with "la langue française," and I've kept all my resolutions, but I've been at it a month now and I make a mistake every time I speak and these natives may as well talk Greek to me unless they speak slowly and distinctly. I want to learn how to say "If you try to put that over on me you'll get stung," as well as "Have you seen the book of my sister?"

I spent two hours in the Luxembourg Museum last Sunday. It's a perfect gem. It's so small you are not bothered by thoughts of what you are missing and a feeling that you must hurry to see it all as at the Louvre. There are not more than 75 statues and 150 pictures, but each one is a delight and just the kind I wish I had.

I get home about six-fifteen and have till seven to read the papers or any French literature I may have, and to write all my letters, because from dinner to ten I have my exchange lesson which throws all my studying after ten. Heinie writes me he saw the Registrar about my credits, etc., and says I can continue in my class, but I was pretty sure I could. Nice of Heinie, wasn't it? Bien, il me faut revenir à la langue française.

[*Paris—Friday, December 5, 1919.*] What happy days these last few have been—for I've been swamped with mail—*three* letters from you, Mother, one from Dad, Helen, Esther, and lots from Princeton with rolls of newspapers about the Yale-Princeton game. Oh, the glowing letters I get from Princeton—the place seems to have gone mad over parties, proms, excitement—everything but work. Helen's letter was nothing but good times. You know I hate to miss a party and if I were there maybe you'd be wishing I wasn't.

I had great plans to go to the Riviera January first and possibly sail from Marseilles, but no, I'm going to sit here and grind to the very limit of my capacity to the last minute. You know if I ever took the notion to attack the diplomatic world, speaking French would double my opportunities. And when English and French are the same to me, then I hope to overcome Spanish (and have an excuse for romping off to spend three months in Barcelona or Buenos Aires).

I'll be the gladdest boy alive to get my trunk again—I'm so tired of washing my one shirt (I *won't* wear these freak French clothes so long as I have one American shirt)—and to be all dolled up once more.

Dad, you hit the wrong target when you write that you wish I were at Princeton living "in the even tenor of my way." I *hate* that expression and as far as I am able I intend to avoid that condition. When impulse and spontaneity fail to make my "way" as *uneven* as possible then I shall sit up nights inventing means of making life as conglomerate and vivid as possible. Those who live in the even tenor of their way simply exist until death ends their monotonous tranquillity. No, there's going to be no even tenor with me. The more uneven it is the happier I shall be. And when my time comes to die, I'll be able to die happy, for I will have done and seen and heard and experienced all the joy, pain, thrills—every emotion that any human ever had—and I'll be especially happy if I am spared a stupid, common death in bed. So, Dad, I'm afraid your wish will always come to naught, for my way is to be ever changing, but always swift, acute and leaping from peak to peak instead of following the rest of the herd, shackled in conventionalities, along the monotonous narrow path in the valley. The dead have reached perfection when it comes to even tenor!

Once and for all, dear Mother and Dad, the only "slant" I've developed is sideburns and the only "designing French girl" is Miss Urbain of Chicago—age twenty-four, weight 165—but a perfect clown and a jolly companion—*Miss Mutt.*

[*Paris—December 16, 1919.*] I'm bursting with news. I've *engaged my passage home.* Meet me at New York, January 29. I'm not willing to come earlier for all of a sudden I find that French has given up combating me and surrendered to my ceaseless attacks, and the rest is all down hill. It gave me a real thrill to sign for my passage home. It's a long time off yet, but it's definite. I'm so happy over it and I know you are.

I was prepared to spend Christmas day moping, but I've changed my mind. Mr. Sanford, the American California University engineer I wrote you about, I like more and more. We've decided to spend the holidays together "Du Midi"—the Riviera,—Nice, Monte Carlo, etc. Both schools close from December 28 to January 4, so I'll have nothing to do for eight days—why not go on this trip? I'll wear my old Palm Beach suit at Nice and be glad to get this gunny sack off my back. It *is* warm, but about as well fitted as an Indian squaw blanket. I'll be back in Paris January 4 for two hard-working weeks; then home. Pack my trunk. Don't forget my Tux or my watch (my wrist watch in spite of all its salt baths still keeps within half-hour of the right time)—and my brown soft hat—and my overcoat—my scrapbook (I really *have* some "scraps" now)—oh, yes, and my suitcase—or a new one—oh, and don't forget my soft shirts—I'm going to embrace 'em when I get within reach. There's no such luxury in Paree, and I've been forced to starched collars—and I'd as soon be forced to matrimony. Did I tell you I got a long letter from Esther? Why not ask her to Florida with you, Mother—pass her off as a daughter-in-law? You might be on the safe side and get used to it in case of emergencies. Still for "yers and yers" I'd as soon take poison as a wife, 'cause I've already begun to think about my next trip—land in Spain and study Spanish.

[*Paris—December 22, 1919.*] After having made every arrangement on the *Mauretania,* the Am. Ex. Co. received a wire canceling all bookings as the *Mau.* has broken out with barnacles or something and has to go into dry dock for treatment. Everybody who booked the *Mauretania* is mad as a hornet, for we must all take the *Adriatic* sailing January 22.

Mr. Sanford and I are all set for our vacation south into the sunshine again. If I hadn't met Mr. Sanford, I would perish of "mal du pays," homesickness, on Xmas day, but being on the move and with a congenial companion, it will be easier to stand.

Yesterday (Sunday) he and I planned to walk out to Versailles, but as usual it was dribbling rain, so we rode out and had dinner at V. and I acted as guide. I had to hurry back, for Madame and Monsieur Lebrettre and I had seats to see Pavlova. Of course, it was beautiful, especially the Chopin music, but I did not enjoy it anything like the Russian Ballet in London, which was wild and reckless and unrestrained. Pavlova and her ballet were too studied and conventional and, while graceful beyond words, were devoid of any thrill.

[*Monte Carlo—December 29, 1919.*] I hope somebody shoots me the next time I tell the truth. Tonight, because I blurted out the truth without thinking, they wouldn't let me in the Casino. It was about the stupidest thing I ever did.

[*Later.*] Still no luck. I got next to the concierge and he gave me the "dope" on how to get in, but it didn't work.

All rather incoherent but it's like this. December 24— at 6 P.M.— my friend Sanford and I fought our way onto the Lyons Express and had the bumpiest, dirtiest, nicest ride ever, because after all it *was* a vacation. So we spent Christmas Eve at Lyons and celebrated by going to bed at 9:30 and sleeping twelve hours. Xmas day was almost as exciting. We strolled around the deserted streets, climbed the top of a near-by hill which is surmounted by a petit Eiffel Tower, and from the top of that had a super-glorious view of the city squeezed in between the Rhone and Saône rivers. But, *the sun was shining*. You, back home, can't appreciate the glory of that phrase. After two months of rain, yes, the sun was shining, and it made the rivers glisten, and the distant obscure Alps appear as if by magic— great white peaks so obvious and yet so camouflaged by the sky that you ask yourself, Are they there or are they not? Nor did that melting light ignore the narrow, funny little byways lined with houses standing since the year 400, for Lyons was a thriving city under the Romans and is dotted with ancient monuments. We had Xmas dinner in a nice restaurant. But even my pleasant companion could not keep my mind off 1916 Central Ave. How far off it was, how lonesome and vaguely uneasy it must be. Eh bien—next Xmas—next Xmas?

On to Marseilles—*oh,* what a lively, interesting, bizarre place, "the most cosmopolitan city in the world"—and I believe it. The streets, balmy all night, swarmed with holiday merrymakers—thousands of Algerians—as many turbans as hats—a hundred different shades of Negroes—Chinese—Indians—a drop out of the East—but what a low joint. Sanford and I, obviously American, were beset and besieged by armies of street walkers. It was my first taste of it, because, as I've written before, Paris during my stay has not come up to its reputation by about 99%. Next day more sun—and *such* sun that I donned my ready B.V.D.'s and dear, old, indefatigable Palm Beach suit, and had breakfast on the sidewalk in an orgy of sunlight. There is a very steep and high rock back of the city—and perched on the point of the highest pinnacle is a church which gave us our first view of the "Côte d'Azur."

Marseilles, crowded into a little valley along the coast, is no less impressive than the 30-mile stretch of *un*describably blue water—not just blue but *blue*—and ships in flocks—tiny ones—big ones—what a thrill it gave me—the smell and the sensation of the sea—"once a seaman, always"—*c'est moi!* So I dragged Sanford down to the wharfs and got another taste of the real Marseilles—squalor, heaps of garbage, swarms of flies and half-naked children, sore-ridden beggars sleeping on the steps, filthy cafés, filthier people. After the monotonous splendor of Paris, the contrast was doubly realistic.

—On to Nice, just turquoise and green pines and foaming surf and glistening white houses and flowers and sunshine—*sunshine*—only it's all that and more. It is a gem of a city. What man, in his utmost effort, has failed to accomplish to make Nice perfect, Nature *has* accomplished. The promenade along the shore is crowded with people from every land, and the hotels and homes are magnificent beyond words. Sanford and I stayed in Nice until yesterday. We climbed one of the near-by hills and through the openings in the twisted pine trees got our fill of blue, white, and green landscapes. But Nice is only one little spot in a great Heaven and is no more beautiful than the other spots. The casinos in Nice are enormous and one sees thousands of people in the concert hall or over the forest of tea tables or in the roulette rooms. The roulette at Nice is a simple affair where one franc is the stake. Altogether I played nearly four hours and had the usual beginner's luck, winning 260 francs but always playing a careful, timid game. Now I was all set to try Monte Carlo. My passport states age nineteen—and a seaman—so I knew better than to show *that*. Sanford had his passport and with a little soft talk and my visiting card I was about to get in when the agent asked me, "What profession?" and instead of saying glibly, "retired Steel Magnate" I blurted out, "Student"—and at once realized it was all over. It was.

This morning Sanford came home minus 200 francs, which helped to soothe my disappointment. I strolled around the grounds overlooking the blue bay and decided it was the most beautiful park I'd ever seen. But some time soon I'm coming back here—when I'm twenty-one—and try my luck. This hotel is beyond my means, so we're going back to Nice tonight. This afternoon I'm walking and hugging the coast to Mentone, on the Italian frontier and some twelve kilos from here. Sanford *won't* walk. Next time I'll stay a month and walk, walk, walk. For a walker the Riviera is heaven.

Going home (Paris) I'll not stop once but gird my loins and grit my teeth and *stand* the 22-hour trip. Sanford is going on to Italy, but it's Paris for me—necessity, not preference. This trip has made me all the more determined to *get* my French. *Everybody*—that is, all guests—speaks French, especially the English visitors.

In spite of all this glorious sun and country, I'm thinking more and more about the end. My "amazing interlude" is almost over. I will be back in the "even tenor" of my way at Princeton and really wondering if I dreamed all this. It's all too fantastic to have *happened* to me. But now it's *fini*. Get out the fatted calf, for, in less than a week after you get this, the prodigal will appear afar off—and, true to the original, leaning on his "staff."

[*Paris, January 7, 1920.*] Bien, this *is* my last letter, mes chères parents. The darned old *Adriatic* was postponed until January 28, so I sail January 17 (before or after) on the French liner *Savoie*—eight days in summer but guaranteed to take longer now. The *Savoie* is the *bummest* boat still afloat, but I guess a salty sailor like me won't mind. I can't think of a darned thing to keep me from leaving with the boat. Still the *Lorraine,* sister ship of the *Savoie,* struck today and all passages were canceled. If that's my luck I'll jump in the overflowing Seine.

Of course, I'm back in Paris after my nice bake in Nice. I found the city scared to death by the Seine River. It's much higher than a cat's back and gives us a chance to see what Venice must be like. The gas company has shut off gas and Paris has frozen up. But I'm in my room only to sleep, so *ça ne fait rien*—it doesn't matter.

Dad, all you wrote about my restlessness is very true. But you are nearly thirty years older than I am—that's the whole point—and when I'm your age I'll be writing my son just what you've said to me and what your father would have said to you if he had been alive when you were twenty. Didn't you have a wonderful trip through Canada and New England just before you entered Boston Tech? My restless nature must come from one of you—I didn't cause it—but whoever is to blame, I'm very grateful, because I wouldn't take $1,000,000 for it. When I reach forty I think I will have had enough of uneven tenor. Gosh, Dad—"don't bring you a daughter." You forgot to tell me not to bring home Mt. Blanc or Sarah Bernhardt—but I won't.

Only ten more days—Whoop la!

CHAPTER III

BACK TO PRINCETON AND THE PIC

It was the custom of father and son to spend the Easter holidays together. The Easter of 1920 Richard suggested their meeting in Washington and proceeding to Harper's Ferry, with its historical associations—John Brown's dramatic episode and, not far off, the battlefield of Antietam. There would be fine walking.

On top of one of the hills overlooking the Shenandoah Valley and the Potomac River Richard told his father of his desire to vagabond around the world after he had graduated, instead of taking the usual three months' summer trip to Europe which had been promised him as a reward for getting his degree.

This was a surprise. Could it be that a refined, esthetic young man who elected to study the Classics, Poetry, Oriental Literature, the History of Painting, who disliked noise and dirt and banality, could crave to be a vagabond? The father knew his son's flair for travel and his restlessness. So after much discussion to develop his ideas, consent was given, with, of course, the mother yet to be heard from. After Princeton, what? had been a problem previously unsolved. This scheme was his solution and he was certain that after such an adventure the future would be of no further concern. His inner conscience, the "still small voice," had spoken.

Princeton—April 2, 1920

My own dear Mudder:—

I'm so curious to get a letter from you telling me how you spent the days Dad was with me. Perhaps I will tomorrow. He 'phoned Hafford yesterday and went to New York this morning. I scarcely saw him the two days he was here, as I'm full up with work Mondays and Tuesdays. Last night, however, we went to a concert together (David Werrenrath) and after had a long walk and a really good, frank visit. I've never spent a more pleasant week with Dad. It was so much better than New York. After I wrote you from Washington, we walked back to the Capitol and had lunch with Congressman Fisher and Senator McKellar and I met most of the Senate. In the afternoon we had a wonderful walk in Rock Creek Park, an interesting wild bit of land.

That night it was warm and moonlight and from the observation car we watched the Potomac all the way to Harper's Ferry, which has been called the most enchanting spot in ten continents and I believe it. We climbed to the top of the old town and looked down on the Shenandoah and Potomac River rapids all shiny in the moonlight. Harper's Ferry is so old and interesting it reminds one of something European and ancient. Next morning we climbed by easy stages to the top of the promontory and the view we got is worth coming miles to see. It must be even more wonderful in flowery spring. It was the sort of view you want to keep on looking at for hours. On top, we had a very important talk he'll tell you about. And then we climbed down to the river again, right through the rocks and bushes, had more fun! In the afternoon we hired a Ford and loped over to Antietam Battlefield. It was a clear, sunny day.

At Philly we had to wait an hour or so for trains and walked into the Bellevue-Stratford to wait. There was an orchestra playing, and playing the very pieces I know and love best. They played Schubert's "Moment Musical," which I heard so often in France and next to "Ave Maria" love best of all. After the concert last night we walked for over an hour and had a good talk. I know he really enjoyed his trip. It was novel and he rested and loafed and met all my friends. We talked of next summer. He likes Mike, naturally.

Soon after the Easter vacation Richard was elected Editor-in-Chief of the Princeton *Pictorial.* He grew determined to make it a lively and influential campus publication. His letters till the close of college are about the *Pic,* essays, proms, examinations. On his way home he stopped at Chicago to attend the Republican National Convention, out of which he got a great "kick."

Before commencement, Richard and Mike and Burnham Hockaday had developed a tentative plan for a late-summer outing in the Rocky Mountains, depending on the reaction of their parents to the scheme. Finding them sympathetic, in July Richard proceeded to Kansas City to join the Hockadays and with a fourth boy, Ed Keith, continued to Browning, Montana, their starting point.

[*Browning, Montana—July 20, 1920.*] We rode to Glacier Park Hotel day before yesterday. We rode back the same afternoon and all four of us declared it was the merriest day ever. None of us had been on a horse in ten years and the effect was correspondingly severe. It took us three hours each way. The daily rains have made the vegetation dense and the rolling hills, checkered in sunlight and shadow and all ablaze with flowers, make an unforgettable sight. I remember how you marveled at the purple heather hills you saw in Scotland. These are much the same. One hill is purple with wild asters, the next yellow with Shasta daisies, the next blue with bluebells. Best of all is a small orange flower that covers the ground for square miles. The only sign of civilization is a lonely steer or a long-haired Indian on his lean horse.

These Indians are worth the trip to see. Lots of them speak English and have the funniest names. One of our guides is called "Raising-hell-for-nothing," another "Pete-bad-old-man," and his wife "Rose-a-long-time-sleeping." Rose weighs about 400. She and Pete are collecting our provisions in a rickety old wagon, followed by their seven dogs. Rose was wearing a big brass and leather belt and when I asked Pete if she would sell it to me he made a sweeping motion which included Rose from tip to toe and all she had on, and grunted, "Ten dollars." But he wouldn't sell the belt unless I took Rose, too. They are just like our niggers, entirely irresponsible, and we've been delayed by their breaking faith.

Our two guides are old at the game and are taking us straight into the mountains where there are no trails and no Indians, only mountain sheep and deer. We've been busy as bees all morning packing and it looks as if our four pack horses will not be enough. We will be off at six tomorrow. Mike and I are reveling in this country. The horses we rode to Glacier were just "Injun" horses— gallop or trot. The hotel at Glacier Park was wonderful. We had lunch there and rested a bit. We'll stop there a day or so coming through the Park, beginning about August first or third. Mike and I have a bedding roll—canvas and waterproof—and five double blankets. We have a world of provisions but four men and two guides for three weeks take food. We haven't been fishing but we have four collapsible rods and we are going to fish in water that never saw tackle before. After our long ride we'll be ready for a mere 25 miles tomorrow. But if we strike a good fishin' place we'll stick. My shoes are *long* enough, my clothes warm. Our party is just right.

We have lots of kodaks and I've got to write up our trip for *Outing* or *Field and Stream*. It's going to be fun riding in this gale. It's enough to blow one off the horse. Well, got to go again.

[*Glacier Hotel—August 3, 1920.*] My wire sent yesterday should have relieved any anxiety as to my safety or whereabouts. Our trip so far has been novel and wild and interesting, for we dived right into the wildest mountains in the West and were like lambs in the hands of our guides, but they managed well and their craftiness and knowledge of the country has *made* our trip. We left Mr. Stone's place with two guides, four pack horses and our four saddle horses, ten horses in all, and followed the Indian hunting spots to camp, the best fishing pools, the best scenery.

We've all had fishing tackle and guns and our fare has been ideal. We've had grouse and squirrels till we're sick of them and rainbow trout till we don't dare look one in the face. I've fished a few times, always with some success. The guides are good cooks and after riding from twenty to twenty-five miles a day, hacking, leading our horses, making and breaking camp with two plunges a day into melted snow, our appetites are incorrigible. We four fellows are highly congenial. We usually ride from nine till twelve—and from two till five. The guides pack the horses, cook, hobble, do all the disagreeable work. We're all asleep and the campfire out by ten and we sleep till *eight*—a terrible camping rising hour, but this is our vacation so we do as we please. We lay over three days one place—on the edge of a pine-surrounded lake, just fished and read and slept.

I've been wretched from sunburn, incurred the first day, and since I've ridden with a towel over my face. The temperature is delightful, never hot, but the sun blisters in a minute. Mike and I have slept in one big bedding roll with eight blankets, and have been comfortable. Our mountains have been in wild country, far, far wilder than the Park. We saw *one* man, a fire guard, our entire trip from Stone's to Java, *but* dozens of sheep and goats on inaccessible crags, a bear and several moose. The Park is humanized and civilized and soft.

We reached Java night before last, and rushed to Belton for our mail. I got *lots*. We spent the night and left for Lake McDonald yesterday morning. The water is inky blue and the mountains surrounding impregnably sheer and embattled, yet the people here say pooh! pooh! when I stand agape at the view and say *this* is stupid compared with that beyond. Two Kansas City girls are here and we six have had a time, swam and danced and soda-ed and played bridge, but we must go back to Java tonight and on tomorrow for another ten days of camping over a different route back to Stone's. So I'll wire again from Browning when I return there.

I was never safer. Dad, we don't have to *stand* in our stirrups any more, and can ride all day and never notice it, and long for the unbarred prairies around Stone's so we can gallop.

Vacation over, senior year begins.

[*Princeton—Sunday night, September 27, 1920.*] Homesick—just as if I'd never been away at night in my life! I've given up ever getting over it.

I was down to dinner at Hamill at Lawrenceville this evening and had a delightful visit with Mr. Henry. The old school was never so beautiful or appealing. We talked of Wesley's entering there three years ago.

My, what a whirl this week has been. It seemed I was drifting along calmly in a canoe at home and all of a sudden go dashing over some roaring falls which are Princeton. Mike and Chan were here and we visited till late. Saturday I saw Profs, got my gym locker, exercised, moved *Pic* furniture, saw all *Pic* men back, had posters printed. Our new officers are a joy. I'm up to my neck in my subscription campaign to get at the students before the *Tiger* and

Prince. Last year we had 300 subscriptions among the students; I'll not stop under *1000* this time. Meeting all the gang in New York for a reunion at two tomorrow. It is fun to be busy. I want to get all I can done before school work interferes. I'll take a course in Shakespeare in place of short story, and Henry van Dyke's course in Poetry, Money and Banking, Speaking, perhaps International Law or Oriental Literature, and French—all stickers.

[*Princeton—September 30, 1920.*] Wednesday is going to be my hardest day, but I find great consolation in the fact that I'm sure to hear from home that day, to be cheered and encouraged and loved. I always need all three, but more than ever this fall. It's going to be a momentous fall, one long remembered, just as this summer will be. In fact, the entire last fifteen months have brought me more contentment and benefit and happiness than previous years. Surely now I am favored by the gods in environment, training and opportunities. I've no right ever to be discouraged.

I laughed out loud, Dad, at your "hope you have love for further adventures." Why, I have traveled far and wide in twenty years, but it's a mere trifle to what I'm going to do. It's what I enjoy most, when I'm most alive and farthest away from the commonplaceness of earth. Whatever little poise I have acquired has been acquired to a big extent from the advantages of travel and the associations it involves.

I'm in the dumps about our *Pic.* We've got our publishing rates arranged satisfactorily—more than last year, but still quite reasonable. Ads are very slow and limited—they always are—but our campus subscriptions are desperate. There are four papers, *Prince, Tiger, Lit* and *Pic,* and last come is out of it. Everyone on the *Pic* board volunteered to solicit one dorm and I felt constrained to do my part. After working the whole board three nights, we've got only 300. *How* I detest soliciting! It's so far beneath the dignity of a senior, and head of the paper, but every ounce of our strength is necessary to meet competition; so last night in the pouring rain I canvassed freshmen all over town. Ever since we opened, all my friends have visited and enjoyed one another, while I rushed hither and thither trying to force *Pic* on unwilling buyers.

My schedule—I got in advanced Public Speaking—includes Spaeth's course in Shakespeare (instead of International Law), Money and Banking, Oriental Literature, French with a *Frenchman,* and Dr. Henry van Dyke's Nineteenth-Century Poetry. I'm delighted with it. First class at nine. I've just the preceptors I want, too. I hope I have time to work and thus enjoy my classes.

But he did not get those courses in without a struggle.

[*Princeton—October 10, 1920.*] My war with the university is progressing rapidly and at present the enemy is retreating, thanks to my visit to all the ten men on the Curriculum Committee. It looks as if I can have the courses I want. As usual luck broke in my favor— it almost always does except in golf—don't know about love yet. Our subscription has passed 525 on the campus and we ought to glean 250 more. Our issue is slowly and exasperatingly getting on. My two best photographers are tearing around the country speaking for politics. We had our first Speaking Class last night—subject, League of Nations. I was astonished at the speaking power of most of the members who have been at it three years, but I need it so much.

I wonder what *Field and Stream* is doing with our story.

October 14, 1920

Dear Dad:—

I decided to let you pay this bill of $22.98 and $3, else I wouldn't have much left. Books cost millions now. We got our issue of *Pic* out after an all-night session Sunday and we find it will be necessary to order 2000, or more than any other publication on the campus, including the *Princetonian.* This is not a letter—but a bill!

[*Tuesday, October 19, 1920.*] I had an unusual experience with my photographic manager. All of a sudden for no reason he resigns from our board, and several other things. I asked him why. He says for three years he has slaved, sat up nights, neglected his studies, read not a line, drifted from his friends, grown thin and developed the worry habit, and his last year he is going to try to be free and live his own life. He didn't try to excuse himself for the awkward position he placed his co-workers in. But now he gets eight hours' sleep and two hours' exercise—can read, visit, write and be free of "wrinkled care." I understood his position so well I could not be very angry at him. He figured out it didn't pay in the long run. I wonder if it does! However, his work has fallen on my shoulders and it's heavy. Life is so short—especially youth—it seems a shame that it makes so many of us draft horses.

The *Pic* is the best *Pic* since its beginning. We think it is the *best* pictorial published by any college in America, and thus the world. You say, "Should that not make you proud?" It would but for the lack of organization, the escaped steam and inefficiency and general irresponsibility. It's a clever publication, though, in spite of the muck it has to plow through.

My engravers, after promises to have my cuts Saturday to the printers, got ill and only got them there this morning (Tuesday) because I went down and stormed till they dropped everything else to do the work. I didn't even trust the truck driver who carried the cuts from one office to the other but rode right with him. It takes six days to print and, with Monday lost, night work at double prices is necessary in order to get our *Pics* out Saturday for a 10,000 spectator football game where we hope to sell 500 issues. The situation required my presence, though I had to cut five classes to do it.

Mike and I went to Trenton Friday night and played bridge at Helen's—had a very merry evening but we are too busy for such frivolities. I'm sending Haff and the Doctor two seats for the Yale game on November 13. There'll be 50,000 people in town and how I wish you could see it. I like the Public Speaking—only made two or three speeches and they were prepared. I'll have to come to the extemporaneous by degrees. It's all lots of fun.

As usual this letter has been a ramble of facts requiring or offering no thought, just impulses, but that's the way I live.

[*Princeton—Monday night, November 2, 1920.*] Your long-lost son, after a long hibernation, comes to—only he has been far from being asleep like Bro. Bear. The Yale game *Pic* went to press last night. Our circulation management is greatly improved this year.

My despair of 1000 paid subscriptions was groundless. We oversold our last edition and had to steal or buy the issues out of the dormitory rooms to cover outside subscribers. We raised the price from 25c to 30c per copy and for the Yale game it will be 50c. Everybody will be in a holiday mood and will pay 50c. We hope to sell 4000 copies. It will be the biggest effort yet.

In sophomore year I studied the utilitarian philosophy of life and decided that was really my philosophy. Expediency! Consider only the result and its effect. If the effect of the result is best, then don't consider the *method* of achieving that result. This is very dangerous, for the philosophy of conventional right and wrong does not enter into the situation. It winks at dishonesty and even at murder if the benefit achieved by committing them is greater than that by not. This tends to make one unscrupulous. I've snitched pictures, and lied for the *Pic* and torn up valuable books—done anything to put out the best possible issue—not to be prevented by any little consideration for personal property. One person is outraged and indignant, but *1000* subscribers and readers are pleased and attracted by the result. Not that these lacks of scruple *now* have much influence, but the tendency is strong. P'raps I'll hang for embezzlement some day.

I'm enjoying Dr. Henry van Dyke's English Poetry course more than anything I take. It demands three 2000-word essays in three months. My Shakespeare demands the same thing. In Public Speaking we have to deliver a 1500-word oration every month, and other essays require 10,000 words. So I'll wield a fast pen this fall.

I've always suffered from overconscientiousness. It really is a fault and source of unhappiness. At M. U. S. I wept if I was absent from school and was distracted if unprepared for a lesson. But I'm snapping out of that.

Well, I must write an editorial—shall it be on prunes or prisms? Any way it must *be* something, so good night.

[*Princeton—Sunday afternoon, November 8, 1920.*] *What* a hectic week end! Yesterday was the best fall day I ever saw, a golden glow over everything. So Mike, who stayed at home also, and I decided to take an outing of some sort. We hired a Ford for twelve hours and about 4 P.M. set sail for Philadelphia—had dinner—went to the theater—home about 2:30. The roads were good and the night was cold and clear. We had our sheepskin coats and blankets. We never spent a more delightful day—had the top down and just us two. We plan to do it as often as possible, which means never again most likely. The college is deserted and quiet for once, all in preparation for the revel next week end when Yale and Princeton play here.

I'm fretting over the piles of class work past, present and due that stares me in the face. I've studied this fall only by snatches, interrupted, hurriedly, and as for steady, concentrated grind, where one *gets* an idea and holds it, not at all. Reading *Hamlet* in an hour or 200 pages of *Foreign Exchange* in two is not much mental training. Mike and Larry exasperate me, for every evening they see their friends for an hour after dinner, study from 8 till 11:30, do their work well and consistently and go to bed just as I'm coming in from the *Pic* office for an hour's work only, so as to get to bed by 12:30. Each day is a struggle for me, and an easy well-ordered adventure, often monotonous, for them.

Everything here went 99% for Harding at the election. But the sun will shine just as bright and we'll all have just as many worries and pleasures as under Democratic rule. Xmas is *not* very far distant—how I wish I could skip till then! Still, midyears come so soon after, dozens of essays and *Pics* in mad succession. So after all what's the use of wishing it were any other time? I know only too well I'll be wishing the rest of my life I could be as carefree and joyful of life as I was my senior year at Princeton.

Today Mike and I arranged a real-estate deal for a whole house for next commencement. It takes care of our two families, eleven beds and three baths. We want it for a week. The house is furnished and it is close to the club for meals.

[*Princeton—Sunday night, 11:59, November 30, 1920.*] My Thanksgiving vacation has been the pleasantest few days I've known in Princeton. *Oh,* what an orgy of rest and sleep—and work, too! It began Wednesday. Everybody in college went tearing away as if Princeton were poison. Poor idiots! Only Mike and Shorty and I knew better. We three went to the Firemen's Ball here in town and

More amused than impressed by the sprawling grandeur of a mythological
warrior, Richard mimics his pose in Berlin.

Bicycles for two. Mike took this picture of Richard in Holland.

had the time of our lives. I read all Saturday afternoon *A Vagabond Journey around the World,* for Mr. Franck is lecturing at L'ville soon and I'm to have dinner with him. Aren't you jealous, Dad? I must finish his book before then. I'll surely pump information from him.

I've read *Hamlet* for a fourth time (and shall many times again, as it is the most inexhaustible piece of literature), and written a 3000 word essay on "Hamlet before the First Act"—all since supper. I could do millions of work under the present state, even if I did flunk my "Money and Banking" mid-term test with about a 20. I never failed a test before, but I've not the time to bother. I'll never be a banker. The next nicest thing to being a whirlwind of occupation is to be in a big comfortable chair asleep. One can't enjoy the last without the first.

[*Princeton—Monday, December 6, 1920.*] Just came back from Mrs. Robinson's funeral. She was taken ill very suddenly and died even more suddenly. In fact, I knew nothing of it till the day after. I'm so sorry. There were few boys she loved more than me—and there are few outsiders I love more than her. Her neat little house was packed to the attic with friends—dozens of her old boys, for everyone that ever was a Kennedy House boy adored Mrs. "Roby."

I've been utterly *consumed* by the *Pic* all week. Sometimes I think I *hate* it all, and yet when I once plunge in I forget all else but the joy of production—producing something live and worthy and readable. That's the only motive. Funny, in college we fight literally for honors and opportunities to work ourselves to death. We get no honor, certainly no reward in money, we risk our friendships and club life and grades in lifting the *self-imposed* burden—and if we are not lifting, feel self-reproachful. Queer! I'm not getting light and careless about my work, not at all, but I do not have any chance to study and the contest now is to get through on wits and not wisdom. The trouble is I'm interested only in the *Pic* and all else here is incidental. But everyone else is the same way. Shorty runs the Y. M. C. A. and manages the basketball team, Mike manages the track team, Larry dozens of things and athletics, Heinie is my circulation manager and is on the crew.

I keep my business department in hot water. I've at last got the best offices in college, had them papered, and $100 in shelves and tables installed, and $300 I've spent on a developing room with electric drying fans and basins. Just now when I'm on the downhill side of my editorship (nine issues done and four to go), the *Pic* for the first time in its life *is* something—*officed* and out of debt and circulating and *anticipated,* up-to-date equipment. And then I'll leave it all for the next board who will appreciate it not in the *least.*

Dad, all the years after my senior are going to be developing, but not so much as this one. I wouldn't want them so "developing." The strain would get monotonous. But college is little more than a push for momentum so that you can spring into life's activities. "Routine of Life?" Life is not *life* if it's just routine, it's only existence and marking time till death comes to divorce us from it all. Oh, to live a life that is *not* routine, *not* in a rut so deep one can't see over the sides to the limitless horizons beyond. Only to grasp the thrills and inspirations *now* instead of when I'm "settled" and uninspired with the energy of twenty. Mike heard a lecturer recently on the pitiful condition of Europe, and the difficulty of passports and passage and all the other possible glooms. He came to me and said, "Dick, what do you think about our waiting till conditions are more favorable?" Bosh! He doesn't realize the difficulty will be half the fun. He doesn't thrill at the hope that the conditions are *not usual.* All the more adventure if traveling is the more difficult.

The more imagination one has the more travel means. I'm going to read history by the library-full in the spring.

Well, believe me, I know what I'll do when I get through the *Prince* and the *Pic*—not till April first, however. I shall sleep and rest and read and visit and live. The undergraduate schools committee asked me to form a Southern Club. I shouted back, "No, get someone else." I was asked to be an editor on the Senior Class Book. Again it was "Never." Mike put my name up for class odist as at L'ville, but well-known lyricists and musicians are in the contest. I haven't a chance as I'm not known for anything so esthetic. As for school days, after next June—oh, fateful month!—I'm not interested. Lots of my friends are going to Boston Tech and law schools, but I want to go around the world.

Gosh, Dad, I suppose business conditions are about as bad as possible. I hope you won't have to sacrifice to get me through school. I'm a rather expensive hobby, I guess. Yes, money-making is the hardest thing in life for the uninspired, but I feel as positive as anything I'll find *something* new and use my imagination to make dollars out of it. I revolt at the idea of being a bank clerk or any other sort of "beginning at the bottom." I'm going to be my own boss from the first whatever I do. I can't work for anybody else and not have the reins. I'll never be happy or progressive that way.

[*Princeton—Wednesday afternoon, December 15, 1920.*] Only three more days and I can let the fires under my boilers cool down and run on one volt instead of ten. The last few days have been exasperating beyond measure. My printing press has been on strike for several days and inexperienced pressmen have taken their place. Our cuts from the engraver were impossible. Some of them had to be made over. I planned to have our Christmas issue out yesterday, but it will be tomorrow perhaps, and at that I've spent three afternoons and evenings trying to keep the pressmen from throwing up the job. But last night about ten I left the press knowing that the last sheet or "form" was ready. All I have to say is, "Ha, ha!" But I realize in a few years I'll look back at this year and smile at the tragic way I looked at such trivial matters, just as now I cannot see how I ever worked myself up into such frenzies about the funny little *Lawrence.*

I was in a grocery store recently buying oranges for Mike, who was ill with indigestion. I saw a big Xmas fruit cake in a fancy tin box, the top of which was decorated with dancing elves. I was in sore need of a cover for our next issue and the cake top struck me as just the thing—but the darned thing cost $7.50 and they wouldn't sell the box sans cake. But by paying $7.50 as collateral I was allowed to rent the top for a few hours for 50c, take it to the photographer and have a print made and take the top back to the grocery store. The cry is "Let somebody else do it, Dick," but nobody else would have thought of the cake top, or of getting it if he had.

Speaking of living one's life, a friend of mine showed me a letter from his father to this effect: The boy, age twenty-two and on the

Senior Council, had written to Baltimore to ask his father's permission to go to a Saturday night dance in Philadelphia costing $3.82 in railroad fare. The father wrote back that after considering it, he would consent. Meanwhile the boy failed in a test, the notice going to the father who rushes to write the boy again that he has *vetoed* his permission for the party. No wonder the boy has absolutely no initiative or individuality, and they have no mutual understanding. I told him the sooner he breaks away and stands on his own feet the better for him.

Princeton—Sunday, January 9, 1921

My dear Mudder:—

Your never-failing wire this morning reminded me what day it is—I'd really quite forgotten in the sweep of activity since my return—but you never forget. I've had such a lonesome, lost feeling every since my return. The six years in which I've developed a will and personality of my own have been spent in New Jersey, and I always come back to it with a sigh of relief and contentment, but this last holiday, so smooth and untroubled and companionable, has opened my eyes to my own home and I love it as I never did before.

Tonight I feel like Conrad in quest of his youth. Nine more years and I'll be thirty and the last vestige of youth will be gone. At present I can look forward to no joy in life beyond thirty. I see there the end of my ability to enjoy and love and *live*—it's only existence for me after that. That's the disadvantage of being one of this ultra-modern generation—we are satiated before nature intended us to be. The thrills and cream of life, as well as the dross, have been sprinkled through the years for you and your age, but they have fallen on my head all at once and the sky is empty and monotonously gray. The automobile, the moving pictures, the benefits of constantly increasing means, travel, New York and Paris, the war and then the world, have come to your generation after you were old enough to be interested in them as they came. But I have fallen into the midst of them and am accustomed to them. However, you are saying, no doubt, that all this proves I am very, very young— discouragingly young, for it's the way inexperienced youth has talked since the beginning.

What a brimming full year this last has been for me. It found me in Paris—my last few busy days—the experience of a sea voyage de luxe—our two weeks in New York—my eventful college term with the *Pic*—the quiet weeks in Memphis with you, Dad and Ammudder, divided by the unusual and successful Montana outing—Glacier Park—St. Paul and home again—my struggle through the fall here to be rewarded by the two happiest weeks I ever spent back at home—all in *365 days*. It seems almost incredible! What man can boast of a 21st year such as this? But it's only a prelude to my 22nd. Nor is the next to be unique for its prosaicness nor any up to thirty. After that, I don't care. You have taught me to avoid self-depreciation, yet I cannot help but think sometimes that I have failed to gain the full courage and strength and poise and control and intellectual development from these amazing years that I should have. While I'm discouraged at having gained only an inch, I do realize I am on the one and only track which leads to an ell. How I should like to read my letter written on my 22nd birthday!

This is *your* day, Mother dear, not mine. I'm in the midst of a race—what an unfortunate time to choose for a birthday letter to one's mother—but the love is here, the sympathy, the admiration.

[*Princeton—Saturday, January 22, 1921.*] I "take my pen in hand" for the first time in about two weeks, but that doesn't mean I have not had my typewriter in hand day and night. Between essays, tests and *Pic*, I've become a human dynamo—and now that I can stop and look back over the past two weeks I marvel that I have accomplished so much, yet got enough sleep, exercise and food. Of course, the *Pic* was an extra big issue. But I forgot the anger and weariness and sweat it takes in the pleasure of seeing it take root and grow and bear fruit. It's the "Vacation Number" and eight pages extra. The senior class is voting now on "most popular," "best athlete," etc., and everybody in my club has flatteringly given me "most original."

Whoopee, but it's got cold—wonderful skating—I've had a short jog trot over the frozen ground and "breathed deep."

If you come to New York for vacation and go to a hotel, I want a room with two beds so I can have Mike and Larry stay with me. I never felt closer to my four roommates, with the shadow of separation beginning to darken. I've made new fast friends this year, foolishly late.

Dad, I got 85 on my Money and Banking essay.

I made out my schedule for next term. When the Dean saw it he asked sarcastically, "Aren't you afraid you are going to be overworked?" I told him I was afraid of nothing of the sort, that I had slaved all last term and the present one and I was tired to death, and also sick of so much practical economics which I did not need and which bores me. So I'm taking Victorian Literature (Dickens, Thackeray, etc.), American Ideals (Whitman, Longfellow, Emerson, etc.), Ancient Oriental Literature (the Bible and Hebrew writings), Advanced Public Speaking (orations and extemporaneous), and fifthly, Modern Painters (1600-1920). It was hard to choose. But I calmly sidestepped anything that smelled of work and essays. I hope to use my time in reading history and travel, in exercise outdoors and in company, so as to be fit to begin my trip and write about it entertainingly. If I feel I have enough material and pictures for a good book, I shall feel it my duty when I return to do that first—other things after. With all that in mind I took five easy, pleasant, cultural, informative courses, and I was *exactly* right. I wish I'd done it long ago.

[*Princeton—February 9, 1921.*] Yes, Dad, we *have* so little time for relaxed conversation. The Ancient Greeks insisted the only purpose of education was to facilitate expression. In that respect mine has been only partly successful. The only way to learn to express is to express, and I've been too busy getting ideas and information to express anything.

I've taken advantage to some extent of my opportunities but the *important* thing is that I *realize* that the reaches of life are infinite, and that a door has been opened from a room with four walls to the great outdoors. With this realization I can continue to experiment instead of hibernating in one confine. The more I think about the idea of the book and lecturing, the more it appeals. I believe I could write a salable book.

I've been asked several times to go on deputations for the Y. M. C. A., speaking on the broadest aspects of life and religion.

I've never had a chance to as yet, but this spring I might go in heavily for it. My work in the speaking course here has helped very much and while at first I was nervous and retiring, they can't keep me down now.

[*Princeton—Wednesday morning, March 2, 1921.*] Saturday I met Mike in New York to see Mary Garden in *Faust*. I'd never seen that opera before and was duly impressed and delighted. Mary is as young and interesting as ever. After dinner Mike, Larry and I returned to the Manhattan and heard Galli Curci in *Rigoletto*. Both performances we had seats in the balcony with all the garlic-smelling wops, but that's the true atmosphere.

[*Princeton—Sunday, March 6, 1921.*] On April first the last *Pic* is buried. I've spent my time this week bickering about the next board, and it's all settled exactly as I would have it. My last issue is going to be a special "Abandoned" number containing the most outrageous and amusing copy and contents we dare publish. Every publication has a last fling—it's an old custom.

Well, our prom was a huge success. I did not have a girl, but as I knew dozens that were there, I had quite enough partners.

Our class begins again tomorrow, and I shall speak on our lost academic spirit in college—which I bewail, but am a cause of as much as anyone. Our interest is every place but on our books. Princeton and other universities, therefore, turn out business men of culture, men who will lead in the material world, but few great college presidents, writers, diplomats, philosophers, professors, research students, in comparison with old universities, where academic training was of first importance.

You suggest, Dad, that I keep the check from *Field and Stream* as a souvenir. I can hardly do that, but their letter of acceptance will serve the purpose. I'm wondering when I shall settle down to the grind again. I was so ground by last term there's a reaction, I suppose, that is only natural.

Spring makes it hard to "concentrate" on other things than play and fresh air. But tomorrow is Monday and I have five classes—none of which I've thought about, so better look to 'em now.

[Princeton—Thursday night, March 31, 1921.] Easter Sunday was perfect here, bright, sunny, and warm. Even Shorty left me to preach in Philadelphia. Feeling very rested, I could not resist the outdoors—put on my walking shoes and followed the canal back through woods and fields to the road leading to L'ville (all alone) and struck across to the old school coming down upon it in the twilight from above. They, too, were having vacation and no lights were on. Never has it seemed so appealing. A rush of emotions and memories came over me as I looked from Kennedy House to Upper and the other familiar haunts of the benign spot. Mr. Henry's great red tulip bed was in bloom, just as it was the first day we went for a walk which began our unusual and invaluable friendship. I was hungry and thirsty and was glad to see a familiar light in Mrs. van Dyke's house. They were at home and asked me in to supper. How the two younger girls have grown! Penelope has become a beautiful, charming girl. Those were such pleasant days, *now*. Well, after two hours' visit I followed the highway home, physically tired for the first time in weeks.

I've spent several hours recently drawing zigzag lines on a big map of Europe. These lines are itinerary—where I should *like* to go. It looks more like a gadfly's route or a labyrinth than a European trip. One would believe this was to be my last trip to Europe and that I was seeing everything this time to make sure. My course in Oriental Literature is fascinating. It's given me a great desire to "do" Egypt. The course drifts to Babylonia and Assyria. My studies in Rembrandt, Rubens, etc., lead the line through Antwerp and Amsterdam. My lifelong desire to travel in Alsace diverts us from the Rhine banks inland. The line gropes south to Marseilles. I *must* go back to that fascinating town. A walking trip starts at Cannes and follows the most beautiful coast in the world to Genoa. Then I shall go across Italy to Corfu, and from the "Isles of Greece" to Athens. I *must* climb Mt. Olympus and sail up the Dardanelles to Constantinople. That's as far as I got. Well, you see, I'm just *full* of wanderlust and when I pore over the map I itch to see it and *feel* it.

Before being done with the *Pic,* four or five of us seniors were planning a theater party to celebrate out of our profits, but I grabbed every cent and $100 besides out of the bank and spent it on my last issue. $950 for one *Pic,* and they usually cost about $500. Instead of our having $75 or so apiece to spend personally I spent all of it and leave the next board *$100* in debt to pay. *But we* had to pay bang-off $1100 of the last board's debts and I didn't think it fair to make *one* board pay for the stupidity and mistakes of all previous boards.. If we pay $1100 of the debt, the others can pay $100.

[*Princeton—Friday night, April 9, 1921.*] I'm utterly lost with nothing to do. It's such a blank sort of sensation. I've been looking forward to it for a year, and it's not at all what I expected. In fact, I really don't like it, but I do like writing to you and shall indulge myself more and more my depressingly few remaining weeks.

At last we have arrived again at spring! The vegetation seems to have recovered from the frost recently and our little town is once more a wonder spot to glory in. I should like to live here. The academic, cultured, social atmosphere, the accessibility to New York and Philadelphia, the sheer beauty of the place, all combine to draw one back. It is a town of 6000, but half the home-owners in it are in *Who's Who*—lawyers, artists, architects, statesmen, financiers, and an unequaled group of educational authorities who are too close to be appreciated. Einstein is coming to spend the spring months as a lecturer. Alfred Noyes and Dr. van Dyke draw crowds. Wilson and Cleveland are stamped on the place. Professor Gauss is the highest authority in America on the literature of the Romance languages. Conklin in biology and Russell in astronomy are better known in Europe than America. I could go on for pages, but my point is that, with all this dazzling mass and source of inspiration and wisdom, I have spent my two years of discretion—with *Pic*. Am I a better man for it or has it been a waste? I've taken and know no biology, no geology, little math, little philosophy, no astronomy, no architecture, no chemistry, no foreign language but French. You may ask what I have had. English, English and more English—French which I learned in Paris—a *good* history course both European and American—a pleasant Horace course—public speaking—and Modern Painting—there are all I've got any benefit from. But I've covered English prose and poetry up and down, in and out, and am better read than 99% of my class in this respect, only might be twice or ten times as widely read if I had *read*—which I've not done—or done too hastily to profit by it.

Dad, you say that in college I have learned "to think and analyze and apply thought and analysis to working out my problems." I hope I have. I get very blue at times because I realize I don't think and analyze, but depend on an impetuous but irrepressibly energetic force to carry me along. I always get there, though upside down sometimes. How many times I have resolved to write oftener and at less length! But I do so dislike to write *anything* half-way. I may be careless about my speech and time and my money, but whenever I pick up a pen R. Halliburton becomes a *very conscientious* person.

I've a picture of my book—a great melting pot of history, literature, personal autobiography, humor, drawings, paintings, photographs, pathos, romance, adventure, comedy, tragedy, all branching off, but an integral part of the most vivid narrative of real experiences of a very live, open-eyed and sympathetic young man on an unconventional and originally executed circumnavigation of the globe, all bound up in a large and richly covered volume with *Wanderlust* in big gilt letters across the front. There! That's rather concrete, isn't it. It will vitalize my trip, experience my pen, exercise my thoughts, and collect in a manuscript all I have learned and all I can extract from a prodded imagination. The trip will be one education. The manuscript will be another. There can *be no failure!* There'll be a Book. No, I don't want a Baedeker, nor a Harry Franck, nor a Mark Twain, nor a Frederick O'Brien, but something of each, plus chiefly me. Above *all things* it will be neither stupid nor monotonous. If a man does not sing, actually or theoretically, when he works, there must be something wrong either with the man or the work.

[*Princeton—Saturday night, April 17, 1921.*] Since my last letter, I've been disturbed by a comprehension and introspection which have never impressed me before, and which I don't like to think about now. It's this! Among the students of every college there are always a group of men who think more clearly, speak more intelligently, seem to be more developed mentally and socially than the great mass of their fellow students. They are mostly Phi Beta

Kappas, influential speakers, serious students. In which class is included none of my close friends or I.

In other words, I see myself satisfied with less than the best, choosing something other than the highest development Princeton can give me. And then I begin to cross-examine myself. Granting that I became determined that further training is best, *now*, just when real enthusiasm for intellectual development has come to me, would the fact that I would be able to lead a fuller life for having got it compensate me for the three or four more years of concentrated effort? And would I then loathe to become a great lawyer, or statesman, or college president or the writer of exalted unreadable literature? Perhaps this is all answered by my choice to edit the *Lawrence* and the *Prince* and the *Pic;* perhaps the higher life has not enough action and freedom; perhaps my *Book* will refute my doubting mind.

Suppose this: Why not Oxford—for a year, to try it? Take a three months' summer trip and be in England in October. After a year there I'll be only 22 then. I could try for a Rhodes Scholarship, which, added to your support, Dad, would establish me excellently. If one year's experience proved unsatisfactory—enough! Please write me what you think about all this. As things stand now, I want to go *all the way around*.

[*Princeton—Sunday night, April 24, 1921.*] *Field and Stream* gave me a very good space—three pages. A number of people have spoken to me about it. Let's hope this is just the first of many more, and that the name of the author will become a familiar one to many readers.

My roommates and I had a 41 Patton handball tournament recently and I won the beer-mug trophy. There is a club dance every Friday night for a month, and I'll be partying myself to death. Still as I weighed *150* pounds yesterday stripped, I'd better do something, else I get too pudgy.

This room has been filled with a howling mob all night. I'll stop and sing some too.

[*Princeton—Friday afternoon, May 7, 1921.*] What a pleasant afternoon for me! I've no classes on Saturday—or Sunday, so Friday afternoon always initiates a good long opportunity to rest or read. While I've still a great amount of work on my hands, Mike and I are taking time to keep up with our trip plans. Shorty is sailing July first with a committee of college picked men to study social conditions in Europe, but his main reason is because his cousin and fiancée are there. Larry is going in the conventional way. Only matrimonial Heinie thinks it a waste of time to do anything else but make shekels and build a house for his Dot. Hopeless! But good old Heinie! No fear about my jumping over the broomstick soon. I disagree with you, Dad, in your estimation of the bachelor—that he becomes a selfish egoist. A man is that or not by the time he is 21 and marrying is not going to change him. If I could find—when a fitting time comes—a wife who would be as stimulating and *interested,* as socially graceful, as my mother, I would be a fool not to marry.

Tomorrow is a big day for us. Mike's track team meets Yale and Harvard, and the Navy row us on the lake. Heinie is captain of our boat.

I've been reading Browning's *Paracelsus,* a consummate poem and psychological study so subtle and so intense it is a classic and entirely beyond anything but a mature concentrated mind—and this work he wrote at the age of 22! And I began to wonder if perhaps I'd best start selling groceries.

I thoroughly enjoyed your remark, "If your ambition is to be superintellectual, living in an *atmosphere of vague idealism,* you should have striven for the Phi Beta Kappa" and "by introspection you can prove yourself a hopeless imbecile." Well, I feel better about Harvard and Oxford.

An agent came around today taking measurements for our graduation gowns. That *was* a blow. In three weeks our final exams begin—I wish it were a million weeks. So sorry I'm a week late with this, but the college authorities are obdurate when it comes to substituting letters home for their essays.

[*Princeton—May 22, 1921.*] I'm in a haze from the week end— just about the happiest seven days I ever spent. *Everything went beautifully*. It sunshone itself to death. Marie was the most popular and by far the most attractive girl on the street and followed around by a flock of men everywhere she went. She has a brilliant mind plus a very demure, shy personality, plus a very stubborn will, plus a tantalizingly attractive appearance. People stare at her. I *couldn't* let my last chance for a Princeton houseparty escape and not take advantage of it. She was so in love with Princeton and I was so in love with her—oh, yes, just for the time being, of course.

It was a relief to find I was able to enjoy myself whole-heartedly again. I was afraid I was getting bored and blasé, but it's all wrong. I'm dead tired after the strenuous week, but very, very happy—it was *so* successful.

[*May 23, 1921.*] Just about a month from today I'm set adrift, with a diploma for a sail and lots of nerve for oars. So many men graduating have their lives visioned and arranged with the greatest precision—four years law—father's law office—four years medicine—three interne—practice. Mine is so much more shaky—one and a half travel, nine months writing. If published and a success, fine. If not accepted, then what? And at the "then what" stage I'll be nearly *24* years old. Well, that being the case it's *got* to be a success. When I stop to think about after June 21, I frankly become afraid, just as a child might when told it is going to be thrown in a pond to *learn* to swim!

Mike and I had great news yesterday from Kansas City. His parents are enthusiastic about his going with me. His methodical-ness and great sense of responsibility are necessary counterparts to my wild imagination and reckless energy. It's a question which type gets the farther or accomplishes the more. Some day Mike will be at the top of a great business where efficiency and faithful obedience mean everything and imagination and inspiration *nothing*. Of course, the question is, How far can one get on that foundation; and the answer is, Just as far as one can get with lots of inspiration and reckless energy.

Tuesday, May 31, 1921

My dear Mudder:—

Isn't it splendid that Wesley's birthday comes at such a beautiful season of the year? It is such a great consolation to have today a day of flowers and sunshine and happiness, rather than cold, gray weather such as, well, January ninth, for instance. Year by year we drift farther away from the time when he was such a vital part of our family, when it was impossible to contemplate the four of us being ever any more or any less, but the succeeding years can never dim the memory of him as he was at fifteen. He will still be so when we are old. He would have been nineteen today, almost grown and moulded. We can remember him always *only* as a fine-looking curly-haired youth. I always think about you, Mother, on May thirty-first and love you more that day. Well, I do not believe he would have us despond because he is dead, but he would have us love his memory.

[*Princeton—June 2, 1921.*] What a long pull it's been since Christmas. I almost recoil from the thought of *eighteen* months abroad. Mrs. Hockaday has two other sons to comfort her in Mike's absence—and you have no other sons. However, Dad will be a great help, for he is a very optimistic reassurer. How alarmingly close the time is coming! How I would like to hold the sun in the sky and delay the summer a month or two! I'm so happy here now, more than I ever realized I could be. Even my exams, of which I had my fourth this afternoon, have not depressed me. I've gone at them with a song and laughed out loud at the questions I didn't know.

The girls at our houseparty were so lovely in their youthful, simple dresses. I hope to heaven I'll get abroad unencumbered by any sentimentalism and not waste perfectly good hours writing letters to some uninterested girl.

CHAPTER IV

BEGINNING THE ROYAL ROAD

Germany and the Matterhorn

AFTER Princeton, what? Richard had chosen *what* by listening to "that still, small voice" which he had been told, many times, to hearken to. However, his faith in the "voice" did not allow him to leave his beloved Princeton without a heavy heart. So strong were his emotions that he actually *ran* from 41 Patton Hall as he started for the railroad station. His mother and father went with him to New York and at once his search for a ship began. Richard and Mike soon discovered that their diplomas were no asset in breaking into the ranks of ordinary seamen. Their search for a ship was novel to them and for a time became disheartening, but they *did* find one at last—the *Ipswich,* bound for Hamburg. And so Richard began the fulfillment of his dreams, the solution of his problem, After Princeton, what?

[*North Sea—July 30, 1921.*] It's been six weeks since I wrote "Dear Mother and Dad," but nevertheless I've been writing you every night since I left New York, and put it all into the brown copy-book I'm mailing with the letter. It's close to 15,000 words long, so you see I can't have missed much.

We have been at sea fourteen days. At 9 P.M. tomorrow we tie close to the Hamburg docks, and my third trans-Atlantic voyage will be over.

Our route, to my delight and surprise, did not go through the English Channel, but north of Scotland. We are now, I guess, in the middle of the North Sea—and what a different sea I find it from September 20, 1919. It was light green and snowy and very rough then; today, calm and deep blue and warm. Starting at the Grand Banks, for nearly a week we had dense fog and low temperature, all the time the foghorn blowing and the icy spray drenching the deck, but two sweaters and three pairs of pants kept me warm, plus nine hours a day of vigorous work. Naturally, at every turn I've compared the *Ipswich* and the *Octorara* and find each has its advantages. The *Ipswich* is 6500 tons and the *Octorara* 1500, and the crews are about the same size, which means the present crew works about four times as hard as the former. The route last year was through the Gulf Stream, with hot, velvety nights till we passed the balmy Azores, and this trip it's been fogs and icebergs and stormy all the way. Our portholes are fifteen feet above the water, yet only for the last two days they have been open, as the waves have smacked against them unceasingly.

Last Sunday and Monday Mike was green with seasickness and simply had to knock off work and lie down. I myself felt as uncomfortable as I could without being really nauseated, but never missed a meal, though oatmeal frequently sufficed. In my notebook I have written at length about our painting and shipping and general work.

I've missed the coil of hemp rope forward we had on the *Octorara,* where I could recline after supper with a book and watch the sun go down and the moon come up over the mirror-like water. The sun does not set in this latitude now until eleven and it's up again at 3:30, and this is a hard steel boat and always dripping wet from icy sprays, so I've had to seek a different evening pastime. I've found it in the notebook, as you will appreciate when you see how long it is. I tried to write an average of 1,000 words a day, which, if I keep up, will total the 500,000 word goal I've set myself. They are just memoranda of thoughts and stories and experiences. I may attempt an article for *Atlantic Monthly* and call it "Two Weeks before the Mast," and compare modern sea service to that described in Richard Dana's *Two Years before the Mast.* Dana and I were both college men—Harvard and Princeton; both of cultured families; both stimulated by the same urge—both followed it to sea; both write about it from American ships, one in 1840, one in 1921; both named Richard; both 22.

I do not contemplate with pleasure the difficulties that are sure to come between Mike and me and to end in unavoidable separation. My trip is my occupation in life. I've "gone to work." My aim is

The royal road is before him as he tramps down a forest highway in the Vosges.

Behind him in the picture but before him in adventure was the Matterhorn, when this picture was taken on top the Gorner Grat. Zermatt lies in the valley.

proficiency in my present task, not to get through on a certain date. It's going to be "speed up" from Mike and "slow down and stop" from me. It's unfortunate, but inevitable.

Our crew has been a joy. There is a Yale junior on board and several high-school men. The talkative Captain Tucker was our illusion, for he's not spoken since the day we signed on, but the mates have been considerate. All during this voyage the wireless has informed us the mark is sinking lower and lower until it takes 80 marks today to equal a dollar in value. However, I am not going to take advantage of the exchange to live recklessly. I shall follow the spirit of my trip. Things have been rather matter-of-fact and would get monotonous if kept up much longer. I was surprised how natural the work seemed and how quickly I became accustomed to the "old life."

I'm glad we are nearing land. At three o'clock we steam six hours up the river to Hamburg, past the Kiel Canal and the heart of Germany.

[*Hamburg—August 1, 1920.*] This note will be mailed along with my Saturday letter, so you will get two at once. I just wanted to back up what my cable told, that we are safe and well in Germany. Mike and I worked it so as to be on the bridge all day yesterday where we could see everything, and there was a world to see. We passed within a mile (west side) of Helgoland and on to Cuxhaven port, the longest string of shipping we ever saw, on up the Elbe. The Captain let us off about three and we did not dock until ten. We were just passengers to watch the scenery go by. It was Sunday and all the river excursion boats were packed to the rail, every beer garden lit up and swarms of people everywhere. There are new ships all about and Hamburg harbor seems anything but dead.

It's hot! And after the icicles of the past two weeks it seems disproportionately so. I am darn glad to get a rest from *manual* labor, but it did me good and no doubt I gained on it.

[*Berlin—August 7, 1921.*] We arrived in Berlin yesterday and, having been directed to a hotel here by Danish friends of ours in Hamburg, got settled within a few minutes after our arrival. We have received the most courteous and hospitable treatment at every stop until I cannot reconcile the Germans' brutality and ferocity in the war with their affability, generosity and kind-heartedness.

Well, I've seen a new world since I wrote last Sunday night. My eyes and ears are exhausted every night from being overtaxed. Mike does surprisingly well in German. The little practical German I once knew has been my salvation. I can understand—that is, my ear catches every distinct word uttered by a German and if I but knew the meaning of the words I could understand everything. In France, a native glides and weaves words together so one must learn to understand phrases.

We certainly made time getting off the boat. Mike wanted to wait till a German sailor could go along with him, but I needed no such attendant and struck out from the dock for the American Express Office where I was to meet Mike at three. They didn't get away till late so Mike missed me and we didn't see each other for two days, which was a very good example to set at the beginning! Soon, thanks to a map of the city, I was showing the police around and could have hired out as a guide.

I spend half my time collecting pictures and information for future reference. Naturally, my own pictures are those of an amateur and not good enough. I'm aiming at an article, "German Impressions in 1921," profusely illustrated with bought and original photographs. I've been scribbling away and have 12,000 words in my new notebooks, but I will not be able to send them to you till I reach England and have time to write the article which I shall send first to *Metropolitan*. I've had to give up attempting two things at once—I mean keeping up with my book notes and collecting data for an entirely different type of article for magazines. I will throw all my energy into book notes and use from them what I can for magazine attempts. I can do neither justice if I try to do both, so I've found. I'm ahead of my 1,000-words-a-day goal. You can get an idea from my first book I sent home what I'm putting into it.

We will leave here Thursday morning on bicycles for Rotterdam. Isn't that a great idea? I noticed so many people in Hamburg cycling that I quickly determined I should see rural Germany and a lot of it in that way. Mike is as enthusiastic over it as I. We'll make about 65 miles a day and stay at farmhouses and small towns. I hope it is half as interesting as my English outing. We walked miles in Hamburg and I know it, and the people in it. The water was terrible so we had to fall into the Hamburger habit and guzzle tons of beer to satisfy our incessant thirst. Both Mike and I were so crazy about the place we stayed from Monday morning till Saturday and hated to leave then.

Beginning last night we have been awe-inspired by the magnificence of Berlin. I must see Paris in the foliage season to say it is still the most beautiful city in the world. The Tiergarten Park here is incomparable. We had a long, slow, rubberneck ride this sunny morning and for three hours drove through more parks and past more memorial buildings than it is fair for one city to contain. The Royal Palaces certainly look moth-eaten and I dislike intensely their rococo style of architecture that abhors a smooth, white wall, but must have gilded eagles and statues and recesses as thick as possible until the whole thing is a nightmare. I never hope to see anything as harmonious and satisfyingly impressive as our own Capitol Building and Washington Monument, clean and classic and powerful. There are more monuments in Berlin than people, and myriads of white marbles banked by heavy green foliage decorate every part of the city. I'm so happy to be in the midst of all this, so fortunate. I'm well and fat. My 1,000 words are yet undone today. My 30,000-word notebook will keep you reading for a week.

[*Berlin—August 10, 1921.*] Still in Berlin and no chance to get away till Friday, but that is only too agreeable to us, for Berlin is full of interest and we need every possible minute.

Mike and I visited the German Coney Island a night or two ago and found human nature to be the same, only worse. I thought Americans were easily pleased, but they are not so easily pleased as Germans. One of their stunts is a mechanism where half a dozen people turn cranks at once; these force air into deflated balloons and the balloon that bursts first awards a prize to its destroyer. The booth operator cheers on the perspiring contestants and makes money literally by the sweat of other people's brows. The park is really beautiful, so many fountains and flowers and bands.

Mike is taking the airplane ride over Berlin today but as anything after my London-Paris trip would seem flat and as I cannot afford the five dollars I'm not going. Yesterday we spent hours in the museums and are finishing up today. Their collection of Greek sculpture is really magnificent but their modern efforts, especially in pictures, are miserable beside the Louvre. The big cathedral, built in 1905, is a gaudy imitation of St. Paul's and as unharmoniously ostentatious as most things German. We went to the theater recently, saw the *American Girl,* a sort of musical comedy. We almost got put out we laughed so hard when the chorus waddled and hobbled on. The music was rather good and one does not miss much when one misses the lines in such a show.

[*Berlin—Friday, August 12, 1921.*] I've discovered fifteen minutes every day I didn't think about before—after I've ordered breakfast and while waiting for it to be served. So hereafter I intend to do all my personal correspondence at the breakfast table. Mother, it's less than a month till September eighth, Heinie's wedding day. There is no one, and perhaps there will never be anyone, whose wedding I am more interested in. It is a great regret that I cannot be there. I want to give them a present of course. Will you get it for me?

Yesterday we spent the morning getting our passports and visés for Holland—two hours in the Frederick Museum and I almost lost an eye at the collection of Rembrandts, Rubens, Hals, etc. It was impossible to comprehend that the pictures we studied for weeks at a time at Princeton and had seen in copies hundreds of times were actually before my eyes in the original.

We go from Berlin to Potsdam, to Magdeburg, to Hanover, to Osnabrück, to Amsterdam, Haarlem, The Hague and Rotterdam.

[*Potsdam—August 15, 1921.*] See where we are now and it's an enchanted place to be. Our bikes are splendid. We've our knapsacks, raincoats and cameras, not over fifteen pounds in all. The ride to Potsdam, twenty miles, was beautiful. We spent the afternoon sightseeing with Mr. and Mrs. Ship-King, my first Lawrenceville roommate and his wife, who are touring Europe. They had a special guide, so we saw everything *in English.* All the apartments of the late Kaiser. The grounds are more radiant and beflowered and better kept than Versailles. In fact, it's the most seductive garden I've ever seen—fountains and trees and marbles.

We went to a dance hall frequented only by soldiers from the large barracks here and had a most interesting evening. Every dance or so the girls danced together. A man could break in by loudly clapping his hands together in the ear of the desired partner. Then the soldiers danced together and the girls broke in. They did a funny little jiggy waltz, polka waltz I believe, such as we danced in 1860. Mike and I found us two rather fat girls and we danced, too.

I'll be so glad when we get some place where I can actually converse. It's exasperating not to know enough German words to make a few remarks.

[*Nenndorf—August 19, 1921.*] You will have to look hard on your map to find where we are this sparkling sunny morning. In general, we are half-way to Amsterdam from Berlin, in a little watering place called Nenndorf where evening and fatigue found us and where we found as beautiful a quaint old hamlet as I ever saw.

I wrote you from Potsdam. The next day we got only as far as Genthin, some fifteen miles west of Brandenburg. Genthin is a very small place but the smaller the towns the softer the feather bed. The first two days the wind took all the joy out of life and between Genthin and Magdeburg it took us six hours to go thirty miles. Mike was so sore and stiff we had to stop and I began to despair for the success of the trip, but next morning the wind had changed and blew behind us all the way. Brunswick was our next stop, fifty miles more, and yesterday, pedaling forty-five miles to Hanover without a stop, we made this town, fifteen miles beyond.

This is the most beautiful scenery in the world, for nothing is so picturesque as intensely cultivated, animated farm land. It would do your heart good, Dad, to see this territory in harvest time as it is now. Mathematically neat, fertile acres, trimmed trees, clean woods, no broken-down fences, no muddy roads, no grass-grown corners, but rolling miles of sugar beets and copper grain and clover. We've come 175 miles and found no elevation more than 200 feet and no depression more than 100, so we've had no heavy hill climbing to do. Sixty miles was the most we've done but we've our second wind now and can do more daily with comfort. I never got such complete satisfaction out of anything before and am happy every minute of it.

For the first time I've got behind with my 1,000 per as I'm too tired and sleepy to do over 500 words at night.

I've taken three rolls of films and surely can get something out of them. My luck is nothing startling. The subjects—goose girls, sheepherders and homely, rural things—are good.

[*Amsterdam—August 22, 1921.*] We are in a *real* city again. Mike and I both agreed we'd never been so quickly and completely taken by another place as we have been by this. It is teeming and beautiful and rich and its endless canals make it a veritable Venice.

Sunday, we had lunch at Deventer and reaching Amersfoort at seven found we had covered 75 miles in eight hours' riding. The afternoon trip was one of the best—all the Dutch peasants sitting in gala attire on their cottage steps—old men with bright-hued wooden shoes and gold earrings. Bicycles are the one means of transportation—fat grandmothers and whole families with the baby carried in a basket on behind. Extremely interesting country with perfect, shaded roads.

The better road from Amersfoort to Amsterdam lay through Utrecht but it was some 25 kilos longer than the straight line to Amsterdam, skirting the Zuider Zee, and, as we wanted to be here as early as possible, we took the straight line and rode all morning twenty feet below sea level. The real Holland. Canals and cows, canals and cows—but such canals and such cows! We had trouble finding a reasonably priced hotel, for nothing is reasonable after Germany.

We are going to the Rembrandt gallery this morning, and I plan to camp there hours; to the famous Isle of Marken this afternoon; and we set sail tomorrow for Haarlem, The Hague and Rotterdam.

We saw Dutch movies last night of the Dempsey-Carpentier fight, but the captions were demoralizing, such as "ik zijn olucht eede ook," meaning "upper-cut to the jaw."

[*London—August 29, 1921.*] It was a happy, happy day, when we set foot in London and rushed pell mell to the American Express Company, dragging our bags behind us, and oh, what a beautiful stack of mail! Irvine and I just sank into a chair and read letters for an hour. We had been looking forward to that hour for six weeks and even then it was twice as delightful as we anticipated.

I've another booklet jam full of notes—25,000 words on Germany and Holland. I'll have 30,000 more by the time we get to Paris and you can read for a week or two of things that happened.

London doesn't seem so interesting as before but I've seen and done things entirely new and enjoyed every minute. While Mike did the Museum and Tower and Abbey, I did the Bank, Cheapside and the Tate Museum. I went back again to feast my eyes on the pictures I studied so hard. There have been several beautiful wings built since you saw it, Mother, hung with pictures of post-bellum subjects.

Every letter was so cheerful and full of good news—just as mine can't help but be—the rain on the farm, the nice, new car, good health and spirits. Aren't we a heaven-blessed trio, thanks to your and Dad's hard work and good sense?

Mike and I have taken pictures by the score. Mine are rotten! So are his. But we are learning fast and if my kodak hangs together through the mauling it's getting I'll be a photographer yet. I'll break myself buying films but it's a worthy extravagance. The other bank-breaking expense is trunk shipping, and it is about over, for tomorrow my trunkful starts for Memphis, Tennessee, U. S. A. It cost me too much. Home it goes and all my clothes in it. I'm keeping a change of underwear and a handkerchief and, no doubt, they will be coming next.

I looked forward to graduation as to a time when I could relax and get more sleep and be *less* busy, but so far it's been just as bad if not worse. Every second of my day has been occupied since I left New York and at that I'm behind, not in time or itinerary, but in self-imposed tasks. My 1,000 words take from two to three hours *every day*—just the only time I could have to relax and read and write letters. They bring my breakfast so fast here I don't have time to get started on a breakfast note.

Amsterdam is the high-water mark: the most delightful and interesting place. I enjoyed the gallery there above all others. We went to the Isle of Marken where the pictured Dutch costume is really worn, and we dressed up in wooden shoes and took pictures.

We bicycled to Haarlem where I sent you a pair of wooden shoes for your birthday, Dad. They will arrive about two months late. I meant well. The ride to The Hague was the best of all: great green estates and homes more luxurious and better kept than any place we'd seen. Nothing but Packards and Locomobiles in this rich, fat country. We could have stopped a month at The Hague, neat and beautiful and parks and seacoast and palaces, but we had spent too much time; so, on to Rotterdam. We sold our bikes for $10.00, having paid $15.00—not bad, was it? We sailed second class from Rotterdam to London and reached here Friday morning.

Mike and I are parting for an indefinite length of time but plan to get together later. I am disappointed that I cannot get to Scotland, but I've got "Pyrenees" emblazoned on my brain and all else is subordinate to that. I had to choose Scotland with its personal pleasure or Pyrenees with its book material so I chose the latter, as I *always* mean to do. I don't like to go alone, but my likes are secondary. Mike and I have a complete understanding that lets each go his own way and meet later on. We have had perfect harmony. My notes are full of amusing things. Mike is worth his weight in gold to a narrative such as mine for his adventures and stories and remarks are always merry.

We went to see *Abraham Lincoln* the other night from a gallery seat and nearly fell over the balcony on hearing the Negro character speaking cockney English. But it was a good play.

[*Brussels—September 4, 1921.*] I'm in Brussels, once more on ground familiar to you. It hasn't changed any—the buildings, I mean. And so far as I can see the people have quite recovered from the German occupation.

I did hate to leave England. I intended going Wednesday but it was Friday afternoon before I actually made it. Troops of friends caused the delay chiefly. Mike will follow me, leaving London tomorrow.

I have said I have no intention of being back by June first as Mike says he must be, nor can I hope to make enough money to travel as rapidly as would be necessary to get home then, nor do I want that sort of trip. Mike wants India and China to be the climax of his trip next June, Europe being merely incidental to him. It's all climax to me.

I think Brussels splendid. The square before the Hôtel de Ville— do you remember it?—is the most interesting I've seen, and the great cathedral and the Palais de Justice are indeed impressive. Everything is closed today but I can examine the outside.

I'll be well into Switzerland when you get this so you know how happy I'll be.

[*Coblenz—September 8, 1921.*] I'm recalling vividly your praise of the wonders of the Rhine for I've been "wondering" myself the last two days.

I took an all-day trip to Cologne. I was disappointed in the city but the church makes up for it. *That* is magnificent, though I don't care for the modern ceiling inside. I climbed up in the steeple and took pictures of the river.

It's marvelous weather, and a waxing moon for my Rhine trip. I climbed on top the Ehrenbreitstein fortress last night and sat entranced two hours—the Rhine and Moselle and myriads of lights in the river valley 400 feet below. It was inspiring to see a great American flag flapping over the famous German fortress as we steamed up the Rhine.

I meant to start walking south today, but I had to ship my pictures and papers to Paris, so that I might walk with nothing but my camera and cane for luggage. I've a fine map of the river, which shows pictures of every castle and town in a long narrow form. I will make Mayence Sunday night—only 40 miles, 20 a day, but that's fast enough on such a scenic outing. Everything of interest lies in that 40 miles. With this crystal daytime and silver nighttime I am indeed blessed, and with open eyes and ears and mouth I'm about to write myself to death in my notebook. My greatest difficulty will be to condense my 500,000 words to 100,000. I must get out and ask questions for my article on Germany which I feel encouraged about. This town filled with Americans is a novelty. The people are very content to have them and they live together like bugs in a rug.

[*Basel—September 17, 1921.*] I've traveled a bit. Things have whirled past so fast I'm lost in a slough of impressions and people and adventures and feel I'll never get them disentangled in my notes. The morning I wrote you from Coblenz I called on an officer, Captain Thomson. He and I began to talk. I told him about my trip and aim. He asked me out to dinner at his own home, an attractive flower-hidden house in the best part of the city. His mother and sister live with him. We had a very pleasant meal. They insisted I spend the night, so I went back to my hotel and brought my "things"—one camera and one cane—out to Captain Thomson's. I slept in luxury—washed my clothes before I turned in to be clean next morning. Next day the Captain, his very attractive sister and another girl took me in their army Cadillac across the Rhine to *every military post* in the "bridgehead," 250 kilometers altogether. It was perfect weather and I never saw such beautiful country.

Mike caught up with me and 'phoned out to the house. I spent the second night there and was escorted to the boat by all three. I certainly was lucky for I *got* Coblenz cold for my German article. Cologne, English; Coblenz, American; Mayence, French. I was surprised to find myself written up in the local paper. I gave no news to anyone except Captain Thomson about myself; never mentioned navy or walking or anything that was printed in the article.

I had planned to walk on to Bingen from Coblenz and wanted to meet Mike for further planning. So we got together at the boat and stayed on till the next stop, about a mile, but long enough to plan a meeting at Mayence. I got off and walked to Bingen, climbed the Lorelei and loitered three hours enchanted by the view up and down the Rhine. You remember how concentrated everything is at this section of the river. I didn't get to Bingen till nine o'clock but it was moonlight and even more beautiful than by day. On to Mayence by train. I missed Mike but next morning we met. I was there to investigate the French occupation and the tales of horror spouted against the Negro troops by the whining Germans. I went to Colonel Coleman, the highest American officer in French territory. He *made* me go with him to call on General Schmidt, the French Commanding General of the 100,000 soldiers in the occupied territory. The General was charming and gave me a major to show me around. We visited the black barracks. The blacks are impudent and undesirable but are perfectly behaved and cause less actual trouble than the white soldiers. From now on, I'm a *"correspondent."* It gets me everywhere.

On to Strassburg, alone, the next morning and climbed the dizzy delicate towers. What a marvelous building! On to Obernai that night and started early next day afoot for St. Marie aux Mines, through the heart of the Vosges; crystal weather, hot sunshine, the Blue Ridge all over, with hundreds of years of cultivation, blue-green valleys, thick villages, blue lakes and sky. I'm too full of that trip to write about it. I climbed the highest peak and, following its backbone, discovered I was walking along the old division line between France and Alsace—"F" on one side of the stone, "D" on the other. I watched the sun set on the French side and the moon rise on the Alsatian, 3500 feet up and with a lake 1,000 feet below me on the one hand and the plain and Rhine on the other. I stayed too long on my perch and got entangled. Having scorned the roads, in the war areas of stone huts and boulders and trenches and barbed wire, I missed my path and stumbled around in the semi-darkness till ten o'clock. I was afraid to tackle the hillsides through the stumpy pines and the blind precipices, so I stayed all night in an old dugout and was warm with my sweater. I had breakfast at Schlucht and made Krüt and the railroad through pouring rain and impenetrable fog. The last day I took great joy in the rain, especially as I had no raincoat, but a hot bath here in Basel last night and I'm perfectly normal.

Mike and I had a momentous talk in Mayence. We are parting for good at Paris. I'm going to Spain and he to Marseilles. I'm desolate to think of going on alone; however, business is business. I'm off to Lucerne now and to Zermatt with my bag, bareheaded—lost my cap in the Vosges.

[*Viege, Switzerland, September 19, 1921.*] I'm lost again—this time in the Southern Alps at a little junction station called Viege or Visp, just where the line to Zermatt meets the Rhone. Mike and I are leaving at ten this morning for Zermatt and will be there several days.

The day I reached Basel mist and clouds began to obliterate all Switzerland from view and my few days here have been spent cursing the fog. I spent Saturday night and Sunday night in Lucerne, saw the Lion, and took the boat trip around the lake, disembarking at Brunnen and walking along the edge to Tellsplatte, through the famous open-sided tunnel and to Fruling at the end and taking the boat back. Surely, as you remember, nothing could be more beautiful. On the way back I fell to talking with an English gentleman who turned out to be the ex-Premier Asquith's private secretary, a most interesting person.

This little town is the most decayed place I've ever seen. Its church vault contains the skulls or bones of 3,000 dead who have been dug up to make room for more—a gruesome sight.

The weather has taken on a decidedly frosty tinge. It's clearing today so I can see the Matterhorn in all its splendor. The trip from Bern to Brieg was a marvel of scenic railway. I'm in Mayence again with my notes. My French is coming back beautifully.

[*Back home in Paris—September 28, 1921.*] Away with breakfast notes! I'm bursting with accumulated thoughts and adventures and, having locked myself in my attic garret and thrown the key out the window, I can write a full size *dinner* note and not be interrupted. I've decided by far the best part of my trip is reaching the cities where my mail awaits me, and yesterday was the second of these high spots. Nothing mattered after I got hold of the batch of letters; Paris could have sunk into the earth and I would not have known or cared.

The reason, Mother and Dad, I went to Zermatt was that I had determined months ago to climb the Matterhorn—which we did! I didn't mention it before because I knew you would worry yourself sick but, now it's all over, congratulate me on the feat. Nothing is wrong or *strained* or worse off for it, and I've had an experience which perhaps I can never match again, for, certainly, I'll never climb *that* mountain a second time. We got there September nineteenth in the densest fog, found the place deserted but for one small hotel. We began to scout for guides and information; found two men who were highly recommended but who refused to climb until the weather was unmistakably clear and safe. September twentieth dawned more foggy than ever so we walked the six miles to the summit of Gorner Grat to get the training. September 21st found us sore but it was clear. The guides still refused to move until the clearness was verified by two days of it. *Again* we climbed the Gorner Grat. It stormed nails and snails that night but September 22nd we rushed to our window to see our mountain pure white, from base to summit, and sparkling like diamonds. Here was our chance and we took it. We begged, borrowed and stole equipment and rented three-ton cleated Alpine shoes from our guides. We had to have heavy mittens, leggings, helmets and sweaters.

The four of us with ropes and ice axes left Zermatt at 1:30 the afternoon of the 23rd and climbed for five hours to the "hut." It was 6:30 P.M. then. It's a two-story shack with Alpine Club blankets and bunks upstairs and stove and table downstairs. We had a good hot supper there. It was the clearest sunset I ever saw, right behind the Matterhorn. We slept till 3:30 A.M. Our guides had hot breakfast for us. At 4:00, in brilliant moonlight, we started to *climb;* before had been merely walking. One wonders from the picture how it's possible to get up so steep and sharp a precipice. One wonders twice as hard when one has to face it. Each of us was attached to a guide with heavy rope. They would go first and help pull us after them. Not only are the rocks straight up in places but they actually *overhang.* In such spots ropes dangling from an iron spike are an assistance, if one can climb ropes. Right along the edge we crawled with a six to eight-thousand-foot drop straight on either side. It was a terrible, weird sensation, with the air near zero, the wind howling around and stinging our frozen faces with snow, with only a twelve-inch snow-covered edge to walk on, and 14,750 feet above sea level. Imagine that, if you can, and you will imagine the fiercest moment of intense living I ever experienced. Of course, it was a physical struggle. I panted all the way up and all the way down, but so did the guide whose fortieth ascent this was. My heart beat only reasonably fast and, now that it's over, I'm proud of such a strong, normal organ. We crawled to the supreme ledge at 9:45 and sank exhausted in the swirling snow; had hot coffee and a bite and in ten minutes were so cold we had to start down—but those ten minutes! Mont Blanc fifty miles to the west—Jungfrau seventy-five miles to the north, Italy to the south and every mountain and glacier in Switzerland in relief about us.

Coming down was as laborious, though not so fatiguing, as going up. Mike and I both slipped on the ice several times but our guides tightened the ropes and stopped our precipitous descent. It was nearly 7 P.M. when we limped into Zermatt—my gray suit in shreds, our hands and faces hacked and skinned by the ice and rocks and our heads bumped and sore from raising them against some jutting stone. But two men were never hailed as such heroes, nor were ever so content and self-satisfied. A hot bath remedied everything and we left next morning at seven feeling we had hit the high spot, in more ways than one, of our trip. It is the most difficult crag in Europe to climb and the most dangerous. Once, yes, gladly—but never, never again. I'm sorry you were not along, Dad. You could have done it, I'm sure, for it was a case of agile arms and nimble feet and confidence, rather than brute strength. My Vosges tramp and the Gorner Grat climbs prepared me well.

I was all set for Paris next day but before we reached Lake Geneva I grabbed my bag and jumped out the window that I might walk, agreeing to meet Mike in Paris. I stopped at the Castle of Chillon near Montreux and had two of my most delightful hours in the most interesting ancient pile I know of. I rambled through the halls and dungeons, but it was near sunset and visitors were being ousted from the castle. The water was so enticing and the air so warm, I crawled up the beach 300 feet and went for a swim past the lakeside of the building and back, pulled onto the sand underneath some overhanging rocks and sat watching the sunset silhouette the Alps opposite. I had a copy of Byron's *Prisoner of Chillon* with me and read it as the fiery red ball hung suspended in horizon clouds. Canto II, Canto III, I read and looked up to find only a semi-circle remained; Canto IV, only the top crescent; Canto V, and the sun sank out of sight. I walked to Lausanne along the lake edge and nearly got arrested for stealing roadside grapes. An obliging motor car took me on to Geneva. I sat up all night to Paris along with the Bishop of London

(St. Paul's) whom I had heard preach there in August. I submitted the premise that the architectural beauty of his church was a mighty competitor of his sermon, at which statement he chuckled.

I found Paris unchanged, as beautiful and vivacious and gesticulatory as ever. I had dinner last evening with Mrs. Keyes. The Keyes and Mike and I are going to the Opera tomorrow night and I shall make a *fourth* attempt to see Napoleon's tomb. Mike's at Versailles today and I've not left my room for I must knock off a million words today and tomorrow.

Don't you worry, Dad, about my "holding my job." I was made to fit it and it to fit me. I've gone at this thing with a seriousness and determination that have characterized the few things in the past which I have reveled in. You are right about the "jocular tone." That is the first requisite. Far be it from me to have the set purpose and serious conscientiousness that have dulled so many travel books and robbed them of spontaneity. I'm keeping as far away as possible from a travelogue. I must develop my own style. My notes will profit by that principle as I've not even a dictionary to *corrupt* me.

At present I refuse to promise myself anything for every day my plans change, to suit my latest whim. When I look at the map of the world, the miles I've traveled already can't be found. It appalls me to begin to realize what enormous distances await me, but the greater the distance, the more to see.

[*Paris—October 3, 1921.*] It's been one damned thing after another standing between me and work—mostly people. I would get desperate if it did any good. My visé for Spain! I collapsed when I paid for it. Mike and I had a comical evening with a Follies queen— will make a good story. I've seen none of my old haunts nor am likely to. This city has such an enervating, hypnotic influence it's a bad place to grind out work.

[*Paris—October 9, 1921.*] Your son is rapidly degenerating into a complete ne'er-do-well. The five days I planned to honor Paris have lengthened to twelve. Mike left for Marseilles Wednesday night after a sad parting and I feel desperately lonesome in the most sociable city in the world.

About a week ago Mike and I met a young Italian girl, accompanied by her grandmother, on a rubberneck ride. The girl spoke English and both she and the old lady proved so charming and interesting we managed to see them several times afterward. Mike was slightly smitten with "Suze" and while I worked over my notes they sight-saw Paris. Realizing how sad I must be with Mike gone, she invited me for the week end to their farmhouse in the country where the two live alone. So yesterday I left Paris and am spending a quiet and sunny and genial day with the cows and chickens. Madame, who is now quite 75, was a lady-in-waiting to the Empress Eugénie.

What a whimsical morning we have had! I put up clothes lines and fetched water from the town pump and spoiled my appetite for lunch by eating all the grapes on the garden wall. We three are taking our lunch to the woods, for in this ideal sunshiny weather we cannot rest indoors. I shall have to employ all my strength of character to go back at five this afternoon and start the week right by being on hand when the library opens. I have about 8,000 words of my article ready. I am calling it "Adventuring in Republican Germany" and making it as humorous and breezy as possible.

Recently I walked the familiar streets of the Latin Quarter with a mixed feeling of happiness and sadness, though why sad I do not know, for every day I lived there was full of new and pleasant experiences. Paris is certainly the most distracting place for an ambitious, unbudded author.

You can let the *Commercial* have the Matterhorn notes and a designated picture. My bag will be empty when the thirty pounds of accumulated junk are sent home. *Metropolitan* will send my article home if they won't use it and you can readdress it as I will direct. I hope it's not necessary to readdress anything but the check.

CHAPTER V

ON THE ROAD TO ROMANCE

in France, Andorra, Spain

RICHARD did not get away from Paris till October twenty-ninth. The forced delay was exasperating and disturbing. He wanted to have his German "Adventuring" story ready to offer the *Metropolitan* and the Matterhorn story for some other magazine. The writing and the gathering of pictures proved a vast undertaking. He managed to write four long letters home during this time, mostly about all work and no play. On October 17, he begins:

[*Paris—ad infinitum.*] Oh, where are the breakfast notes of yesteryear that came so frequently from Germany! Still, how can there be any breakfast notes where there is no breakfast? For in Paris a flying cup of *café au lait* and a roll at the corner saloon take less than five minutes.

I've always heard the writer's life is calm and independent. It's not true. No bricklayer ever worked any harder than I am doing. But don't worry. I know just how far to go. And it all makes me throw back my head and sweep away the side issues that threaten to clog my progress toward my goal—and you.

His next letter was a bit brighter. "I've had a sort of recreation today away from work—took a long walk and at *last* got to Napoleon's tomb. I'll be glad to get away from Paris—it's grown stale."

Before he had posted this letter, the American Express Company delivered a huge bundle of mail, in which he found much to cheer him. He added a long postscript. He gave his mother some Paris fashion notes. "I guess it's too late for Paris styles *now,* but in case: every well-dressed woman I see is in *black* from head to foot, with much shoulder cape. Dresses neither one length nor the other. Large straight-brimmed black hats—although the best I've seen were dull

99

blue or tan with an eighteen-inch streamer of thick curly cock feathers fluttering over each shoulder. There are a number of red heels on the streets, but it's not really the mode. Paris women always look stunning. . . .

"You are quite right, Dad, about one's style of writing and I'm quite conscious that I'm making a bed I must lie in always. One cannot change one's style any more than one's height or color, so I must make the best use of mine and always improve it.

"Paris seems as reckless and spendthrift as ever, but it would take an earthquake to make it otherwise. These cold days, the streets are packed with red-cheeked hilarious French and just to watch them makes you gay. . . . During my prolonged stay here, I have made enough money to buy my bicycle, so now I'm leaving Paris."

[*Orleans—October 30, 1921.*] Hooray! Another breakfast note. You never can tell from the writing paper where I am but it is Orleans *this* time. I left Paris with a mixture of regret and relief at three o'clock Friday and cobble-stoned on my bicycle to Versailles. I was sorely tempted to make a third visit, but only rode into the lower park from the roadway and looked back from the lake up the vista that leads between the trees. The autumn foliage was unusually colorful and made the half-hour "lost" a very sure gain. Just beyond I saw an army kite balloon about to ascend, so I crawled onto the field and asked if I might go up. The soldiers were not enthusiastic but finally decided I might. We went only 1,000 feet but the view over Versailles was magnificent.

I got only to Rambouillet the first night on my way to Chartres but had a most interesting evening in a country hotel. On to Chartres yesterday, stopping and chatting and taking pictures. At a school house I was asked to make a speech about America in French. I don't think my children understood me too well, but anyway my funny ungrammatical phrases amused them highly.

For any conception of Chartres Cathedral read Adams' *Mont St. Michel and Chartres.* It's a book we ought to have in our library.

I'm going on to Blois today in a roundabout way to take in the châteaux. From yesterday I'm already bewildered by the number of them I saw—many not listed on map and in guides.

[*Tours—November 4, 1921.*] Bring forth the atlas once more. It needs a little exercise. I'm still rolling down the Loire, or rather zigzagging back and forth across it, for my path has been anything but straight. You can find Orleans where I wrote last. I followed the river to Mer on the north bank and crossed over to the Château of Chambord which, being the first real one, took me off my feet. It's so enormous, yet so delicate! I run out of all superlatives in describing these castles. Each new one outglitters the one before.

My *bicycle* outing is proving a farce for I spend so much time prowling around the estates I never have time to bicycle. The days are so short I scarcely get started before it's dark at 4:30. Chambord took all the wind out of Cheverny to the south. I spent the next night at Blois and half the next day at the remarkable Blois Château. There I put in so much time taking photographs of sheep on a sunny hillside and their accordion-playing shepherd that I saw only Chaumont on the south side before night. Chaumont appealed to me most of all so far. It's high on a bluff with a magnificent view in both directions. Medieval fortress outside and Renaissance inside. It was very much inhabited so I could not see all of it.

Amboise that night and its château next morning. Chenonceaux that noon—then I liked *it* best—built on arches across a sparkling river with dense autumn foliage on both banks. Then to Loches, quite far south. This *was* the best and I spent five hours there where I meant to spend one. It's the *real* medieval castle with thick walls and a 150-foot moat and battlements and drawbridges. It takes you straight back to the Crusades and with its harsh and belligerent look was a great contrast to the lacelike châteaux I'd seen before. I came on to Tours in the afternoon and am delayed again by this interesting city which historically is unequaled in France with the exception of Paris only.

This trip makes the German tour take second place, for in all the world there is not such beauty in landscape and architecture as here in Touraine. I may try to put together an article in Barcelona but the Loire is the most written-to-death river in the world. I may save my wind for Carcassonne and the Pyrenees.

[*Nantes—November 6, 1921.*] If it's true the Nances came from

Nantes, I'm among the spirits of my ancestors this morning, and what a bright sunshiny morning it is! My small hotel overlooks the Loire and the sun is up and shining into the water.

I got my pictures (negatives) at Tours and feel very encouraged. I've enough to illustrate my trip beautifully. In fact, I shall send half a dozen of the best ones to the *Times*—"Lorraine in Automne." They might be worth $25 or more.

Well, my Loire Expedition is all but ended. It's been the most delightful trip I ever had. From Tours I followed the north bank to Luynes, Cinq-Mars and Langeais. The last is remarkable for its furnishings which have not been changed for over 300 years and it's the only château of which this is true. I spent the night at Azay-le-Rideau to the south. It poured that night and next morning the Renaissance masterpiece was drenched with autumn leaves, thick on the walks, covering the moats and lakes, and very appropriate to so aged and crumbling a building. I saw a herd of cows and sheep at some distance from the château and nearly ruined myself crawling over barbed-wire entanglements to get where I could photograph them with the château in the background. It will be a professional picture—if! Ussé was the next one. It's the most elaborately carved and most artistic of all. Chinon, next. I spent three hours exploring its extensive ruins. Its history is the fullest and though it has almost disappeared above the ground, what's left is worth coming to see. I thought Richard Cœur de Lion's body was here—finding it was at Fontevrault, I hastened there. I spent that night at Saumur, where the château is not so good after the others. I just rode around the walls at Angers and rushed into Nantes for last night.

This is the most interesting and *paintable* country in the world, just one romantic landscape after another. It would be almost worth while getting married just to take a bride over this same course. I shall do what is incomparably better—take a mother over it. And I assure you, I shall be an excellent guide.

[*Again at Nantes—November 7, 1921.*] I planned to go on to the coast by train but yesterday dawned so remarkably clear and warm I could not resist an outing in such weather and started off by bicycle, but loitered so along the road I got no farther than St. Etienne. Both the Marne and Orijon are as picturesque as Holland when it comes to windmills. Every ridge is lined for miles with strings of white stone mills and on a day like yesterday, with the low but strong sun flashing on them and the gusty wind whirling all of them at a terrific rate, I was struck by the unusual beauty of the landscapes. There was a small plateau above St. Etienne and four of the biggest mills were on it. After lunch I climbed up to them and, finding them grinding furiously the grain that had waited so long for a windy day, spent a very interesting two hours and took several pictures which I pray will be successful.

Night came at Savenay along with a train, so I checked my bike and put it on the car for Bordeaux. Early that morning I combed the town for information about boats for Bordeaux and after two hours and twenty reiterations from twenty different sources was convinced there was no boat. So, very disappointed and exasperated, I bought a railroad ticket. I had to "change cars" at Nantes where I arrived at 11 A.M. The "connection" is at 11 P.M. tonight. I nearly exploded when I learned it, but here's a good chance to sit in a café and write letters to half a dozen people, Mike, Marie, and several copyright owners whose pictures I want for my book.

Well, that's why I'm back in Nantes, very much against my will, especially since I've an all-night ride on a third-class coach before me. It's often the case, though, that at such a late hour I can find a bench for myself and stretch out. I can sleep on even a boxcar but I can't sleep standing up in a boxcar.

By no means, Dad, have I overlooked the "spiritual" qualities of this trip. They come unbid, however, and it has been of great distress to me that I've not been able to write about them while they are still strong. Being mostly alone this way, I think and visualize and imagine more than when I have company.

I'm inclined to let meditation spoil my notes, but must not, for it's joy and effervescence and spontaneity, I am convinced, that the public wants and not philosophic travelogues.

Don't worry about my lack of clothes, Ammudder. One might worry about my lack of desire for clothes. But I am clean always and old clothes do not look so old when there is a shaven face and fresh shirt (always the same one) to go along with them.

Now I've got to go and get a seat on the Bordeaux train before these wops beat me to it. I may go *first*-class if they don't watch me too close. So good night.

[*Toulouse—November 13, 1921.*] I got my train at Nantes and had a cold, uncomfortable ride to Bordeaux, and instead of its getting warmer as we went south it got decidedly colder; springlike in Nantes and ice and frost in Bordeaux. My plans to work there a while were shattered by the first breath of chilling air, for what must it be in Andorra with snow in Bordeaux? But I had to see that very attractive town, get my pictures developed, etc.

I pushed off on my bike in cold and sparklingly clear weather with a strong wind behind me straight down, or up, the Garonne to Agen pedaling and not exploring as I had done in Touraine. I went on to Toulouse next day where I spent a delightful morning and late that night got to Carcassonne, considered by many the most interesting sight in France. It's a perfectly preserved medieval fortified city: walls, moats, dungeons, drawbridges, just as it was in the year 1000, and perched 400 feet on the top of a knob where it can be seen for miles. All other such fortified cities are in complete ruins—only a stone or two or a grass-grown wall—but here is an entire city, not only in perfect condition but an example of the best and strongest elements in medieval building. It was a Roman camp first and every succeeding conqueror added to its strength until the very sight of it must have disheartened any attacker. The double lines of wall are one mile in circumference and contain 52 great towers. The houses inside are scarcely less ancient, so that the whole place is a picture reality of a thousand years ago.

In brightest moonlight I saw it first and walked around its walls to look at every angle. In the detail-obscuring light it seemed more romantic and bulky than by day. I spent the next morning prowling about with my camera in clear sunshine.

Just after lunch I met, without doubt, the high point of chance acquaintances on my trip—a Boston physician and his wife, loafing in Europe where and as long as they please. Dr. Watson is a Harvard graduate, taught and lectured twenty years in the Medical School, is the author of plays and books on travel and surgery, an authority on art and literature. He is the most wonderful raconteur I ever heard, and an intimate friend of every author and statesman and soldier from Lincoln to Harding. He knew General Sherman and Longfellow and Lowell and Roosevelt and so on ad infinitum. He did at my age just about what I am doing and so took a fancy to me. We three spent the afternoon strolling about. They had been within the walls at an excellent hotel for three weeks and never tired of the remarkable sight. They had me to dinner, the best meal since I left America. My train left at eleven and I was loath to go for it was a most stimulating evening. Mrs. Watson is as intelligent and charming as he and made me decide if I could find so poised and brilliant a woman I'd marry her whether I loved her or not.

Wasn't it odd—this refreshing afternoon right in the midst of those ancient and storied walls? It put a new urge into my desire to progress with all my might along the road of intellectual attainment in the hope that some day when I'm 75, as Dr. Watson is, I'll be as useful and delightful as he.

Back to Toulouse last night to change for Ax-les-Thermes, just above Andorra. I hope to get to l'Hospitalet by tomorrow night— how, I do not know. I'm prepared for the cold.

[*Barcelona—November 20, 1921.*] Oh, happy day! I'm at last in Barcelona which has been to me, for four months, what Jerusalem was to the Crusaders. It is not the city itself the reaching of which is important, but what it signifies: warmth from now on, the civilization of temperate zones and their similarity to our own country gone for good, the Pyrenees, which have been a never-ceasing prod at my back, overcome and left behind to freeze themselves to death if they wish—that's what Barcelona means to me, the first complete rest and relaxation since July sixteenth. Of course, when one has as much at stake as I have on this tour, one can never really relax and forget, for if there is nothing pressing to be done for the moment, the ever-growing mountain of undeveloped notes keeps my working day at the twelve-hour level.

Yesterday morning at Seo d'Urgel I slopped through snow and pouring rain to the autobus that took me to Calaf on the main railroad line, thence to Barcelona. We sloughed in low speed over terrible mountain roads made bottomless by heavy rains, from 7 A.M. to 5 P.M., with an hour out for lunch; then, five hours more on a reeking, creeping third-class coach here, to arrive in pouring rain. It did not stop for twenty-four hours. I was more weary and exhausted than I have ever been before and from nothing but sitting. Well, I had to slop through the streets, not knowing three words of Spanish, looking for a hotel and being denied a room on account of my grimy, muddy appearance. I'd burned the sole out of one shoe in Andorra and it had cracked and fallen off, leaving me to walk about in my stocking foot.

I was getting desperate when I found a room and slept from ten to ten, to be waked by a *blazing* sun, and lilting music outside my window. After dressing, I went out and found a square full of Sunday dancers, like "Jimmy" in the funny paper. An Algerian oboe and an Oriental tom-tom drew hundreds of people to dance a queer Spanish figure—circles of three to thirty holding hands (almost no women) and stepping and dipping as they revolved three or four steps to the left, then as many to the right. It looked unutterably stupid, but I joined in and found the "dance" perfectly fitted to the syncopated music.

Afterward, I noted what looked like another American who, like me, had been dancing. We were both a little embarrassed, but agreed not to tell. He was Paul McGrath, a young architect from Chicago, in Spain to study its architecture. He speaks Spanish fluently, is 27 years old, the best company since Mike left, as solitary as I; so we have been inseparable except while I am writing, and we will go to Valencia together as soon as I'm through.

Paul and I decided to take a walk of several miles and headed for a hill 600 or 800 feet high that juts out into the bay, from the top of which I was sure the view of sea and city would be worth the climb. We passed something which made me think of you, Dad, and a remark you made several years ago as we walked past the fountain at 59th and 5th Ave. in New York before the Plaza: "Why must they have a statue of a nude woman always in the most conspicuous place?" I learned why here today and I'll send you a picture of the reason. There is a figure of a woman atop a fountain in Barcelona and the sculptor decided he would properly clothe his lady in the latest fashion. The latest fashion was 1875 when bustle dresses had come in, so the stone figure has a great bustle dress on—high collars, tight sleeves and floor-sweeping skirt. It is comical! I pray my picture of it is a success, so it may tell you that the reason women are always left unclothed in statues is because whatever style they are dressed in goes out in six months and leaves them very démodé.

When we finally reached the top of the hill the sun was shining from the sea onto the white walls and roofs of Barcelona. It made such an extraordinary panorama we spent a half-hour looking at it, until the sun's sudden drop into the ocean made it too cold to sit longer. So down into the city to join in the Sunday afternoon parade along the Clief Boulevard. I think 400,000 of Barcelona's half-million people were promenading: hundreds of soldiers in gay green and red uniforms all dressed up to fight the Moroccans.

It's been an extraordinary week. A Cornell professor I met in Zermatt said of a certain noted travel writer, "He was like the little boy who walked ten miles to see the circus and then couldn't get in." I resolved then to *"get in"* as well as walk the ten miles, and so far I've seen, everywhere I've been, not only the big show but the sideshows and special performances.

I hesitate to begin on Andorra. It's as if I were to say, "Now, I shall write you about France," for my article will run to 10,000 words, I'm afraid, and be hacked and condensed to keep it that low. The past week has been like a sweet dream except the bus-ride nightmare, events so far removed from things usually imagined, an experience so different, so strange, so distant from 1921, that I am not right sure it really happened.

After I wrote you at Toulouse I spent all afternoon getting to Ax-les-Thermes. My hotel proprietor discouraged me greatly—"It could not be done in November, never had been done, you would freeze, etc., etc., etc."—but if I must go, there was an auto that went as far as l'Hospitalet every morning to fetch mail and I could ride up in it for a very small sum. Naturally, I jumped at it.

Next morning I rushed about buying a heavy wool vest and mitts. I found the car and got in. I asked the driver exactly how much the charge would be. He shrugged his shoulders, "Oh, I don't know," from which I gathered it was a matter of tipping. On arriving at l'Hospitalet, the driver told me the bill would be 80 francs. I laughed in his face. "You've as much chance to get 80 francs from me as 80 million." Just before arriving at l'Hospitalet I had given the chauffeur four very important letters to mail at Ax when he returned. Well, the chauf and I went to the mat. He was furious. "Remember, I've your letters. I shall hold them until you pay the 80 francs." That made me see red and inspired me to fight fire with fire. I jumped to his car and took out the spark plug. There were no others, and no garage at l'Hospitalet. "When you give me my letters you may have your spark plug." So we exchanged; he had to, and I paid him 30 francs.

After getting this unpleasant situation off my hands, I went to a hotel. I was again disturbed about making this trip as there was heavy snow and zero weather. I looked around for a donkey to ride and found one, but the owner hesitated to let it go, and it took considerable persuasion to change his mind. We started climbing along a snow-covered trail at seven o'clock and by one had reached the crest.

Night at Soldeu and next morning on the sunny Spanish slope in the clearest, sunniest day possible that thawed everything. We followed the narrow gorge that led to Andorra all day, and at three had reached the capital, a dirty collection of ramshackle houses. "Andorra" consists of a few scattered dwellings strung along the valley. I saw the wildest scenery imaginable, the Pyrenees all snow covered above me and the greenest of sunny gorges beside me; brightly dressed people and mules—no roads—no wagons—no change in anything for a thousand years. If my pictures are good they should sell anything, for the subjects, both scenery and people, were all my highest ambition could ask for.

At the capital I called on the President of the Republic and we spent about two hours, both in our stocking feet before the kitchen stove of the White House, talking about Andorra. He was a simple, naïve old man who spoke very bad French patois, but I learned everything from him. What if I'd not been able to speak French? Forty times I thanked fate that I could, for no one speaks English in Andorra.

It poured rain next day, so I spent it reading the one book in the entire town about the country, written in 1846, but as authentic now as then. I visited the schoolteacher that night for more dope and next morning took several photographs of the President, who insisted on regaling himself in his official robes, though I preferred him in his wooden shoes and normal costume.

That afternoon my donkey "Hannibal" and I wound down the most beautiful valley to Seo d'Urgel, the Spanishest of Spanish. I visited the ninth-century cathedral and inadvertently watched the initiation of a new member into the order of priest. The doors were barred to the public but I was in a dark corner and didn't leave when they chased out the others. I nearly lost an eye—vivid robes and incense and fur and candles and chanting, impressive but frozen and haughty.

A remarkable week.

The urge that made me seek that little country with determination played fair and, yes, except the Matterhorn, I would gladly give any month of travels for that one week.

[*Barcelona—November 25, 1921.*] Tuesday night, Wednesday, Thursday, Friday and Saturday I worked twelve hours a day and finished "Andorra" at four o'clock this morning, but it's *done* and never would have been had I not sailed into it with that sort of energy. I'm sending you a carbon copy. It's as good as gold somewhere, and my thirteen pictures are *beautiful*. I'm sure you'll agree this story is by far the best. It makes me very ashamed of my German yarns but I hope that may always be the case—always ashamed of the last one—otherwise, I can never improve.

The last paragraph goes like this: "My mule and I had reached the southern gate that leads on to civilization and as I turned to look back once more at the magnificent panorama the sun broke from the clouds and the wind blowing from the north brought to me the graduated rumble of the distant cataracts. A wave of sadness possessed me as I beheld for the last time the green and happy Valley of Andorra and there was a sigh in my voice as I gave the mule a prod and cried, 'Spain, Hannibal, Spain!' "

It has poured in never-ending torrents since Tuesday, but little I cared. I only prayed it would rain itself to death while I was kept in and grow clear again when I emerged. I saw a light opera with exquisite music. The 30-piece orchestra played with their hats on, but *how* they played! Everyone sings in this country and sings well.

My "chapter" on Paris will be one of the best. The Rhine, the Matterhorn, the châteaux, Carcassonne, Andorra and Paris! This writing experience was just a dream and a hope once; it's no *dream* now. Climbing mountains seems not to hurt—I've ceased to have a "pump." The only ailment I can find is writer's cramp.

[*Barcelona—still Barcelona—December 3, 1921.*] *Two* weeks ago tonight I reached here and tonight I depart (really) for Valencia farther down the coast. I am delighted here. I find notes on every hand. It's unusual, it's romantic, it's balmy and bright—it's *Spain!*

Paul and I have walked, walked day and night, to the hills behind the city for the beautiful seacoast panorama. Yesterday we saw it by moonlight and twinkling lights. We've been to typical Spanish theaters and found them exceedingly novel and entertaining. I have never seen such beautiful women as here, dressed in Spanish costumes and dancing with castanets. They are charming but off the stage they put on Paris fashions and kill all their unique attraction.

Spain of architecture and sunshine and art and music is the rarest thing on earth, but oh, what a miserable, misspent, unsuccessful mess it is when it tries to be modern and civilized! Its modern architecture is nauseating, its street cars and industry and army are jokes, and in consequence it has dropped to a most insignificant place as a world power, to be feared about as much as Andorra. But in the old and unsullied Spanish atmosphere it is a delight to ear and eye, and since it is the first country I've touched where things are *absolutely* foreign, I am spellbound by the strangeness of it all. When I get south I am sure to find the Spanish atmosphere to a much more accentuated degree.

I have been walking on air since I mailed my manuscript with thirteen pictures and captions and a letter to the editor. If he writes you, turning me down, send it to someone else. I feel confident, as usual. Nothing like air castles. We can't have stone castles without them.

[*Valencia—December 5, 1921.*] I sit by an open window with the sun streaming in and look out upon myriad towers that awe me with their beauty.

Paul McGrath and I left Barcelona Saturday night on a third-class coach and after fourteen hours of scrambling reached Valencia more dead than alive, but his splendid company and the riot of sunshine that greeted us made the trip worth while.

Valencia is far more interesting than Barcelona, which is a modern commercial town. This is *real* Spain and oh, how appealing it is! Paul is out sketching this morning and will be for days, since it's heaven for an architect or artist and he is both. I've an article on Spain formulating in my head, so I am photographing right and left. I spent yesterday climbing crumbling church towers for pictures.

This is orange season in orange land and the country is ablaze with green and gold. This afternoon I'm taking my kodak and shall walk about the country, for the roads are impassable for our proposed bicycle trip.

I shall push on tomorrow for Madrid. I don't like the long trip or being alone again after having such a splendid Spanish-speaking companion, but Paul and I plan to join up again in Granada. We sat in the park while the band played melancholy plaintive Spanish motifs, and watched the colorful crowds pass by, soldiers and generals everywhere in rainbow uniforms and inefficient bearing. As Paul remarked: "What could be more inconsequential than a Spanish general?" He has a mandolin we lug around to charm the rail coaches and scenery with our music and singing.

[*Madrid—December 8, 1921.*] The long trip here was worse than I anticipated, for nothing could be more nerve and spine racking than a Spanish third-class railroad coach. All Spanish trains are locals and it took 22 hours to go some 300 miles. I had to change three times. Never have I seen such bleak country. One might compare it to suddenly jumping from the Florida coast to the Bad Lands in Utah, and why the city's founder chose this dreary spot I cannot see except that it is in the geographic center of the country.

When I arrived here at ten today in a car loaded with noisy soldiers and filthy peasants, I was in no mood to appreciate the beauty of any place. I found a pension and, having slept all afternoon, will be ready tomorrow to do the town. I miss the warm sunshine of Valencia and I miss Paul. The wan sun tried to break through the mist this morning and shine for me on palace walls where lines of beggars and bums were asleep.

I bought a ticket tonight for the Royal Opera House and am going more because it's in Madrid than because it's *William Tell*. Each night I wonder how I've got along so well during the day on my four words of Spanish, but language soon loses its significance to experienced travelers and if one let a lack of it interfere with progress in all countries where the language is unknown, traveling would be a waste of time. I'll soon get on to it. All the stimulating people I've met in Europe speak several languages.

These Spanish are the best loafers on earth. No wonder they are so far down the international scale. They lunch from one-thirty to three, dine from *eight-thirty to ten,* and all theaters begin at ten or as soon after as there's a crowd. They never go to bed. At 3 A.M. in Barcelona throngs of people ebb and flow and life is as animated as in New York at ten. People promenade in the streets purposeless, just walking up and down day and night, but it all gives a liveliness to Spanish cities which, though it is only surface, is pleasant to take part in.

I'll be here five days, or more, two days at Toledo and then bump back to oranges and olive trees.

[*Madrid—December 10, 1921.*] It looks now as if I'll spend Christmas in Spain—which is just as good a place to spend it as anywhere except at home.

Yesterday I walked about 30 miles and covered every important section of the city, up and down the Prado, through the parks, so that by the time night came I fell asleep over my notebook and gave up all idea of any night activity. This morning I hurried to the Prado and what a triumphal monument to art it is! It is smaller than the Louvre but I believe it has more masterpieces than any other museum. Velásquez was my favorite artist after my course in painting at Princeton, and my original map of wandering took in Madrid just to see his paintings. Whatever happens now I can leave Spain happy, for never have I been so gripped by pictures as by Velásquez'. He paints air and sound and life. Passing from his life-like canvases of earthly things out into the Rubens room, I was repelled by the latter's merely decorative pictures—Venuses and cupids and nymphs chased by satyrs, all up in the clouds, all pink and baby blue. The Murillo room positively angered me—saints and crucifixes and Heaven, sighing virgins surrounded by cherubs sitting on clouds with "Heaven is my home" expressions. Nothing insipid about Velásquez. In fact, one of his best pictures is a burlesque on the classic Bacchus and Greek god type.

A soldier p-rade was passing as I left the Prado, so I followed it several miles after a picture but nothing turned up even though I went to the very barracks itself.

[*Madrid—December 14, 1921.*] I had dinner last evening with the English Consul at his apartment. I had explained my lack of dinner coat so he wore street clothes, too, though the other gentlemen were properly dressed as well as their wives—all English but me. I was not ashamed over my clothes but it was the first time in my life I was embarrassed by an unmistakable inability to keep up with the mental level. Everyone else spoke Spanish, French and Italian. Their grace of conversation and expression quite bewildered me, as did the rapidity and subtlety of their wit. After dinner we went into the music room and listened to the Consul, who is over 55, sing in beautiful baritone to his own accompaniment almost anything we asked of him. His nephew, a captain in the British Army, then for an hour played his own compositions. The other guests all played or sang in turn until I felt like disappearing under the rug. They gave me new inspiration to study until I can hold my own in any company.

This morning, I called on the American Consul and found him delightful and normally American in his intelligence. Yale 1908, graduate of Harvard Law, rich, polished, sailing upward in the foreign service by leaps and bounds, speaking five languages. I'm having dinner with him this evening. But you just bet I don't hold my hands and wail over my ignorance.

I spent a most delightful day at the Escorial Sunday. It's the grimmest, most melancholy and most awesomely enormous pile of cold, unadorned granite on earth, I suppose. It took all day, as I spent the last two hours in a climb up the mountain behind so as to get a picture looking down on it—which turned out splendidly as all my Spanish pictures have.

Every day I'm thankful I came to Spain—just another hunch that worked well, for, though I thoroughly dislike the Spaniards, the country is intensely interesting.

A letter from Paul says he's waiting for me at Granada, so I'll go to Toledo in the morning and head for Granada the night of the next day. I dread that ride but there's no other way.

I made an all-afternoon trip out to the military aviation field Monday in search of airplane pictures of Madrid, had to walk two miles each way from the end of the trolley, found the General and he was delightful. He gave me an hour of his time and showered beautiful pictures on me, just what I want to illustrate "Spain."

[*Granada—December 18, 1921.*] Back in *sunny* Spain once more but more dead than alive after the 26-hour trip from Madrid. To be in Granada is worth any trip and any inconvenience.

Toledo! There *is* a town, the oldest in Spain and perhaps the most unusual. I spent a night and a day there and enjoyed every minute. The cathedral is the second largest in Spain, and the ancient bridges over the river that surrounds the city are famous everywhere. The Tajo River forms a "U" about Toledo with deep perpendicular banks, and the top of the U is fortified with Roman walls.

I was taking a midnight moonlight walk all alone and passing under the walls of the local madhouse, when I was startled by the weird, inhuman noises emerging. Not knowing what it was, I was doubly terrified.

I had to go back to Madrid to get the express south again, changed cars twice and reached Granada goggle-eyed at seven yesterday.

Spain is mostly a deadly, dreary country geographically but the section around Granada is an Oriental garden. I shall be here till after Christmas, for Paul is going to stay a month and I would not care to miss his company on Xmas Day just to save two or three days.

As usual, the sun is pouring down radiance in a navy-blue sky until it hurts one's eyes to look out the window. Paul and I are snooping around to find a bull fight this morning and will visit the Alhambra this afternoon and evening as there's a moon.

What do you think of calling my book *Ulysses, Jr.* instead of *Wanderlust?*

[*Granada—December 21, 1921.*] Granada grows on me day by day. Paul and I agree that it is the most satisfying spot we have met on our travels. He knows Italy, and I, France. Day after day the sun pours in a flood over the Alhambra where we hasten each morning, he to sketch, I to make notes, three hours before lunch and three hours after, until the sun dropping behind the snow-covered mountains brings a chill which ices the pools and makes an overcoat comfortable.

I found the head director of the Alhambra a jovial old man, speaking French, who, seeing my enthusiasm, led me through dilapidated corridors and roofless chambers unknown and unphotographed by the public in general. There is not a foot of the old pile I have not investigated. The exterior where visitors walk is patched and repaired and seems remarkably preserved, but it's only a gilded shell. Behind is rack and ruin where weeds and mould and bats flourish undisturbed by passing feet. Near the Alhambra is the roofless, unfinished Renaissance palace of a Spanish king, built nearly three centuries ago. A flight of steps leads up to the top of the wall from which a splendid view of the famous "Court of Lions" is visible. I was assured I was the first person to photograph the court from *that* inaccessible position. I bought a copy of Irving's *Alhambra,* read it— perhaps in the very room it was written in—and see before me the scene described.

I have chosen one of the sunniest terraces for my workshop, backed by a 30-foot wall covered with orange vines and blossoming red rambler roses. I have Granada and the sun-struck silver mountains to look at, with palms and fountains and ancient marble water basins about me. I sit in a low wicker chair and use a marble bench for a table and, interrupted only by an infrequent December visitor, read and write in unequaled beauty and comfort of surroundings.

This afternoon, after "hours," Paul and I wandered into the gypsy quarters, in caves on the side of a hill. They swarmed in pestering droves about us, fortune-telling, dancing, begging, but what could be more colorful than Spanish gypsies?

This city and its Oriental palace must be a paradise in spring, but we think it well-nigh perfect now with no one here but us. The fountains splash, the blue sky reflects itself in the marble-edged pools, the sun glistens on the oily deep-green leaves of the orange and citron trees—all for us alone. I could stay here for months and never tire of doing what I do each day, for never have I been so happy in a quiet, restful way.

[*Christmas Afternoon—Granada.*] Three thousand miles away from home on the day of the year when your son would prefer above all other days to be at home! You have been in my thoughts continually for your message of love and encouragement has sparkled in my brain.

Last night at midnight I knelt on the stone floor of the ancient Spanish cathedral among a throng of worshiping strangers and prayed that Christmas Day would find my mother and father in better spirits than on any previous anniversary. The church service was Catholic and impressive with its music and voices echoing about the dim-lit vaults, with its great choir singing the age-old carols and the reverberating organ rumbling and subdued, in glorifying the nativity of Christ.

My company left nothing to be desired. There was the comforting presence of Paul, and we had with us a most charming and welcome American woman, Mrs. Plimpton, whom we had met in the Alhambra gardens in the morning. She is the mother of two grown sons and the grandmother of two growing boys. She suffered the same tragedy as my own sweet mother, the loss of her younger son. He was killed in France in 1918. Her husband is dead; she feels homeless and disconsolate and travels desperately in search of forgetfulness. Her tenderness and circumstance reminded me strongly of you, Mother. I loved her from the first and when I told her of you and of Wesley she loved me.

We strolled along a less boisterous street of Granada after church last night and confided to each other our views on the philosophy of religion and happiness as if she had been my mother and I had been her son.

This bright sunny morning Paul and I decided we would not work one bit, but, as usual, climbed to my flowering Alhambra garden, and there enjoyed our rest fully and read the pile of American newspapers that came from Chicago. We met Mrs. Plimpton in the afternoon and we three, for the last time, strolled through the marble halls of the Alhambra, and across the valley to the Summer Palace to watch the sun set in a blaze of Christmas glory. We go now to have Christmas dinner with Mrs. Plimpton at her hotel, the best in the city. We had been wondering for a week what good fortune would be ours for the big meal, but never dreamed it would be so American and so homelike.

Three hours later—and what a splendid dinner it was! Turkey and rich wine and a big box of candy she had bought for us. Everybody was in his element. Mrs. Plimpton has keen and strong blue eyes that remind me of yours, Mother, and what do you think? When I left she put a sealed envelope into my pocket. I was afraid it was money but not being sure I could not refuse it and she asked me not to look till I was alone. The envelope contained 200 francs. I feel uncomfortable for I told her how simply and adventurously I was traveling and am afraid she *might* have suspected I was trying to work her sympathies for charity. What shall I do? Keep it and show my appreciation by letters and thoughtfulness? We three leave by the same train in the morning, she on her way to Gibraltar and Africa, Paul and I to Seville.

I've not had a bad Christmas, have I? I hope yours has been as happy.

[*Seville—December 29, 1921.*] Paul and I took third-class for the long, tedious trip here, but we sneaked into Mrs. Plimpton's first-class compartment and rode half way before we were kicked out. At Bobadilla where we changed cars, she for Gibraltar and we for Seville, I lost my camera in the hurry and scurry. So I'll *have* to get a new one now and will use Mrs. Plimpton's money to help pay for it.

Seville is so sunny and blossoming it quite remedies the ills encountered in getting here. We spent yesterday in the cathedral, the finest monument I've seen *yet,* and so enormous St. Paul's looks doll-like beside it. Only St. Peter's, in Rome, is bigger. Its colored windows reflect color and at sundown the white pillars and vaulted ceiling are patched thickly with bright reflected spots of light. The gardens of the old Moorish Palace here rival the Alhambra. Today

I sat and napped and dreamed there in the sunshine from nine till five, not even leaving for lunch, as half a dozen oranges plucked from the tree overhead sufficed.

[*Cadiz—January 1, 1922.*] Seville proved rather disappointing. The cathedral and wonderful Moorish tower are worth a day and the tropical gardens of the Alcazar a day, but as it is out of season for bull fights, Seville's chief attraction was lacking. Paul and I played about the parks and streets looking at the moving crowds and amused ourselves. Rather than endure the train to Cadiz we took a small tug by river to San Luca near the mouth. It was a balmy, muddy ride, a change from railroad filth and discomfort. But we were on the train from San Luca to Cadiz when the Old Year went out. Paul and I both swore off Spanish trains for our New Year's resolution and I hope to keep it for a while. Cadiz is fascinating, topographically and historically.

We have been almost living off oranges in Spain. This morning I bought a dozen huge, fancy ones for twenty cents in our money. We will take a long walk about the seawall which almost surrounds this town and fill our lungs with salt air. The sun has crossed my window as I sit here but has gone now and left me chilly; one look at the glowing blue sky above the narrow little street assures me that the sun will not be hard to find again.

[*Gibraltar—January 5, 1922.*] If my last letter seemed a bit weary this one should show that I've recovered, for Gibraltar would give the Wandering Jew himself a jolt. So many sensations have come my way since I wrote last, I am quite lost in them and only careful notation will unravel them.

The Monday after, Paul and I sauntered here and there over and about Cadiz absorbing the great mass of color in this most Spanish of cities, following the coast and docks, rowing about the harbor in a small boat and going that night to the theater.

Early Tuesday morning, long before sun-up, Paul and I dressed and I packed. He insisted on going to the boat with me and I was glad of it. It sailed at seven and we parted. He was a splendid traveling companion and I shall miss him. I had been told the little boat went straight to Algeciras (across the bay from Gibraltar) but it stopped at Tangier, where I got my first glimpse of real fezzes and Moors. Had it occurred to me to inquire I would have bought a ticket to Tangier and visited it, but I'll see other Oriental places enough. The sea was *extremely* rough and I was on the very verge of real seasickness for the monotony of a meat diet and Spanish olive oil cooking has put my stomach on the bum and made it a ready prey for a heavy sea.

How awesome the Rock appeared from the sea! The lights twinkling from its harbor and terraced city reminded me of Ponta Delgada in the Azores. It was quite dark when I ferried across the bay, and the black silhouette of the Rock against the starriest sky I ever saw was very beautiful. Standing in the prow of the pitching spray-swept ferry, I felt all the urges that seethe in my restless spirit rise to the surface. A glorious stimulation came over me to drive on with this aim of mine to a fine finish. It made me grateful, more than ever, that such good fortune is mine, and, likewise mine, a capacity to enjoy and profit from it to the full.

After dinner I went for a walk about this very English town where uniforms swarm on the streets and our own tongue is used exclusively. Before I knew it I was well up the mountain, vestless and hatless as well as overcoatless, with the twinkling Bay and boats below. A gate barred my path, but I stole through it and followed the path past all the "forbidden" signs until I stood on the very tip of the ears of the crouching lion which the Rock resembles and saw beneath me a panorama that I have not words to describe. The wind tore at me for trespassing but I sat as long as I could stand the elements.

This morning two other Americans (Oxford Rhodes scholars) and I completely circumnavigated the peninsula, keeping close to the water, and then this afternoon, with a soldier, I reclimbed to my nest. I saw the gun galleries that honeycomb the rock, etc. I'm going back tomorrow and spend the day with a rented kodak and stay for another night view. The rock is *covered* with blooming hyacinths. I am going to a subscription dance tonight and begin my struggle with ships next day.

[*Gibraltar—January 9, 1922.*] This letter is going to rank among the three most startling that your son has ever written to you. The first was the one from New Orleans about my runaway plans. The next was from Paris saying I had safely climbed the Matterhorn. This, the third, is from Gibraltar saying I am in *jail* in a British military prison (part of it is a hospital) with a cot and four whitewashed walls and one little barred window. But don't be unduly alarmed, for it is not a very serious matter and day after tomorrow should see me clear of it.

There is an American Consul here and Paul McGrath, who caught up with me again, is near by. I'm in the "jib" for being caught taking photographs with the Consul's camera in forbidden parts of the fortress. And since my first trial this afternoon came to nothing because of the lack of one witness, I'm put here for safe keeping until Wednesday at ten when another trial will be called. Of course, it is my first experience in court and quite a novel experience for me. The judge suggested I hire counsel, but I insisted on being my own for I feel quite capable of taking care of myself. The military authorities try to believe that I'm a spy and insist there is something "more serious" than at first appears.

[*Gibraltar—January 11, 1922.*] Out again. It's all over, but oh, at what cost!—£10—$46—(I have half that much) or one month in jail. *Believe me,* I paid the fine—with Paul's aid. Anyway, I got $46.00 worth of adventure out of the experience. I'll just about make the grade to Marseilles financially since disaster broke upon my head.

But back, 'way back, to the beginning of this novel and expensive experience. The day following my last letter, I went up with the American Consul's camera after having been shown about the day before by a soldier who knew where everything was. I photographed many of the views through the openings in the galleries—hidden guns, perspectives this way and that. Then down the perpendicular east side where the whole sweep of the mountain was before me and where I took another roll of pictures, reveling in scenery of heights and distant mountains and sea and ships 1300 feet below, that would make any photographer's heart beat faster. The steps zigzag halfway down and then a path leads around the rock, ending at the city on the opposite side. The setting sun shadowed the east side but flooded the

east bay with light, making every sail sparkle against the blue Mediterranean. On this precipice, descent of which was almost as difficult
as the Matterhorn, and as steep, dwarf palm bushes grow thickly and
among them, springing from the very rock, narcissus and hyacinths
and lilies make a complete covering and sicken one with their overpowering odors.

It took me all afternoon to climb down as I stopped every few
rods to sit on some protruding rock and just look. It was fully dark
when I got home. After supper I climbed past the guards again
and up to "Best View" where I was thrilled as I was when I saw it
first. There were the stars which, showering to the horizon, met the
myriads of lights from the ships in the harbor.

Those two night views from Gibraltar will go down in my history
with the sunrise view from the Matterhorn as the greatest visual stim-
ulations to date. Next day I hurried to get my rolls developed. They
were *perfect*. At once *Geographic* began to burn in my brain. I
rushed to the library and ransacked it for information and at five Sunday morning got up to finish my picture-taking in spots neglected the
day before. An early start was necessary for the sun shines on the east
side till four only, so I almost ran the three miles to the path that
winds up to the zigzag steps. Standing on the south point, I snapped
the Cape below, bristling with guns, and began to get very careless in
my enthusiasm, so much so that I did not hide the camera as two
civilians passed by. They went straight to the signal station and told
the commander, who sneaked up and saw my camera. I expected to
be handcuffed and thrown into the sea, but they allowed me to return
to my room unaccompanied. First thing I did was to place my old
negatives in the gutter outside my window, but I did not hide the
new ones.

Monday morning about 11:30 I was in the corridor of my hotel
writing notes when three plain-clothes police came up to me and
asked if I were Halliburton. "Yes." "The Police Chief wants you."
The Police Chief said, "Go to your room with these three detectives
and bring *every* scrap of paper you can find—bring your suitcase,
books, everything!" Back to the room we came, all four of us. The
new negatives were on the bureau. They went into one "Inspector's"
pocket without his even looking at them. We returned and it did

my heart good to hear the leader of the trio say, "We report that we have every article and paper in the room, including the pictures." They decided their case was not ready and sent me to the block house. Paul, who arrived in the midst of my difficulties, was allowed to see me through the bars and I told him where the old negatives were. He must look on the morning of the trial, and if they were still there, he was to let me know by a broad smile; if not, by a broader frown.

On the day of trial Paul came in all smiles. They questioned me for an hour or two, became satisfied I was no German spy, and the American Consul said my passports were *not* forged. The judge did not think much of my defense, but having all the negatives, he let me off with a fine of £10 or 30 days in jail.

Well, your son has pulled through uncut, but very *burnt,* and the burnt cat avoids the fire.

I almost forgot that the arrest took place on January ninth and was a novel birthday present. Twenty-two seems dreadfully old. I'll be middle-aged in no time.

[*Marseilles—10* A.M., *January 18, 1922.*] Paul left for Ronda after he saw me free and had paid part of my fine. I stayed to hear from a wire I'd sent to Tangier, inquiring about French boat sailings. There was nothing for a week. The train took four nights and three days but it was cheaper and got in four days earlier. Also Gibraltar wasn't so attractive as it used to be. So, the morning after my release, I, too, followed on to Ronda and met Paul. Mrs. Plimpton had given me her kilometer book with 800 kilos therein, more than enough to take me to Madrid, and artist Paul put my picture in place of hers and "stamped" it properly. Ronda quite rewarded the day there. It's built on top of *two* enormous rocks with perpendicular sides. The rocks are about 200 feet apart and the gorge between them, through which a river plunges, is 500 feet deep. It is an awesome sight from the bridge up and down the chasm. Paul and I climbed down to the bottom and came back for a moonlight look.

Paul carried my bag to the station and we parted for good. I shall keep in touch with him and visit him whenever I am in Chicago. I got to Cordoba at nine and should have stayed to see the wonderful mosque but I was so set for France I would not have stopped to see Heaven.

Now, for the good news! You remember I lost my camera at Bobadilla on a car that went to Cordoba. So in dreadful Spanish I asked the station master about it. "Yes, it's here," he said. I nearly swallowed my tongue as he went to get it while the train with my bag on board was "all aboarding." "This has been here two weeks," he said. "Is it yours?" "You bet it's mine," and I grabbed it and flew for my moving train, weak with joy. It was not mine at all but a handsomer machine than mine and brand new. I'll discuss the moral question at length—now that I have the machine.

My dread of the third-class trip was strangely softened by the recovery of "my" *$43.00 camera,* and the long, hard, cold night and day to Madrid were not so bad.

I made Barcelona in 36 hours and Marseilles in 18. I really should have rested at Barcelona but I wanted to get it over with. It's the longest I ever went without sleep and while I could scarcely talk straight enough to ask for my mail, strange to say I wasn't sleepy. Of course, as you've drummed into me, Mother dear, "one's mental state is in proportion to one's physical." When I opened Dad's cable and saw both my articles had failed, I sank into a chair more despondent than I've ever been in my life. The world had come to an end. My trip was a blank failure. I'd sacrificed reason and pleasure and company in vain. All the bushel of fine letters from you and everybody else could not console me. The few dollars from newspapers and *Travel* were poor solace to my expectations.

I plodded to my room to sleep from noon till noon, got up and shaved, had a hot bath, put on fresh clothes, had a big meal and laughed heartily at my own desolation of the day before. My pictures were perfect. It had stopped raining and before I knew it I was whistling for dear life and searching in vain for my troubles. It was a hard lesson, but I shall profit in the long run for having been jarred sensible. Well, I'm as fit as a fiddle. I'll jump on my old bike with my knapsack and get to Nice as fast as I can, for it's always ten degrees warmer there than here. There I shall stick till my three articles are done and send them to you, Dad, to copy and forward, saving me many dollars and days.

I hope the lump of copy I sent you written in Paris will show you what kept me there so long. I'm sorry now that I am not those three weeks ahead, but I couldn't know then that I was working in vain—

not quite in vain. Too bad I'm not in India with the cool weather. My hands and feet are so cold I should like to sit on the Equator for the rest of my life. Mike writes enraptured letters from Egypt.

Marseilles—January 18, 1922

Dad:—

You foresaw my disaster way back on October 30th when you said: "If the article is returned its length will be the reason." Your prophecy came true. You certainly prepared me for the bump, Dad. But it was good training and *lots* of it.

Truthfully, I've felt no more physical inconvenience since the Matterhorn climb than before. I'm going to scale Vesuvius at Naples and Olympus in Greece but they are mere stairsteps to the one and only. I promise not to try Everest, though Fujiyama in Japan would be fun.

Please, Dad, when I send you manuscript, *damn* it as well as like it. I value your estimation highly for I find you are usually right in knowing what is above or below the line of conviction and sanity. Don't think it's fine just because *I* wrote it. Look from an impersonal view as if you were the editor, judging its faults and virtues. I hate to admit it, but you're right about too much work making me weary. I've slowed up. Result: I've got behind in my notes. Oh, Dad, you say, "This voyage over land and sea is nothing but an unusual post-graduate year instead of Princeton." This trip is my *work*. Some Princeton grads from '21 went into banking, some into theology. I went into traveling and *writing* and I take it as seriously as they do. It must be my *income*. You have set me up in business by furnishing me with money for my education. I must make a success of these articles and then of my book. No, it's no vacation, it's no postgraduate year, it's serious business.

I'm off again as soon as possible, as well and as enthusiastic as ever, even if jolted sadly.

[*Marseilles still, dammit—January 22, 1922.*] Yesterday I bought a front-row seat to hear Alfred Cortot in concert with a 100-piece orchestra and got the thrill out of it that I always get from professional music. He played the Schumann concerto among other things—

pianists always do, thank Heaven! But he played it more inspiringly than I ever heard it. Perhaps it was because the emotional French audience respond to music with all their souls and this reflects on the artist. The 2500 people in the auditorium were still as death and then went into hysterical applause, for Cortot, being French, is one of the country's idols. In the orchestra, which is a Marseilles symphony and performs every week with some star, the organ and harp were given conspicuous importance and a quartette of those two instruments, a first violin and Cortot was the most beautiful thing I ever heard as well as the most unusual combination.

This morning I climbed the same steep and rocky hill surmounted by a church that I climbed with Chard Sanford on December 27, 1919. The same wonderful view, the same blue sky and sea, the same cypress-covered hills which extend to the foamy breakers.

My notes have profited by some 3,000 words during this delay and I have carried them now as far along as Cadiz, which is all before the big Gibraltar task. Why it is that words in letters roll from my pen as fast as I can write, yet stall and strain and struggle in my notebook, I do not know.

[*Nice—January 28, 1922.*] Back on the sunny Riviera! In the Savoy hotel, which, in my absence, has doubled its size and *price* so that I can't stay.

My bike trip thus far has been only half a success. While cloudy, rainy days cannot lessen the colors of the Mediterranean and the shore, they can make the roads hub-deep in mud and take lots of joy out of bicycling. Next morning after I wrote you I got off, carrying my suitcase on behind with a young library of books which altogether must have weighed 50 pounds, and rain and strong head-on wind did not give me a very propitious send-off. But the same wind that beat me backward roused the blue sea into beating furiously along the roadside, and the heavy clouds gave a deep blue to the green pines along the way, so I trudged on, enjoying a full dose of salt air, to Aubagne, and then came south over a real mountain of granite and cork trees. With my heavy luggage I had to walk uphill but the five miles down was a regular roller-coaster with glimpses of the sea through the trees here and there where I expected them least.

I had gone so slow that darkness came as I arrived at La Ciotat and its beautiful position on a small bay beckoned to me to rest there. The heavy wind rose violently in the night and dashed waves against the quay until the spray came to my hotel window. Madame and I had a long talk in French before the big, open fire and for the hundredth time I thanked fate that I could speak it.

Next morning the wind was still high. It had poured rain during the night but go I would and did, right along the coast and the worst roads I've ever seen. The high road to Toulon ran inland, which I did not want. I had lunch at a small place and quite late came toward Toulon harbor through La Seyne and looked down upon almost every boat in the French Navy anchored here and there in the bay. The city was swarming with sailors and full of amusements, but I was too tired for anything but bed.

Next day to Hyères, a favorite English winter resort, where one sees the gawky-red, but sweet-faced English girls contrasted with the slightly over-dressy and over-cosmeticized French women and the baggy-clothed English men in golf knickers beside the inevitable black coat and striped pants of the Monsieurs. Speaking of pants, I tore the entire seat out of my new pair the first day's cycling, but they were repaired skillfully. From Hyères I went to Cape Lardier on the opposite side of the peninsula from St. Tropez. Again the roads were terrible but the scenery indescribable, the sea every shade of blue and purple and the vegetation fresh and dank from a month of rain. A clear sunset inspired me to take a swim, or dip rather, for the water was certainly cold, but equally invigorating. I was the only non-French guest at the rather pretending hotel that night and I've never spent a more delightful evening. The 30 people or so one by one formed a circle about me as I leaned against the table and told of my adventures. The rain, my being foreign, my amusing French and wild stories made them ready to listen, so for nearly an hour I "entertained."

Next morning it was pouring, but on good roads I wheeled through Fréjus and St. Raphael for lunch, and then to Cannes for the night. The St. Raphael-Cannes road is a terror for grades, but the most beautiful stretch of azure scenery in the world, I'm sure. Seeing a short, rocky peninsula with the waves seething about it, I walked out and sat as close to the water as I dared in the rain, but well-wrapped in my coat, and watched the water break at my feet and felt the salt wind whistle about my head.

This morning it was again raining, so I put bike and me on the train and came here to recover my luggage I'd sent ahead from La Ciotat and to get settled at my old hotel for the day and move tomorrow.

The stars are out tonight and I hope a solid month of rain is over. This noon I sat next to the widow of General Bell of the U. S. Army. We chatted away and I suggested she and I go to *Herodiade* at the opera this evening as she was all alone, but she had been previously invited.

As I went to my room I bumped into an American girl who had been installed in it by mistake, and I moved to another. The unexpected introduction was enough. She lives in New York and knows lots of people I know and more I'd like to; so we went to the opera this evening and enjoyed it thoroughly. We had a walk in the clearing weather, tea and dancing this afternoon. She pays her part and I pay mine. I'll run over to Monte Carlo tomorrow and try my hand again at roulette and then get to work on my articles in earnest.

[*Nice—January 31, 1922.*] The day after I wrote you Pauline Frieder, who, by the way, has proved quite as worth knowing as anyone I've met yet, and I bought third-class round-trip tickets for Monte and the most beautiful Sunday you ever saw. They all but held me up at the Casino on account of age, but finally let me in. Oh! what an enormous gambling den! There must have been 5,000 people playing every manner of something-for-nothing game. So Pauline and I had a hard time getting seats.

My heart never beat so fast from excitement, for we each had 200 francs in chips and were out to win our fortunes. My stunt was to play black and red only—no numbers—always play one color until it has won twice, then change over once and come back. With beginners' luck we piled up francs from the first and in ten minutes had doubled our money. "It works," I was sure, and had visions of yachts, etc., right off, but my victory was premature. We were playing black, and red began to come three times, four times, and each time it continued

I stacked chips on black, thinking after five and six reds it *would* come black, but the darned thing came red *eleven times* and absolutely *stripped* us of every chip.

If I had had another 100 francs in chips I might have recouped by keeping still to black, but we let bad enough alone and, feeling very blue, we got out of the place, bought a half-pound of candy, found a bench in the gardens overlooking the sea and there had a candy jag and drowned our sorrows. But it was the most nerve-racking emotional excitement in the world. I was in a welter of perspiration when we left.

Yesterday—you might well despair of such imbecility—I went back, vowing to win back what I'd lost. I played small and safe and for an hour clung to my 50 francs, but bit by bit it dribbled away. I bought 100 francs more and was almost out of them when, with only five francs left, I began to play on two colors. Then my luck turned. Time and again one of my two chips won and soon I had 260 francs. I resolved to play my 20-franc chips twice more to double my money and stop when bang! zero came with two 20's out. You should have seen me get away with my 220 which meant a net profit of 70 francs and leaves me still 130 in the hole, altogether.

I am going back today and, if the columns still work, I'll recover everything. If yesterday were only a flash I'll stop short. I can see how people go mad over the tables. A man next to me yesterday lost 3,000 francs in twenty minutes and was wild-eyed. It's the most intense thrill I've known. I've worked late at night and am up to Gibraltar in my notes.

[*Nice—February 3, 1922.*] If my other letter takes a boat before this one you will be in suspense, I'm afraid, about my Monte Carlo venture, but if that is the case, let this page put you at ease again, for Monte and I have played quits and are not speaking. My luck does not encompass gambling nor is my temperament suited. My last fling proved that whatever my calling is, it isn't playing roulette at Monte Carlo. I bought more chips and played small stakes, but lost. A man observing my tenseness and ignorance gave me a handful of plaques and told me to play as he did. We went from table to table playing according to luck, and winning steadily. Well, he decided he wanted some tea, so we separated. I cashed in and was quite a bit winner—but I didn't feel very proud and I left satisfied to quit.

I've written nearly 6,000 words since my cure and now, fairly in the swing, will begin to eat away great piles of work. I've almost finished my Gibraltar notes and sometime today will tackle the article.

Yesterday morning Pauline and I took an hour out and climbed a hill overlooking Nice for pictures. And this afternoon she's invited me to tea with other American friends.

It's been dazzlingly sunny for several days and the promenades are packed with lazy, idle, spendthrift people looking for pleasure with all their might and showing on their hard faces that they can't find it. Nice is a second Atlantic City where tailors' wives and horse-racing touts gather in droves and think they are being very swell. Monte is certainly the most elegant, aristocratic place in the world and the jewels and shops quite awe one.

CHAPTER VI

to Egypt and India

AT NICE, Richard was faced with a situation that disturbed him greatly. Whatever route he might choose to take from there, he would find himself reaching India in summer, which, to him, was unthinkable. He offered two solutions to this situation. One was to come home after seeing Italy, Greece and Constantinople, and go straight to Cairo in September and on to India in winter. This was the less satisfactory. The other was to circle around the Mediterranean, have his mother and father meet him in Italy in July, and visit with them till the time to sail for Cairo. He opens a letter on February sixth without the usual salutation to his parents. "This all indicates that *at last* I have a thought. In short, I *think* I'll come home! Wait—wait! Let's not get excited unduly for it's all just a *thought* to be deeply pondered over by you and me." In not more than a dozen lines, he presents his first alternative. Then he goes on: "But here's one, perhaps even better: Go back to Marseilles, on to Cairo, then as spring advances come north through Palestine, Asia Minor, Constantinople, Greece and Italy by July fifteenth there to meet YOU— *both of you*—and we three loaf in North Italy and Austria until September fifteenth, when I will start east, arriving in India early in November. Yes, that's best."

Expatiating on this second alternative, he devotes as many pages, in this letter and his next one, as he had given lines to his first suggestion. He then cabled his second plan home.

He writes: "I am permitted to use the airplane picture of Gibraltar for 300 francs. Gosh! So I am waiting before I start Gibraltar and have begun on 'A Merry Christmas in a Moorish Castle.' When this is done, I'll write on 'Don Quixote, Jr.'

"I had a most delightful day yesterday. Early in the morning I took the train to Monaco and prowled around the city at the rock.

In Barcelona this bustled lady with the parasol was used by Richard to prove to his father that statues are better undressed.

No. 27313

Colonial Government of Gibraltar.

(Department) _____

(Date) 1/1/1922

RECEIVED, from *Richard Llewellyn* the sum of

Ten Pounds ——— Shillings

and ——— Pence being amount due as per margin.

£ 10 . 0 . 0

Jno Stevens
Treasurer.

It cost a fine of ten pounds sterling to take forbidden pictures on Gibraltar, but Richard got a receipt for his money. (He got the pictures too.)

It's extraordinary. I didn't appreciate it before. I took the cog railway up the cliff above the sea to the Grande Corniche road, 2,000 feet above Monte Carlo, and followed it on foot to Nice, twelve miles. The views are astounding from that height. I have 20,000 words of best notes *yet* on my bicycle trip, Pauline, and our interesting but hard luck at Monte. I read them to her and she suggested some changes.

"A letter from Ammudder containing $100.00 was forwarded from Rome. It was more than dear of her.

"I'm trying to put the brakes on my volubility habit. Unleashed through more than *two* years of travel it would make my book run to six volumes! The more I think about *Ulysses, Jr.* the better I like it for a title, for as I develop my notes they become more and more adventure and less and less 'wanderings.' But also I'm coming to the realization that any plan I make is liable—almost certain—to be changed."

Later, not having heard from the cable home, he writes a short letter: "I have been pacing the floor all day, wrestling with the situation. The news about my Andorra article was a blow. The ocean itself is not so blue as I am tonight. So I shall not try to answer your letters till a night's sleep makes me more philosophical and cheerful."

Next morning he continues: "I've not mailed this yet, as you see, for I knew twelve hours would cheer and clear. I've read all your letters again and, of course, the worst is not so bad as I thought. A weekly story asked for by Mr. Mooney [President of the *Commercial Appeal* Publishing Company] is fine—that will almost pay my expenses—and with a magazine article accepted occasionally, as there will be, I feel much encouraged. Just now, I'm tired of work. With my letters, and 20,000 words of excellent notes, and two stories, I've truly been on the job."

His father had to cable him that his second plan could not be worked.

Marseilles—February 11, 1922

Dear Dad:—

The cable came. It was short and to the point. I walked miles along the seashore and debated the situation. I am going to Cairo and be in Egypt till April first, then whether I go north from there or east will depend on information, inspiration and my guardian devil. In all events I'm going ahead and shall travel toward the rising sun. I have too much confidence in my book idea and shall not give up.

While I was glowering in indecision, Pauline, who had first thought that for you to come to Italy was just the thing, sensed the situation and snapped me back into action. So I'm leaving for Marseilles and will finish this letter tonight. . . .

I reached Marseilles and began to look for a job or in lieu of a job a cheap passage to Cairo. As I begin to sense the prospect of moving on, I get less blue, and, once in motion again, I'll be happy. Nice and Monte Carlo lulled me into inaction. My small winnings at roulette and Ammudder's $100 aided and abetted the sunshine and the beautiful setting.

I sent you twelve registered packages from Nice containing a ton of pictures, notebooks and manuscripts.* The mail did not really weigh a ton on the scales, but it weighed all of that on my shoulders. This is the first time since I left home that I've been absolutely caught up and I feel like a boy out of school. My notes are up to date, every story is written up, everything mailed and my baggage light again. The past seven months are a closed chapter, and from now on it will be Chapter II.

I left Nice just as all the world was coming in, as the annual spring carnival opened yesterday, and last evening were the first parade and ceremonies. I've never seen such gorgeous floats and costumes and display. There were ten people waiting to grab my hotel room. They are welcome to it. My friend Pauline and I joined the masked mobs and spent quite a merry hour but, in consequence, I got to bed at 3 A.M. She is a most delightful and stimulating friend and a half-hour's walk with her, or tea, revives my lagging spirits always.

Sarah Bernhardt was in Nice recently and I saw her once—was

---

* Among these packages were a 4,680-word article on "Don Quixote, Jr.," a 3,200-word article on "The Rock of Tarik," a 1,650-word article on "Alhambra Adventures," and closely written notebooks galore; also books, pictures, etc.

so thrilled I went back again. She is too remarkable to be human. She never left her chair the entire four acts yet held her audience spellbound by her dominating personality.

Well, it's 12:30 so I send this much as the close of Chapter I and shall write more tomorrow beginning Chapter II.

To be continued.

[*Marseilles—February 18, 1922.*] Chapter II. What a satisfactory day this has been! Early this morning I mailed the last of Chapter I and wired Rome to forward all mail to Cairo. Then I went straight to the Consul's office and received super-courteous treatment.

The Grace agent, a Mr. Lenwright, an Englishman, asked me to dinner at the British Club. There we met two other Britishers and had a most delightful two hours. Then Mr. Lenwright told me of an American and his wife who were traveling through all the inland waterways of Europe in a houseboat and took me to see them and it. They proved intensely stimulating. He's a Columbia grad, Ph.D., named Ogalvie, about 33. His young wife is from Murfreesboro, Tennessee. They live alone on the boat and are just starting up the Rhone, down the Rhine, down the Danube to Egypt where they will go up the Nile next winter. Mr. Ogalvie and I spent the entire afternoon together and I'm to see them again Monday morning.

I have to look the other way, Dad, when I come to the place in your letter where you kill the fatted calf for the return of the prodigal son next Christmas. If it had come sooner I doubt if I could have sent my long cable about India. The infinite miles between me and home will not let me be back by then if I keep my face toward the rising sun. After all, I know you understand, this trip is not travel altogether, but a graduate's desire to be seeing and feeling things that stimulate his pen; that it's been over-stimulated has been the trouble.

I'm absolutely sure your hope will not come true about my wanting to be still a while after I get home. I can be happy if I can always be in action or motion, say as an elevator boy, but I know if I must have a life behind a desk it will be a dismal and miserable failure. Perhaps it's lack of physical concentration, perhaps it's a nervous habit, but it's consuming, whatever it is.

[*Marseilles—February 23, 1922.*] The best of news! I sail Friday on a French freighter for Alexandria.

I decided upon consulting with Mr. Ogalvie. He said he would see the manager of the Fabre Line. Ogalvie has the most irresistible personality and after initial rebuffs got the manager's consent to my sailing as a passenger for $15.00. Not bad for a five or six-day trip. It's almost too good to be true. Should he change his mind, I think I'll take deck passage. It's of no consequence whether I dine with the seamen or the captain.

[*Marseilles—February 25, 1922.*] One last word before I sail. My freight boat stunt *did* prove too good to be true. It postponed its sailing till Thursday next and changed its destination to Algeria and Bierut so, after careful figuring, I decided to go "sur le pont," that is, "deck passenger," meals included. This way the boat is mine. I'm in the air all the time. I bought a big blanket which I can use at night. It cost $1.70, so I could afford it. I bought also two dozen oranges, so you see how comfortable I'll be. The nights are a bit cool but the days are already blazers.

Our trip is seven days. We don't stop, either. I've collected a young library—*Innocents Abroad, The Three Musketeers, The Count of Monte Cristo,* and Voltaire. I chose them because I wanted something absolutely diverting.

I told the Ogalvies and my other friends good-by this morning and am all "packed" now. I spent yesterday at Aix where there is a remarkable collection of tapestries and old churches. I couldn't stand this killing *wait* much longer but feel very happy just now, realizing I'm actually off.

[*S.S. Harvraise—February 26, 1922.*] At last I am back on the sea. A fish that has been on dry land some months could not make that remark with more satisfaction in its heart than I do. Especially since it's the *Mediterranean* Sea, which is "new field for me."

It really surprised me last night as we pulled out of Marseilles to realize that I was just as eager and excited at being on the water again and headed for new adventures as when Mike and I steamed out of New York Harbor last July.

Marseilles is beautiful from the sea: myriad lights sloping up to the base of mountains and the cluster of white granite islands at the mouth of the harbor, including Château d'If.

It didn't take me long to catch on to deck passage life and I had a plate and spoon and wine bottle all ready. When dinner sounded I stood in line with the crew and the three other deck passengers, Arabs, to receive the allotment of food. The cook *almost* poured soup on a ten-franc piece but not quite. My tip began to work immediately and he gave me a china plate for the tin one and a bit better service. After each man was served he took his plate to some favorite spot about the boat and ate in picnic fashion. The food is nothing to complain of. Just as we had baker's bread and breakfast food and condensed milk and canned fruit, all characteristically American dishes, on the *Ipswich,* so now we have fresh bread and the inevitable lettuce salad and wine, without which these seamen would starve to death.

All today I've reclined in an improvised deck chair and watched the islands pass by. At sunset we are passing between Corsica and Sardinia, about eight miles across, and numerous lighthouses are blinking on both shores. A plank makes the back of my chair and an unused stand for coils of rope, the seat. The blanket renders it fairly comfortable so that, if this faultless weather keeps up and my books and ink and paper do not give out, I'll be content to keep my place in preference to that of any of the six first-class passengers who pace the deck for lack of something better to do.

[*On Board—Monday, February 27, 1922.*] We've been in sight of land (Italy) all this day, and a more rugged, varied coast isn't. From my deck chair on the poop I've seen everything and thanked fate again and again that this very pleasant mode of transportation was found. People who have never been to sea except in a first-class cabin on a big liner can never know the full charm of the ocean, for they have seen it only under disadvantageous circumstances, where the great size of the vessel gives the life of a hotel, not the life of the sea. But sailing as a deck passenger on the blue Mediterranean on a small freighter allows one to reap to the utmost all the peculiar sensations which only the sea can afford.

One would never think it was February, judging from the sun which blazes away in a cloudless sky, burning my skin (as usual), heating the decks and giving the unrippled water a profound and oily blueness. It seems incapable of the obstreperous tantrums of which the *Aeneid* accuses this ocean, when the waves rose high and the troughs sank so deep that spots of dry land were exposed on the bottom, to which the ships of the Trojans fell with great damage.

[*On Board—Tuesday, February 28, 1922.*] Last evening was the best yet. Although the days are blazers the nights remind me it *is* February; they are so clear and starry I regret that the cold wind makes the deck chilly as a bed. But last night I spread my blanket in the hollow of a coil of rope atop the "poop," and piling on rope as well as blanket and pulling the cover tight about my neck and leaving only my face exposed to the sting of the wind, I managed to keep warm. Then, after I had exhausted all the poetry I knew by heart, and looked for the Great Bear, the Lion and the Unicorn, and all the other animals an imaginative mind can find in the stars, I fell asleep. The situation brought back to me a little poem which I learned from a third-grade reader when going to school to Ammudder, along with Napoleon Darnell and his brother Rezneat. It was lost absolutely since 1905, but it came back to me last night as I looked for figures and shapes in the planets. This is it—a charming bit of sentiment, I think, and I'll not forget it again.

> "At evening when I go to bed,
> I see the stars shine overhead;
> They are the little daisies white,
> That dot the meadows of the night.
> And often when I'm dreaming so
> Across the sky the moon will go:
> It is a lady sweet and fair,
> Who comes to gather daisies there.
> For when at morning I arise,
> There's not a star left in the skies;
> She's picked them all, and dropped them down
> Into the meadows of the town."*

If I ever have a child I shall certainly teach it that little poem. And so, how philosophic it is to find it better to be in a freight boat and

---

* "Daisies," by Frank Dempster Sherman, by permission of Houghton Mifflin Company.

spend the evening in such a manner than to be on the *Olympic* where one must be on review all the time. Indeed, what vagabond could ask for more than I have? Good food and wine, a comfortable bunk, good books and good thoughts to keep my mind occupied, the boat to myself, enough water to keep clean, enough sunshine to keep warm. Again and again as I lie on the deck under the blue and brilliant sky, spending my time between reading Dumas and watching the wheeling sea gulls, these lines come to me:

> "Sun and wind and beat of sea,
> Great lands stretching endlessly ...
> Where be bonds to bind the free?
> All the world was made for me!"*

It's a very strange coincidence that today, the 28th of February, should be the very day I begin to read *Monte Cristo,* for in the story the two great events of the book, Dantès' imprisonment and liberation from the Château d'If, were both on February 28th. The book is all about Marseilles and Paris and I feel as intimate toward it as if I were reading a book laid in Memphis or Princeton.

I enjoyed the *Innocents* more and more. Mark Twain had my idea exactly 50 years ago, but we cover different fields entirely and he is Mark Twain and I'm only me, so he's in no danger! I like him best when he's serious. He is certainly a realist. But for his fine flights away from burlesque he might be successful in making people believe he was himself a boor, lacking sensitiveness and culture; always "in need of a spittoon," "of someone to take his muddy boots off the mantelpiece." Mark is right. His very carelessness and roughness are assets. I'll read more of him when I get home and study his later style.

[*On Board—March 1, 1922.*] I can see no longer in my deck chair. The sun went down in a great ball of fire, inch by inch, into the sea and immediately the new moon appeared overhead. It is so clear and beautiful my heart is filled anew with thoughts of home as well as thoughts of the immediate future—Egypt! I've been still all day and must take a stroll about the deck.

[*On Board—March 3, 1922.*] There was nothing new to write yes-

---

* "Adventure." From *Verse,* by Adelaide Crapsey, by permission of Alfred A. Knopf, Inc.

terday, except that it's getting hotter. We see land again tomorrow morning and dock, so I'm told, about noon. I forgot to say it was night when we passed through the Straits of Messina between Sicily and Italy, so I failed to see the classic Scylla and Charybdis by which I first was impressed when reading a schoolboy primer about Jason and the Golden Fleece.

My Egypt plans are fully stated in this letter. That is to say, they are *nil*. I find I have a much more adventurous time if I let it take care of itself. This is truly a new world I'm coming to.

[*Cairo—March 7, 1922.*] Hurrah! Mail! Your letters tell me you are well and as "even tenored" as usual. I take a new lease on life.

My freighter reached Alexandria at four Saturday. I was the only one to go ashore and I went with all possible rapidity for I was tired of the idleness. Only my books kept the last day or two from deadly dullness.

These native robbers began to swindle me out of all I had at the start but I learned how to treat them likewise at the start. I reached here about midnight. Next morning I spied a Y. M. C. A. and in half an hour was installed in the dormitory. The other men are all English but very pleasant companions.

Sunday I prowled to my heart's content. I picked up a really delightful Arab lad who knew the bazaars and other places of interest like a book and proved not half bad company. This being my first taste of the Orient, everywhere I look I see a new world. Cairo is truly that after France. Sunday night I called on the U. S. military attachés. A Colonel Allen proved delightful and proposed to take me for a drive, but his chauffeur had gone, so we walked instead, up and down the Nile, till midnight.

Yesterday afternoon I began anew to prowl—mosques, minarets, alleys, dives, everything. And I was so completely affected by my colorful and novel surroundings I forgot time, space and *myself* for hours and walked a dozen miles before I realized I was dead tired and suffering blistered feet. I had planned to go to the Pyramids but it was threatening rain.

Cairo is a huge city, 800,000. Its European district, a model of solidity and magnificence, opera, monuments, etc., seems doubly impressive beside the squalor and congestion in the native quarters close by. I'm beginning to get the atmosphere which can be got only by one traveling slowly as I am.

Mother dear, your entertainments keep you occupied and stimulated. I wish I could find something to *un*stimulate me. The restlessness I've suffered from for some years seems to get no better and at times makes itself felt in lack of physical composure. I frequently must leave the theater because the effort to sit still so long destroys all pleasure in the performance. Yet, when I'm walking about in the air, if alone, my mind is as clear as a bell and ideas, well connected, simply buzz in my head. I write chapters, make speeches, form plans. You must not be alarmed about all this. It's nothing new. I've never been in better health. Only yesterday the Secretary here said to me, "Your travels seem to keep you in fine trim. I never saw anyone look more rugged." It's because I'm so sunburned, and well slept and fed, and feel an exuberance that bubbles over and churns about in my head and my toes. My restlessness is not due to any run-down condition. I don't know what it is. I suppose it's just me and must be endured along with blond hair and big feet.

I got the two letters from Marie you forwarded. She went to Lawrenceville for a prom and her description of it made me homesick. She was in Kansas City and met all the friends I have there.

I spent *last night* on top of the *Great Pyramid* and am just back but unable from weariness to continue.

[*Cairo—Friday, March 10, 1922.*] Mrs. Plimpton came and I had dinner at Shepherd's with her and met Colonel Allen as she and I were parting. Yesterday morning I "did" the museum and I spent the afternoon in Shepherd's gardens with Mrs. Plimpton and the evening in the Colonel's car in a long and beautiful drive up and down the edges of the moonlit Nile.

Today, early, I went to Memphis and Sakkara and got back late. I'm dead tired tonight from twelve miles of walking through the most fascinating stretch of rural Egypt—date palms and crops of everything such as an Iowa farmer never dreamed of. Without seeing it one cannot conceive of the sharpness of line between the fertile narrow river verdure and the absolute desert, each is so extreme. There was no cotton planted yet; the barley and wheat and cucumber crops are on now. Then vegetables, then cotton, all in twelve months.

There's nothing left of Memphis but a name. The step pyramid of Sakkara was interesting and, decidedly so, were the famous tombs opened in 1850 and found exactly as they were in 2000 B. C. I've not yet been able to conceive dates in this country, nor to grasp the fact that this building or pile antedated the Christian era by as many years as have followed it. As yet the night's rest on top the big pyramid has been the rarest adventure, but no details now.

Do not be surprised to receive a cable saying I'm on my way to India. Your last letter, Dad, has about made me abandon the plans I've struggled with so long. The killing time idea is frankly repugnant in spite of all I can do. Of course, the fact that it's summer in the East has motivated everything.

[*Cairo—March 16-17, 1922.*] My sweetheart Mother, rest easy now. I'll never swim the Hellespont *this* year, but I had a fair substitute. I swam the Nile at Luxor. I am enjoying and marvel of Egypt more than any country yet. I shall have full notes on it. I have been restless under the recent uncertainty but now that I'm all set again I'm as calm and determined as ever before. Let me tell you what precautions I am taking. First, I'm being *revaccinated* and *reinoculated*. The doctor said it was not necessary. I said it was. So tomorrow I take both. I shall go to Kashmir and keep north all the time. I can get material enough without visiting the elephants and tropics of Colombo and south India.

I have often thought of the fact that without doubt it was Ammudder who first started me when I was a little boy on this would-be path of literature—at least, a love of reading and books.

You always stimulate me, Dad, with the philosophic way you look at the worst. Dumas says, "Life is a chaplet of little worries which the philosopher counts with a smile." You truly seem to do that. Only years of experience, I suppose, can bring such equanimity of mind. Perhaps I'll have it some day.

Well, I've written three letters from Egypt and said nothing about Egypt, and as I am written out now you must wait for my notes for the details. As I've said, the night on top of the pyramid was an inspiring adventure. It was a full moon. I climbed up at ten o'clock and beheld a truly wonderful sight. The Nile and then the three miles of verdure, then the knife-like edge where the desert begins, the other pyramids about us and the sea of sand behind. The moon went down about four, and the darkness gave new tones to our surroundings. The sun rose over the minarets of Cairo and struck the sides of the near-by pyramids slantingly so that they sparkled like gold; a haze spread all over the velvety valley, dotted with groves of palms and lakelets of irrigation water. The desert took on changing colors and a long caravan crawled toward and past us as I watched. It was 10 A.M. before I came down—twelve hours on top. I had a blanket but couldn't sleep for the cold but had so much to see I didn't want to. Next morning I walked out among the groves and villages and took a few good pictures of the pyramids through the palms.

The trip to Luxor was a fright, yet interesting going with the natives and their luggage of vegetables and livestock. Everybody ate sugar cane and threw the pith on the floor so that a mat of pith six inches thick accumulated.

The ruins of Karnak at Luxor are the most awesome structure imaginable. I climbed to a "pylon" of tumbled stones to get a picture above the forest of enormous columns and on the way down lost my balance and fell about 40 feet. Three score natives came yelling and running to me expecting to find me in pieces but I landed in a pile of debris and was only shaken and jarred. They couldn't believe I was not killed. I went back by moonlight and it was doubly stirring.

Next day I walked to the Tomb of the Kings chiseled out of granite and sculptured in the walls with whole volumes of hieroglyphics, colored and embossed. It was truly beautiful. The other temples on that side of the river are in better preservation than Karnak and more delicate, but not so impressive.

Crossing back, I swam the Nile and had an amusing adventure. The swim was not difficult. The difficulty lay in the problem of recovering my clothes! Next day I went in a boat to Edfu, which is the best preserved building of antiquity—2,000 years old and in perfect state except that the early Christians carefully chipped out the faces of the hundreds of gods carved in the rock walls. Had I not been feeling rather low from some ill-eaten food, I would have joined a caravan going to the Red Sea.

[*Cairo—March 22, 1922.*] I'm off tomorrow for Port Said but with little enthusiasm, for I've been head over heels in a great plan to fly to Bagdad and cross Persia and Afghanistan by caravan. After devoting three solid days to it I've given up. Every authority said the latter part is mad and the former can be had for a price only.

With this letter I am mailing you a manuscript, "Camped on Kheops" which has occupied me off and on for nearly a week.

I had dinner Sunday with the President of the American College here, the father of a classmate, and there met another classmate who I did not know was in town. He's teaching at the college and is very enthusiastic about it. He and I have had tea with girls two or three times, a dance or two, and dine together tonight. I needed some company.

Egypt has not been so adventurous as I should have liked but intensely interesting. The town here has been in an uproar for days over politics—riots and mobs and cheering all day long. The students cause the trouble but fly like sparrows when two police charge them.

Your cable "Approve—careful—well—love" was very encouraging. I *shall* be careful, rest assured. I will not hear from you again till I reach Calcutta, at least two months from now. That thought saddens me.

Upon Richard's arrival at Port Said he found the American oil tanker *Gold Shell* just arrived and in need of one seaman, and he was immediately signed on. His letter from Calcutta telling about this long trip across the Indian Ocean, round the toe of India and up to Calcutta—a non-stop voyage—is missing. He found this a restful experience after the strenuous days in Egypt.

The nine other seamen were Greeks with whom he soon made friends. Their names were long and hard to pronounce, so he gave them nicknames. His name, being equally difficult to them, was abbreviated to "Boy."

A chapter in his *Royal Road to Romance* entitled "The Garlic-Eaters" details the incidents of this trip. The only thing out of the usual was a burst of flames from the stacks just after dark. Everyone on deck thought the oil-laden steamer was afire. Much excitement prevailed as the men instinctively lined up into a fire-fighting brigade. The flames subsided as quickly, and it was learned that a careless stoker had cut off the air below and the heated oil vapor had ignited in the stacks when it came in contact with the oxygen of the air.

The paragraphs at the end of this chapter bring him into Calcutta:

"On Easter Sunday, with the thermometer hovering around one hundred and ten in the shade and the wind burning one's skin like a blast from a furnace, the *Gold Shell* docked at Budge-Budge on the Hooghly, a dozen miles below Calcutta, and the seamen, confined to the boat since they left Texas, fifty days before, hurried to dock her in order that they might put their feet on dry land once more.... The peg-top trousers, the green silk shirt, the heavy red tie with brass stick pin, the squeaky tan shoes, the checked cap cocked on one ear, the hair close-cropped by each man for his neighbor, and the *Gold Shell's* crew was arrayed in all its glory, prepared to sweep noisily upon the seaport, paint it red and leave it enriched by their hard-earned, easy-spent wages....

"That same morning I left the *Gold Shell* for good. Not until the hour of separation did I realize how attached I was to that clumsy old tanker and her blasphemous crew. Slim and the bo's'n were not aboard, so I didn't get a chance to say good-by to them. However, the very next day a letter from Slim addressed to the Y. M. C. A. reached me and I reproduce it verbatim:

"'Burg-Burg [Budge-Budge] April 20. Dear frend Boy.... I arrived on the Gold Shell well. I am not drung but in my happy feelings. Where you go lass nite. Micky said he woked up in Y. M. C. A. with tatood chest. If you got tatood I beat you up. The short legged animal [his name for the bo's'n] is ashore today hisself so nobody work. They say the ship is going to take six cargos to Ramgoom [Rangoon] and I see you maybe when you come back from the Himmalyammas [Himalayas]. Sweet Caporal [the tom cat] was ashore lass nite but came back today not drung but grouchy. Take care of yourself. I close my letter wishing you the perfect of health—Frendly.

"'Slim Dourateliasinous.'

"A postscript from Micky was scrawled at the bottom:

" 'Hello Boy—This is just to bawl you out for letting me get tite last night and that damed tatoo stuck on me. . . . Slim and me have laughed ourselfs sick over the cart race. The bosn aint showed up yet but I'm back on me durty job. Wisht I was going out in them jungles with you Boy—I aint never seen no canabells. By-By matey.

" 'truly and sincerely—Micky.' "

[*Calcutta—April 23, 1922.*] I finally got hold of the Tutweilers last Wednesday.* Mrs. T. left the sixth of this month but Mr. T. I met here in his city office and he said, "If you care, come out to Jamshedpour and stay as long as you like." I accepted.

My plans are well under way. An American here spoke so enthusiastically of a certain Dr. Lapp, medical missionary at Dhamtari, 300 miles southwest of Jamshedpour, and of the absolutely uncontaminated-by-Europe region he lives in, 30 miles from a branch railroad, that I wrote him and asked if I might pay him a visit.

I bought two tailor-made white cotton suits. They were necessary for Mr. Tutweiler's. I *live* in my boy-scout short pants and shirt so that the heat concerns me not a whit. With my helmet I prowl about at midday all over town and am honestly not the least uncomfortable.

I've been working steadily on my notes and enjoying it; all *Gold Shell* notes. I didn't realize before how thoroughly happy and satisfied I was during these three weeks, what fine traits lay under the harsh exterior of my shipmates. I have a deeper affection for this boat than for either of the other two. On the *Ipswich* I had Mike and didn't bother about the others. This time I cultivated all the crew. I got a letter from one of my special Greek friends that is a masterpiece and which I'll quote in my notes.

This afternoon in a cool drizzle a Mr. Conger (American business man) and I went out to the Temple district and splashed about; we saw them burning dead bodies and sacrificing goats and other malodorous things, but the rain put the damper on the funeral pyres and the general enthusiasm.

---

* Richard had met Mrs. Tutweiler in Memphis where she had visited the Halliburtons. Her husband was manager of a steel mill some miles out from Calcutta. She had invited Richard to be their guest when he came there.

[*Jamshedpour—April 28, 1922.*] Let me discuss the season here, which I know is causing you worry. Yesterday at Jamshedpour the official temperature was *one hundred and twenty* degrees, in the shade, of course. I can scarcely believe it, but it's true. It's so dry my clothes crinkle and the perspiration is gone as soon as it comes. The sun at midday is scorching, but I'm hid under my cork helmet. Truthfully, I'm not the least uncomfortable and walk about, ride horseback, even dance, with not so much sweat and lasting discomfort as at home in July when it is ninety.

Dr. Lapp, the medical missionary at Dhamtari, wired me, "By all means, come." I leave here Monday. Whatever I find there will be the result of a chance conversation and following what I hunched as a good idea.

The settlement here is a dry, barren place with some 300 foreigners, who gossip themselves to death, play bridge and ride horseback. I'm getting eager for the north, but will see Dhamtari first.

[*Dhamtari—May 7, 1922.*] I'm leaving here this noon for the big city again. The past week has been one long delight—*unusual*. I swear at myself for having stayed so long at Jamshedpour killing time when such country as this was accessible.

The missionaries met me, and more delightful, hospitable people do not exist. They are Mennonites, a sort of Quakers. They will not "take up arms or go to law" and refuse to allow a Hindu to become a Christian if he has two wives and refuses to "put away" one wife. It's real India here, a region of wilderness and aboriginal life where a white man is stared at and natives are in constant fear of tigers and panthers. This mission is doing a wonderful work.

The first night we took a walk a mile away from Dhamtari. Native villages swarm with naked children and half-naked people in mud houses. Frugality is the dominating spirit—have nothing, need nothing, want nothing but a little rice. The tom-toms were beating for a marriage celebration; a weird piercing pipe sounded indistinct and melancholy. The sun set behind a row of palm trees bordering the edge of a waterhole where bullocks swam and water carriers with pots on their heads filed in silhouette along the bank. From the jungle squawking birds filled the air with their noisy quarreling for berths in the rookeries. For the first time I felt I was in *India*. We slept in the yard that night, right under the moon and stars—such stars!

In this dry and parching weather the air is clear and brings the planets very close. All night the *tom-toming* kept up. Next day we drove in a Ford ten miles farther into the jungle to Mr. Lapp's own home, to see the Girls' School and Orphanage. Indian children are no less pretty than our own: expressive eyes, thin lips and noses, glossy black hair. The girls are sometimes really beautiful. A strange man being led into the compound caused great excitement and there was much smiling and giggling. I couldn't help but smile back, to the obvious horror of my Quaker-bonneted missionary escorts. The widows' home, the famine camp—never have I seen so much suffering, one sickening invalid after another; they live on when Americans would have died a dozen times. One approves of the medical missionary when one sees such suffering and such ignorance. Dr. and Mrs. Lapp have been here twenty years and kept me going with most gripping stories.

My second afternoon we took on guns and bearers and went for a walk through the jungle. The night before a panther had killed a bullock 100 yards away and we were on the lookout for him. In the sandy road, along the open fire belt, we saw tracks that would make you believe a circus had walked past. Monkey tracks, wild-hogs, innumerable deer, and then, all of a sudden, a huge tiger track not an hour old. We scared up rabbits everywhere but didn't waste shot on them. Two deer dashed across the opening 'way ahead and a wild-cat jumped before us not 100 feet away. I shot, but missed. At a tank we ran into a score of enormous monkeys. They are half-tame as no one shoots them and we came within 50 feet of them before they ran. They must have weighed 125 pounds each with four-foot tails. They swarm everywhere and sometimes become so bold they must be shot. Dr. Lapp had to kill one recently because he would knock down the milk women and drink their fresh milk. About the same pond, a hundred different kinds of birds come to drink, ducks and pigeons and clouds of doves. We watched kingfishers hover over their prey and then drop upon it. I was entranced at this big dose of wild life.

Next morning there was a Christian wedding at the little church

In helmet and shorts and carrying a cane Richard is best man at a wedding in Dhamtari, India.

After a tiger hunt in India, Richard is photographed with the trophy of the day.

and I went. Two hundred Christians sang hymns in Hindu, and after the service we were all decorated with flower garlands and rose water. My picture was taken with the bride and groom.

At twilight in the Ford we, Dr. Lapp and Bro. Smucker and I, took guns and drove another ten miles deeper into the woods, left the car and walked three or four, reaching another tank where animals come to drink during this hot, dry weather. Dr. Lapp climbed a tree while Smucker and I hid in a pit that had previously been made for us. It was bright moonlight and each of us had a gun. We could hear the animals in the dry jungle crashing through the brush but for an hour nothing came. We could see faintly the space between us and the jungle. About nine o'clock two small deer came out and crept toward the water on my side. About ten Dr. Lapp's gun fired—a second time—a third time. "Wild-hog," said my bearer, making tusks with his fingers. Then I heard Lapp call to Smucker: "I got Old Stripes, but wait a bit." I couldn't wait but grabbed my gun and hurried up. Smucker stopped me. "Not so fast, he may be only pretending he's dead till we get up to him. They do that." So, all together, we cautiously closed in. A big tiger lay still right under Lapp's tree—quite dead. It took us half the night to get it home. Next morning the villagers came swarming in to see the beast. . . . It was a great night.

I came back to Dhamtari in a bullock cart and went to the leper colony. It was indescribably horrible—500 inmates, some without hands or feet, burying one another, incurable, in constant agony, raw stumps of limbs. I'll dream about them for a long time.

At lunch hour I took a picture from the roof of all the boy orphans saying grace before their meal. They were lined up and stood with closed eyes and folded hands like little angels.

I leave at noon today, or will try to, and reach Calcutta tomorrow, and go off Wednesday morning for Gaya where Buddha got his inspiration.

[*Calcutta—May 8, 1922.*] I had a very cheap ride home, second class, for $1.50 (600 miles). I found a young American working his way around—just left yesterday for Darjeeling, returning Saturday. He is going to Benares as I am and I'm trying to get in touch with him. I may go ahead, stop at Gaya, and meet him again at Benares.

I've wonderful copy about my boat trip but suppose you have enough for a good seaman article for the *Commercial*. My Dhamtari pictures are good and I will write an article. *More* must be sold by the time I get back to Calcutta. I've paid "my expenses" from Gibraltar here but can't keep up. I'm getting restless to get off another article to you. I've never been so well and strong. I'm sensing adventure ahead. Amen.

[*Calcutta—May 13, 1922.*] I'm off at last, within an hour, for Benares. David Russell of Ohio arrived and I'm glad I waited for him. He is three years younger than I, but he *is* a companion and seems willing to hit for Kabul, Kashmir and Katmandu. It will be so hot in the Ganges Valley we shall not tarry long. He will meet me later at Agra.

I'm leaving my suitcase here at the Y. and carrying only my knapsack, but it's loaded to the brim. I've had big inside pockets made in my khaki shirts to carry my passport and wallet in so that they are always on me—the only real valuables I possess.

David is carrying two bags and must deposit them if he wishes to keep up with me, the flying infantry. I've a water bottle, my camera and knapsack—that's all and I'll be gone six to eight weeks, but, of course, you will hear from me every week. Get out your map and follow me to Benares, Agra, Delhi, Lahore, Rawalpindi.

[*Agra—May 18, 1922.*] Two days at Benares, Lucknow, and now Agra. I arrived last night, but have not seen the Taj yet; going out right now.

This is all just as fascinating as you could wish it to be and I was never so content and enthusiastic. I'm well and fat—hot, yes, but accustomed to it and indifferent toward it, though my helmet I never abandon.

[*Delhi—May 21, 1922.*] Last Saturday night, eight days ago, I left the Y. in khaki clothes, with one knapsack, cane, helmet. I took the special mail train for Benares, without doubt the most amazing city I've seen. As an Indian city primarily, it is not of unusual interest, but as a religious city it is a pageant, a carnival of funerals—one vast array of temples and sacred shrines and wandering sacred cows, priests and burning pyres, strung for miles up and down the muddy Ganges.

Waiting for the daytime heat to subside, I took a guide from the Dak Bungalows, which are placed at each station to accommodate English people for a very reasonable rate; beds are supplied, baths, food. You must have your own bedding. We went straight for the river. I had read about Benares but reading can never prepare one for *that* place. Even at six o'clock when all religious activity had ceased, thousands of pilgrims and citizens were bathing and dressing along the river banks, which, for five miles, are terraced with stone steps and lined with once magnificent palaces and temples. Priests throng in droves, and holy men in a g-string and red dyed hair growing at every angle from their wild-looking heads. There were enough sacred white cows and bulls roaming about to supply meat for all the starving population of India for a month. The city reeks with filth and rotting flowers. Flowers everywhere. Some of the shrines are littered with them where the devout pilgrims have cast them in worship.

Our first afternoon, we trailed down the temple-lined, staircased alleyways—color! color! color! Blazing turbans, blazing, bejeweled women, naked children, ostentatious, Oriental wealth and unspeakable swarming misery. We went to see the famous Kincolfoleries. Those gold and silver cloths made me ache, I wanted them so. Elegant and rich beyond words. Piano spreads I priced from $500.00 to $1000.00. Each of them weighed from ten to fifteen pounds. The same shop had shawls with gold thread tassels and embroidery that were just *made* for you, Mother.

Well, as night came on in Benares, a wedding procession came. Tom-toms and native wailing bagpipes preceded a crowd of friends, all dressed in brilliant clothes. The bridegroom was on his way to the house of the bride, was dressed in elaborate scarlet robes, and seated on a horse hidden under brocaded tapestries. A gold and red canopy was carried by four bearers, torch lights were everywhere, and a mob of Hindus followed behind. My heart beat fast at the sight, in such a way as when I heard the death roar of Dr. Lapp's tiger, or when I saw the sun rise over the minarets of Cairo as I stood at dawn on top the big pyramid, or when I walked down the glittering valley in Andorra, or beheld the mountains of Switzerland from the Matterhorn. Something within responds to the new flavor of the thing—a violent, gripping sensation that is not permitted those who lead the even-tenor life. It's such sensations, such heavy concentrated doses of living, that make you realize you *are* alive.

Next morning, at sun-up (the thermometer jumps from 70 to 100 when the sun peeps over the horizon), I got a small boat and rowed slowly up and down the swarming banks, close by, far away, stopping, photographing. Solitary priests, sitting facing the sun, prayed with fixed eyes under huge umbrellas; old, shaven-headed widows standing waist deep in the water extended their hands beseeching death. I saw the bodies burning all day long, carried in a wooden cradle and wrapped in cloth, piled on top of half a cord of wood and consumed; then the ashes, and often half-burned limbs, are thrown into the Ganges and everlasting life is assured.

After our long boat ride we visited a score of temples, all seething with humanity and odors; groups of lads shouting out the Hindu religious literature; people sprinkling water on the feet of waddling cows; bells chiming, and the hot sun pouring down onto it all to illuminate and heat the darkest corner. I had heard that Ghandi, the most famous of Hindu political agitators, was imprisoned in a penitentiary near Allahabad, so I got off the train there and called at the jail, but he had been removed to Bombay. I was going to interview him in his cell. Anyway I was shown about the Indian jail, 2500 criminals, only two whites. On to Cawnpore, where I took the midnight train to Lucknow.

Lucknow has the most bizarre architecture. It was pictured in the *National Geographic* some time ago in color—beautiful, fantastic plaster buildings. I saw it all and the Mutiny Memorials and went back to Cawnpore. I had no ticket and the moment I stepped in the express train for Agra, bang! *two* conductors asked for what I didn't have. So I had to buy a ticket to the next stop, twenty miles away, and rode 200 miles. I stayed in Agra three days. Agra is a gem. I have heard about the Taj, seen pictures of it, but *nothing* can reproduce it.

It takes one's breath away. It is so beautiful it hurts. I spent six hours looking at it the first morning. That night the last of a moon was due to rise at 2:30 A.M. Alone I walked the three miles and wandered around the inclosure till twelve when I hid. I was determined to see what I had come to see.

Words fail me to describe these magic hours—all, all alone with the Taj! A light burned over the graves under the dome, two guards slept outside the doors, two were inside the wall gate—that was all. Only I was awake. The slanting beams gave a mellowness and softness to the marble dream that defied comprehension. The odor of flowers was everywhere, roses and lilies and fragrant shrubs. The park is drenched with water and while the surrounding country is a desert at this season, the trees and grass here are emerald green and make a luxurious setting for the most luxurious building on earth. It's white as snow though 300 years old, in perfect preservation and built with such niceties time will never touch it.

For three hours, I roamed about the garden, on the glittering side, on the black side where the moonlight gave a glowing edge to the domes and minarets. There is an elevated marble pool halfway down the walk from the entrance gate. I took off my shoes and stockings to bathe my feet. How cool the water was! Then, in the moonlight, I took off my shorts and shirt and dropped into the refreshing lily-padded water. It was too warm to catch cold, just romantic and magic. For half an hour I sat by the pool with my clothes off, dabbling my feet, the moon pouring itself over everything, the garden about me a fairyland, and the Taj above me. I was transported out of this world. It was a taste of paradise.

The Taj by moonlight is a common sight—but the early hour, the sleeping guards, the solitude, the flowers and back-to-nature disregard of clothes! Thousands of people pass the pond by day but no one has ever bathed in it at 4 A.M., alone, enchanted. At sunrise, I climbed to the top of the entrance gate and watched the first beams strike the great dome. The light came fast. It was soon bright and golden. I had seen that aspect the morning before, so I took a cab to go home after a row with the keeper.

That experience will always be half-lost. The sensations were too unreal to last. I know it happened, felt the weirdness of it, but it was like a dream—next morning it is hard to recall. My pictures of the Taj are truly beautiful.

There are a dozen other tombs in Agra that would be world famous but for the dominating Taj. The marble carving, inlaid ivory and exotic architecture are so elaborate and profuse one becomes satiated with beauty and scarcely looks twice at other walls and mosques that are glories of richness and design.

On reaching my lodging, the proprietress said to me, "Another young fellow has arrived." "David Russell?" "Yes, that's his name. He's here now." I was so in need of a companion with whom to talk and enjoy this amazing country, and he proves a made-to-order one.

We came to Delhi yesterday, without ticket, and saw the biggest mosque in the world this morning, deserted. Friday is their Sunday so we missed seeing the 15,000 that worship there on their Sabbath. We go to the fort and palace this afternoon for another overwhelming dose of marble and jewels and unbelievable ancient luxury. Tomorrow we spend the morning doing the rounds outside the city—tombs, antiquities, etc. Then we leave for Simla (in the mountains, northwest of here at the end of railroad) where I will receive two weeks' mail.

We shall fight it out there about Kabul and Katmandu. Permission for the latter, if not the former, will suffice. My tempo sagged for a while, but the past ten days have been rousing. I've long ago ceased to worry about the loss of Italy and Greece. This is *so* much better.

The bugs are eating me up and we must be off at sunrise tomorrow.

CHAPTER VII

THE GOLDEN PERIOD

Kashmir, Ladakh, Udaipur, the Malay Peninsula, Angkor

Simla—May 24, 1922

My dear Sahib and Memsahib:—

What a difference in temperature a few miles can make! I slept under two blankets last night and my teeth have chattered all day but, after the heat of the plains, this is a most delightful discomfort.

Simla is magnificent. Eight thousand feet up in the mountains with snow-capped Himalayas all around. The entire Government of India spends seven months of the year here. It has a most official and dressy air, all up and down hill and strewn about, and filled with fashionable people. I've only my shorts and a short coat, so I'll not be invited to dine with the Viceroy.

David and I had a most adventurous ride up from Delhi—played our waiting-till-last-moment start and then dashed into a first-class compartment and slept de luxe all night, changed for the Mountain Railroad and rode first again. Halfway up the ticket taker came around and made it very embarrassing by asking for tickets. "Sorry, lost 'em," was all we had to offer, but we almost never got by the gate at Simla. We had to give our histories, and may hear from it yet. First-class fare is 60 rupees, $20.00. We paid 0 rupees. We may get caught fair and have to pay over half our fortune.

I saw the Afghanistan Consulate yesterday—about Kabul—out of town. I saw the English authorities today about Katmandu—come back tomorrow. They are a dopeless bunch.

[*Rawalpindi—May 29, 1922.*] We leave this morning for Srinagar, Kashmir, by freight truck, walking the last 60 miles of the 200. We waited at Simla five days for that darned Afghanistan Consul and he never did come but finally we saw his secretary and have com-

153

municated officially by mail. We hope he will get the passports—
then, through the Khyber Pass to Kabul!

We are all eagerness for our Kashmir trip. Everyone says it is
paradise. Certainly, the Punjab in May is quite the opposite, but a
dry, parching heat that doesn't matter so much. . . . I detest these
notes, but being pressed so for minutes, they are the best I can do.

[*Uri, Kashmir.*] Our truck left Rawalpindi loaded much over
its one-ton capacity with natural results—a breakdown every few
miles, especially as the road to Murree climbs 6000 feet in 20 miles.
We barely got to Murree by sundown, found a military Y. and were
lodged and dined free of charge.

How bracing this Himalaya air is after the thirsty Punjab! We
were cold all night but thoroughly enjoyed it. It was downhill all
morning, so our old truck got along fairly well, but on the uphill late
this afternoon gave up the ghost and left us stranded at a Dak Bungalow 120 miles from Rawalpindi. Tomorrow morning in another car
we go to Baramula, at the head of the Vale of Kashmir, get off and
walk two days to Srinagar.

The trip this far has been extraordinarily beautiful. A gorge all
the way and a most spectacular road along the cliff (see November
Geographic, "A Pilgrimage to Amernath"). The wild flowers are in
full bloom and wild strawberries and blueberries and mulberries
growing everywhere. But everyone says, "Oh, this is nothing. Wait
till tomorrow."

All today we have had the Himalayas in the distance—22, 23, 25,
27,000-foot, snow-covered mountains that appear unbelievably high
and huge. These Indian trips are going to compensate for anything
and all I may have missed in Europe.

I am so glad to hear "Gibraltar" is to see day. The pictures there
are a big help. Have you had time to hear from the other two Spanish
articles?

[*Paltan, Kashmir.*] We left Uri at five this morning with the
weather at five above freezing, drove 40 miles in two hours and left
the old wreck at Baramula, the gateway to the valley. We are
sorry we did not walk the last 40 miles. It was extraordinarily wild
and verdant: magnificent trees, flowers clinging to the walls of the
canyon, a boiling torrent at the bottom and always a snowy Himalaya

to close the distant gap. Our walk was across a flat, the real "Vale of Kashmir." It's quite beautiful, the road lined with great Lombardy poplars, the land covered with emerald rice paddies, or, where the plant has not sprouted, still pools of water to reflect the amphitheater of snow that entirely surrounds us.

The eighteen miles went rapidly, for the day is disagreeably chilly and walking was a pleasure. Our bungalow is lost in a garden of the most brilliant roses, wild and cultivated, growing in great bushes and perfuming the air. Waist-high purple iris grows like weeds all over the inclosure and over the hills where they are not crimson with poppies. I'm lying in the shade of some unknown but gigantic tree with roses all about me, a line of poplars narrowing down the avenue and a big, white mountain, as always, at the end. Doves in hundreds are cooing themselves to death everywhere. In fact, their noise becomes an annoyance. The petals I've inclosed will be only dust when you receive them but were once a rose from the Vale of Kashmir, which makes them a most extraordinary rose ruin. Will I *ever* be home in April? The last spring I was in Memphis was that of 1915. I've never regretted being in India "out of season." India is so extensive, what is out of season one place is in season another. It's scorching and parched at Rawalpindi. I'm shivering in cool verdure here.

I knew nothing of India's past till I came this way. Delhi is one of the most historical places in the world. The remains of seven empires that have risen and fallen are in evidence around it. The British are establishing an eighth. One asks, will it follow suit?

[*Srinagar, Kashmir—June 5, 1922.*] I was up all last night getting off my article and am half-asleep tonight, but it must be.

Kashmir is so much more beautiful than anything else in the world, everything else looks like back alleys. Our walk through the valley was a joy. Myriads of poppies and iris, lush verdure everywhere, thousands and thousands of poplar trees planted in rows through which the snow-topped mountains rise. Every glance is a photograph—a rainbow of color. The Vale of Kashmir is twice as wonderful as it is reported. A poet or artist couldn't stand it. He would perish from too much beauty.

We ran right into luck from the very first. We had a free tent surrounded by American people who supplied us with everything, including meals. That was good, but then we accidentally met a Mr. Catlin, American, living in a de-luxe houseboat on Dal Lake. "Come on over," he invited us, "and live with me." So we did; all free, private gondola, rich food. All yesterday we were on water with six oarsmen behind us. Garden after garden, fountains and flowers, such as Versailles or Potsdam never dreamed of, built by the builder of the Taj Mahal and as beautiful in their way. Water flows all over the land, the snows are melting and all the country is a semi-swamp, verdant beyond imagination. Streams everywhere and lakes that mirror the blue sky and white peaks. This city is all canals and rivers and giant mulberry trees and maples and willows; all the flowers known are in Kashmir.

During our few hours not spent floating in lotus-covered lakes, we've been preparing for a long mountain trip. We had planned to go to Leh, 270 miles northeast, right in Tibet, but today we learned that all the limited passports have been issued. So I'm riding 50 miles tomorrow on horseback to the summer residence of the Tibet Consul to ask for a special dispensation. If we yet fail, we will take the Amernath trip in *Geographic,* not a fifth so interesting nor so unusual as Leh. Before we go I'll write you definitely. We've no news from Afghanistan yet and I'm getting apprehensive.

[*Srinagar—June 9, 1922.*] I know you are eager to get this letter to learn what move I am to make. David and I start over the mountains into Ladakh, and *hope* to get there. The country is so sparse and the natives so inhospitable to Europeans that the number allowed to make the trip each year is limited to twelve. All twelve had long ago applied and we have been spending our time here trying to persuade two of the members who were undecided to drop out and give us their places, and at last succeeded.

We are located beside a snow-fed canal with willows and giant chinar trees shading us. The distant snow mountains reflect themselves in the water and the perfume of honeysuckle and jasmine is everywhere. The last few days Mr. Catlin has given us entire charge of his gondola, supplied with pillows on which we sit while being rushed through the water by four to six oarsmen. There are a few streets in the native quarter but away from the center all transportation is done by canals which, banked by flowers and trees and grass, are beautiful beyond words.

The "agents," who are giving us $30.00 worth of supplies free in exchange for mentioning them in our articles, invited us to dinner recently. We had dinner under the trees beside their boat and danced on the grass afterward. Next day four of us played golf on the world's most picturesque golf course. I found it very strange trying to hit a ball for the first time in two years. Yesterday we climbed to the top of a thousand-foot hill overlooking the city. Right on top is a B. C. Hindu temple that is visible for forty miles up and down the Vale. The view from the summit is one of the most extraordinary I've seen.

There is no valley in the world like this—an "emerald set in pearls," it has been called. It is loggy with an over-abundant supply of water all the time. The rice paddies cover mile after mile, are under water; the trees grow in variations and magnitude as nowhere else, and the long lines of poplars, along every road, divide the valley into checkerboards. The river winds through the city and, while like a mirror here, it begins to fall at the end of the valley and roars downward in a never-ending cataract all the way to Rawalpindi. To one side the Dal lakes, calm and lotus covered, are seen, but as I ever reiterate, it's these mountains that most awe me—20,000 to 26,000 in a complete circle about us. The Vale is oblong, 5260 feet above sea level and as near flat as land can be.

This Ladakh trip seems a delay, but its interest makes it a jewel. Get a book on it—I've one, *Where Three Empires Meet* (British, Chinese and Russian)—and learn about this fantastic place where every woman has three or more husbands, where the Buddhist religion rules the country in a strange way, a sixth of the men being priests, and all prayer being done mechanically. I'm *seeing* something.

Leh, our present destination, is 500 miles from Rawalpindi and the railroad. That is 270 miles from here. We cross a snow pass of 11,500 feet and a desert pass of 13,000. Ladakh is the highest country in the world, Leh being 11,000. Grain is raised at 15,000. We are carrying a cook who will be coolie, too, two pack horses for the three of us and some provisions, though we plan to buy most of them on the way, as that is much cheaper and saves transportation charges. All in all we plan to spend a little over a dollar a day each for the twenty-five days we are to be gone.

Ten days here I can scarcely account for and yet no notes beyond Agra. Mr. Catlin is a splendid talker, has done everything and been everywhere, and we listen to him from dinner to bed time. He leaves tomorrow, too, after three weeks vacation here and we shall be sorry to part.

It's dawn outside. I've had so much to do the last night and yet more to do today. We will take the first stage by boat, leaving about dark and arriving sometime after midnight where we get our horses.

[*Srinagar—June 12, 1922.*] We saw Mr. Catlin off in a blaze of baggage and though we had him to thank for one wonderful week all free, we decided we partly paid for it in having to listen to his very eccentric ideas. I never heard a more forceful, brilliant talker, and he quite convinced David and me to his views for the time being. He promised us jobs if we ever applied for them.

As soon as he left we got busy on our equipment. It was 10:00 P.M. before we got away in a boat belonging to a merchant whose rugs we admired. Our last hour in Srinagar was spent in his shop overlooking the "Grand Canal." It was full moon and clear mountains. Things seemed doubly beautiful, but he did have one rug, 17x7, that, whatever the light, was the most beautiful carpet I've ever seen. He had tea and cake brought in on a carved walnut table. The wood carving here is exquisite and dirt cheap. A screen that took a carver two years to do was offered for $100.00.

We had an eight-hour ride in a scow. Sleeping under the moon with two boatmen poling us through Dal Lake and up the river fifteen miles to Gunderbal, all the beauty of a Kashmir night was ours. We had dinner on the boat and found our cook very good. We planned to start up this Lider valley yesterday but were unable to get rice for our cook and as it is too expensive to feed him on our food, I rode back to Srinagar and got 30 pounds of rice. So we got off today after six hours' wrangling about horses and coolie—got off with two pack horses, a coolie and a cook.

We are 6500 feet tonight and go to 8500 tomorrow, to 11,500, to

13,500, and then into Ladakh. This valley is narrow and fertile and beautiful. I'm in Agra with my notes, but I'm in Memphis with my heart. Never have I been in better spirits.

[*Kargil, Kashmir—June 18, 1922.*] Gosh, but I'm far from home! Tonight David and I are camped 130 miles from Srinagar. It's a wonderful trip, this! Like nothing else in the world and my only worry is that I'll not be able to tell people about it and do it justice.

I wrote you several days ago that I was never so well. The very next morning I awoke sick as could be—a bit of bad food, but I walked fifteen miles just the same. At our next stop I was all in and lay on my blankets wishing I were home with all my might. Finally I took a big drink of Mr. Catlin's brandy and got well immediately, but we lost a day from our marches.

It has been ever-changing, magnificent scenery, dense vegetation, snow mountains and dashing torrents leading up to a 12,000-foot pass called Zogi La, where we walked over a dozen miles of snow and camped on snow one night. It's been utter barrenness ever since, except for occasional oases fresh and green, with wild roses and young wheat. The great mountains, all snow-covered, rise up to 20,000 feet all about us. We have never been lower than 10,000 feet since the pass. The snows are melting fast now so that the valley streams are wild and roaring, nor have we been out of their sound one second since we left Srinagar.

This country was all a part of China once and the people are still Chinese, but it was conquered by the Indians a century ago, so is now under English supervision. Our camping ground tonight is a true garden. Clover and iris are thick underneath and wild roses in three shades riot everywhere. The second highest mountain in the world, "K2," we see tomorrow, 28,600 feet. We live on eggs and chickens we buy along the way and as we walk about twenty miles a day, we eat up everything in sight. We buy a lamb tomorrow and will have a change. We nearly had a disaster yesterday. Our pony, carrying tent, beds, furniture and utensils, walked right off the edge of the trail and rolled head over heels into the rushing river. Our coolie just wrung his hands and wailed over the loss of his pony and we wailed over the loss of our equipment, but we jumped into the icy water and by drenching ourselves managed to save everything in the nick of time for the water rushes past at twenty miles an hour. Luckily the horse fell in a cove so he was not immediately swept away.

We make only two miles an hour. The trails are so dangerous, steep and rocky the heavily laden horses can't go faster. Each noon we camp from eleven to three in a shady place and sleep or read while the sun is hottest. It's damnably hot by day and almost freezing by night.

I've an article all but finished, "A Tale of the Taj Mahal," and will have others on Kashmir and Ladakh. I'm writing on the grass by candle as our table was wrecked by its plunge in the river. Sweet perfume is all about and Himalayan stars overhead. Best of all, the smell of egg curry and rice for supper is pungent.

[*Leh—June 26, 1922.*] At last we're in Leh! Perhaps, to say we are 450 miles from the end of steel signifies best how utterly removed we are from civilization. We have been the flying cavalcade since I wrote you from Kargil and arrived here last night, dead tired, but very happy to have accomplished this adventure. We have been getting up at 3 A.M., breakfasting in the dark and off with our two pack horses, our cook, our coolie and ourselves, by 4:45. It is hard to conceive how slowly we have to go and how laboriously. On foot we might make three miles per hour but our laden horses must be constantly spurred on over the rocks and prodded up defiles and over 13,500-foot passes to make even two miles an hour; so that a twenty-mile march in a day means ten hours' restless motion.

We saw Leh from six miles across the desert that, at 12,500 feet, spreads before it. It looked only a mile away but it took us three and a half hours to arrive. Distances in Ladakh are strange and wonderful. One can see every detail of villages ten miles away but they are very elusive.

The religion of the Lamas is too weird to comprehend. They are a sect of Buddists, only more so. Their salvation is entirely mechanical, gained by the repetition of prayers, or the turning of water wheels, or wind-fluttered flags containing written prayers. The roadside is edged with long lines of mud shrines, ugly, decayed, but by passing each one the traveler gets that much closer to Heaven. There are

prayer walls, too, some of them over half a mile long, eight feet high
and thirty feet broad, with the surface entirely covered with millions
of small, smooth stones each inscribed with a small prayer. Over
two-fifths of them bear the characters which, translated, mean "Oh,
flower of the lotus, oh." That is an especially holy prayer, though the
priests themselves can't say why.

Ladakh has 36,000 people, 18,000 males and of that number one in
three is, or will be, a priest. Leh has about 6000. The monasteries
suck the life out of this desert country, yet are tolerated and revered
by the poor people. The monasteries are perched on the most inaccessible crags that can be found. We visited one after an hour's climb,
stiff and exhausting. The village that supported it had scarcely a
hundred people but the monastery had as many priests and they were
all squatted in a room reading aloud, in a droning voice, from their
sacred texts, printed on long pieces of cardboard. Everyone stopped
and stared as we entered. They do nothing but meditate and read
and eat and wear red robes. This temple to Buddha is extraordinary,
a score of wood and bronze images all seated and with rows of copper
jars holding oil, water and meal before them. The walls are covered
with devil heads, and bright flags and shawls. We were shown down
the private path of the monastery, cut tunnel-like through the rocks
and canyons. We'll visit other monasteries here at Leh.

The Great Festival has been postponed again and is six days off,
so David and I argued an hour last night whether or not we'd stay for
it. I want to stay. He doesn't. It's a shame to come so far and miss
the great event, yet six days here seem a terrible waste. It will take us
two or three days to check off Leh, so the actual wait is not so very
long. There's a local religious festival on this afternoon and we're off
to it now....

The festival proved delightful and a treat. We, being the only
whites present, were given the seats of honor and saw everything.
The Lama religion is reincarnation and all that and each big monastery has its incarnation. A new child is made the god as soon as the
old one dies. The local incarnation is four years old and as sweet and
spiritual a child as you ever saw. He was carried to his throne by the
head priest. Everyone salaamed to earth as he passed. There was
dancing and music but the child fell asleep, he got so bored. Later I

entered the monastery and took the little god's picture. He stood quietly in a shaft of light and I hope it's good. It's a funny place.

Lamayuru, Kashmir—July 2, 1922

Dear Memsab and Sab:—

"Sab" is the way "Sahib" is pronounced by these funny people. It's correct to drop the "h." Sa-ib soon equals "sab." We are three days out from Leh on our homeward journey.

[*July 5.*] And now six and back to Kargil, healthy and happy, healthy chiefly because we've walked over 500 miles this trip and happy chiefly because we are homeward bound and only five more days to Srinagar. We were at Leh five days and I never enjoyed five more, though it *was* cold as Greenland—naturally would be at 11,500 feet. After I wrote you there, we met a Mr. and Mrs. Kumick, missionaries for thirteen years in Ladakh, who told us that what we had seen at the local festival was really more rare than what we might see at Hemis, so we left on June 30th. The Leh affair happens only once in a lifetime when the Buddhist incarnation is established at the head of the monastic community. I went back after the festivities were over and had a most interesting hour with the priests and their little god, and helped put him to bed. Poor boy! Only four or five years old, he has been taken away from his parents because he was chosen as the reincarnation of the head priest who died shortly before this child was born. Strange to say, he has a really divine face and but for dark skin would greatly resemble the child pictures of Christ.

The natives, still unfamiliar with devices of white man, were in holy terror of our cameras and we did not get good pictures till I bribed one of the head chiefs to force some of his friends to pose.

The polyhusband idea is really dying out and it's just such travel writers as I am that keep it going in fiction.

Our missionary friends had not been out of Ladakh for thirteen years, not even to Srinagar. They had never seen an airplane and few motor cars. In 1909 they left civilization and are going back to England now for a year's rest. They gave us fresh milk and potatoes and green things from their garden and had they not had a very sick patient in their house would have boarded us. We have never lacked good food, however, for it is cheap and our cook prepares it well. We bought a live sheep four days ago and it's all gone now, so we're buying another here. A 40-pound sheep costs *90 cents*. Dried apricots, rice, eggs, fresh flour bread, potatoes and puddings keep us from starving though it just does, for all-day tramps in this high altitude give us equine appetites.

The first day we made 22 miles, and again every two miles represented an hour's march, for it was in deep sand or along crevasses or over mountains every foot and very slow with our two pack horses. That night we met the Hebers, missionaries coming to take the Kumicks' place, who tried to discourage us at Srinagar, but they were glad we are enjoying our trip and had us to dinner.

We made 25 miles next day but our cook was so slow at lunch we did not arrive at our camp till ten that night. It was wonderful moonlight and these wild fantastic crags and canyons had an appearance we'd not seen before. It had been a trying day. We were too tired to eat supper, simply rolling ourselves in our tent and blankets and sleeping till 4 A.M., and were off again at 5:30. We climbed 5000 feet that day and rushed it for eighteen miles as we wanted to get to Lamayuru in time for a picture. Lamayuru is the weirdest spot in Ladakh, built in the face of a spire-like rock with a monastery perched recklessly (500 years ago it was built) right on the peak.

To reach the monastery, we stumbled through dark tunnels, up ladders and precipitous steps, through a maze of dark hallways. We were led into a great hall where over two hundred men and youths were reading their sacred books. A huge image of Buddha leered down at the rows of brass bowls filled with oil and grain offerings. The room was fantastically carved, and gaudily colored. As in the temple at Leh, terrible demons made grimaces from the walls and ugly masks hung from the ceiling.

We planned to do 30 miles the next day but this country is so sparsely populated horses are not always available when wanted. We crossed one pass 14,000 feet high, nearly as high as the Matterhorn, but with peaks soaring up 10,000 feet higher all about you. It's hard to realize the height but for the rarety of the air. On the downward ride we met a party of Dutch going to Yarkand to climb unclimbed peaks. They had 30 horses, equipment. With them was a Miss Dunbar, American woman about 60, a life-long globe-trotter, who was about to take this tremendous trip alone but was forced to wait till associates came. She is gray and asthmatic and frail, but Leh she had to see before she died. She certainly is plucky.

My old navy shoes that have served me so well have made almost their last mile. They were old when I sailed last July and have performed miracles. I had them nailed together at Leh, but 130 miles of sharp rocks have caused a relapse.

We are buying a new sheep, getting more sugar and other provisions here, and will make six or eight miles before night. Two days puts us at the foot of the notorious Zogi Pass, which, though only 11,500 feet, is the barrier between the rain and snow of Kashmir and the deserts of Ladakh, so that it is always either impassable from snow and glaciers or disagreeable from slush and swollen streams. It's a 25-mile tramp across.

[*Rawalpindi—July 19, 1922.*] Yesterday I was a very happy man and quite appreciated the Bible proverb, "As cold waters to a thirsty soul so is news from a far country." Four weeks' mail awaited me here on our return from Kashmir, and all the important documents about Kabul and Katmandu were tossed aside until I could examine my letters from home. They are so cheery and refreshing.

Nothing had been done about our passports and nothing will be unless we go back to Simla, which is out of the question. The Afghan Consul, in reply to frantic wires and special deliveries, has disdained to notice us. There is a fair chance for Nepal and we are driving for that. Tonight at 2:30 A.M. we slip into a train for Peshawar and will at least take a day's trip into the Khyber Pass.

I have not written a letter for many days, but my articles are letters to you telling you about the places I see and enjoy. For the past week, day and night, I've dug at them. I wrote from Kargil, halfway home from Leh. The very afternoon I sent my letter we got under way with our horses and cook, sending them on ahead, while we bought supplies. They turned aside to rearrange the loads and we passed them unknowingly. After an hour's hurried tramping we grew alarmed at not overtaking them. Two hours, three hours—we were *running* for it was nine o'clock and very dark. Seeing a light at last ahead, we breathed a sigh of relief for we had had visions of our entire train falling into the river, baggage and all, as often happens on these narrow, slick trails. We hallooed to our coolies, but an Englishman and his wife hallooed back. It wasn't our party at all. The men assured us no one had passed, so we knew we were in front and not behind our ponies. We were wet with perspiration at 12,000 feet, but the woman gave us coats and dinner and sent a man to look for our bunch. He returned later with a mournful procession. One of the ponies making a false step had slid off into the Indus and was lost with our pots and pans and food. All our clothes were on the other horse. We had not even a match and as the temperature, after dark, goes to 45 degrees we would have suffered.

Next day, we made our 25 miles but very slowly over rocks and flooded rivers, and arrived at camp after 10:00 P.M. Being in the snow pass we decided to use the Bungalow, but it was full. However, one occupant let us sleep on the floor of his room.

We crossed the Zogi Pass next day in snow and rain and slush and once more entered the verdure of Kashmir. The change from naked, desolate Ladakh to the indescribable lushness of Kashmir was startling as we looked upon it from the high pass.

At Sonamarg, the end of the day, we arrived wet to the skin, no food all day, dead tired, but called on Mrs. Coan, the wife of the Y. director at Lahore whom we had known in Srinagar. She was tenting there, as some people do, for it is the most glorious place for scenery on earth. She put dry clothes on us, gave us a hot supper, packed our pockets with bread and nuts, had us back to breakfast and sent us down the valley in wonderful sunshine, rested and fed and happy. After dinner, David started again by moonlight, walked 25 miles more to Srinagar. I felt that too much so I started with the train at five next morning and got in at four in the afternoon. Meanwhile, David had made all arrangements for our residence. I paid off our ponyman and cook, dumped our equipment over to the agency and felt as free as a lark and glad to be "home."

Really, the Scind Valley, which we traversed approaching Srinagar, is the most exquisite bit of exquisite Kashmir. One has never seen nature at its best till one sees this valley, painted with flowers, sprayed by turquoise blue torrents, shaded by pines and walnut trees and plane trees in every shade of riotous green. It's truly an earthly paradise that will haunt me as long as I live.

We took a completely furnished houseboat just like Mr. Catlin's, all to ourselves. You see Srinagar is just another Venice. One-third of the population live in river boats and *all* visitors, for the boat can be moved about every place to suit taste or convenience. Most of them float among the lotus flowers on beautiful Dal Lake, but we were in for business and had ours moored in front of the *library*. We had a bedroom and bath each, a dining room and a sitting room with kitchen-boat attached, a good cook, a butler, a bath attendant, and an oarsman for our private gondolier; three strapping meals a day, endless fruit (Kashmir is one great orchard), electric lights and bedding—all, *all* for $1.15 a *day each*. That price covers everything, but at that the cook, who was owner of the boat, made 50 cents.

We spent the first 24 hours bathing and resting and delousing our clothes. The next day we sacked the library and with ink and paper all about us have slaved away, stopping day and night only for meals. I first got my Taj article done. I'm sure you'll like it. It's short but represents hours and hours of work. I had to take valuable day time out to bother about photographs, but made up for it in the wee morning hours. The minute it was done, steam was up and I slashed into "Outlandish Ladakh." I wrote in the utmost comfort in our all-window sitting room. Our boat was under weeping willows and quite cold at night. Birds were everywhere. In fact, between them and the endlessly variegated and picturesque water traffic that passed our window, only concentration held our eyes and minds to the paper. Five days and five nights we splashed ink. Having contracted for a truck seat to Rawalpindi on Monday (today is Wednesday), we *had* to be there. I should have written "Kashmir," too, while I was so delightfully located, but my curiosity about our Afghan passes lured me away.

Our last night the wife of our agent had us to dinner in their 100-foot palace boat—grand dinner and then an evening of music. The woman is a full-blooded Indian but a credit to any man. When these Orientals *are* polished they put Europeans to shame. She plays beautifully (they have a grand piano) and he plays and David plays. One guest had his Hawaiian guitar and another sang. Only I sat like a block.

Next morning we had half a million odds and ends to finish up. Leaving at noon, we had a good ride in an army captain's car and sped over the 40 miles of poplar-lined avenues we had walked over coming up. We had a pleasant night at a rest bungalow at 75 miles and made the 125 miles yesterday, to arrive at night. Mr. Catlin, passing through, had put in a word for us at the best hotel in town. When we arrived the proprietor gave us a twenty-rupee suite and has had us into his private dining room for the four best meals we've had in India—all free and glad to do it. He wanted to hear some of our tall tales.

We slept on a station bench when we were here before—variety, variety!

I'm so sorry about Laura. Tell her I am. It wouldn't be home without her. Tell her I've developed a worse appetite than ever, especially for raisins and for oatmeal. On our Ladakh trip we put raisins in every dish—potatoes, bread, meat, everything. It's hot as forty hells in India now. Rains, but before it rains one is quite draggled by humidity.

[*Lahore—July 27, 1922.*] You would laugh if you could see your son at this moment. I'm seated on the front steps of the Lahore post office panting after the hardest day's work in a year. This mail business won't wait for anyone. It closes irrevocably at a certain hour once a week and if you are one second late your foreign mail does not go for *seven days*. I've had this fact in mind that long, yet was up all last night in the rush and got my manuscript and pictures registered today only by threatening to murder the entire force if unaccommodated. But they are off and I've two hours for ordinary mail—thus this letter.

Unable to persuade the best hotel to come down from fifteen rupees to five, we went to the Dak Bungalow the same day and by night had all passes and truck rides arranged for the Khyber trip next day. We left at five and drove 30 miles right into that most historic pass in Asia. It is mostly sentiment, rather than scenery, in the Khyber. Being midsummer and about 180 degrees in the sun—

honest—all the camel caravans were conspicuous by their absence. They come through from Kabul in the winter. The road is a military motor highway and a wonder, though the railroad is being pushed through so fast it will soon be passé. Two-thirds of the British soldiers in India are in the Punjab, for all the trouble comes from the Afghan side. Everywhere one looks are camps, camps, camps. Our pass allowed us to go within four miles of the Afghan border. We were received there by the Major in charge, provided with riding horses and a military escort of Indian troops, all tasseled and colorful, bearing spears, and wonderful riders. We rode right up to the sign "Afghan Border" with its skull and crossbones. The enemy snipes at night and soldiers get killed from ambush occasionally. The Major dined us and sent us home in an army truck. It would have been an awesome day but crags and rocks were fed to us so vigorously in Ladakh, more desolation in the Khyber was not very exciting.

The minute I arrived at Lahore I started on "The Paradise of Asia," Kashmir, and worked like a fiend. My style is rushing from the breezy and piquant to "strained grandiloquence" and poetic sentiment and I can't stop to save me.

David collapsed with sunstroke! He was very ill yesterday— fever 106, but it's down to 103 today and he will be up and about in four or five days. Meanwhile, I have to spend my time between nursing him and rounding up prints by day and working on the finishing touches of manuscript by night. I would have been off to Delhi yesterday morning but for the emergency. I feel splendid while everyone else I see is droopy and pepless.

Rest at ease, my dear mother and dad, about "criminal minds, diseased bodies." I'm in the bridal suite of the best hotel in India and I've learned how to ride only first-class with viceroys and rajahs. In fact, I'm missing too much of what you are afraid I'll get. Lahore, I've seen. It's just like other cities—marble tombs and malodorous streets and heat. I've had enough of them and find my mind on China more than India.

[*Delhi—August 2, 1922.*] Since I wrote last at Lahore I have had a most adventurous though exhausting week. I left David rapidly recovering from his sunstroke, got to Delhi on a night train, and left immediately next morning for Jaipur, one of the intensely interesting native states. I tried riding free by day and certainly had a hard time doing it. They wired Jaipur to be on hand to nab me, but I got off at the station before and walked down the tracks, only to find I was twelve miles away from Jaipur, rather than four or five as it looked to be on the map.

It's all beautiful country, for the monsoons have broken for fair and everything is drenched in water. It's spring now in India. Crops are sprouting, flowers blooming and the air is cool and soft as I never believed it could be a month ago. Jaipur is just what you think India should be before you get here—elephants in the streets, gaudily clothed people all weighted down in heavy silver jewelry. Every house is fresco painted with crude pictures of rajahs and warriors. One sees no Europeans, or their clothes, or their manners, or hears their speech. It's real unadulterated India.

I took a vehicle out to Amber, the old palace of the rajahs—magnificent if one were not fed up with such things. The next night I left for Chitor where I spent a day in the fortress which was once the mightiest in India and today, all in ruins, is extremely impressive. I climbed the Tower of Victory.

On to Udaipur a short distance on a branch line. It is called the "City of Sunrise" with entire justification for it is the loveliest spot. Kashmir is a district, a state, but Udaipur is only a spot, a jewel. Lakes everywhere, and islands and hills are brilliant green from the rains, and beside the water, all tufted in trees, are white pavilions and palaces. The Rajah is the richest in India and holds the title of "King of Kings." His capital shows evidence of wealth, for more magnificent buildings one cannot find, though, as always in India, they are matted with pigeon filth.

The islands which the palaces overlook are walled with carved marble and covered with bright-colored, fairy castles half-hidden in palms. I took a long walk through the near-by gardens and ate pomegranates off the trees for lunch. It began to pour as I was on the point of photography so I got nothing, but the two bought pictures will suffice. Never did I hate to leave a place more but my money was nearly gone.

I was inspired to collect an article on Udaipur, Jaipur and Chitor and call it something like "The Jewels of India," but it approaches so closely the usual, stereotyped travel article I refrained. My articles have, I hope, been unusual, about unusual places. Why slip back?

A wire from Nepal awaited me here. It was unfavorable, so I've lost both Kabul and Katmandu. However, my India trip has been satisfactory even if out of season. If China and Japan are as much so, I'll be happy.

[*Calcutta—August 6, 1922.*] David and I had a very busy last day together in Delhi and separated regretfully.

This last adventure was a grand finale to my train experience in India. My conscience was beginning to smite me for maneuvering the railroad company out of so many fares, but now I *was* broke and ride I must. Anyway, my book will bring many tourists to India! I succeeded in climbing into a first-class sleeping compartment unobserved and was relieved when the train got in motion. My relief was not for long. A train guard suddenly opened the door and found me cleaning up in the wash room, but he apologized nicely and I forgave him.

Next morning with daylight the round of ticket collectors was to begin, so I went to the new guard and pleaded my case, successfully. He let me continue free all day but with the coming of the second night I was a passenger to Calcutta on the tender, partially covered with coal. A second-class ticket costs 70 rupees ($30.00) and I had no rupees.

Calcutta seemed depressing and flat. I slopped through the rain to Amexco unspeakably weary and sat on the steps from seven to nine waiting for them to open. When they did, out came my mail and for two hours I had a happy time. The check for *Commercial* stories saved my life.

A Mr. Reed in Amexco—Princeton, 1917—had me to dinner and theater my first night and next morning took me around to see a Mr. Adams, head manager of an American shipping company. "Have you a boat for Rangoon, Mr. Adams?" "Yes." "When does she sail?" "Wednesday." This boat, the *Ellora* arrived today and I was on hand, believe me. Adams and I went on board together and in less time than it takes to tell it, I was accepted, *not* as a worker

At the crest of the Zogi Pass, bound for Leh, 11,500 feet, a land of eternal snow.

On one of the many waterways of lovely Kashmir, Richard and David found a completely furnished houseboat, with four servants, which they rented for $1.15 a day each.

but merely signed on as seaman to get around red tape. I will pay $1.50 a day for my upkeep. It's a two-day trip, though this monsoon weather is the devil and delays everything. How is all this for luck?

I've had my last illness for ever and ever. Think of it, right through four months of Indian summer when everybody is all in from malaria or something else as bad, I've felt like a million dollars all the time. I'm thinner than usual, but what of it when I'm so hard and healthy? I don't know what I'll do with Ammudder's $100 for if the *Commercial* pays me for all my articles and Dad can sell a few on the side, as he's done, I'll be independent.

That is certainly sound advice, Dad, about the maintenance of individuality by each party in matrimony. I wonder if I shall ever have the experience of reconciling my eccentricities to the eccentricities of a wife.

I'm weary of Calcutta and shall sail *down* the Hoogly with a very different emotion from that with which I sailed *up*.

[*Rangoon—August 14, 1922.*] Look on the map for the Khyber Pass and then look at Rangoon and see how much nearer home I am now. I was supposed to sleep on the second-class deck, but a soldier with a wife and three children had two cabins, one shared by himself and his son, so when he heard my plight he offered me the third bunk which I took. I had awful food, mostly curry and rice, and was served in the saloon *after* the other passengers had finished, but what did I care, especially as I was guardian for a big basket of apples?

As I was going on board a fat Hebrew asked if I was going to Rangoon. I said "yes." After making sure we were friends he admitted he was not going but merely sending two big baskets, one apples and one cheese. Would I take them along and turn them over properly at Rangoon? I was a bit indignant at his approach but when he said "apples" I thought twice and agreed. There were twelve dozen apples when we left but only about ten dozen when we landed this morning for I kept alive on them.

It was awful weather and took us three days and nights rather than the usual two. It's still terribly hot. There's the big golden pagoda to see here and the elephant lumber yards—little else.

I'm quite intact. Marie sent me *Cytherea,* a recent American novel.

I read it and have been depressed ever since. I'm keeping my eye peeled for more articles. Of course, there's material for them everywhere.

[*Rangoon—August 19, 1922.*] What a strange week *this* has been; not very exciting with adventure, but unusual socially.

My trip to Mandalay was a terror—twenty hours in a third-class compartment. Mandalay is hardly worth the trip. Kipling made it famous but never saw it. There are Buddhist temples, etc., but very much like Ladakh.

I called on intimate friends of a member of the Consulate, the wife of a man he had visited for a week in Mandalay and their daughter whom he had fallen violently in love with and almost married. He told me everything about them except that the entire outfit was mulatto—half English and half Burmese. At the girl's house, a full-blooded Burmese woman met me at the door. Naturally, I thought she was the servant. Imagine my embarrassment when I learned she was the *mother!* I about fell through the floor. His girl is fairly white and for his sake I made a date with her but we just had a ride in a victoria.

I got back here yesterday and *sail*—deck passage—in fifteen minutes for Mergui on the lower Burma coast, change boats there for Victoria Point, the southern tip of Burma, go up the bay in a launch and walk across the peninsula, catch the railroad on the east shore and arrive in Bangkok in about ten days. More details later. I'm keen about the idea. It's been done but once or twice by Americans. It takes five days.

[*Bangkok—September 3, 1922.*] Well, another long-laid dream of mine has come to pass, though it proved something of a nightmare. The Malay Peninsula has always attracted me geographically. Years ago as a kid at M. U. S. I pondered on the map over that strange formation of earth and sensed adventure there, though in my most ambitious aspirations I never suspected I should one day walk across it.

Now that it's all over and I am normal and happy in Bangkok, it does not yet seem to have been an ordeal. Time as well as distance lends enchantment. Nevertheless, for a dozen books, I'd not do it again. It was a great adventure; that's what I wanted. And when I finish this letter I'll start on "Byroads to Bangkok" and then a second article on "The Singular Siamese," so among the three (this letter making the third) you will get a complete understanding of this golden period of my adventure.

Of all the things in the world I hate, most of all is to be a tourist. All tourists go from Hongkong straight to Singapore and on to Rangoon. All round-the-world tourist steamers go that way. Mike did it, David did it, but I'll wager not five Americans have done it as I have, which, perhaps, illustrates good American common sense.

This entire expedition came rather unexpectedly. At Rangoon I felt blocked. I would *not* do the usual Singapore trip, but the rainy season discouraged anything else. Many routes were studied. Then a man in the Standard Oil Company suggested this possibility, saying there was a trail from Victoria Point to the railroad on the other side. His information was vague, but I had a strange intuition that it was possible, and as it is only 40 miles, it couldn't be so bad.

The first boat I boarded at Rangoon took me to Mergui. We left Sunday morning and got in Tuesday morning. The chief engineer befriended me and I slept de luxe on his cot and dined first-class in his cabin. He was a hard-bitten old Scotchman and drank more whisky than I could water.

Mergui is a wild, half-savage, true native Burmese town unchanged by British domination. It is full of snakes and jungle and banana trees. The entire coast is spangled with vivid green islands that make the Mergui harbor one of unusual beauty.

Mergui contains about a dozen white men. I met them all and slept at the house of one of them. There is only one white woman in town. All the men keep native women who act as cooks and housekeepers as well. They are a reckless, low lot, adventurers all, existing in that disconnected jungle village because it is disconnected.

My host was a young fellow who had married a native woman because she owned a rubber plantation. He had spent all her money and was chafing to get away. They have two children. All the men have children, little half-breeds doomed to be ostracised by black and white both. That is the saddest part of it all.

Out of Mergui, the *Daracotta* was only a little tug, but for fifteen rupees—$5.00—I had a berth on the saloon seat and meals with the other two passengers. We threaded our way through thousands of islands, a tortuous, picturesque trip, and in two days reached Victoria Point, one of the world's jungle beauty spots. Before I got off two British residents came on board and we all had breakfast together. They learned of my adventures and the younger one, Mr. Ainsworth, a true British gentleman, suggested I come to his island and stay while I was getting my bearings. I was glad to accept. I found it a little paradise. The island was four miles long and three broad, covered with an awful tangle of jungle trees and creepers and vines and flowers. The beach is sand and lined with coconuts and fuzzy evergreen trees. It's very hilly and along two sides the hills form a precipice over the water.

Mr. Ainsworth is 30 and owns the island, soul and body, and all the natives on it are his subjects. He has two Chinese servants. The coconuts fall on his roof and roll into his lap; bananas rot everywhere for lack of consumption; wonderful tropical fruits grow all about; lemons and limes keep you supplied with refreshing drinks.

Naturally, he was extremely interesting and a million miles above the other white men of that world. Living absolutely alone, he dressed for dinner every evening, clean white shirt, flannel clothes and pumps. He insisted it kept up his morale and self-respect. So I dressed, too, in clothes of his, and we had a formal dinner on his jungle island. The second day we went exploring right through the heart of it. It was all so new and vivid to me. Brilliant flowers glimmered in the forest gloom, so unusual; beautiful giant trees tangled with vines and trailers and parasites. Cool streams splashed and gurgled along the glades, parrots screeched, and always the ocean boomed, boomed not far away. For beauty of vegetation, I've never seen its equal. I realized I'd make a life-long friend in Ainsworth.

It was arranged I was to sail up to the Pukchan River, 65 miles, in Ainsworth's dugout with a board deck and a banana-leaf curved roof. So, at 5 A.M. with two boatmen, I got away with a dozen bananas as supplies. My boatmen I had to pay in advance to get—six rupees each. They slept all night at anchor and let the night tide get past, so I made them row against it all morning; but in the afternoon the water backed up again and a strong wind rushed us along to arrive at Taplee at 5 P.M. One of my boys spoke a little English and through him I talked to the head man. Taplee is in Siam where the money is a tical—50 cents U. S. A.

At first, I wanted an elephant but that cost $6.00 and could not be had on account of rain and streams out of banks. After much rowing, I got a coolie for a guide across. I spent that night on a mat in the second story of his house, with mosquitoes eating me and lizards playing tag all over me. Next morning, my coolie and I started on the trail, a semi-invisible path.

The horrible and wonderful experiences of this semi-aquatic adventure will be told in my article. I will not repeat here. It's still a nightmare. The last eight miles of that day's twenty were along a good trail serving a rural population, so we moved very smoothly. My low brogues—imagine that! low-quarters for such a trip—got so stretched and loose they stuck in every mud hole and were sucked off, but I found rattan creepers and bound them on.

The sight of the railroad was a gleeful one for it led soon to the station at Chumpon, my destination, where I learned the next train for Bangkok left in two days. But I found the division engineer the only white man in town, an agreeable Englishman, and he invited me to stay with him the two nights and days I must wait. I did so and had my clothes washed, was fed and rested, all free of charge, and had a most genial time in addition. He was not an Ainsworth. He kept two native women, drank and smoked continually, worked as little as possible. He had gone through the war as a boy. He said frankly that he sought happiness and insisted he had found it in this separation from complexities of Western life.

"It's easy money," said this intelligent, well-bred, well-educated, handsome young Englishman. I shuddered at his philosophy—why, I do not know. Perhaps he is right. Why grind and pant and slave! To what end? Why seek fame and fortune, why seek anything? You never find it. Ambition is a devil that is never satisfied but only torments one. This man had deliberately acted on that philosophy. A selfish one, to run away from life and responsibility, to be sure, but why assume responsibilities if it only makes you bitter and aged and unhappy?

I realized then how far away from that I am. One doomed to

seek, seek, all my life, never content with what I have, despising it after I have it, seeing a higher place and greater fame every step upward, loading myself with responsibilities and dreading lest I misspend my gifts—gifts of parentage, environment, education, pride. There's a question! But it's no question to me. I may get happiness from you and your friends, but from life, never, for it's an overpowering, brooding enemy, that I must strain to preserve myself against. That's the result of refinement and education. It oversensitizes one. There is no choice in the matter, however. To go my way is weariness to the final exhaustion, but to turn back one inch, to be for an hour what my host is—I would despise myself to the point of madness.

Well, that's a moody state for one to be in who is dining tomorrow with the American Ambassador and in the midst of one of the world's most strange and curious cities.

I *bought* a third-class ticket to Bangkok and it took twelve hours. I got a good picture of Siam along the route and I'm bursting with copy: paddy fields and tall coconut trees, graceful and scattered; banana jungles; water, water in canals, and bloodlust temples and pagodas at every village. The country is deep green but splashed with screaming yellow splotches, the robes of the innumerable Buddhist priests. The people are ugly but well-formed, dress only in a sort of baggy bloomers, chew repulsive betel-nut which turns their teeth black, though it does not destroy them. But for Siam, "singular" Siam, let it go until my articles arrive for it would be repetition.

I called on the Consul—Princeton, 1912—rather interesting. He is the man who wrote *Outwitting the Water Demons of Kashmir*, Maurice Dunlap. He sent me over to a Mr. Williams, Secretary at the Legation, where I met the Ambassador and was invited to luncheon tomorrow. Williams is Princeton, 1917. Princeton! That magic word! The key to any social door. Williams is a brilliant young fellow, 26, who has served four years in diplomacy and quite fired me with its virtues.

Yesterday I was busy every second. In a week or less I'm off— where, I do not know. If the French Consulate recommends, it will be across country by boat, caravan and rail over Cambodia, via Angkor to Saigon. Angkor is the greatest temple existing in Asia and one of the most inaccessible. The trip will take two weeks and put me in

Saigon the last part of September. The *Commercial* will publish two articles on Siam and it will clear my expenses here.

I'm going to work like a hive of ants for a few days and will write you my plans as soon as I have any.

[*Bangkok still—September 11, 1922.*] Damn! And thank God! *This* is off my chest! I've devoted all my time to the article and none to you. It's a long one and I intend it to run in two installments, 3,060 words and 2,600 words.

Bangkok is magnificent. I've been here a week and have been entertained so constantly I've done only this inclosed story when I meant to have had a second one by now. It's dinner and luncheon every day and I could be booked up for another entire week, but I'm refusing everything. I've met everybody but the King. It's a heaven of hospitality. The Ambassador (I've dined with him three times) and I are calling each other Eddie and Dick. I've been motored every step. I've seen everything of this extraordinary city. The inclosed article is to go in the Bangkok paper for $20.00 for reduced manuscript.

I'm interviewing ministers, diplomats, et al., getting material for a second article on Siam. I have wonderful pictures for it.

I'm in the air about Angkor yet, but have had no time to investigate.

[*Bangkok—September 12, 1922.*] I'm off to a little place on the south Indo-China coast called Kep. Going by boat and by motor bus from Kep to Pnom Penh, then to Angkor beside the big lake and then back to Saigon. I worked all last night on my "Singular Siamese" but I've not finished as I had to spend today saying good-by.

I'm going "deck." I'm loath to leave Bangkok. I will write all about it and me on the boat.

[*Pnom Penh, Indo-China—September 16, 1922.*] I'm going back a few days to where I left you with my last long letter from Bangkok.

As I wrote, I found the Consul to be a Princeton man. Likewise, the Secretary to the Legation, through whom I met the United States Ambassador. The latter is not a demi-god, as I always supposed ambassadors were, but his wife is one of the most charming women I ever met. On the fourth, I went to the legation for luncheon, a very happy one. I sat next to Mrs. Brodie and she and I soon became fast friends. The Consul, the Standard Oil manager with his wife, and the American Advisor to the Siamese Foreign Department (Dr. James) completed the table. It was a real Siamese meal—rice, to be sure, but two dozen different kinds of curries to make it tasty.

The next day Mr. Dunlap, the Consul, took me to call on Dr. James. He is the highest foreigner in Siam and completely controls the foreign affairs of the country. He gave me an hour, and a more interesting one I never had. For lunch I was the guest of the Railroad Administration Advisor. Later they took me to the club for tea. I was considered a curiosity and made to relate some of my adventures. And that night I dined with an Australian and his Smith College graduate American wife, who is the daughter of the Chief Justice of the Philippines. She is a brilliant woman and made it a most stimulating evening.

Next day I was the day guest of the British General Manager of the Siamese Merchant Marine. He took me in his speed boat in and among all the wonderful, teeming canals that *are* Bangkok. Thousands of native houseboats and little rowboats and produce-laden rafts, moving between squalid, teeming rows of houses on poles, or, at times, through narrow water lanes where the palm fronds meet overhead and the parrots screech in the branches.

And the morning of the next day I spent driving with Mrs. Brodie in the ambassadorial motor. And the day after that I left on a small French boat which calls at a tiny place called Kep twice a month. The ship was an ex-private yacht and carried one second-class and one first-class passenger. I approached the first-class passenger, a clean-cut, blue-eyed, white-toothed gentleman. He was delightful and we became friendly at once. I spoke to the captain about food and was fed with Mr. Schneeberger (sounds German but is really Swiss). So I traveled strictly first-class for two nights and two days.

Yesterday noon we stopped two miles off the coast in a regular storm. A big steam tug took me and 50 coolies and baggage and the Bishop of Pnom Penh, who had come aboard. We went toward shore with the tug dipping under water every few moments in the gale.

It could not dare approach the small wharf for its wild dancing, so a *dugout* came for us and, after straining and struggling, the Bishop and I got into it. That few hundred feet was the worst I've ever seen. The waves rushed completely over us and drenched us to the skin. But we made the shore by a miracle.

The motor bus left not until this morning so I took a walk down the booming jungle coast, looked over the Cambodians, a scurvy, decadent imitation of the Siamese. I had dinner at the rest house, wrote a while and went to bed in a long chair, as they wanted $1.50 for a bedroom.

France has worked miracles in her colony here. Every old straw village has been razed to the ground and new stone houses and parks and immaculate streets built instead. The road up to Pnom Penh is hard stone and the motor bus simply flew over it.

I leave tomorrow morning at eight for Angkor. I'll be there two or three days, then back here for Saigon, where I meet Mr. Schneeberger again. It's good to be back in a civilized place, where the language is comprehensible and I can ask for what I want without going through gymnastics. You see how smoothly and happily things are still going. Surely no trip was ever made around the world so merrily as mine.

[*Saigon, Indo-China—September 22, 1922.*] Je suis en France encore, for this city is a little bit of Paris. Last Saturday I wrote you an old-time letter at Pnom Penh. Sometimes things have to be done, even if it takes all night. The French mail left Monday and if I did not get my "Singular Siamese" article off on it there was no telling when it would go. So I wrote you first to put myself in the proper mood, then rolled up my sleeves about five in the afternoon and worked like seven devils till five next morning.

Shortly after, feeling rather sleepy and groggy, I went on board a first-class river steamer with my usual deck ticket. My own deck was one horrible mass of niggers, animals and food, so I went up on top the boat till the inspector left. Then I came down, appropriated the captain's own deck chair and, the most comfortable person on board, slept all day.

There were two nice-looking English women on board, a matron and her daughter about 23, which is getting oldish for a girl and, doggonit, for a man, too (though if I were 36 the *Commercial Appeal* would still call me "Memphis boy"). It's a novel trip up. The river flows downstream six months and upstream six months, depending on the wet or dry season. It was filled with Java weed, a water herb which grows as it floats on the water. We entered the great lake about dusk. It's 100 miles long now and looks like the ocean, except for treetops growing thick all over it. In the dry season it's a sea of mud with almost no water at all.

I did not speak to my English friends all day. The mother looked rather uppish. Anyway, I wanted to sleep. That night I. was waked up and to my astonishment told to get off as we'd arrived at Angkor. A high wind had come up and such a heavy sea was running we almost never got into the sampan alongside. But for my encouragement, the two ladies would not have gone at all. It was 1 A.M. The agent had said "tomorrow morning"; I'd supposed seven or eight o'clock.

Well, I never had such a ride. It rained in cloudbursts, the sampan leaped and rolled; it was black as coal and the two ladies shrieked every time a wave broke over the boat. I had my hands full. It took us two hours of rowing through treetops to reach the shore where a Ford awaited us. The driver was a native and came so near running us into the river alongside once or twice my own nerves began to find a limit. At last I took the wheel and though I didn't know the road, which was part under water and all through the jungle, I got us to the bungalow in low gear—fifteen miles of it. Yet the advertisements read "de-luxe steamer drops you at the gate of Angkor." It was dawn when we finally arrived and I sat in wet clothes and watched the sun rise over the Angkor towers a mile away. We three, having gone through it together, became fast friends, and so the Giddeys and I started off in company at seven next morning.

As for Angkor, it's the most wonderful building in the world, and the biggest, the most delicately decorated, the most magnificent. All morning we climbed and strolled about its extraordinary corridors and courts and towers. Such magnificent carving I've never seen or can ever be seen, for the Khymers, who built the temple (one of a score, all of which stand), surpassed the Egyptians and the Greeks.

No one can grasp what Angkor means for it's been accessible only since 1910, but, as the years pass, Angkor will be recognized as the first architectural wonder of the world. It's bigger than Karnak and as delicate and artistic as the Pantheon, yet almost unknown. There have not been 50 Americans who have seen it.

It was a strenuous morning so they slept all afternoon and night while I roamed about, and the next day we started out in a motor (I as the guest of the Giddeys) to see the other ruins which are in dreadful decay as the gourmand jungle has absolutely devoured them. Trees a hundred feet high and three feet thick grow right on top of galleries and roofs, with their roots running down the sides and into the ground. I've a picture to prove it.

Another temple called Bayan had 51 towers, has about 30 now, each topped with a four-faced giant, each face eight feet across, looking to a quarter of the compass. You can't escape their gaze. Think how much these sphinxes know—all the wisdom of a thousand years is stamped on the faces. No one but them knows what became of the Khymers, of whom not a trace remains.

On the way to Saigon (we changed at Pnom Penh) we three had a jolly time. I traveled on *deck,* but first deck with the Giddeys, and had my meals alone. I slept in a chair on their pillows. Next morning at Pnom Penh my left foot, for some funny reason, began to swell up like a balloon and hurt like the devil. I had a bit of fever. Everybody said I'd been stung by a poisonous insect.

In misery with my foot I limped to the Consulate and saw the Consul who remembered Mike and Burnham and Hub Peet. The last was sick here with malaria for two weeks and his parents came up from Singapore. *My* parents not being accessible, I won't get sick, though if I could see them by that means I'd be glad to be *awfully* sick.

I had dinner the day I arrived with Mr. Schneeberger, my friend from Bangkok, and would like to see more of him, but my foot hurts so I can't walk and am poor company. Whatever it is, bite or abscess, it's coming to a head very rapidly and will be opened tomorrow. I've never had anything hurt so bad. I suppose I shouldn't grumble as it's the first ache in ages. But all that will be gone long ago when you get this. Despite my foot, I dined with the Giddeys night before last and had a pleasant hour above the table and a miserable one below.

[*S. S. Cadaretta, nearing Singapore from Saigon—September 28, 1922.*] Another little jump is almost over—three days of fairly comfortable travel on a 2500-ton freighter. Never had a squall all the way down—not enough to agitate the ocean. Before leaving I got my foot lanced. Never have I felt such relief. By afternoon I was walking on it again.

I lunched with Mr. Schneeberger and killed time all afternoon. I got in a rickshaw and just rode for three hours. I don't know when I've been so blissfully calm and composed. All my duties were done, my house was in order, my foot had stopped its wracking pain, my indecision about my plans was all over. For better or worse I *had* decided. It was a cool afternoon and the shady, beautiful streets and parks of Saigon were fresh and green from the rain. My coolie thought I was crazy. Whenever he looked around I waved my hand in any direction. It made no difference. I slept in the hotel on Schneeberger's lounge. Up at five and by six was aboard. We sailed at eight, to reach Singapore in three days.

[*Two days later.*] Hurrah! I knew I could! I knew I could! I'm on my boat as I planned to be and I pay $9.00 in place of $25.00. It was too easy. I was as nice as pie to the captain yesterday, admired his pigeons, looked at his postcard collection and was friendly in general because I knew the final word was with him. This morning the two American agents came aboard. I was as tactful as you would have been and let them know one at a time who I was, my college, my situation. When the three got together there were *no* blackballs and, glory be, the ship sails tonight for Java, so I'll not be delayed. It's four or five days to Surabaya.

It's pouring rain and hot and stuffy here. You see we are almost on the Equator and I'll cross it tomorrow for the first time. I am going ashore with the captain to the agency at eleven and spend the rest of the day seeing Singapore. My old enthusiasm, somewhat jaded with my swollen foot in Saigon, has all come back with my good luck here.

I hope Captain Fauntleroy has not said, "Hold, enough," with our articles for they are coming faster than ever. There'll be over 32, besides rotogravure pages. So today, September 28, 1922, at this end, all was never so well, rested, normal. I don't know "good-by" in Malay, but I know "piggy" means "go," which I must do.

[*At Sea, Exactly on the Equator—October 1, 1922.*] I mailed you a letter at Singapore, a day or two ago, but a little love letter written with Mr. Neptune on board won't hurt. I've often wondered where I *would* cross the line and always supposed it would be on a voyage to South America, but to Java is as good as any. And it's not hot at all, delightfully cool, in fact. I'll sleep on deck tonight right under the biggest stars I've ever seen, and I'll need a *blanket*. I had always thought one was only half alive, on this line, from heat.

After all I had two days in Singapore. Mr. Donaldson, U. S. Rubber Company's Singapore manager, took me for a long motor ride about the island and out to his lovely home to tea with his wife. One of the sub-managers had me to dinner, and we had a very pleasant and argumentative evening. We drove till 1 A.M. and I almost *froze* in the open wind.

I went to the "Y." Everything was dark so I just prowled around till I found a vacant room on the top floor and went to bed.

Next morning I bummed about, the afternoon I spent in the Raffles library reading up on Java, and after dinner went back to the *Cadaretta* which sailed at 4 A.M.

Singapore is not an interesting place, though, during the tire and rubber boom, it was rolling in money.

It was this morning we sailed, in fact, and all day it's been a regular excursion—islands, islands and birds on every hand. It's 7 P.M. now, still slightly light. I've moved out of my stuffy cabin which I had never used and put my bag in the ship doctor's cabin. He dressed my lanced foot today and it's almost healed over. My Saigon stay was killed by that blamed bite. I'll never forgive it.

I've sat under the awnings on the captain's promenade deck all day and tried to write notes but the water is so strangely beautiful and the scenery so constant I've not done much.

CHAPTER VIII

Java, Bali, China, Siberia, Japan

[*Surabaya, Java—October 4, 1922.*] I'm among the Dutch again and very glad to be among anybody as long as it's on shore. I'm wild for exercise. I've not even walked ten feet since crossing the Siamese Peninsula and the absolute inertia on this recent ship voyage has stagnated me completely. I'm going for a ten-mile tramp tonight some place—any place. It will be dark so it won't matter greatly.

At two o'clock today we sailed into Surabaya harbor. I was on shore ten minutes after the anchor dropped, for I knew the Consulate closed at four and my mind had been on that place all day. Taxi drivers swarmed about me and said there was no other way to get to the city, which lies twelve miles *inland,* except taxi which would cost fifteen gulden—step right in! But I knew better and, as always, found the usual cheap way—in a cart. I kept asking, "Wo ist Konsul Amerikanish?" I can't speak Dutch, but German isn't far off, so I'll use what I know. When I found him, he had no mail for me, but was obliging and gave me information on Java.

Surabaya is just a commercial place, full of shops and packed with motor cars. The island is rich beyond measure, all belonging to tiny little 11,000-square-mile Holland. We leave at 5:40 A.M. I hope I wake up!

[*Surabaya—Thursday morning, 8:00 A.M.*] I *didn't* wake up and I missed the early train, but there's another at 9:30 so I use this time to postcript my letter.

After dinner last night I went in search of a Mr. Powers, a rich American to whom I had a letter from Mr. Donaldson of Singapore. Powers lives in an obscure suburb, miles out, but I was in need of exercise so I just walked to the place, though it took me two hours. Powers has lived in Java 40 years and knows what's what. I'm to call

184

Monday evening (today is Thursday) and meet his wife and get information and letters for Bali, which he knows like a book.

Coming home, I got hopelessly lost but the country was wonderful in the moonlight so I didn't mind. However, I came into town from the *opposite* side I left from and reached home at 1 A.M. I must have walked eighteen miles, at least, but it made me feel fit. I've walked so much that nothing under fifteen miles has any effect.

[*Surabaya—October 8, 1922.*] Letters, letters, letters, letters! Oh, what a joyful bundle all mailed in one big envelope from Hongkong. The Consul was out but I ransacked his apartment and *found 'em!* The poor servant thought I was either a desperate character or mad. Now, that I'm shaved and bathed, I'll enjoy them all over in answering them, but before that let's have a word or two about Djokjokarta.

The trip was a holy terror. I had to go third-class. East Java is a paradise in season but it's not rained here for six months and the land is burned to a crisp and dust a foot deep. I looked like a coal miner when I got to D. and so went to a native hotel, only four rooms, but clean. I was the only guest. I just moved about a bit and went to bed at eight o'clock. Next morning I had a long walk everywhere.

Djokja is an extraordinarily interesting place. I've not been anywhere where the people are so interesting externally as here. They all wear skirts of batik such as I'm sending home (mine is a table cover), rich blues and browns, with a tight-fitting turban to match. The men wear a jacket of white cotton, and the women thin organdy. Their colors are all subdued, not screaming as in India, and they are the neatest dressed people I've seen anywhere in Asia. There is heavy foliage everywhere, trees arching over every street in the European quarter, while in the native quarter it's a mad jungle of alleys, each group of houses having a high wall around it and shaded by dense groves of bananas and "flame of the forest," a brilliant red-blossoming tree that is well named. People swarm in these walled groups; a bit of rice and a few bananas are all they want. The ground's the richest on earth, so that they simply doze and have food dropped into their laps. It's never cold, clothes are unnecessary. Why work? Why worry? The men lie around and smoke; the women, each with her fat star-eyed baby swung on her hip by a cloth sling, make batik cloth or sell peppers in some shady lane. That's life for them!

That night I went to a native theater and was delighted. I'd seen the Siamese and the Cambodian dancers and fully enjoyed the Javanese. I can't say it's exciting but it's graceful—just posturing in a slouching position with a slight movement of the hands, the fingers of which they turn back until they touch the wrist—rather a snaky suggestion. They kept up the monotonous music and dancing for an hour. I got tired and went across to an "operetta" in Dutch, half native actors and half white. I decided to see it from back stage as I had done in Bangkok but the rajah in the play put me out. If I had to be humiliated, it was best that it be done by the star of the piece. I went around to the front door then and stayed through one act. It was so unendurable I left that, too. The native orchestras are most amusing. They have no written music. The orchestra consists of three or four different-ranged and toned xylophones, a tom-tom and a series of iron gongs. The head xylophonist carries the so-called tune, just improvising as he goes, while the rest of the players "accompany" him as suits their fancy. You can imagine the jargon, yet, strange to say, it *is* music. All the tones are soft and melodious and everything seems to blend, no matter what notes are struck.

Next day—yesterday—was to be a memorable one. Borobudur! The spot lies 30 miles from Djokja and there is a railroad only 21 miles of the way. After going five miles I found I was on the wrong train, and, after walking the five miles back rather than wait three hours for a return train, I again reached Djokja, madder than seven devils.

But I got away again and reached Muntilan at noon. "One hour's walk," said the station master, "to Borobudur. Last train leaves for D. at five." But I had gone too far to change my mind. I opened my collar, took off my coat and simply flew. The sun had gone behind clouds and a light rain fell, so it was quite cool. Wonderful, verdant country, tobacco, bananas, sugar cane growing in a riotous profusion. The rains had reached this part and it was in a fresh mantel. I can see now why people rave so over the beauties of Java. With the smoking volcanoes rising sheer on both sides, and these teeming, steaming fields and groves, it swarms with batiked, half-naked people, entirely naked babies, and endless buffaloes, ducks, bullocks, snow-white rice birds, carts, animation and life everywhere.

Borobudur is built over a squat hill and not on a level as is Angkor. The former rises high above the surrounding fields and can be seen from Muntilan. But after Angkor it was simply *nothing* to me. A great archeologist is quoted as saying, "It is the most stupendous achievement of man I have ever seen in so small a place." He can't have seen much. I was thoroughly disappointed, but then I'm temple-weary and would probably think it supreme had I seen it first.

I tarried on the way back to look in on a shadow play—dancing figures on a screen with native music. It was so fascinating I almost missed my train—had to run for it, in fact. The exercise was great, even if the temple was not. Eighteen miles! I'll be in great shape for Bali.

I procured a book about the island and a map and shall take it on foot or horseback—150 miles across.

Now for a bit of conversation. Mother, my ideal of girls certainly has changed and it will change many times more with every advancement in age and experience.

Of course, Mother, you *know* I'm careful. My unbroken health proves it. I happened to notice, while I was washing my socks before a mirror, how unusually well I looked. The heavy lines of sleeplessness and worry that sagged under my eyes at Princeton last June are all gone. I'm not any fatter but who *could* be, living as actively as I do?

So, you did like *If Winter Comes*. I thoroughly enjoyed it, too, but it depressed me. *Cytherea* is the same thing, only much worse. Those two books are enough to drive any man to celibacy.

[*Surabaya—8:00* A.M., *October 9, 1922.*] I am only too fearful, Dad, that what you say about the ultimate extinction of the white race is true. These Asiatics are slow and sluggish in progressing, but progress they must and progressing they are, and while we increase by hundreds, they increase by millions. Already their disrespect of the white, their arrogance, is terrific in the East. A vast debacle is smouldering against the Caucasian and when once these hordes begin to resist in concert, what is to stop them? One sees thousands upon thousands of half-castes in Asia. They do not tend to whiten the brown man, but to brown the white.

Language is a difficulty at times, yet I seem always to get there. At Djokja, the native proprietor of my hotel and I could not understand one single word, each of the other. Yet I lacked for nothing, made my wants understood and was as normal as if I'd been in the Peabody Hotel.

As long as *Commercial* takes my articles I do not bother about there being so few receptive magazines. It's the *money* I want for continuous work on my book. I shall live on the payment for my articles and where the checks come from is of no consequence. You are right. My fight with the book will be to keep it inside one volume. My notes, when complete, will not be far short of 400,000. I look forward with enthusiasm to compiling the book and suppose you are right about my working 24 hours a day. After the book is sold, what? Another book? Things always fall in line for me of their own accord and I am not the least worried over the uncertainty of the future. It's no use making decisions, they won't stand a week. . . .

Yes, I've got past the discouraging point over the unsuccess of my articles in a bigger field. I feel happy that some have found a buyer. After all, my original idea was *apprenticeship* on this trip, and as an apprentice I've made some progress, as you say, toward mastering the trade. I, too, can feel a greater fluency and boldness than when I began a year ago, for a year ago I was slaving in Paris on my "Germany" story. As so often, Dad, our minds, though 10,000 miles apart are again en rapport. I know you never are surprised to hear what I've done.

[*Surabaya—October 10, 1922.*] Just a note. The company refuses to sell me deck passage to Bali and second class is $72.00. But I'll get around that some way, either buy a ticket to the first port and once on board "talk" to the purser or captain, or else buy nothing and then talk. The first may be the better as I'll get smoothly on board.

[*Banjuwangis, Bali—October 12, 1922.*] I just landed on this wonderful island from Banjuwangis, the last east point of Java. I had a comfortable trip all day yesterday from Surabaya—6 A.M. to 4 in a second-class compartment with a third-class ticket. Last night I spent at Banju and wrote a much belated letter of thanks to my friends, the Giddeys. This morning the Dutch agent took me on board the ship where I bought a deck ticket, the very thing the agent in Surabaya refused to sell me. It was only five hours, but a marvelous five, volcanoes and islands everywhere, the clearest water I've ever seen.

My letter to Mr. Edgar, the American, I presented at once. He is a Standard Oil agent and very decent, has a nice house, and I've had a drink and a bath and tea and am now being motored to the end of the road up the mountain range where I begin the tramp to the lower side. I spent the night at 2000 feet.

[*Leaving Bali—October 21, 1922.*] This is my first letter written in pencil. I won't be able to think clearly without my old pen, but even with lead I can communicate to you that I'm still well as can be and going strong. My pen is gone for good this time. It was almost useless, tied together with string. Having bought it my junior spring at Princeton and having used it constantly since, I'm sorry to part with it at this late stage of its circumnavigation. If my articles henceforth are weak and stupid I'll blame it on the new pen.

Another very eventful stage of my journey is almost over for I'm waiting at the sea shore for the weekly boat to ferry me across the Strait of Bali to Banjuwangis where I'll catch the train tomorrow morning.

In Saigon when I was struggling with the problem of where to go next, my *heart* pleaded for Hongkong, because it brought me nearer home, but my head sternly demanded Java—and Bali. You know which conquered. I'm so happy it turned out this way, for in Bali I've seen the rarest and most novel things and have enjoyed and profited more than in any other place I've been, India excepted, of course. I had plenty of time to "do" the little island right. It gave me time to roam and see and comprehend.

Mr. Edgar motored me from Banjuwangis to Poemahan (inland) where, as the sun set, I climbed the mile or so to Gitgit. The view over the tropical Java Sea, the terraced rice fields and the graceful, inevitable palms everywhere made a magnificent picture from 1500 feet. There is a rest bungalow but I preferred the stars and the soft ferns. The young wife of the Dutch custom's officer with her two babies was summering there and we had a pleasant evening, though our only means of conversation were a smattering of German on the part of each. Her babies were cute, aged one and three. The elder spoke only Malay. The mother gave me a list of Malay words, so I was quite equipped linguistically and found it to be invaluable in my expedition. I dined among the natives next morning and at six was off for the 4200-foot climb up a path. From the top, the two lakes were visible and I rested an hour looking at them and the novel natives that passed. There are only 50 whites on the island and 1,000,000 natives. They wear no clothes above the waist, neither men nor women. In the country the farmers wear a loin cloth and the women a cotton skirt. The Holland-bred native officials have daughters and in order that they might be modestly dressed, and not be shameful, decreed that *all* women must cover their breasts. So in Banjuwangis and Den Pasar they do that when a white man is seen, but in the country they still cling to nature and unaffectation.

[*Later—tonight.*] The boat came in and I'm now on board after another exasperating conflict—with the captain this time. He remembered that I came over deck before. He was dining with a dozen first-class passengers when I stopped on the first deck to speak to a Dutchman I'd met in Den Pasar and to look at a basket of native junk a vendor was selling. The captain suddenly shouted from the table to ask if I had a first-class passage. "No, I have not." "Then, get off the first-class deck." His tone was so insulting and the situation so embarrassing I vowed I'd be obstinate and finish my harmless examination. Three times he howled at me and finally came over from his chair, purple in the face, and with clenched fists ordered, "Get forward with the pigs where you belong." "The pigs are not all forward. I have the misfortune to be addressing one." I've never seen a man so mad. He lost complete control of his temper and simply bellowed. This line is notorious for its tyrannical attitude. It has a monopoly— why be civil?

[*Surabaya again—October 24, 1922.*] This is certainly an interrupted letter. I got to Pasoerau safely and a truck was obliging.

Tosari is 6200 feet high and disagreeably cold though one looks down on the Equator. At three that morning I started with a guide the climb to Bromo Volcano. It was very severe and I tore my shoes to shreds. About sunrise I got to the Sand Sea that surrounds the cone and about half past seven reached the brink. It was an awe-inspiring sight to look down 1000 feet into the roaring crater and an hour was not too long to look at it. I got back well-blistered and worn out but in time for the bus down to the coast again.

As I began to write several nights ago, my Bali trip was a great success. The third day, having walked through wonderful mountain country and a forest of palms, all thickly peopled by colorful hand-some brown people, I reached Den Pasar.

I left Den Pasar along the south coast to Karang Asem and fol-lowed the beach—blue water with palms overhanging it and won-derful swimming for 25 miles. I spent a night with a fisherman and over a week with a family of salt workers. I went with them to Den Pasar where a big cremation holiday was on and I never saw such strange doings. They fought over the corpse, 500 young men, half of them pushing it to the pyre and half of them pushing it away, symbolizing the human unwillingness to give up life. There were native music and feasts and parades for two days. After I said good-by to my salt-worker friends I climbed 5000 feet to look into one of the grandest sights in the world. The old volcano of Bateor is 25 miles in circumference and was once *all* lava, but it has cooled and only a cone, like an island, in the middle of the lake is still active. The crater all about the cone was once water but it's dried to only crescent shape now.

The second day I prowled around on the dry floor of the crater, visiting the villages, some half-buried, some surrounded by the lava of 1905. I got back to Banjuwangis a day early and spent it with Mr. Edgar. You know the rest. I had walked about 150 miles of *heavy* walking and much climbing and after Bromo am enjoying this *"rest"* though I'm so uneasy and on edge about boats it won't be rest till I sail.

[*Surabaya—November 1!!! 1922.*] I'm still in this forty times damned city, the ninth day since I got back from Bali, eating my heart out to get away but succeeding only tonight. A British ship sailed for Hongkong at 6 P.M., the twenty-seventh. At 5 P.M. I went calmly aboard dressed in my best and established myself as stowaway in an open cabin. Just as the boat sailed a Chinese employee came in and tattled straight to my chief enemy, the purser. I was put off with the pilot in the darkness into a little skiff. The ship sailed on and the pilot and I were rowed to the houseboat where the pilots live.

At last, an American ship was announced to arrive Tuesday. I was on hand to step aboard the *West Mohammet* and grab the captain like a long-lost friend. It was arranged that I am simply to go aboard tonight in the darkness and get off at Singapore. No one is to know who and what and why I am aboard. The captain is a good sport and I am wild with joy.

[*Singapore—November 8, 1922.*] My last note from Surabaya saying I was leaving turned out correct for once, though until the ship was six hours at sea I was in an anxious state of mind. I stayed secreted with door locked in my stuffy cabin, nor did I dare breathe until we passed the pilot boat. Then I came out and was "discovered" and brought to the first officer. He was "horrified," the captain gave me a stern lecture, etc. We left Thursday and arrived Sunday at seven. I got ashore to the Y.

[*Hongkong six hours north, South China Sea—November 15, 1922.*] My ship will dock early tomorrow morning and I shall be waiting on the office steps when the mail clerk arrives. This is the *first* reason November sixteenth will be momentous. The second reason is that it means *Hongkong*—not just the interesting city itself, but the back door to home. Ever since I left New York, Hongkong has been the goal, and many a time have I looked at the map of the world and wondered was it physically possible to reach this tremendously faraway point. And now I'm there! I feel so thankful for my safe delivery here that I must say so. I was getting desperate from delay in Singapore. I had Ammudder's $100 I've been hoarding, and could easily have paid for a passage, but I wouldn't. I'm trying to live on my "income" from the *Commercial* and occasional articles sold, so I can honestly say I "worked my way." I swung on to my purpose— and was rewarded.

I went to the Consul and explained he would have a destitute bum on his hands unless he helped me to get away while I still had money. He was born in Jackson, Tennessee—a Mr. Blackard—and knew our family. That turned the trick. He put some force behind a request and they agreed to take me on the *Van Overstraten* as deck passenger at fifteen dollars gold. Once I was on board, the chief steward proved a human being and gave me a roomy second-class cabin. She's a big ship, but the ocean has been raging and we have pitched up and down all the way till everybody else is deathly seasick and I'm pretty weary myself. The propeller is out of the water half the time.

[*Hongkong—Morning, November 17.*] Yesterday we drew into this spectacular harbor and I stood on deck with my teeth chattering and reveled in the first *cold* I've known since last February, the first day it has not been blisteringly hot. It was really a queer sensation. We ferried across the teeming harbor, the fifth largest in the world. I called on Amexco and the clerk asked if I had a basket to carry my mail in. I needed one. Up at the Consul's office, I sat for four hours reading it, all so cheerful and newsy and encouraging.

My friends the Giddeys are here. I'm getting my clothes patched up before I call.

I worked on my Bali article last night and then had a vigorous walk about the hill. The Taj article did look fine in the paper, didn't it? Just use your good judgment, Dad, about "selling" Bali. Very happy "we" sold two stories since last I heard. Perhaps they'll go easier now.

[*Hongkong—9 P.M. November 17, 1922.*] I'm going to Canton tomorrow with Mr. Peterson, a traveling acquaintance. I 'phoned the Giddeys and will dine with them at their hotel on top the mountain. P. and I took the cog and went to the top—it is an overpowering sight—Gibraltar all over. However, thousands see this—none see that. One looks down into a great titan-surrounded harbor with thousands and thousands of water craft dotting it—mostly Chinese—and 200 steamers at anchor. We saw the sun set over Macao Island and the lights in the harbor begin to twinkle—walked down.

With 22 articles printed (presumably) and $290 from magazines I've made—or rather *Dad* and I have made—$730 so far, beside the $100 or more I've picked up along the route, I'm not spending so much as *Dad* and I are making, and hope to have enough surplus to pay my railroad fare from Frisco home.

That was a fine letter from Helen Pendergast, wasn't it? She is in a class by herself when it comes to mental congeniality with me. She is the only real girl "pal" I've ever had, and I've got more stimulation and happiness from her company than from any other girl.

I seem doomed to be the "Memphis boy"—of course, long ago Captain Fauntleroy got my letter requesting justice. I always feel sweet sixteen again when I read my headlines, sort of infant prodigy.

[*Back from Canton—Tuesday Morning, November 21.*] Well, Canton proved wonderful. It's not so, Dad, that I am satiated and that "sugar is no longer sweet." I got a real thrill out of Canton. Really I've never got such satisfaction out of any other two days. Canton is the epitome of China—all the wildest legends and pictures and colors one has heard rumored about China are found in Canton— streets lined with lacquered and gilded shops, ivory carving and jade shops, fans and silks. The streets are only from four to six feet wide and present a forest of banner advertisements that cloud and obstruct the view down the canyon. The river on which Canton is situated is the home of 60,000 houseboats and 250,000 people. There are *square miles* of houseboats, with towering Chinese junks appearing in the midst of them. No matter where you go—how obscure the street, it is packed with moiling, active, hard-working people.

The Chinese differ greatly from the Indians. One passes a shop in India and finds the proprietor dozing over his goods; but here there are noise and cries, the sound of the hammer or spindle from every shop. The Chinese seem to have inexhaustible energy. They slave all day and half the night, eat a bowl of rice and sleep under their work tables. There *is* a civilization in China. In India there is only what's left of one. At night the Canton streets are filled with music processions lit by lanterns, all weird and truly Oriental. Jade Street is one of the best—one mile of jade and amber shops—but it's *high* as heaven. Of course, you can jew 'em down, but even at that jade is no pastime for a vagabond. I had Ammudder's money and after a day's bargaining, I spent it on the alluring stones which I'm mailing home. I never enjoyed "shopping" so much.

I went to Macao, the Portuguese place where fan-tan is played so much. It's the Eastern Monte Carlo. I sailed on the now famous *Sui An*. She was pirated by 60 bandits and all the American and British passengers stripped of everything. I'll send a new departure story about the whole affair for the *Commercial*. It was the most outrageous holdup Hongkong has ever known and the colony is extremely excited about it—but I'm poaching on my own story, "Piracy à la Chinoise." I thoroughly enjoyed the experience. Fan-tan is *lots* of fun and I really won at it. I got "home" Monday and went shopping in Chinese shops to replenish my suddenly reduced wardrobe.

Dad's cable about Ladakh awaited me also. Rather nice, isn't it? I'd rather break out in the *Geographic* than any magazine except the *Atlantic*. I wonder how much they give us, Dad?*

[*Shanghai—Monday, November 27, 1922.*] Last Tuesday afternoon I went for a long and wonderful walk with Miss Giddey and another girl. We climbed down the Pacific side of the rock to the beautiful Repulse Bay Hotel and had tea there and danced. It's without doubt the most splendidly situated and beautiful hotel in Asia. We came back along the shore in a bus just at sundown, with islands and fishing fleets and Chinese junks filling every picture. I do love those junks.

I arranged to sail next morning on a Jap liner for Shanghai and to pay $20 gold for it. It was my *first* boughten second cabin on a passenger ship since the old *Savoie*. I hated to spoil my record, but the maddening effects of Surabaya were still upon me and I had no more energy or courage left to fight for a cheaper passage on a freighter. I hate second class—one feels second rate. I'd much rather go deck on a freighter and be no class at all.

Shanghai is fifteen degrees colder than Hongkong but just snappy without really hurting. I went, as usual, straight to the Y., where I'm garreted. At once I copied my piracy story and took it around to the editors (plural). I made a mistake. They all said it was all right for the home town but not for them; they had already covered it. One semi-Chinese paper wanted me to take an editorial job with them. It's a new and prospectively profitable paper—only after-

---

* The *Geographic* paid $250.

noon—and if I had the time I'm sure I could work it up to something. The initial salary was to be $300 Shanghai a month—$150 gold—but I declined with thanks. Shanghai is about as Chinese as Pittsburgh, so I'm pushing on as soon as possible.

Out of Shanghai, Richard visited Hangchow. "Hangchow is indescribably beautiful. The Chinese say, 'Heaven above and on earth Hangchow.' Lakes, pagodas and shrines all hidden in foliage and hills. It's very much like Udaipur in India."

He returned to Shanghai and then went to Peking, taking inland water routes as far as Hankow.

He groaned over the days it was consuming and his temper was made no better by getting stuck on a sand bar in the Yangtse for twenty-four hours, but after all there were compensations.

[*Hankow—December 7, 1922*] However, this has been a most worth-while delay. Hankow is China with a capital C. No, or very few, foreigners, so that the things Chinese are left in their original dirt and color. The banks along the Yangtse River swarm with coolies and dogs and babies and houseboat dwellers. I've spent two sunny mornings just looking—it's fascinating. Surely there are no people so interesting as these. India as a country, its topography, architecture and vegetation, is in a class by itself, but for individual human nature China has them all beat. They are irrepressibly good-humored—all thorough rogues, but also good sports, so that you can't help liking them. I feel helpless in writing about China. You see with your eyes whole volumes every day. The river trip was great. I had four Norwegian missionaries in my cheap quarters, learned a lot and had good company. The watercraft, the water life, the mighty Yangtse should have an article, but I've no time to write it.

[*Princeton Court, Peking—December 11, 1922.*] I expected to find Peking terribly cold. It's a joyful disappointment to find it perfection—crisp and dry and sunny. I'm plunged into friendly hands and welcoming homes. Yesterday Mr. Lenning Sweet—Chan's older brother who runs the Princeton Y. here—and his wife took me for a long trip, rickshaw, into the western hills. After dinner with friends, Len and I got on bicycles and rode for five hours visiting pagodas and wonderful old temples. I thought I was temple weary, but those created a new enthusiasm, so artful and so surrounded by Chinese atmosphere. Princeton Court is all Princeton men—none of my class, but that matters little. I've never been happier on my trip.

[*Princeton Court, Peking—December 14, 1922.*] There is nothing like Peking. The Altar of Heaven is the most spiritual monument yet, even more than the Taj. One stands on a great round altar surrounded by thick forests of firs and all one can see is the great vault of heaven. I never saw anything so conspicuous as the heavens there.

Last night a friend and I went for a long walk about the walls. This morning I gave a fifteen-minute talk to 500 Chinese students at the Y. chapel with an interpreter. I talked about the sack of the *Sui An.* This afternoon I'm teaing with Mrs. Harry Franck. He is out in the wilds. I met her at Lawrenceville last year. I've managed to see lots of sights—the Winter Palace, the Forbidden City, and so on. It wouldn't seem I've had time to sleep and eat, but I have.

[*Princeton Court, Peking—Tuesday, December 19, 1922.*] And I swore I'd leave Sunday! It happened that by waiting until tomorrow I would have the opportunity of calling on the Generalissimo of the Chinese Army, and such a rare treat should not be missed.

Saturday a Miss Hill—Vassar grad—and I went to the Great Wall. It is one of the most impressive sights I've ever seen, wriggling and climbing for 2500 miles over the rocks and ridges of barren Mongolia. It was terrifically cold, but I was swathed in furs and enjoyed it. On Sunday I went to call on the young American tutoress of the Empress of China—you can imagine how interesting *that* was. I spend tomorrow at General Fing's army camp and leave tomorrow night.

[*Harbin, Manchuria—December 25, 1922.*] Back in Hongkong I wondered where I'd be on this day. Harbin was about the last place I would have guessed, but it's as good as any or rather as bad as any, for I don't care where I am since I'm not at home. What a violent contrast, today and this day last year! Then it was oranges and sunny Spain and the Alhambra; and now it's bitterly cold and sleigh bells and Russia. It is toward Vladivostok my face is turned, and it's a set face for I'm encountering difficulties at every step. I think Len Sweet's overcoat decided my mind, for he offered it to me if I were going to Siberia—and I half went to Siberia just to get the coat. It is a splendid one—long, heavy-furlined, and a big, all-embracing fur collar. I felt so prepared and well armed in it. I'm not sure yet that I shall get through to Vladivostok, but a good fight is always worthwhile. On Sunday I went for a walk about the city wall with Miss Ingram, the tutoress of the Empress. The Royal pair were only married a day or two before, and this girl and the Emperor's tutor were the only Europeans present at the great ceremony. I saw some of the parading. I learned much about the internal affairs of the court.

It was twenty-four hours to Mukden. I spent the night in a little Russian hotel, below zero outside and suffocating inside with the windows nailed down and strips put in the cracks. I reached Harbin late at night and found myself in a city as Russian as Moscow itself. All the pictures I'd seen in geographies of Russia were there. The droshky with the arched yoke over the horse's neck, the domed churches and tall fur caps and knee boots. Next morning it was twenty degrees *below* zero, but I was hidden in my fur coat, had on heavy underwear and thoroughly enjoyed the tang and the purity of the sun-flooded air. I went straight to the Consulate. The Consul would do nothing. Since we have no official relationship with the Soviets I was told they would assist me to Vladivostok *only* if I had a letter of recommendation from the Consul. That was Saturday morning. Everything closed that afternoon. I simply had to kill time, so I went to a Russian church as their Sunday begins on Saturday at five. Everybody comes in and prostrates himself before numerous statues, kisses the feet of oil portraits and then stands during the entire service, which may last two hours. I stood one hour and gave up. The music, though, was wonderful—rich, deep bass voices that made the very building shake. What a contrast to the extraordinary service I attended at Granada last year!

I called on the secretary of the Y. He proved a fine fellow, with a charming wife. I spent the evening with them and learned volumes about the political and social situation in this cockpit where Russia, China and Japan are glaring at one another like tigers. I went to Christmas service at the Y. chapel, and in the afternoon Mr. Haag took me to see the poor refugee devils, packed 150 into a barrack, where they had fled to escape Red rule. We called on several families living partitioned off by mats, and just barely living, but they all said it was better than life in Red Russia.

Saturday night I met at my hotel an Englishman who had lived some time in Harbin and knew the Bolshevik officials in the Bureau. He offered to accompany me when I needed him, so this morning we went back together. He got hold of the Reds he knew best, slapped them on the back, gave them cigarettes, etc. and we could have had the crown jewels for the asking, much less a simple visé. My pass was rushed through—no questions asked—everything went smooth as silk till the bill came, 25 yen or $13. That floored me, but it was too late to turn back.

At dusk I went for a walk with my English friend and his partner, a glorious walk, twenty below, but crisp and dry, so that one would never dream it was so cold—until a nose or an ear froze.

[*Vladivostok, Siberia!—Friday, December 29, 1922.*] Just *think* where I am! The very name Vladivostok always gave me a thrill whenever I thought about it. Now that it's a very important part of Bolshevik Russia, it's doubly interesting. As often I've so much to talk about I don't know where to begin. Instead of things getting more dull and commonplace as I advance, they get more novel and enthralling. But why shouldn't they when one is in Vladivostok, in Siberia, in the coldest month of the coldest country, and in the midst of the red, red Bolsheviks. I must say I've had excellent intuition on this journey. If the guardian angel that urged me on would come around I'd present him with a gold medal.

But let me go back. I wrote on Monday night, December 25. Next morning your cable came: "Greetings, well, love." I was the happiest man in Manchuria and simply burst with joy as I slid the mile or so over the ice, shouldered my lordly way into the packed Soviet office and pushed aside many smelly, brow-beaten Russians. They gave me back my passport, stamped and viséd all in a space about two by three inches—not big enough, I felt, to be worth $13. My success with the visé gave me such renewed self-assurance that I persuaded a Russian bank to cash a $50 express check, which, in my pocket, just about filled my cup of confidence.

Then I had a most delightful afternoon. In the Englishman's apartment I met a young Russian whom he was tutoring. The Russian asked me to his home to tea where I met his refugee family. They were of the "intelligentsia" class that the Bolos hate so, and had to flee for their lives with what money and property they could. They showed me pictures of their old Russian estate, many square miles of farms and woodland and a beautiful, ancient home. Everyone spoke almost perfect English and played the piano or violin, and sang. As usual in musical festivals I felt very insignificant and uncultured. My Russian friends had a picture of the old Czar in every room and the boy almost worshiped before it.

When I left Harbin, regretfully, next morning at nine, third class, I had a compartment with three Russians. They insisted on stopping every crack of air, it was suffocating, and I had to move to more airy quarters. A grand conglomeration of fat-cheeked Manchurian Chinese and rough-looking, fur-hatted Russians in boots and great reindeer coats were aboard. I used my big fur coat as a mattress. In fact I've used it for everything but food. I had no difficulty at the border.

It was a long but interesting 30 hours to Vladivostok. At the Y. great luck and small luck met me. I found I had missed the *weekly* boat to Japan by *one day!* This meant a six-day wait, but since I *have* to wait, I am waiting in the snuggest, most pleasant home in Vladivostok. Len Sweet and Mrs. Sweet gave me a letter to Mr. Lewis, Y. secretary at Vladi for all Siberia. I found Mrs. Lewis at the Y. and was invited immediately to reside with them. Their home is a delight—and she and he both are. She is an Oxford graduate, educated in Europe, and speaks six languages, including Russian. He was in the Y. service in the Ukraine, at Constantinople, in Armenia and at Archangel during the war and she in Y. W. C. A. work in Moscow and Poland.

I have my own room and know of nothing better than to sit and

listen to my hosts tell me about the devil Reds. I'm lost in the entanglements of Vladi's recent history, it's been so many colors. The
city has been Red only since October, but the streets are still crimson
with flags, and swarm with soldiers. What picturesque streets!—
like a procession of bears, for *everybody* is swathed in hides and fur—
fur boots, hats, gloves, not to mention greatcoats. Vladivostok is ma-
jestically situated on hills overlooking a narrow long harbor. The
harbor is frozen solid five months in the year and only by heroic work
can the ice breakers keep one channel open.

This afternoon I had a long walk with my camera on the frozen
harbor, taking pictures of the old Russian fishermen, fishing through
holes in the ice. The view back was splendid—all Vladi with its
domed churches rising in tiers on the hill. It's a ramshackle town
built helter-skelter and at present dreadfully run down. The Reds
dominate the place body and soul but, as it was the last stronghold of
the Czarists, it is still a point of friction. Every week a long train of
boxcars packed with enemies is sent across Siberia back to the interior.
How they survive, I don't see, for it's unendurably cold. Executions
and arrests are the order of the day, though things have quieted down
almost to "normalcy" since October. The Reds rule like iron and
are a thousand times more autocratic than the autocrats they destroyed. They are giving up their wild theories one after another.
They see it's impossible to enforce them, that the economic laws
against which they revolted must prevail in the long run. In a few
years if the Bolos remain in power, as it seems they must, Communism
will resolve itself into a sane sort of government like England or
America. The Russians are too human and capable for there to be
any other outcome. If the Reds would only stop preaching world
revolution they might have a good chance to be recognized.

[*Still Vladivostok, dammit—Thursday, January 4, 1923.*] It's been
an ever-increasing conflict between my urge to get home and the
urge to "see through" what I've begun. The two emotions have
made me very unhappy at times, but now there's only one force;
the other is completely dead. I *have* seen it through. Now, I've only
to come home from the party.

Well, Yokohama is very, very close now and I think my endurance will hold out to there. Once more I'm swamped with experiences and talk.

First, about the ferry boat to Japan. Since I wrote last we have had an *awful* blizzard, and when it's fine weather at twenty below you can imagine—or rather you can't imagine—what a blizzard is. The ship was due in Monday; it's Thursday and she's just here. On New Year's Day she was so buffeted by the storm and so endangered by freezing spray she had to turn back to Japan. She limped in today, a fairy ship of ice. And she's sailing tomorrow at noon—and with me on her, though I've wondered at times if I could overcome the mountain of combined Bolshevik and Japanese passport nonsense even by tomorrow. It cost me $25 gold to pass through here, but it's been worth much more than that. A courier at the Consulate led me around to the endless bureaus to complete my visé. It would have been hopeless otherwise.

New Year's Eve I went to a mass meeting of Bolshevik workmen, which waxed tremendously exciting at twelve o'clock. New Year's Day Mr. Lewis knocked off and we decided to take a walk in the blizzard which had been brewing all night. We filled our pockets with sandwiches and left about noon. The thermometer registered 35 below and the wind cut you in two. We climbed to some of the forts behind the city and I can safely say it's the coldest place I've yet been. I suddenly found Mr. Lewis's ears, nose and chin as white as this paper, frozen solid, but we rubbed snow on his face and brought back the color, though they swelled dreadfully next day. I escaped as I was swathed in fur collar and muffler. I could write a letter just about the market here where the refugees sell all their property to live.

[*Kyoto, Japan—January 9, 1923.*] *See* where I am on my 23rd birthday! You'll soon have a middle-aged son, but the point is, you'll soon *have* him. I got off all right, loaded down with 40 pounds of European mail. I've never been so seasick, never; this was terrible—a small boat and wild weather—twelve hours late getting in. Ice so thick we feared the boat would capsize it listed so. Learning I was near the famous Ama-No-Hashidate peninsula (we landed at Tsuruga),

I dragged all my mail bags there and spent a day and night. It's glorious; under two feet of snow, yet warm.

[*Yokohama—January 12, 1923.*] I'm in the sailing place at last, and sailing is in sight. Meanwhile, the *President Taft* is off in an hour and I want just to send a hello. Day before yesterday I went to Nara. What a beautiful, breath-taking place—stone lanterns and fantastic pines and shrines in such profusion and artistic setting as I never saw. Japan certainly has the monopoly on scenery. It's dead of winter—what *would* it be in spring? I left Kyoto at midnight so as to pass Fuji at sunrise—it *worked,* beyond description. That snow-covered cone is as majestic as the Matterhorn. It is worshiped by the Japanese, as it should be. Everybody climbs it in July—it's everyone's religious duty. There have been several parties gone up recently—it's only 12,700, you see, and I'm going to Tokyo today to interview one of the climbers. It would be a grand finale to a grand trip and I would come home after a proper climax.

To be sure, I'm thinking along lecturing lines, but first I must catch up on my notes and articles and bring everything into concord. I couldn't talk intelligently otherwise. I mean to accept all bids to speak in public.

It has been a terrific key I've played on since May, 1921,—my nerves and muscles need a rest dreadfully. I'm not ill—have forgotten what that means—but I'm beginning to realize I'm tired *of* the strain more than tired *from* it, and I want only to rest myself to death and exercise, when I get home. I need systematic exercise worse than anything. It's been sudden violent exertion and then nothing but moving confinement for days. It's not low speed I want at home but a dead stop for a while, if that's possible.

I'm not thinking one foot beyond my book at present. It is going to be a heavy and long, but a pleasant struggle to prepare it for the market.

I'm afraid I've only half a personality. When it comes to formal society I am utterly at home. I could talk to Buddha himself and with ease. But put me in a crowd of light-hearted, bantering men and I'm tongue-tied and miserable. I'd give everything to be a "jolly good fellow." They make wonderful traveling salesmen!

I've not written much about Japan. I'll save it to tell. It's bright and charming, but I'm flying too fast for deep impressions.

[*Yokohama—January 23, 1923.*] As usual I am buried under news, perhaps the most astonishing news yet. However, by this time you have become as quietly accustomed to the shocks of my novel adventures as I, and nothing any more is really astonishing.

Another dream has been realized, another "complex" satisfied. I climbed Fujiyama on the seventeenth—alone!—and am the first person in the history of the world to have undertaken the expedition single-handed in winter. Back home writing beside my comfortable oil stove it seems only a dream, an amazing interlude. I wouldn't be sure it had really happened did I not have photographs to prove it—to the world, as well as to myself.

I believe, when I wrote you last, I mentioned my desire to climb Fuji and the newspaper article I'd seen about Lees' climb. I went to Tokyo and found Colonel Lees. I spent the afternoon and evening listening to his long arguments *against* my going. His arguments were sound. It was dark of the moon. The climb *up* took twelve hours, and the January daylight was inadequate by six hours or more. I had absolutely no clothes or equipment, no knowledge of Japanese or snow climbing, and no money.

I left his place resigned to my luck of being in Japan in mid-winter. I went to Nikko instead, the tourist paradise. It has the most extraordinary temples and shrines, and is superbly situated, but I was so Fuji-obsessed I hated the lovely place. From the train I could see the peak, as I'd seen her coming up from Kyoto, snow clad and solitary and tenderly beautiful with her gentle sweeping curves. I simply couldn't leave without closer investigation; so I went back to Colonel Lees and, paying a deposit on his ice axe, snowshoes, and fur-lined flying coat, announced I was going to climb up only as far as prudence and good weather and common sense and sunlight permitted. I bought iron ice-spikes for my shoes, a sweater, etc., and, having spent two days vainly trying to get a companion, went back toward Kyoto and got off at Gotemba, the usual halt for Fuji climbers. I spent the night and half the next day hiring a motor car, a cook, supplies, charcoal.

Well, my coolie and I were motored nine miles and walked four more to the base, 4500 feet. There is the first hut of a series of ten that serve the upward trail. We slept there till 4 A.M. Something said to me as I told my coolie goodbye in the pitch darkness that I'd get to the top with such weather. It was day, about six, and the sun burst right out of the Pacific as I watched from my high perch.

My crampons (ice shoes) were perfect. I never slipped but stomped anywhere over the iceberg I chose to. The snow was entirely covered with glittering ice. I had on two underwears, a woolen shirt, and two sweaters encased in a new, unwashed, stiff khaki short work coat to keep the wind out; woolen gloves with fur gauntlets over them, a woolen ski cap, two pairs of wool knit socks, heavy high shoes, Japanese straw snowshoes and crampons. I was clothed for the North Pole, luckily, for that's where I went.

I made my plans to get as high and far as I could by *two* o'clock. At that hour I meant to turn around, but I got to the *top* at 12:30. It was not easy by any means, but neither did it seem dangerous—just a long, steep, out-of-breath tramp, weighted down by clothes and food and camera and foot gear, but so filled with astonishing views of the sea of clouds beneath me and the glistening white island peak above that I quite forgot fatigue and time.

The summit was intolerably cold. I froze my nose and ears trying to take pictures of the crater—and succeeding. Ten minutes was enough. One glimpse into the crater was enough. By one I was well on my way down. I loafed then and rested on the ice, propped against my axe. It was dark when I arrived at Tarōbō—thirteen hours both ways. I was dead tired and my shoes, new and Japanese, let my toes slide forward and the pain of walking was unpleasant. I thought we'd *never* reach Gotemba. A hot tub bath restored me to life at the hotel and twelve hours' sleep did the rest. I reached Yokohama that night and was laughed at when I said where I'd been the last day or two. But my prints, which turned out fine, verified my tale, and the stunt is now the talk of Yokohama and will be of Tokyo, for the biggest newspaper there (English) has bought my story.

I'd have written at length without the Fuji business, but, of course, that dominates all else. I may be the postman of this letter, but what of it, it's been such fun to write? Oh, of course, I'm absolutely recovered from the climb. My toe-nails are coming off and my nose is sore and peeling, but these battle scars are very minor.

[*Yokohama—January 29, 1923.*] I'm signed on a ship, a big and fast ship, and I sail for Seattle the thirty-first. I wirelessed you this afternoon I'd be there February tenth and I shall!—for my ship is reliable and laughs at storms. There is such a strange feeling inside me tonight. I always looked forward to this hour expecting I would feel like dancing and shouting for joy, but I don't. It's a feeling of bottomless calm and serenity and relaxation. I shall sleep as I've not slept for eighteen months, when I was constantly on the firing line and did not dare abandon my vigil. But now the war is over, and I think I've won.

I called on an illustrated magazine with several very good pictures I'd taken at Ama-No-Hashidate and at Nikko. The editor admitted they were all unique—he offered me *free copies* of his dumb publication for *three* months for five photographs. Nothing doing. I'm past the day of frantic delight over notice from condescending editors. I'm beginning to condescend myself! Out to Colonel Lees' for tea and much comparative talk. He and his niece were delighted over my success.

I went to Tokyo and got my Fuji story money. I was interviewed there and next day, Sunday, a long article on your son appeared on the front page and a big picture on the back. That, added to my heralded Fuji climb, made me the topic of conversation everywhere.

Having heard the *President Madison* was arriving I was at the dock with all my papers. The mate was agreeable to sign me on.

[*Seattle—February 11, 1923.*] I had to work so hard on shipboard that by night I was dead tired and I postponed finishing this narrative till we landed yesterday. It was a great voyage—21,000-ton ship, ten days. I am staying with a friend I made on ship, son of a Lawrenceville man. Love—love—I'm in America—will wire from every stop—Denver and Kansas City.

[*Union Pacific train in Idaho, en route to Denver—Tuesday, February 13, 1923.*] There's no use writing but the impulse to do so is habitual and must be obeyed. I'm so full up with many things and the dubs on this train are so unresponsive looking I've got to write to somebody or bust. Of course, I planned to write on the trip, but the work was so fatiguing, the hours so impossible and noise and constant interruption so confusing, I never got further than started.

We sailed out of Yokohama harbor on a brilliant day. Instead of being high up on the forward deck as on freighters, our quarters were in the bilge of the boat, down a dozen ladders. The very first night we worked till one, getting the forest of booms and numerous hatches in place. I was more dead tired that night than after my Fuji climb. We were pulled out at five next morning and every morning after, and set to work manicuring the decks before the passengers were up. It was cold, very cold, but exhilarating to breathe the salt air. The *Madison* made eighteen to twenty knots an hour. I always got a fierce satisfaction at looking over the side and seeing the foam racing past at 23 miles an hour, day and night, and realizing how fast I was flying home.

There were 250 men in the crew, most of them quartered on the bottom of the ship along with us—and oh, what a despicable lot! It seems the sea enmeshes the scum of scums, makes social derelicts out of them. The captain was a savage old man-eater and, while tyrannical beyond reason and brutal without thought for justice, just the type necessary to keep such scoundrels pulling together under the yoke. I've become the worst autocrat in spirit you ever saw.

Indeed, the *Madison's* crew was a madhouse, speaking a language so debased as to be almost incomprehensible to Mr. Webster. If you have worried about the life I've led the last two years affecting me unfavorably you may find relief in this letter. Instead of debasing me it's refined me. My sense of superiority has been aroused and given a consciousness. Whether happiness follows is yet to be disclosed.

The size of the boat kept us steady enough through three days of terrific weather when the waves were breaking over the decks and spray over the funnel. Even then we worked on the leaward side scrubbing the decks with big limestones and sand. There was lots of painting, window washing and other *brain builders*.

You may know how thrilled I was to see the first lighthouse. It was clear weather, and Rainier and all the other beautiful snow-covered mountains of Washington stood out like Fujiyama. At dusk,

Saturday the tenth, we docked. We men were being paid off next day at two, so I began to get ready—gave or threw away enough oily grimy clothes to start a store.

I called on Mrs. McPherson, widow of the late head-master at Lawrenceville and *what* a powwow we had! I stayed till after one o'clock. She is the grandest old lady I ever saw, about seventy now, but keenly alive, if pathetically lonely without her worshiped husband. She knew me instantly—what I had done at L'ville, who my friends were. It was a reunion of memories. No one, excepting Mrs. Robinson, could have rekindled old, lost, yet beloved Lawrenceville memories as she did. When I finally left she took my hands in hers and said what I knew was true, that it had been one of the most memorable nights, the most Lawrencevillian, most Dr. McPhersonesque nights since she left Foundation House.

At Portland I went to the *Oregon Journal* and met the feature editor, a friend and admirer of Mr. Mooney—so much so that when I said Mr. M. had published some three score of my yarns, he bought my story without *even looking at it* for thirty-five dollars. So my purse began to regain its self-respect—my money from the *Advertiser* in Japan and the fifteen dollars I earned at sea and this new thirty-five. I bought a ticket to Denver.

Richard sold a story in Denver to an editor to whom he was introduced by Governor Sweet, and then went on to Kansas City where he was greeted by Mike and the other Hockadays. Mrs. Hockaday, with motherly compassion, patched and darned and cleaned him up till he was more presentable. With the proceeds of a story sold there he bought a ticket to Memphis, and completed the last stretch of the road that had led him around the world.

When the "books" were audited and a balance struck, it was found that Richard had earned about three hundred dollars more than he had spent on his vagabond journey. This was immensely stimulating to him and inspired him with confidence in himself as nothing else could have done. He now had a mass of manuscripts, notebooks and photographs from which would emerge his first book, *The Royal Road to Romance*.

CHAPTER IX

FIRST VENTURES AT LECTURING

THE surge and urge that drove him around the world had not abated in the least. The quietness of home life allowed him to relax from the tensions of the previous months. During this interlude he did not seek public places, he avoided any attitude of young hero, his social contacts were intimate. He took long walks with his father, had long talks with his mother. He took regular exercise at the Y. For a month there was little discussion of his next move, but by then it became apparent that he was awakening to the need for fresh action.

In his characteristic manner he called a family council. He acknowledged his great happiness at being home, and his surprise that, so soon, he had begun to feel the symptoms of restlessness. The trail now was to lead him to his greatest adventure yet, in New York. Somehow, that seemed to call for more nerve than climbing the Matterhorn or Fuji! There was no fear of the ultimate result, only the dread of the beginning of the struggle. Anyhow, to sell articles for magazines or manuscripts for books, he felt he should go where they are bought, and that was New York, not Memphis. To this argument, his mother and father lent ready agreement.

So, on the twenty-eighth of April, 1923, with a typewriter, his manuscripts, notebooks, photographs and memories, he fared forth.

On his way to New York Richard stopped at Flint, Michigan, and bought a Buick roadster, which he drove the rest of the way.

[*101 W. 72nd Street, New York—May 10, 1923.*] It's nearing two weeks since I left home. It seems two years and nowhere in the wilds of Asia was I more homesick than I am tonight. No one with whom to discuss what seem momentous problems—only a little garret room with 7,000,000 people outside I don't know, and don't want to.

Things have been galloping since I wrote Monday, mostly dis-

209

appointments. It would seem I'd get used to rebuffs but as yet I've not. Successes give me little satisfaction; failures, real depression. I'm located at the Y. on 57th Street. I put my car in the garage Sunday night and take it out Wednesday morning—price three dollars, a dollar a night, and that's the cheapest in Manhattan.

By noon yesterday my typewriter, stationery and everything were in order. I seized my Gibraltar pictures and went to the Hearst Syndicate for a cordial reception but negative answer. They wanted only scandal and gossip, but they sent me to the *American*. I told the editor I had *all* the dope about Chinese bandits. He wanted my story in three installments and gave me two hours to bring in the first specimen. I was 'way down town and dashed wildly home, wrote a thousand words and had it back on time. Another hard-boiled sub-editor saw me and condescendingly took the first 1000 words for $10.00, threw me out and called off the rest—all without reading it. But it was $10.00 and I'll need all I can make.

This morning I went to the Bell Syndicate and they are all interested. I'm to go back tomorrow and produce samples and pictures for ten articles of about 1500 words apiece. I called on the McClure Syndicate—out.

I saw Doran this afternoon and had a long talk with Captain Fauntleroy's friend. Here was, and is, the blow of blows: It is impossible to get the book out by Xmas unless I have the manuscript ready *now*.

I'm working on Andorra to try to market it with a magazine—less money than syndicates but more noble. I'll know tomorrow.

I had tea with Marie this afternoon. She is more mature, naturally; looks terribly exhausted and no wonder, going the gait she does. We went to the Ambassador and talked so hard we forgot to dance.

Things are coming to a head so fast I can scarcely digest it all. Dad, I get such stimulation and gratification from your letters. Don't let a week go by without one for they have become a sort of anchor for me. The best thing, the thing that helps all the rebuffs, is the joy I take in my work. My fingers itch to get at the typewriter. *We'll* get there yet—you and Mother and I. Who and what can resist our united determination!

Richard finds part of the Glory that was Greece in the ruins of the Temple of Zeus.

Athens crowned by the Acropolis. This picture, taken from one of the heights to the east of the city, is referred to on page 387.

For a while now his letters were recitations of his daily contacts and contests with editors and publishers and lecture managers and others to whom he hoped to sell his wares. It is patent that he lacked co-ordination, and there was no one at hand sufficiently sympathetic to direct his efforts.

[Y.—*Monday night, May 14, 1923.*] This is a picture of your son in New York, simply spinning! Time flies so fast I can't keep up

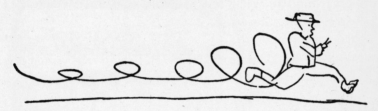

with the days. I've been on the crest and in the dumps as encouragement and bumps come my way. To date I've made only $10.00, but I've "prospects," like the man who promised to pay his board bill when he sold his book which he was going to write as soon as he had the inspiration.

The Bell Syndicate encouraged me so I went to Scribner's with my letters and had a most delightful reception from them. The book manager gave me an hour. I talked and inquired and he answered all my questions, advising me by all means to syndicate if I could *now* and get my name advertised, and as soon as possible bring them sample chapters. Well, then I go back to Bell with an I'll-condescend-to-accept attitude and found they'd turned down everything. Oh, but I was sunk! I didn't know what to do next. I've been revamping my Taj and Alhambra stories into what I call "Moslem Nocturnes."

Friday I knocked off work to go to Princeton with Larry. We parked at 41 Patton and my heart skipped about ten beats with emotion. We danced till six and I was surprised how much I enjoyed it. The new dances are really lots of fun.

I typed all yesterday; then, feeling very lonely and stuffy, I got dressed and motored out to the Keyes'. It's glorious on Long Island and the Keyes always stimulate and dust me off.

Today I went to Scribner's and handed in my "Nocturnes" and

"Don Quixote, Jr."; to McClure's again, in vain; to Brentano's and got ensnared for two hours. There were books, books, books, books— 10,000 authors—dozens doing what I'm doing. I must do it *better*. Then, back to McClure's, for a hospitable reception. The editoress is delightful and was *very* enthusiastic about my pictures and adventures. *But* it's just like the Bell case, I'm afraid, where the editor was enthusiastic, too. I'll hear Thursday and from Scribner's in ten days. Tomorrow I begin to get my *Geographic* material in shape—Fuji and Bali. I'll take my Gibraltar pictures down, too. They would interest Mr. Grosvenor.

[*Sunday night—May 20, 1923.*] I wish I could start with a row of exclamation points to indicate that events of great import are to be told, but, darn it, such is not the case. The McClure Syndicate followed the lead of the Bell—great encouragement and then regrets. I was never so deflated. Scribner's sent back my Taj article: "skillfully written"—*but*. I've one more big trump card to play, the *Geographic,* and I'm leaving in half an hour for Washington. I'm preparing my sample chapters for Scribner's. I've decided definitely on a name at last. It's appropriate, it's catchy and it's *non*-travelish: *The Royal Road to Romance. Wanderlust* just won't do.

Marie and I motored to Allentown Friday afternoon and came back Saturday morning. Spring weather and Jersey roads! The Buick works better every day. Your fine long letter, Dad, cheered me up tremendously. If it weren't for letters and some social diversions I'd ossify! I typewrite in my sleep as it is.

[*Y.—Wednesday night, May 23, 1923.*] Mother, I really smiled out loud over your suggestions about Marie and me. We had a jolly sociable time on the Allentown trip and I enjoyed it no end. She talks about her "Bill" and I talk about my book. Isn't that amorous? I haven't time for any amorousness.

Well, I've *been* quite a bit already since I wrote last—to Washington and back. A Mr. Franklin Fisher is the head who accepts or refuses manuscripts for the *Geographic*. I spent *two* hours and had a glorious time. He called for the material and requested me to let him keep the Bali manuscript for further examination. Then came Fuji.

He said, "Only last year I bought an article on climbing Fuji in summer," but thought it might be possible to run the summer climb and winter climb side by side. Then we looked through my odds and ends of pictures and he took eight, one of Gibraltar, one of Carcassonne, three of Vladivostok and three of Japan. We got along fine. It may be a month before I hear.

That off my chest, I went out to see the Lincoln Memorial. It's too impressive for words—one grand sweep from the Capitol to the Monument to the Memorial to the river, all in line. It's as majestic as the Louvre-to-Arc de Triomphe panorama. Washington was beautiful as I've never before seen it, all in spring clothes.

I wrote my preface to *The Royal Road to Romance*. I'm going to write a first chapter, collect my pictures and descend on Scribner's again.

[*Y.—Wednesday, May 30, 1923.*] I abominate this life but it's necessary, perhaps for two weeks more. Things have gone *so* much more slowly than I hoped for. I get terribly impatient at the way my book is progressing. New York *has* been inhospitable. It's every man for himself here. They trample on those that fall down, but by no means have I fallen down. Things are very much *up* at present. My enthusiasm has been given an awful crack or two but that only makes it stubborn.

A letter came from the *Geographic* saying they were "considering carefully" my stories. Such letters help. Last Wednesday I went to the Pond Lecture Agency. They threw me out—*too late* for anything next season, would talk to me about the *following* season.

Then I went to the Feakins Agency. He was willing to listen. We went to lunch and looked over my pictures. Mr. Feakins said he could do nothing till he heard me speak; so I rushed back to the Y. where there is a talk given in the lobby every night, and got permission to have the floor next Tuesday night (yesterday). Then he had to leave town and I couldn't change the date, but his son and partner in the bureau was on hand and seemed favorably impressed. It was the worst ordeal I ever endured. The lobby is huge; people were passing and talking and sitting and departing, a piano banged in the reading room, and a bagpiper advertising something or other stopped outside to compete with me. It was almost impossible to hold contact and, in consequence, it was *not* an impressive talk.

Well, that's the lecture part. Mr. Feakins kindly sent me to the *Boy Scout Magazine* and I *may* have dropped into a career in consequence. The editor listened attentively, looked at my pictures and articles and, after talking to me for an hour, suddenly said: "You are just the man we want. You dropped from Heaven to answer a serious call for just such a person." He made a luncheon engagement with me for Monday at the Algonquin to meet higher-ups.*

Friday I left early in my car for Hoosac—straight up the Hudson to Albany, then northeast to the Vermont border, nearly 200 miles. It was a most beautiful ride. Henry's† school is ideally located in this lovely, green, mountainous, cultured country. The boys are picked with care and a finer lot I never saw. I talked to them for 45 minutes. That was why I went, to get practice before Tuesday. So you see how busy I've been, and I see no relief for some time. Every spare moment is put on the book.

[*Y.—Monday, June 4, 1923.*] Well, I wrote you what a miserable speech I made at the Y. I reported at Feakins' Thursday. He was back, and his son said he realized how hard it was to do one's best at the Y., and recommended one thing or another. I was simply sick. But I didn't give up. I was sent to a Mr. Powlison, President of the Child Welfare Association of America, to get another place to speak. He was all hospitality and accommodation and said he could get me a *dozen* places. The first offer was at an Orphan Asylum! The sooner the better; so I took it and invited Powlison and persuaded Mr. Feakins to hear me. He *had* to be on hand. The talk was 7:30 at "Sheltering Arms." Two hundred waifs from five to fifteen years old. Powlison and Feakins sat in the back, two competent, hard judges. I *had* to make good or wait a year to lecture. The kids were a tough lot, but I threw myself into it. I told the wildest stories in my repertoire. I acted them out. I knew I had them, for not a

---

* This Boy Scout proposal seemed to offer great possibilities for lecturing, traveling and some motion-picture work. Richard was encouraged to follow it up for a period of two months or so. There were many conversations, but it finally developed that the scheme was too ambitious and had to be abandoned.

† The teacher he had known at Lawrenceville.

person moved. Their eyes were big as saucers, and I saw that Feakins saw *that*. At the end there was uproarious applause. Powlison rushed up and said it was the best talk he'd ever heard made to children. He insisted I come to his office. "I want you in *my* work," he said. Feakins was obviously pleased.

I drove Powlison* down to 14th Street and then Feakins back to his hotel. He talked about everything else but what I wanted, but he told me to come to his office today.

From 8 A.M. till midnight yesterday I worked hard and got a chapter done. I am going to the Ritz to a dance tonight, friends of the Keyes. I've been to the theater once and the movies once. I have neither time nor money for such. My garage bill was $15.00.

[Y.—*Wednesday, June 13, 1923.*] Well, my dear Dad, if I'm an imaginary son, being so far away, here's something to whet your imagination on. I landed my lecture bureau at last and have got my first engagement for next fall! It's only a $25.00 engagement but it's a *start* and that's the vital thing up here in this cauldron of competition and exaction. It was a long, hard struggle to overcome Feakins' indifference. Dogged perseverance won the day. We're working on circulars now.

I took fourteen of my sample chapters to Scribner's Monday and will hear tomorrow afternoon. Someway, I'm very calm about it. I've so much on my mind and had so many rebuffs that one more won't concern me. It will add the necessary incentive to my writing.

I had an amazing experience Monday. I woke up absolutely broke, not five cents. My garage bill, my trip to Hoosac and necessary clothes had eaten up my last dime, so I had to get busy. I took my pictures to the syndicates and was thrown out; same thing at the *Times* and *World*. I took my "Pure Prom" cartoon to *Life* and *Judge*—same thing. But at the *Tribune* I had better luck and sold four pictures for $40.00. The magazine section took the cartoon for $25.00 more. So I am in funds again.

You are quite right about distractions hurting my book, yet this

---

* Richard was introduced into the Child Welfare Association by Mr. Powlison. Like the Boy Scout movement, it occupied an appreciable amount of his time and thought for a while, but he finally decided that the work would not be to his liking.

lecture business is vital. I'm going to Princeton Saturday to reunion and to look around for a room. If Scribner's takes me on, I can leave New York very satisfactorily, though the circulars must be finished, too.

[*New York—Monday, June 18, 1923.*] I picked up *Travel* tonight, July number, and it's *there!* Malay. 4300 words and five pictures. Quite splendidly illustrated. I'll pile down to the editor's office and collect before the check goes home.

Mr. Walter Armstrong very kindly sent me the literary supplement to a London *Times,* dealing with travel books. The phrase "trivial diary of a globe trotter" was not without its effect on me. *That* I *musn't* have.

I often look out my window and shake my fist at the New York skyline and soundly damn the entire place, yet harsh taskmasters develop careful and determined students.

[*Y.—June 19, 1923.*] Thanks a lot for the check. Along with it came a much-needed word of encouragement. I needed that worse than the check. Scribner's turned me down and, of course, I was rather blue. They spent three hours telling me why and offered such constructive criticism that I was glad, almost, that I'd failed there. They shied at the "youthfulness and immature style." I may fail several times again, profiting and improving each time, until at last I have a finished product.

I'll be ready to tackle the next publisher in a few days; then while he's reading I'll turn my attention to endless other imperative things. Lawrenceville has booked me for December fifteenth at $100.00.

Saturday I motored to Princeton. Instead of motoring home, I motored into a garage and put it *in storage* till I get down there.

[*June 25, 1923.*] Things certainly have been humming lately though I don't seem to be getting anywhere. The *Geographic* sent back *everything*—too much copy about Bali and Fuji on hand. They wished to buy twenty pictures at $2.50 per, but I won't take it. I took my final draft for a big six-page folder with illustrations down to Feakins for his visé. I bowed to his insistence on a photograph for advance advertising—had some taken today and tried to look as ancient and worldly as possible.

Everyone, including Scribner's, says, "Develop your action and leave philosophy to Plato." *The Royal Road to Romance* is getting day by day more lightly active and less thought provocative. Perhaps that is best for the first book. Obviously, it's the only way for me to *get* a first one. I'll save my philosophy for later on.

With the circular off my hands, I can turn all my concentration to the book. A first chapter, and Matterhorn, Gibraltar, Taj, Kashmir and Ladakh, Angkor, parts of Bali, Fuji are the only chapters I'm going to submit to the Century Company. My first chapter is about to drive me demented. Everything at a publishing house depends on that. It's all Scribner's read. Perhaps I won't have one; start off with Chapter Two.

Yes, Dad, lecturing *has* been in my mind for a long time. I've always had a feeling I could talk in public if I could ever let go and lose myself but I never dared let go. My Feakins experience of talking in public gave me the first assurance I could do what I'd always half felt I could.

About the middle of July his mother and father met Richard at Princeton and rented the home of one of his friends until September. The three took delightful short motor trips. Richard went regularly to the college gym and enjoyed an abundance of good health and spirits. Except for an occasional run up to New York, he devoted himself to his book. Now for the first time he arranged the chapters into a running story. His Buick was the subject of a family council and the verdict was guilty. His parents drove it home.

[*New York but in Princeton yet—September 13, 1923.*] You know exactly what I've been doing since you left—the same as before, only lonesomely. We had such a good time, the *best* we ever had, together. I used to lie awake nights on my trip and long to be situated just as we've been here in Princeton.

I'm going to New York tomorrow to see *Asia* magazine. I've worked hard and consistently all week, and gone to bed at the stroke of twelve every night. It's fine living so close to meals; I just slide down the banister to breakfast. I'm to get paints for Mrs. Lawrence (the artist) in New York, so she can carry on with the lecture slides. The librarian is drawing my maps.

I dissipated Saturday night. There was a block dance on the street just under my window. I couldn't possibly work, so I went.

[*Address me New York—September 15, 1923.*] Thursday night Mrs. Lawrence and I showed our slides again. They are enormously improved and really very beautiful. The three maps are finished. When she finishes the paint job, then I'll travel to Philadelphia myself and sit till the mounting is done and bring them back in a *box!* I'm not going to New York till that's done.

Oh—what else do you think? The editor of *Asia,* his wife and I spent yesterday evening together. He's Princeton, 1906; she, Smith, 1910. I showed them my pictures and we had a regular powwow. He bought my good picture of Fuji. It's nice to know any editor intimately.

[*Princeton—September 17, 1923.*] Good news came along with your letters. Mr. Huff of the Philadelphia Forum writes, "Thank you heartily for the article. It will do splendidly and I shall use it in the November issue. It looks as though I had two dates for you— Germantown and Wyncote. I expect to have more later." Before we sent Angkor there was only *one* date. He sent me a fine letter to Mr. Froelich of *Asia,* with whom I was breakfasting when it came.

I *must* make enough to support me in the Princeton Club neighborhood and atmosphere. My self-respect is not so infallible that it is not affected by surroundings. I want to give it all the stimulation I can afford.

[*Princeton—September 22, 1923.*] You remember my speaking of Cecil Crouse? He and I were very good friends in Princeton. I met Irene Richardson through him. The other day he wrote that he was going to New York and wished to know if I had settled my plans for living there. I wired back that I would be delighted to room with him. Cecil is the best amateur pianist I've ever known, but I do not believe we'll have a piano. I hope not. It was *his* Princeton orchestra that played at the Savoy Hotel in London one summer.

A letter from the Century Company says please name the hour and the book editor will be delighted to lunch with me.

The last set of pictures came yesterday from Mrs. Lawrence. Monday I'll take the entire lot to Ran at Philadelphia, fight out our troubles and see that they are properly mounted.

[*114 East 39th—October 2, 1923.*] This is my latest portrait. You see I'm in New York at *last!* And I'm much happier than I thought I'd be.

I went back to Philadelphia Friday and my slides were ready, *beautifully* mounted. I bought a neat little leather  case for them. It holds 140 and weighs two tons when full, but I won't have to carry more than half of them.

When I got to New York Sunday evening, lugging my damned typewriter and the two-ton slides, I found the room waiting and Cecil established. He is a magnificent roommate, light-hearted, lovable. He's a member of the Princeton Club. My name comes up October eighth.

Feakins had good news for me: Kansas City, January seventh and eighth ($150.00 for two); St. Louis, January 9, ($100.00). Nellie Green gets me to Westover at $100.00. A friend in Taft School sent a contract to be filled out at $75.00. I'll go to Shady Side on my way home from Pittsburgh at $35.00. The circular is worth its weight in gold. So far we have $1160.00. I'm going to throw all my efforts with Feakins.

[*New York—October 15, 1923.*] An acceptance from Culver ($100.00), and three how-much-and-when inquiries, so you see how cheerful I feel this morning. I have just come back from Feakins' office and he's cheerful, too, about *my* working so hard.

Tuesday evening after Cecil and I had dined at the Princeton Club, where I'm now a member, I met Mr. Henry at the Manhattan Opera House and saw Pavlova dance her "Oriental Impressions." They were beautiful, but tiresome—as Oriental dances *are*.

A letter this morning from Dr. Pahlow* said he would be glad to introduce me at Doran's, where I already know Mr. Overton, thanks to Mr. Fauntleroy and Hamlin Garland. It may be as good a house as any.

I'm wonderfully well. I still have trembly spells but it's *not* physical exhaustion; it's nervous. Once I'm organized and going I'll calm down, maybe, but I'll never reach the "even tenor."

I am not so sure, Dad, it's any advantage to keep on too intimate terms with the ordinary things in life. I had nothing *but* ordinary things for eighteen months and they developed in me a fierce hatred for them. The closer I am to the "angels" the happier I'll be.

I *am* getting a bit nervous as the time draws near for my lectures. Success is so vital but, as before, I'll *not* miss it.

[*New York—October 23, 1923.*] My début at Mr. Henry's school, Cathedral Choir, was about 80 per cent successful. I had great luck in the opportunity to use it as the goat. The room was small, the boys (from nine to fourteen) receptive, the whole occasion easeful and intimate. I saw my pictures, experimented with time and lights. The talks and stories were effective because I had the complete attention of the audience. The little fellows have no sense of repression and talk to you and meet you with surprising frankness and sincerity. I always come away from the place strangely stirred. They are all just babies and *crave* affection. If you give them the slightest encouragement their arms are about you in a flash.

Well, I learned from that evening's talk that I must cut, *cut, cut*. My next is Ogontz, Wednesday evening, October 31, and before then I must write out my entire lecture.

The Pahlows want me to speak at the Ethical Culture Club and I shall, on November sixth or eighth. It's gratis but a brilliant lot of students. It will give me experience. Don't worry about Destiny choking off the book. I'll choke Destiny first.

[*New York—October 30, 1923.*] I never realized it was really fall till you wrote me about it. One never sees a tree in New York. Cold,

---

* Dr. E. H. Pahlow was a professor at Lawrenceville while Richard was there. He and his wife were devoted friends of Richard from then on.

hot, wet, dry—all seems the same to me. How I crave Princeton. Speaking of that idyllic little town, I spent Saturday afternoon and Sunday there, chiefly to see Professor Kennedy, but also to see a tree.

[*New York—November 5, 1923.*] I paced the floor Tuesday night rehearsing "Young Ladies!" etc. Wednesday at two I left for Ogontz—a perfectly beautiful place; one of the teachers took me all over it. I dined at the head table with Miss Sutherland, and a cold reception I got. She was indignant that such a *child* had been sent down upon her and wouldn't speak to me for several minutes. You can imagine how comfortable I felt, gaped at by 200 flappers. Her first remark was, "*Well,* I *must* say you are the *youngest* lecturer that has ever spoken at Ogontz." I replied that I hoped to be worthy of that *distinction.* I had more than usual difficulty to get going; and then, confound it, once I got going I couldn't stop. They applauded tumultuously, nevertheless, and I'm sure Miss Sutherland felt I'd given them her money's worth.

She said afterward she knew the girls had enjoyed it, *but,* while she had been entranced, herself, she felt almost two hours was too long to remain even in *that* state.

At five Saturday I went to tea at the Plaza with Emily Keyes and another couple. Cecil is discouraged and means to go home to Philadelphia. I'm longing to get at my book but this very morning Mrs. Watson, my delightful friend of Carcassonne, telephoned so persistently that I dine there tonight that I gave in and at four must get going.

Don't you worry, my sweet Mother, about Gails and Tesses and Barbaras. People are necessary to me now. I've *got* to mix with them.

[*New York—November 12, 1923.*] Thursday I appeared at the Ethical Culture School as the guest of Dr. Pahlow, who received me with the courtesy only he is capable of. My audience was about 400, I talked 25 minutes, they seemed to enjoy it, and today I received a letter from the class president requesting me to come back.

And then Saturday! Cecil and I went together to Princeton by train. *What* a sight! Fifty-five thousand people packed into every nook and crack. Glorious sunshine, riots of orange on the Princeton side, splashes of crimson on the Harvard. We lost five to nothing but the crowds and cheering and exhilaration were unforgettable. I went to Cap and Gown and saw Heinie and Dot and Larry.

I had my lecture at the Newark church the next night. There was room for 700 and 200 *stood*. There was a special program for Armistice Day that lasted an hour, the worst hour of agony I ever went through. My heart pounded, my hands went cold. One thing followed another: choir, community singing, prayer, announcements. Such suspense is killing but once I got started I was absolutely at ease, more so than I've ever been. I had a responsive audience, my stories were appreciated. The experience was worth many times the $15.00 I received. And there won't be much income tax to pay at this rate.

[*New York—November 18, 1923.*] For the first time in my lecture career, I talked, Wednesday evening, without stage-fright—at an enormous Boys' Club here in the slums. They were young and responsive so it was real fun after the distracting stage-fright I went throught at the church in Newark. Lecturing is a tempestuous, nerve-racking business. I went alone to Brooklyn on Saturday, and Lord, what a crowd!—2000 people, *packing* the auditorium, but they had not come to hear me, rather to see the Jackie Coogan movie which followed. Everybody in Brooklyn was there, from squirming four-year-old brats to sensitive old ladies who looked sour as lemons and were shocked at my lively stories. It was an *impossible* audience. As I walked on the introducer said, "One hour! Not a minute over." Seeing the clock hand approaching the fatal three-thirty, I hurried too much and fell back into inarticulation. There was applause when I left the stage, but a roar when Coogan took it.

[*New York—Saturday night, December 1, 1923.*] I believe more has happened to me in the past week than in any other week I've ever lived. Each week I think is the climax but it's always flat compared to the following one.

There was a prom the night after the Lawrenceville lecture. I was delighted to hear it as I knew the girls would be there from various schools and could carry home the idea. My talk never went better, one hour and fifteen minutes with *no* pictures. The boys applauded with long and sincere enthusiasm. Dr. Abbot was obviously pleased, said it was the best talk of the year and invited me back next year. He put his arm through mine and escorted me to the prom as his guest. The boys were wonderful to me. I met everybody and had the time of my life.

Back to New York Monday to attend a banquet at the Astor Hotel in honor of Sir Hugh and Lady Poynter. He had been lecturing at Town Hall on Kipling, Baldwin, Burns-Jones.

Wednesday night I dressed and went to a coming out party at the Ritz—2000 people there—a terrible writhing mob. Next day was Thanksgiving. I went out to Larry Keyes'.

I'm inclosing one of Feakins' new circulars. Please note where your son's name is—*first* among the newcomers and sixth on the entire list. It was 45th at first.

[*Back from Buffalo—Wednesday night, December 5, 1923.*] Too bad we couldn't be together last Thursday, but at that we were about 10,000 miles closer than we were a year ago, when I was in Shanghai. Strange, that word seems as foreign to me almost as it ever did. The entire trip is losing its realism and becoming fiction, and my book is still unwritten.

I spent Monday getting ready for Buffalo. It was to be my most exacting audience, and I had to be at my best. It was pouring down rain at lecture time, so I had not more than 100 in the audience—very close to me, intimate and intelligent. A reporter was there for an afternoon paper. He brought me home in his car. He was going wanderlusty himself, so I expect an enthusiastic report. A dozen old ladies and gents came up to congratulate me after the speech and several asked me to go home with them, but I was set on getting back here. The $100 was most acceptable. My investment is about to pay dividends.

Richard went home to Memphis for three weeks in the Christmas season. He thoroughly enjoyed himself, but it was quite evident to his parents that he had been going on his nerve for too long a stretch and they urged him to take the strain of lecturing more easily.

[*New York—January 21, 1924.*] Whew! and gosh! This is the first moment I've had to myself since we said goodbye nine days ago. All went along smoothly and pleasantly with my St. Louis and Kansas City lectures. I found Culver beautiful and efficient; stayed at the hotel overlooking the lake and could see the cadets skating on the ice. Some 300 turned out to hear me. General Gignilliat is most distinguished and delightful. I showed the pictures after my talk and they seemed thoroughly enjoyed. Monday morning I walked over the grounds, and spoke again in the gym, to the whole gang—about 800. I was limited to 35 minutes. The short speech was ten times more effective than the long one. I shall always remember Culver pleasantly.

Arrived at Ann Arbor, I took a taxi to Shorty's. Harriet was waiting for me in the cutest, newest house you've ever seen. Shorty arrived shortly after and we had a most delightful reunion. I've never talked so much in a month as we talked those three days.

New York, Saturday morning, straight to Feakins' office to find four new engagements. With these signed up I won't be far from $2500. Watch it hit $3000. Feakins was in great good humor.

Froelich of *Asia* had not yet read my story, but he received me cordially, nevertheless, and *what* do you think? He asked me to be *Secretary* to the Asiatic Society of America, the society that sent Roy Chapman Andrews to Mongolia and that publishes *Asia*. He had heard about my *Pictorial* success and wants me to do the same sort of thing for the magazine and society. I would work on part time only. The salary is only $120 a month. I thanked him and asked for a week's consideration. I know, however, what I shall say—No! I can do *nothing* on part time. I've got to give a thing all *my* enthusiasm or nothing.

You may be sure, Dad, I'm awake to the condition of my nervous system and shall do all I can—chiefly by leaving undone all I can—to restore it.

[*New York—Sunday, January 27, 1924.*] I'm back "home," tired and sleepy but enormously satisfied and happy and encouraged.

The head-master at Exeter was out but the second in line, a grand old man, ex-senator from New Hampshire and new dean of the

school, asked me to tea with him and for a walk over the frozen snow.
My audience was not just the boys but everybody, about 200 students,
some 500 in all. I did only fairly well, was exceedingly nervous for
some reason and had great difficulty in controlling my articulation. I
can never explain or understand the variations in my stage presence.
One night I am cool as ice, composed, unfaltering, and the next
night the lecture creaks and groans. I got applause, but I had that
sickening sensation that comes of doing only half one's best.

I asked about daily chapel and jumped at the invitation to attend
at seven-thirty next morning. During the night it snowed *two feet*
and we had to plow through it. The dean and I sat on the platform
with 750 boys, fine, clear-eyed fellows, before us. The leader asked if
I would say something, but I declined—I'd had no breakfast—but
when services began the first move was for the boys to raise the roof
with united applause—for *me!* It's a custom. Every visitor, distinguished enough to rate the platform, is honored by the "Exeter
Greeting." It *was* stimulating. So I changed my mind, and said I
would talk, and I certainly *did,* vigorously and briefly—five minutes—to efface the botch of the evening before. I was introduced as
an ambassador from Lawrenceville, and I believe it was the best
speech I ever made, chiefly because I was angry at myself. The response was wonderful.

Mr. Keep, the head-master at Farmington, met me at Hartford
and drove me the twelve miles to his school. He and his wife were
the quintessence of courtesy, but kept every student miles away from
me. They gave me not the slightest chance even to *see* a girl. I dined
alone in a huge, empty dining room. My audience was close, eager
and giggly. I laughed as much as they did. *Everybody* had a picnic.
I tried to stop twice, but there were shouts of "No," "Go on"—so I
did to everybody's amusement. If every lecture could be like that one
my life would be a riot of joy. I reveled in it. But even then, Mr.
Keep would not allow me to meet any of his darlings, except the
three Memphis girls, Miss Mann, Miss Summerville and Miss
Mallory, who asked to be introduced and with whom I was permitted
to converse for a few minutes.

I slept like a rock that night. I reached Waterbury at noon. Mr.
Taft, brother of William Howard, had confused my train but sent

his limousine after me. He met me with the utmost cordiality, escorted me to my quarters in his house and made me feel royally at home. He is a gaunt, disarming, Lincolnesque figure, exceedingly human and simply worshiped by the boys. I do not wonder. The school is charming, only a third as large as Exeter. Burn Carter, my Princeton (1922) friend and clubmate who got me the engagement and at whose house I would have visited had they not had a two-day-old baby, took me to lunch. He has just written a book, fiction, philosophical and introspective rather than dramatic. In the afternoon we braved the zero blizzard and went for a frigid walk, talking about books and Princeton and careers.

Now I'm back and with every possible and probable debt paid I'll have over a hundred dollars left and the slate clean.

New York—January 31, 1924

Mudder:—

I've been gone from you *nineteen* days and I am lonely. Sometimes when I feel unusually depressed or unusually elated, without any immediate cause, I get terribly homesick for you—and tonight is one of those times.

I've not been idle since last I wrote. Monday I was off to Philadelphia again—got me a room, dressed and was met at Norristown by the club president. Mr. Huff got me this engagement. The ballroom was packed. I did not stand on the stage, but down on the floor—more intimate. To my surprise I *never* received better attention and scored a *complete* success. Half the audience must have come up to speak to me. Now I'm prepared to address any audience on earth. I'll land the Philadelphia Forum next year and the New York Town Hall and the United States Senate, maybe.

Once back, Sunday afternoon, I've *eight* uninterrupted days and I shall certainly put them to good use on my book as it's the longest stretch I have.

[*New York—Thursday, February 7, 1924.*] Woodrow Wilson has been the all-pervading, omnipresent personality here in New York since his death. The papers have contained nothing else, and all,

Rugged and rocky and desolate beyond belief was Richard's description of the Isle of Skye, in the Hebrides.

While waiting for his breakfast at Chichen-Itza, Richard acts as nursemaid
for an Indian baby, whose cradle is a box.

without exception, pour forth endless tribute. Yesterday I had lunch with Irene Richardson and at three we went to Madison Square to take part in the Commemoration Ceremony. There were 10,000 people packed into the auditorium—addressed by a number of eloquent speakers, John W. Davis, Dr. Fosdick, Rabbi Wise and others. It was most impressive to see all New York stop still at 3 P.M., and all pedestrians stand uncovered for a moment. New York is the coldest-blooded place on earth, usually, yet no other city can be as emotional when the occasion arises.

Fortunately I'd persuaded a boy named Van Cleve, junior and Cap and Gowner, to accompany me to Hill where he'd gone six years. We passed through Phoenixville,* Dad, en route to Pottstown, and I thought of you as I looked out over the big steel mills there. Hill is delightful. Van and I dined alone, as I wished to tax my strength as little as possible. Mrs. Edwards, the head-master's wife, was my very gracious hostess. I can't say I was at my best.

Yes, Dad, there's too much "even tenor" to the Bali article as published in the *Forum,* but I'll *un*even it for the book.

[*New York—February 21, 1924.*] This is going to be a happy letter, for nothing but good things have happened since last I wrote.

I had an eventless trip to Boston and Lowell, but a most eventful engagement. I had not had the slightest idea how big or how many. The manager said no one would introduce me—just walk out and begin. There was a flare of footlights and searchlights. The stage was big as the Metropolitan. I couldn't see anything at first but things cleared presently and I saw a *sea* of faces—*4500* people—*every* seat taken. It was a most astonishing sight, and thrilling. The lecture went along beautifully, and the pictures. I knocked over the water pitcher in the dark, which pleased the audience mightily.

At Poughkeepsie, I attended the Vassar prom with Martha Love. It was lots of fun. I've never seen so many fat girls. Everybody was *too* healthy.

Tuesday, again, was a rare experience. I met the two Keyes girls

---

* It was at Phoenixville that his father had worked in the Bridge and Iron Company's office.

in Jersey City at noon and they took me to their convent. The twenty nuns cramped my style at first, but as they giggled and unbent, so did I. The girls were from six to eighteen—a rather hard variety. Everyone had a *grand* time, including me. The abbess was as human and gracious as anyone I ever saw. We were friends immediately.

Yesterday I dined with Henry at a near-by restaurant. We went to *The Show-off*, a Main Street comedy at which we laughed till we ached. After, we went to the drawing room of George Gaul, an old friend of Henry's and a Lawrenceville boy, now playing the leading rôle in *Seventh Heaven*, which is in its second year. We then had supper at the Algonquin. Mary Pickford and Doug sat next to us. They held hands for an hour.

[*New York—Thursday night, February 28, 1924.*] My musical critic friend, Alan Houghton, asked me to the dress rehearsal of *The King of Lahore* at the Metropolitan. It proved exceedingly interesting—not the opera so much as the audience.

Cecil is gone. Irene Richardson and I decided to mourn his loss over the supper table. She's very merry company and we sat till after ten.

Tuesday night I went with Houghton to the Metropolitan to see the American Ballet, and Wednesday night with him again in the same wonderful seats for *Samson and Delilah*. A more beautiful and thrilling opera I never saw, packed full of glorious music. I walked home on air.

This morning Henry 'phoned me saying he was taking the entire school to *Coq d'Or* at the Met.—had an extra seat. It's always fun with the kids—they're so bright and eager—and all know me from my visits and talks. I helped herd the boys back to school. It seems I'm gadding a lot, four theaters, four operas and a concert in two weeks.

[*New York—Tuesday night, March 4, 1924.*] I've been rehearsing my lecture, for I took a notion it needed pruning for the Philadelphia Geographic tomorrow night. This is the most important engagement of the year, and I must take no chances.

This afternoon being bright and springlike, I had a long walk down Riverside Drive to look at the American Battle Fleet lined along the river. I spent two hours on the *Tennessee*. They are all new and beautiful ships. It quite stirred my wanderlust again.

Dad, you are *exactly* right about this summer being my chance, one and only, for my book. And just watch me make use of it. Once I'm settled and *undistracted* it will just flow along and by August there'll be tons of stories for you to type for me.

[*New York—Sunday night, March 9, 1924.*] I reached Philadelphia at two Wednesday afternoon and went out to see Cecil at Haverford School where he's teaching. He was very much on hand and looking like a man out of jail. I've never seen him so happy. I helped teach one of his classes. It was pouring rain—a vile night for a Geographic Society lecture, but I refused to be dismayed and about 400 people swam to it. They were *real* people, intelligent, traveled, geography lovers. Mr. Bryant, the President, is a trustee of Princeton and introduced me gracefully. He said that every speaker they had, had borne some special distinction and mine was to be their youngest!

When I got back to New York early next morning I hurried down to the Battery and over to Staten Island, and on the *ferry boat* I got more seasick than I've ever been in my life. However, the greeting I got at the Academy cured me. I was sick again on the ferry coming back but I managed to catch the four o'clock train from Grand Central and got to Norwalk before the afternoon was over.

I was dead tired, uncomfortable. A taxi took me to Hillside School where the headmistress had forgotten my engagement—something new on me. And to make matters supremely complex, a basketball game was scheduled for the gym where I was to speak. I was in no mood for this sort of thing anyway. At nine the basketball game was over and I began talking to an assortment of uninterested girls. I cut it short and left for home. Next morning I awoke with a pain in my side, nauseated and faint. I stayed flat all that day and the next day, miserable. But it was fun just lying quiet. Haff spent the afternoon with me yesterday.

[*48 W. 73rd Street, New York—March 19, 1924.*] All right, Mother, I'd rather be a literary figure than a conspicuous politician, or a successful business man. Just now, however, as the end of the season begins to approach, I'm much more concerned with a rest and relief from people, than with being great. May first looms ahead like the pearly gates of heaven. I've eleven more lectures to give.

I am relaxing more and more, and feel steadier than I have since I've been east. George Gaul keeps hammering at me about this. He is a restful person to be with.

I've had a real shock. The 'phone rang the other day and David of Ladakh and Kashmir was on the line—just back from Europe. Of course, I was glad to see him. He has not changed a whit—still looks about fifteen and like the Prince of Wales. I took him out to dinner. We went to Jersey City where I spoke at a men's club.

It takes more than books and time to read, as I'm sure you'll agree, Dad; it takes *mood* above all things. I try to make good my traveling hours with a book, but trains are not conducive to concentration.

[*Wellington Hotel, Chicago—April 1, 1924.*] I went to the most beautiful concert I ever heard, Sunday, conducted by Mengleberg, a Dutchman, with Levitsky at the piano. The orchestra played Dvořák's *New World Symphony* with such expression that everyone walked out in a trance. Music frequently leaves me perfectly cold; Heifetz did the week before, but Mengleberg touched everybody's heart.

I gave a poor talk at West Pittston. When the president first saw me she asked if I had not brought my "poppa." I told her, no, that I'd left him at home to take care of my children.

Akron had been informed of my lecture, through daily publicity, and the ladies had sold 400 tickets and were miserable for fear I'd disappoint them. I gave the best performance yet, cool and calm. They were a *most* enthusiastic and relieved lot of ladies.

To Ann Arbor next day. Shorty met me and took me home to his attractive wife and house. We talked a mile a minute, of course.

After reaching Chicago last night I slept twelve hours and feel fine and rested. The great moment* is at ten o'clock Thursday morning.

---

* An appearance before a meeting of presidents of women's clubs.

[*New York—Thursday, April 24, 1924.*] I gave a very indifferent performance at Gelman and then went to Washington for Sunday, the thirteenth. The Freer Art Gallery is a gem, but disappointing if one cannot appreciate all of Whistler, as I can*not*. The Japanese cherry trees were a riot of color about the lagoon, and everybody was promenading.

One evening last week George Gaul took me to *The Miracle, the* play you must both see when you pass through. The Century Theater has been transformed into a cathedral—well, the entire performance *is* a miracle.

Yesterday I spoke at a small woman's club some ten miles out of Philadelphia. Women are so strange—some were genuinely charmed by my talk, which was short, some were fired to go wandering, some never left the auditorium, and several did not choose to speak to me afterward because I was only a "young tramp" after all.

I had lunch today with Major Vivian Gilbert. He spoke very pleasantly of his Memphis visit, his audience there, and my parents. He's sailing Saturday for England.

May is about here. Before long I go away—away to where? But my circulars are not out, and until they are I can't leave. I'm pounding away at them. The Philadelphia Geographic Society gave me a report in their bulletin that ends by saying, "Mr. H. is blessed with a remarkably fluent vocabulary; he has the youth and enthusiasm necessary for violent forms of travel."

[*New York—Friday night, May 2, 1924.*] I'm home again from Boston. Whee! it's over—and I'm glad. The end was a blaze of glory at the Harvard Club. My best speech was the last one. Tuesday night I spoke at a big barren hall in Boston, "Rogers," to about 300 outdoor lovers, the Appalachian Club. I must have antagonized them somehow. They had little appreciation of the unconventional. The presiding officer had the nerve to report to the Harvard Club chairman that I was *bum*, and so the chairman was long-faced when I made my appearance for the Club occasion. I was dined at the big head table with twelve old grads of the 1872 class, and all through dinner my host kept telling me how hard the chairs got after 45 minutes, and how terrible the acoustics were. I was also permitted to know I was greatly honored to be allowed to speak in the *Harvard* Club, and that their standard was unapproachably high. My audience was the *biggest* of the year—my subject and advance publicity did that— about 300 splendid, cultured gentlemen. But I was hot under the collar when I began. That saved the day. I spat my words at them sharp and crackling. I was determined to make the Appalachian officer ridiculous. I completely lost myself for an hour and a half— displayed more fire and verve than I realized were available. The applause was long. Half the audience spoke to me and said it was the best lecture of the year. As many more congratulated the chairman for his "good choice." If I could be mad *every* time I spoke, I'd soon be famous.

Bob Campbell (of my class at Princeton) had two of his girl friends ready in a taxi by eleven and we four danced at some hotel. Then he and I sat before the fire and talked till dawn broke over the Charles River. I walked to the club where I was staying in broad daylight, strangely happy and relieved that the hardest and most hectic year of my life was over, but realizing it had been a glorious, vivid year withal.

CHAPTER X

RICHARD counted the year as ending with the close of the lecture season, as lecturers do. It was the *start* at lecturing that had made the time so hard and so hectic, and so vivid and exciting, too. With the clearness of his young ambition he had long since, as his letters show, envisaged lecturing as a part of his determined occupation. Travel and adventure "for to admire and for to see, for to behold this world so wide"; authorship; lecturing—these three elements were to make the uneven tenor of his dedicated way. And he *must* succeed with each part. So it was of immense interest and of the most practical importance to him to note the reactions of his audiences. When the response was warm, he exulted. When it was indifferent or adverse, he sought the cause, that he might correct it.

As a matter of fact, the year was not quite over. While he was still struggling to finish his circular for the next season, he was engaged to speak before the Eclectic Club at the Waldorf-Astoria, three hundred "conservative, mature women." He records a hit at this last, the forty-eighth lecture of the trying but "glorious" season.

"There was a gasp when I was introduced. Never before in the club's history had they had anybody like me for a speaker and, as the president said, it was lucky for me she didn't see me before making the contract—she wouldn't have dared employ such a *very young* man. I told her about you, Mother, and your being president of the biggest club in the South. That melted her, and she introduced me as 'Mr. H., the son of,' etc. At the end they cheered, and I had to climb up on the platform four times for 'curtain calls.' I was the guest of honor at the luncheon in the big banquet room. Three other club presidents were there and all three want me for next year—and right here in New York, too. Several of the Eclectic women asked about my book, and they all said, 'If you write it *just* as you speak, it will be perfect.' And that is to be my guide."

233

His lecture folder finished, he left for Siasconset on the island of Nantucket, which he had selected finally, after the uncertainty expressed in his letter of April twenty-fourth, as ideal for work and recreation.

"The boat trip was superb—around the end of Manhattan, under Hell Gate Bridge and down the Sound—bright, sparkling weather. I dumped my trunks straight from the boat onto a truck, sat on top of them, and had myself driven the eight miles across the island—wavery, intensely green, grassy and flowery, but no trees except scrub oaks—to 'Sconset.' I'm going to love the place, I know. It's like nothing I've ever seen—tiny, flower-hidden doll houses, strung along the beach cliffs. I overlook the ocean, so there's nothing between me and Spain."

The room from which he looked over to Gibraltar was in a homely little hotel where he stayed until his acquaintances, the Buckleys, came. He couldn't imagine a more healthful, invigorating climate. He would utilize it to the utmost, he wrote home before the end of May, for his two-fold purpose—"to write, write, write; and to build up reserve strength for next winter. . . . The air is wine and the sun glittering on the moors and ocean, and there are wonderful tramps across the treeless moors. If I can't write a book here, I can't write anywhere."

He stuck to these two ends relentlessly, refused to be distracted by anything else, denied himself society, except to call on Dick Barthelmess and his wife, to dance once or twice at the Casino and to dine with the Froelichs. He kept assuring his parents that he was taking care of his health.

"I'm at the Buckleys' now [June 23rd] and have a delightful room, third floor front, with enough sunshine and breeze and light for a dozen New York apartments. I lie in bed and watch the sun rise out of the ocean, and, through the door, I can watch it set over the moors. I sit at my north window desk and look right down into the blue surf, jump out the window and go bathing on our private beach, get three man-size meals a day in the best house in town, with as nice and agreeable people as there are on the island. The fog and rain are all over. For three days the sun has blazed. I'm holding down everything in my room with weights, lest they blow away into the ocean. The swimming is wonderful. I could write pages about the quality of air and sunshine here."

But, after all, tonic air and exercise were side issues. With that intensity of effort which always characterized him when he had a job to do, he was driving ahead with the book. No one could work harder than Richard Halliburton. He was lost in the world of his royal road, seeking the gay, quick-spirited words, cutting, discarding, getting an easy continuity, waging war on dullness, imparting to the written page the direct effect of personality which marked his lectures. "It's a good thing I have to get up in the morning for an 8:30 breakfast, else I'd never go to bed. I can always work best late at night."

By June second he had done fifty pages of typing. By June eighth a hundred. "The first chapters are the most difficult. Once I'm to the Matterhorn, my troubles are over." By July first he was out of Europe and working on Egypt. "I marvel at the superabundance of my notes. They were a nuisance to keep. I'm happy I stuck to it. My entire trip is there. I shall not lack for material. I gain in fluency every day and in optimism."

On July twenty-first: "I'm moving fast, am about out of India. Malay, Siam and Angkor are nearly complete. I'm absolutely sure to have the first draft by the middle of August and will then have till October fifteenth for rewriting and polishing." On August third he was in Java and Bali. "I see such a vast improvement of style as I go along. The thing I want and must have is *speed*. The reader must dash through the book—not in time but in *spirit*. When it's dull writing, I know it's dull reading, and no matter how vital it may seem, dullness rings its knell."

The relentless absorption began to tell on him. "For nine weeks I've not left my desk. I don't take any heavy exercises or long walks. So long as I'm quiet inside and out I feel—or rather don't feel—anything. The moment I get tired or in a tension the old troubles begin. The more the summer advances, the closer I cling to my wonderful room and delightful work. It's nice being in a shell—I'll break out soon enough in the fall."

But, alas, he broke out of his shell in his next letter.

[*Sconset—Sunday, August 10, 1924.*] This letter is going to give you a bump—and perhaps some satisfaction. It seems that at last I've discovered what it is that's been causing my trembles and debility this past year, and, that being the case, a cure is consequential. Last Monday I motored to New York and got there so tired I was nearly sick. Next day was frightfully hot and I was so exhausted by boat sailing time I could scarcely get aboard. My pulse was beating a mile a minute and I felt very bum in general. The day after I got back (Wednesday) Ammudder came and while waiting for her boat I crawled around to the Nantucket doctor and asked him what the devil was the matter with me. I told him of my extreme nervousness—the abnormal stimulation that kept my pulse beating and kept me so weak I could scarcely wiggle. Without even looking at me he said I had all the *symptoms of goiter*. I asked him to examine my heart. He did and assured me it was as sound as a dollar—neither a murmur, nor overlarge—but exceedingly nervous, in keeping with everything else. There *is* something raising hell with my nerves and it *might* be goiter, though to save my life I can't find any swelling and neither can anybody else.

I'm acting *right now*—going back to New York Tuesday and see a goiter specialist. If he agrees with the Nantucket M. D., I'm going hot foot to Cleveland to Dr. Crile, the best known man in the country for goiter operations. I'll leave everything here and return just as soon as possible. As it is now I won't be able to do anything. The doctor here says goiter always overstimulates. Overstimulated is exactly what I've been for a year without knowing it. You would want to come to Cleveland, Mother dear, and be with me the few days after the operation.

Now if it *isn't* goiter, I'm going straight out to Battle Creek and find out just *what* it is. I felt well enough, no aches or pains, and I look like a purple brick, I'm so sunburned. So long as I was quiet the fatigue didn't bother me. I've really been worrying all along with this absolute rest; it didn't seem to help matters as I supposed it would. So in a way I'm very glad this thing has come to a point in time for me to rectify it. Ammudder being here helped me make up my mind to act. She is very much concerned and is writing you this afternoon. She will go to New York with me.

Well, you know now all I know. I'm not the least alarmed—in fact I'm greatly relieved, and I hope you'll be, too.

This interruption in my book hurts terribly, but it can't be helped—I've been working slower and more laboriously lately and I stopped altogether since August first. I haven't much more to do.

A rather cheerless letter, but there's no advantage in dodging such things. I've been lying on my bed scribbling away here, and it's getting uncomfortable, so I'll stop.

[*Hafford's, New York—Wednesday night, August 13, 1924.*] You, of course, received my telegram and learned what the Life Extension diagnosis is—hyperthyroid. Going there was a very wise move. They examined me from head to foot—blood, urine, eyes, nose, teeth X-ray—found my blood unusually rich—heart sound except very rapid—*no goiter*—but a marked oversecretion of thyroid that gave rise to all my discomfort. They say that there is a very definite treatment and that Battle Creek is the best place. It's very reassuring to know exactly what the trouble is and has been ever since I got home from Japan. It's got to be remedied if my work is to continue, and, as I said in my telegram, now or sooner is the only time to do it. With food consumption normal, more rest and quiet than ever, I've kept getting weaker. It's going to take a positive rather than a negative treatment.

It takes ten days for the full typed report to be delivered, but I can get an oral report tomorrow, and will carry this to Dr. Eggleston at Battle Creek or whoever has me in hand, and we can begin treatment at once. I think in two weeks I can have learned what's what, what to eat and do, and return to Siasconset and *do* it.

Today I'll just lie low and work here at Haff's on my book, which you may be sure I brought along. Please don't be upset about me. When I walked into the Extension Bureau yesterday, they wanted to know what such a healthy-looking person was doing in *there*. Write me at the San.

[*Battle Creek Sanitarium—Saturday night, August 16, 1924.*] The

old familiar paper. I suppose we ought to leave a few of our millions
to the San. out of gratitude. I wired you this morning as soon as
landed. It being Sabbath, Saturday, everything was closed; but I saw
Dr. Eggleston and he had *just* received Dad's letter and was expecting
me. We talked for a quarter of an hour and will go to it in earnest
tomorrow.

I did not greet the San. with much enthusiasm this morning. The
idea of my having to come here at all and having to disrupt my beautiful summer plans nearly kills me. But I'm here and I'm going to
go at getting back to "normalcy" with all the determination I've
gone at everything else. I'm so afraid you're worrying unduly.

Dr. Eggleston is his same gentle self. He said to do nothing but
rest today, so I slept all afternoon and am going home now to rest
some more. I've done exactly the right thing in coming here—should
have done it in May. I've painfully scribbled away at Bali at odd moments during the last week and now am in China. Feakins counted
up $2300 in engagements, so I've *got* to be back on high in time. I told
him to postpone my October 21 date. The next one is not till November 10—thus I gain three more weeks.

The San. orchestra is playing in the lobby (I'm in the foyer), but it
only gives me the blues. I *do* hope you both can run up to see me if
only for a day. I've about starved to death for affection. Glad I've
got my work along—I can hide myself in that, and I shall run along
and do it.

[*Battle Creek, Michigan—Monday night, September 8, 1924.*]
I'm a bum son. Any son is, to go three weeks and not write his lonesome, anxious father. It's not been for lack of interest, Dad, but lack
of permission from Dr. Eggleston. I've not written any or read any
and done my best not to think any—just existed mechanically since I
got here, as that seems to be the remedy for my trouble. The remedy
is remedying slowly.

Here's *good* news though. I've *finished* the first draft of the
Book. I wrote a few pages finale and it was typed last night. This is
one big burden off my chest. I counted up the words and had about
145,000—not so bad as I expected. *Now* I need you, Dad, to help me
cut and prune.

I've written Feakins I fully mean to fill my engagements because I fully mean to be physically able to. It will be a cruel and hateful blow to me if I'm not. But I'll have my complete manuscript to play with and that will be a pleasure indeed. The pictures for the book will be in New York and it will be further pleasure preparing them.

Of course, Ammudder has told you all about everything. How we enjoyed her visit! She practices perfectly a philosophy I read recently that went something like this: "If you would rest, and feel you could rest in some place afar—and can't *get* there—then rest where you are."

Don't get discouraged even *yet*, Dad, about your inability to raise boys. *This* one is going to be a prize winner, despite everything. All this present mess is one more lesson I hadn't learned and needed to.

The "trembles" did not long impair Richard's health or interfere with his working schedule. Having gone at too fast a tempo on too high a key, he must slow down a bit. He did, and though the symptoms recurred at times, he enjoyed, through the rest of his life, a health that carried him over the world on four major trips, and through many bustling lecture seasons.

From Battle Creek he went home and, late in October, he and his father went to New York. There he revised his manuscript while his father kept professional typists busy. By November tenth, all was completed and ready to be submitted again, but in more professional shape than before. The lecturing recommenced.

[*The Drake, Chicago—Monday, 6:00* P.M., *November 10, 1924.*] I'm here, safe and set for the fray.

S'pose you got home from New York smoothly, Dad. I had a quiet night, a leisurely morning of packing, got my slides, checked my trunk and went aboard. We ran into a regular January blizzard upstate and I found Chicago several inches in snow. I'll rehearse a bit tonight and be all ready, and will write you again tomorrow how I get along. Dr. Seabury gave me some nerve exercises which I'm practicing on hard. If I could only follow *all* his instructions, I'd get strong again. Dad can tell you, Mother, what Seabury and I have done. I bitterly regret having to part from him just now, but it had to be. Seabury pounds into my head: "Live by artistry, not by emotion." He says I've lived, lectured, thought, moved, entirely on emotion, until emotionally I'm bled to exhaustion. Now I must live by artistry until my depleted emotional state can recuperate.

Didn't Dad bring home a nice lot of rummage, Mother? You should have seen our clean-up after he and I delivered the Book—pictures, manuscripts, circulars, etc. We tore the old manuscript to pieces, shortened most of the stories, eliminated one or two altogether, had it all neatly retyped, had the whole bound and boxed and mailed to Boni and Liveright, with our prayers and with great relief. If they don't take it, there are others. About a ton of material was discarded and while in the eliminating mood I pounced on my trunk and dragged out clothes I've been carrying around since freshman year at Princeton. It's darn near empty now. With my derby, cane and gloves, I'll look like the Prince of Wales. I must admit I don't tremble so much when I'm well dressed!

I wish I weren't so optimistic about my book. I feel lost without it. But I'll get busy on another right away.

Letters from November 17, 1924, to June 8, 1925, are missing.

During the Christmas visit home Richard decided that since he was getting such a good response from his lectures, and still had faith in finding a publisher for his book in spite of declinations, he would make a second trip out of which new lectures might come and a new book, too. After studying the maps of the world he developed the idea of reliving the life of Ulysses from the fall of Troy till his return to his island home of Ithaca. He devoted most of his spare hours to working out the details of this plan.

At Cleveland Richard finished his lecture dates in the spring of 1925. He had traveled well over the country, fulfilling his engagements without physical distress or discomfort. He had occasional attacks of depression when his manuscript would be returned to him, and would be tempted to chuck it out the window and forget it for good. But a new publishing house would give him new hope.

On his way home from Cleveland it was convenient for him to stop off and call on the publishing house of Bobbs-Merrill. He met some of the editors and continued on to Memphis. He had been at

home but a few days when the following telegram was delivered
to him:

NEW YORK, APRIL 24, 1925.

RICHARD HALLIBURTON
PARKVIEW HOTEL, MEMPHIS, TENN.
ORGANIZATION ENTHUSIASTIC ABOUT YOUR BOOK AND FOR ACCEPTANCE IF
YOU WILL CUT IT. SHALL WE SEND MANUSCRIPT TO YOU OR ARE YOU
COMING NORTH? PLEASE WIRE REPLY.

T. R. COWARD.

Mr. Coward, now president of Coward-McCann, Inc., was at this
time the Bobbs-Merrill editorial man in their New York office. D. L.
Chambers of the home office (Princeton, 1900) had, some little while
before this visit to Indianapolis, seen an announcement in the bulletin
of the Princeton Club of New York that Halliburton '21 would speak
to the members on a certain evening about his travels round the
world. Something in the way the announcement was worded aroused
his interest and he suggested to "Tim" Coward that he go listen, if
they would let a Yale man in. Unexpectedly Mr. Chambers arrived in
New York in time to hear the conclusion of Richard's speech himself.
He and Mr. Coward were quite carried away by it. They had never
heard anyone talk so rapidly or with such contagious enthusiasm.
Afterward Richard told Coward about the book, and he asked to see
the script, which was read both in New York and Indianapolis.

[Lafayette, Indiana—June 8, 1925.] I've never in my life enjoyed
more ten days of pleasant and profitable activity. Indianapolis gave
me a royal welcome. Mr. Howland* is an affable, lovable, understanding gentleman. We worked together beautifully. He's keen
about the book and gave me almost *too* free rein to keep it in the
singing, capricious spirit I value so highly. The jacket and cover were
about ready for my approval. I had a great time "selling" my product
to the salesmen. I talked for half an hour. Five dollars was decided
as the price, and 24 *full* sheets of pictures, printed both sides, 48 in all.
I'm quite satisfied with *that*.

Mrs. Howland is Irvin Cobb's sister and very much of a person-

---

* H. H. Howland, at that time Bobbs-Merrill editor; later editor of the *Century
Magazine.*

ality herself. We dined together Friday night and nearly talked ourselves to death. Mr. and Mrs. Barrett—he was master at Upper House
when I was at Lawrenceville and is now *head*-master of the Indianapolis country day school—motored me all afternoon. I gave the
school's commencement address Tuesday—100 boys and their parents
and friends. I was furiously busy with a hundred details between-
times.

All Thursday in Chicago I worked over movie outfits, and Friday
bought one, tripod, filters, extra films, and everything. It weighs a
ton, but there'll be plenty of coolies to carry it. I had lunch with Philo
Higley and his sister and got into our Ford.* The Higleys live in a
million-dollar house at Hinsdale, Illinois. I had supper with them
and left at midnight for St. Louis for Larry's wedding. Of course I
had a wonderful time. It was the most elaborate wedding I can
imagine—and the hottest. Heinie and Dot and Shorty and Hattie
and everybody were on hand and we had a grand reunion.

Back to Chicago. Philo and I, amid bags and lunches and movie
machinery, set sail Sunday morning. We made about 125 miles after
eleven hours on the road. The old thing about fell to pieces, and it's
in the shop now being patched up for the next spurt to Columbus via
Indianapolis. We *may* get there. But it's free and fun and hot and
breezy, and we don't care. We'll stop at Washington and Princeton.

Any more girls, Mudder?† The days will simply fly till July
fourth and then what a time!

[*Uniontown, Pennsylvania—Wednesday night, June 10, 1925.*]
See—we're in Pennsylvania, much to my surprise. Going is terribly
slow as the darned old Ford is constantly falling to pieces, and this
evening, having climbed up here, is so completely exhausted it may
never get beyond. But we felt the same way about it at Dayton night
before last and at Zanesville last night, so we may survive to New
York. The loss of time is my only concern. We hope to make Wash-

---

* Philo was an old friend. They bought a used Ford to make a trip to New York as a
sort of a lark.

† The missing letters would explain that his mother was sailing for Europe on
Independence Day to chaperone some college girls; that Richard was going on the same
boat and that Roderic Crane of Omaha was going with him for a month or two on this
new "Following Ulysses" trip. "Rod" was a classmate of Richard's at Lawrenceville, and
had gone to Yale when Richard went to Princeton.

ington—200 miles—by tomorrow night. It's all a gamble and really great fun. I'm sunburned, as usual, but used to it. We've no lights and no starter, but we've new tires and that's worth a lot. I haven't had a chance to use my movie machine yet, too pressed for time. Feeling better. Philo and I drive half and half and relieve each other. The roads are perfect, sun bright and country beautiful. I saw Howland for a moment in Indianapolis. So far as I can tell, all's well.

[*The Shelton, New York—Wednesday night, June 17, 1925.*] This is just about the first honest-to-God hour I've had since leaving home quiet enough and alone enough to write more than a one-league letter, and I've been gone three weeks last night.

Here I will stay, looking forward to July fourth as Independence Day in more ways than one. If this Odyssey of mine doesn't lift me I'll be surprised.

Our Ford trip was a pleasant adventure, though we certainly had our troubles. Fortunately we went in a spirit of *expecting* trouble so were not discouraged. The day after Summit the ancient car went to the hospital. A mechanic did *really* fix things and it climbed great mountains like a Packard, while we dashed on to Philadelphia to see Mr. Huff of the Philadelphia Forum. We left Huff's at midnight and made the 35 miles to Trenton in just *one* hour, so you see the old tub was moving. Next morning we stopped at Lawrenceville, watched commencement exercises and came on to the commencement jam at Princeton. The campus was gorgeous. We started on again Sunday noon for New York, and came bumping and rattling down Fifth Avenue to the amazement of all.

An hour with Feakins. To my inexpressible delight Mr. Leopold DeLima, the young man who first helped me with my slides, was in the office more prepared and more eager than ever to push my cause. The circulars were going out fine. Both Feakins and DeLima are most enthusiastic over prospects with the book out. Next to Bobbs-Merrill's New York office, for an hour's talk with Coward and the sales manager. Then to lunch with George Gaul. He's determined to go to Europe and wants to go with me. I can't imagine a more pleasant companion. So he and Rod and I will have cabin 273, a big one, at the end of the boat on *your* deck, Mother. I'm delighted over the arrangement. You'll *love* George. He's staying in France and England three months.

The Shelton, New York—1:00 A.M., July 4, 1925
Dear Old Lonesome Dad:—

In about ten hours more we're off, and when the ship sails down the Bay I'll be thinking about you and hoping you're comfortable and busy and as happy as possible with Mother and me both gone. She came this morning and she and Rod and I had lunch. She's so sweet and charming and I'm so proud of her.

I leave my affairs behind in perfect order. My movie machine is working smoothly. I've read every book in the library on the field, I've lots of notes, a clear vision of what I want and where I must go to get it. I'm properly soaked in Odyssean lore, myths, gods and classic atmosphere, and am eager to get on the ground. Rod and Gaul and I had dinner and got acquainted. We three and Mother's seven are going to have a great time. Intense work, new sights and scenes will work wonders. I'll have all the glamour of my last trip and none of its strain.

CHAPTER XI

IN THE WAKE OF ULYSSES

THE letters that follow until mid-August Richard wrote to his father back home alone in Memphis.

[*Paris—July 17, 1925.*] Our departure from New York was smooth as silk for everybody. Right off I knew it was going to be a jolly crossing. We were all in the humor, and it was the "first time" for all ten except Mother and me. We had one big table and a merry time at each meal. The girls were all very sweet and bright. Mother enjoyed herself completely.

Rod and I are off early tomorrow for Innsbruck just because I remember how much you loved it. A day there and on to Vienna.

Rod is fine company, enthusiastic and willing to do his part. Paris has seemed more charming than ever, though I've seen darn little of it.

[*Constantinople—August 4, 1925.*] After leaving Vienna we took the boat down the Danube to Budapest, a lovely, but not specially spectacular journey, and on, that same night, to Belgrade, the dull, dirty capital of Serbia, and then 48 of the worst hours of train travel I ever put in. Every fifteen minutes we were viséed or inspected or annoyed for tickets.

Constantinople! A completely distinct city, like only itself. The first night we were here I had a Taj-Mahalish experience in Santa Sophia and climbed the great minaret at dawn and helped the Moslem muezzin greet the sun as it burst out of the Bosporus and call all the faithful to prayer. We've seen bazaars and boated and climbed. I've had a Turkish bath in Turkey, too. A most novel experience. Today we took 200 feet of film. I hate the damn camera but we've crossed the Rubicon with it and must see it through.

How much more smoothly this journey goes than the last! I have definite dates and places and plans and I like the security of it for a change.

[*Athens—August 15, 1925.*] I'm the maddest man in Greece; I arrived yesterday to find the idiot American Express Co. had forwarded all my month's accumulation of mail to *Naples*—though why Naples and not Liberia, only God knows.

Also the proudest! You have the honor to be the father of the *first and only American in history* to swim the Hellespont. Leander was the first Greek, Lord Byron the first Englishman, and Richard Halliburton the first American. Of course, I was headed straight for the Hellespont the moment I sailed from New York. As with the Matterhorn, I said nothing about it in advance for obvious reasons.

The morning after I wrote you from Constantinople, Rod and I caught a little Turkish steamer and sailed across the Sea of Marmora, through the Dardanelles to the town of Dardanelles, sometimes called Chanak, on the Asiatic shore. Straightway Rod and I complicated matters dreadfully by lugging our movie machine to a hill overlooking the Hellespont and taking a picture of the place I was going to swim. A few Turkish forts were in range. Between nagging police and a sailboat incapable of sailing upstream against a rousing wind, and a six-mile current, we lost three days in a row.

On the third day the wind became so violent we gave up temporarily and went to Troy, twenty miles away, in a wagon, and from sunup to sunset prowled over and about the most romantic and storied ruins on earth. Delaying too long to get home by light, we slept all night on the Scæan gate where Helen pointed out to Priam the armies of the Greeks, where Hector said goodbye to Andromache and through which the Wooden Horse was dragged to Troy's destruction—truly a fine place to sleep.

Back to Dardanelles next day for more visés and fruitless requests to sail across to the European side—all a ruse, they said, to take forbidden pictures of their secret forts. But at last we got permission to cross over to the Gallipoli Grave Yard (30,000 British soldiers killed in the campaign). We were threatened with immediate execution if we went nearer Abydos, where the forts are. Once at Gallipoli, we spent the night with the British caretaker and next morning at dawn began to buck the six-miles-an-hour current that swirls around the peninsula of Abydos. We simply defied the police and felt we'd take our medicine if only we could swim first.

We reached a mile above Sestos after seven hours' rowing. I made Rod and the two sailboatmen pull for dear life while I steered and sailed, one mile an hour for seven hours, against wind and current. Leander swam directly across from Sestos to Abydos, but having a violent current and a wind that was whipping the water into a sea of whitecaps, I went on a mile and three-quarters higher up—a longer swim by that much, but longer time to get across before the current might sweep me past Abydos point. We lunched on sardines—no breakfast, and climbed a hill to take a sweeping panorama of *my* battlefield.

The exercise of climbing in the scorching sun had the usual physical effect on me. My knees shook when we got back, and my hands trembled so I could not have held a glass of water or lit a cigarette. I said to myself, "You're a physical wreck—can't climb a 150-foot hill without prostration and on top of it you presume to attempt a difficult and dangerous swim. You can't even *walk* five miles." That did me good.

So after a round of pictures—movie and still—we up-anchored and I paddled out into the racing current, the first swim in three years. I didn't know whether I had got more than two hundred feet, when I was the most surprised fish in the Hellespont to look around, after a *solid hour* of swimming, and find I was about a mile from shore— and a mile and a half below my starting point. My difficulty was with cold—the water was icy—and the waves beating and breaking over my head kept me swallowing salt water until I was thoroughly nauseated. But I was amazed at the ease with which I swam. I doubled, trebled my speed. As we approached Abydos point I had to fight to make any headway at all, going southwest about ten times as fast as I went south. But seeing the shore so close I stuck to it and presently my foot hit solid ground. Rod dragged me into the boat, gave me a swig of brandy and I was live as ever. He got pictures all the way across.

I can't explain it, and yet when I finished I could have done it again and faster than before. My physical state becomes an enigma to me more and more: completely exhausted by nine holes of golf, and yet capable of the endurance required for this hard swim.

Back at Dardanelles we found a Constantinople boat in the harbor and jumped aboard her before the Turks could find out what crimes we had committed. In 45 minutes we were steaming over the very water I'd swum in. That night on the boat my sunburn began to torment me, but except for this I had no other ill effects. We reached Constantinople in the morning, changed boats at once for an Athens-bound steamer, traversed the Hellespont for a third time, and arrived here yesterday afternoon—to learn that I had drowned in my attempt.*

Well, one more of my great aspirations is checked off. Only Olympus remains, and after writing here for five or six days we're off for the mountain. I've not dared open my eyes here in Athens. I want to clean up before plunging into Greece. I've no interest in modern Athens. It doesn't exist for me.

Some letters after August fifteenth and the first part of the following letter of August twenty-second have been lost. Richard's mother is back from Europe now and he addresses both parents:

. . . the age-famous Vale of Tempe, the most lovely and classic scene in Greece—only five miles long, but *what* miles! We took mules and spent the night in a village; went 25 miles by mule next day and slept at a monastery; got a late start and slept with shepherds on Olympus' side three-fourths the way up. Off at four and got to the "impossible" Throne of Zeus, a great rock chimney, at seven. Here the soldiers and shepherds who had come along would go no farther, but one of the little monastic shepherds, a boy thirteen years old named Lazarus, insisted he'd go; so we three climbed. Our shoes were old and soft and clung to the rock face. On top we found Miss Frazer's name, the Miss Frazer who introduced me at the Chicago Geographical Society. Two men and two women had climbed before us, and that's all. We had a thunder and lightning storm, which seemed only appropriate. Jupiter was in a rage over our sacrilege and for revenge he kept us on top all night, unable to descend for clouds!

* The New York *Times* had so reported.

Down and back to the monastery next night, and next day back to Larissa, a night there, and next day and all that night, under a full moon, again in the Vale of Tempe.

Thence over a spectacular motor road to Delphi, the home of the oracle and the national shrine and treasury of ancient Greece. We saw the ruins by the same full moon. Rod sat over the now extinct crevice where the sacred fumes rose to intoxicate the sibyl and let a beer bottle supply the gases—and when properly befuddled prophesied all manner of good fortune. We spent one entire day climbing Parnassus, 8000 feet. I saw the sun rise from that celebrated mountain. It was a fatiguing journey as we were tired to begin with, but it was rewarding. We got back Friday night. The moon was still bright but waning. I tried to get into the Acropolis Saturday and Sunday nights in vain. Monday I was free to climb over the darned walls and spend a night alone in the Parthenon. The gates were locked and the guards unbribable, but I reasoned that if a Persian army could sneak up and over the Acropolis walls, I could. So I found their very path, and the rest was easy, and overwhelmingly beautiful. Never was anything so divine, so chastely perfect, as these haggard ruins. I'd been up to the Acropolis ten times since, but in the moonlight everything seemed changed.

The Olympus and Tempe pictures are beautiful. I've expressed my movie camera back to you, and *not* with tears. I'm free as a lark, and have learned my lesson.

To the casual, the materialistic, the non-classicist, Greece is just a hot, barren, backward, sterile waste of rocks and cactus. It takes intelligent imagination to find glory in these rocks, and to be awed by the crumbling, prostrate fragments of stone that merely indicate where a marble temple stood. I feel in ancient Greece the most uplifting force in the history of our civilization. In so many ways the Greeks were infinitely superior to any other race that ever lived. Their supreme development in all the branches of art, which have been our standards of perfection ever since, is admirable, of course. (In architecture and sculpture especially they make all succeeding generations seem like blacksmiths), but it was their development in the art of living and thinking that captivates me. Imagine what it must have been like, an entire race of people with none of the inhibitions of modern civilization. Philosophy and moral science have only been restated since ancient Greece, not bettered.

I've done all the heroic, physical "stunts" I've the least desire to do. I've wanted to climb Olympus and swim the Hellespont for 25 years. I'll be content to stay in the valley now. There are other wonderful mountains, but I've climbed every one that ever held any lure for me, except Popocatapetl in Mexico.

I have resigned myself to make very little out of a $5.00 book. I've set my heart on the publishers selling 5000 copies, the first edition. I'll be surprised, very, if it goes over that unless they bring out a cheaper edition.

Athens—September 10, 1925

My dear Mr. Howland:

I have spent three days at Rupert Brooke's tomb on Skyros Isle— the very first American, so far as I can learn, who has ever braved the dreadful journey thither. It is a semi-desert, inaccessible, barren "corner of a foreign field." Some day I'm going to write a little book on Brooke's life and death. . . .

I cling to the hope that there is a proper map in *The Royal Road to Romance.* If there isn't, the book will remind me of an exam I flunked once in Navy navigation school. We had a long, tedious, intricate, logarithmic problem in range-finding to solve. It took an hour of furious figuring. To get the exact spot of the enemy's ship we had to divide the final result of our calculations by two. I did all my figuring exactly to the inch. My figures were neat, my pencil a lovely gray shade, it was absolutely flawless—and then I forgot to divide this beautiful result by two and shot my shell twice too far. So, without that map, our travel book will lack the final, vital twist. . . .

But I've almost forgotten about the old book in my impetuous collecting of the new.

[*Athens—September 17, 1925.*] This is *not* another all-day-and-night letter, this huge bulk, so don't despair. It's opus No. 1 of my present interest, and I hope longer than its successors are going to be. It's taken me longer than it took to climb the darn Olympus, I had so many reference books in French and German and English to plow through to get the points of information. I read up for five days, I wrote it in two. Please have it typed and put away, Dad. Along with it goes a big burden off my chest, as I tackled the hardest story first.

[*Athens—September 24, 1925.*] Here is exhibit No. 2, and Chapter IV in the new book. I think it's pretty good and like it much better than Olympus. I'm finding myself more and more in a dilemma—to stay on here and write more stories, enjoying the wonderful library, or hurry on to Sicily. I'm writing with more ease as the days pass and wish I could remain a *month* and write Parnassus and Tempe and Hellespont and Troy and Rupert Brooke and Constantinople and Marathon. I'm going to do Tempe anyway. I think the inclosed story doesn't show that my long period of literary inactivity and general discord has undermined my imagination and dramatic touch as I feared it had.

[*Athens—Wednesday, September 30, 1925.*] Here's another one—Tempe. Coming right along, aren't they? In reading over the copy for mistakes I see where I could improve it right now, but it would take another precious day. The legends I insert are such obvious insertions. They must either come out or be put in the key of the main story. A good rest from it, and I'm sure I can make quite a poem of this rough draft which will go logically after the thunder-and-lightning Olympus story.

My dilemma about leaving Athens or staying and writing was decided for me most emphatically in favor of the latter. By chance, in the Amexco here, I got in touch with a young Greek who has lived at Ithaca and whose family still live there. They speak English, are Homeric scholars and made to order as hosts and guides for my pilgrimage. The Athens son, John Splyris, insists on escorting me—eighteen hours from Athens—and establishing me in his home; so we'll go there next week. Ithaca is the all-important place. Over *half* the Odyssey takes place there and I can't take too many pains with it. By waiting and going with John I'll see it exhaustively. I'm itching to get moving, though. Athens is ever interesting, but so is time.

I suppose by the time you receive this, you'll have a copy of our book on the table. My imagination cannot comprehend it at this distance. Even so, I feel a thrill down deep within me.

I'm all right. The moon's full again, so I'll go up to the Acropolis again tonight.

[*Athens—Tuesday, October 6, 1925.*] And still they come, my stories. This is No. 4, and the last of the Greece proper anthology, except one on Marathon. I took a bus several days ago out to the famous battlefield and walked back along the same route the marathon runner came to report the victory to the Atheneans. I have a good story in it.

I go tomorrow to Piræus and sail through the Corinth Canal, and through the Bay of Corinth to Patras. John Splyris is sailing with me. Athens certainly has a spell, and I'm not overly happy about pulling loose.

Richard went to see all the scenes of Ulysses' adventures but not in the same order as Ulysses. To avoid doubling back and forth, he visited the various points in the same vicinity at the same time. Roderic Crane was called home before Richard reached Naples.

[*Naples, by gosh—October 20, 1925.*] I've been on the move so constantly since leaving Athens there's been no time for either moss or letters to grow.

I left Athens very calmly as the successive delays had given me plenty of time to accomplish everything. The boat trip through the Corinthian Canal and Gulf delighted me. I spent most of next day getting to Olympia where the original Olympic games were held for 700 years, and saw there the celebrated statue of "Hermes," Praxiteles' masterpiece. Back next day to Patras, and the morning after I reached Ithaca. I had a sixteen-mile muleback trip the same afternoon, a 40-mile exploration the following day by foot and motor car, and a full morning the third day. I saw every inch of the island. My Greek friends entertained me royally and made my stay pleasant and easy. In Patras again, an Italian steamer took me away overnight to Corfu, one of the most important stops of Ulysses. One day there was sufficient to see all I needed to. I hurried on to Brindisi, reached Naples yesterday morning at seven, and at nine was off for Pompeii. I climbed Vesuvius by the cog railroad in the afternoon. Of course, it was interesting, the view superb, but it was all aside from my main theme so I just *saw* it.

This morning I went to Amexco and got your terribly welcome letters and the *Book*. The mail contained so much of vital interest—Feakins' and Chambers' and Howland's letters were *so* important—and the book's advent—all at once. I had one of my faint spells after four hours with it all and had to dispossess my mind of everything, walk down the quay, dine comfortably alone, before I could go back in a normal condition to finish all that the mail contained. Today I cabled Chambers and Baker* to express my satisfaction over the book. Howland has left Bobbs-Merrill to become editor of the *Century Magazine*. I cabled him congratulations.

The Book! I like the size and *especially* the full size of the photographs. The brown cloth binding is *awful*. I wanted dark blue. The end-papers are original. The free, big print I like very much and, all in all, I'm about as well satisfied as I expected to be, so far away from the factory. It seems surprisingly young. My lack of variety in expression, my roughly connected ideas, etc., strike me as never before. Of course, I am trying to see how severely critical of myself I *can* be—and I find it very easy. The printed page is so heartless and unadorned. The bubble of the book is its charm. When I stop bubbling it begins to creak. I fully believe I have the raw ability but need discrimination and restraint. However, it's a happy day and a dream come true. I can never have any more dreams like this one.

The Royal Road to Romance he had dedicated to the four Princeton roommates, "whose sanity, consistency and respectability drove me to this book."

[*Naples—October 27, 1925.*] I'm sure the moment that has given me the most contentment and happiness, since I got back from Japan, was the moment when I opened Dad's letter and read that, at long last, the Book was in your hands, actually, in three dimensions. I got

---

* Herbert S. Baker, then Bobbs-Merrill manufacturing man in New York.

far more pleasure from knowing that *you* had hold of it, than that I did. You've both worked and wept so hard with me over it, we had such pain and discouragement and so many battles, physical and moral, to fight.

I loved Capri. I waited till the shipload of German tourists had departed, and then, with an English lady companion, went swimming in the Blue Grotto. We were turned to silver fishes surrounded by white fire—but you saw it and know how lovely it is. I went on to Sorrento and drove to Positano and tried to row out to the Sirens' islands as they are important in my Odyssey, but no boatman would risk the terrific sea. So I went to Amalfi, had tea at the Capuchin Monastery Hotel where I hope you stopped. Then next morning on finding the weather fairly calm back I went by boat to Sorrento, back to Positano. The sea was slightly quieter. We got a big boat, rowed by four fishermen, and embarked on the most thrilling voyage I've ever had. The sea and sky did everything in the catalogue. I've never seen water rage and boil as it did against the Sirens' rocks. The rain poured, then suddenly departed, leaving a huge rainbow. I got a whiz of a story.

I wrote Mrs. Brooke (Rupert's mother) I would visit her about December first at Rugby. Her letter to me was very sweet and appreciative.

I tried in vain to get my gray suit, now filthy beyond endurance, dry cleaned. The shop wanted *ten days*. I got me a bowl of hot water and a table and soap and brush and proceeded to scrub my coat and trousers as one would the kitchen table. They are dry this morning, and they look like the devil, but they are *clean* and after being pressed may show signs of life. At worst they can't be as unsightly as before.

[*Messina, Sicily—October 31, 1925.*] See where I am now—Sicily—and what a lovely place it is! Tomorrow will be November, yet it's warm and sunshiny here with flowers everywhere. Messina is a dull and unbeautiful spot itself, left so by the terrible earthquake in 1908. Every house in the place has been built since then, and even now most people live in barracks.

I left Naples four days ago for a beautiful motor ride with my Blue Grotto friend. Messina is the famous Scylla and Charybdis place, of course, and I've been playing around with them. Yesterday I had the idea of swimming from one to the other, but the currents were so terrific because of the tides, and the water so cold, I didn't get more than a mile before I saw I'd never reach the shore. I had a boat and four boatmen with a *light rope around my waist,* which didn't help swimming any. The old myth is based on reality—there are several dangerous whirlpools on the Sicilian side and a big rock that once bore Scylla's cave on the Italian. I'm off this evening for the extreme western tip of Sicily, Trapani, where Polyphemus' cave is located. Then back to Messina to take boat to Stromboli, the volcanic island north of the city where I may have to stay five days as the boat service is very infrequent.

[*Malta—November 17, 1925.*] And see where I am now—Malta—right in the middle of the Mediterranean, and a fine place it is. Near by is the island where Ulysses spent seven years held by the nymph Calypso, and so it is an important stop for me. I've never spent a more full and varied week.

Getting back from the Cyclops' land, in western Sicily, I got a small boat at Messina and went to the little island of Lipari where I stayed all night in a fourteenth century hotel. At four next morning I got another boat to Stromboli, Æolus' isle. It's just one great volcano rising straight out of the sea and thundering and flaming day and night. I had to stay five days at Stromboli because a storm came along and the rowboats couldn't be launched, for the waves, to take me out to the steamer. But it was a lovely little island. I climbed the 3000-foot volcano and passed a day looking down on the most spectacular scene I've ever beheld. At night the molten lava streams down a 2000-foot terrace into the sea to make the world's wildest fireworks. All in all, it was a well-spent five days and will add greatly to my story—not to mention some fun I had on the side.

Back to Messina and straightaway to Catania. I got a motor car and rode ten miles up the lower slope of Mt. Ætna to the usual starting village, and next morning at six, with a guide, two mules, a muleboy and some friends, started up. The November air was like wine, and the chestnut groves all along the way were a striking golden contrast to the great wastes of black lava on both sides. The last 2000 feet was all snow. The hut where one sleeps was 800 feet below the 10,000-foot summit. We climbed this last distance, but the wind was so strong and so cold and I was so ill-prepared for it, we just had one look over the crater rim and hurried back. We spent the night under a mountain of blankets at the hut, saw the sun rise, and slid home again down the lava ashes. Had I not climbed the Matterhorn and Fuji and Olympus, Ætna would have been thrilling, but, except for the terrible cold, it was not especially interesting. I'm glad I climbed it all the same.

Here in Malta, the American Consul, a Harvard grad, and a Miss Adams, an altogether charming person, took me to lunch in a 400-year-old palace and motored me all afternoon all over the island. On the way back our hired chauffeur was going a bit fast, a twelve-year-old boy ran in front of us and we struck him with a sickening thud. I've never experienced a more dreadful moment. Our wheels did not go over him, fortunately. However, when I got back to him he was bleeding in a dozen places and his clothes were torn to grimy shreds. I picked him up, unconscious, and we dashed to the hospital. He came to on the way and to our relief could move all his limbs. The hospital fixed him up and dressed his badly gashed little body. We went to see him Sunday night and found him quite all right. But it was all very heartbreaking. Why he wasn't killed I simply do not know.

Sunday Miss Adams and I took a boat and went to the neighboring Isle of Gozo where Calypso's cave is located. A pleasant day and a picturesque island.

Yesterday, Monday, I saw the museum and read in the library, and this morning I take passage for Tunis, and a 36-hour train ride along the north African coast toward Tripoli. Half way is the isle of Jerba, the land of the lotus-eaters. It's important, accessible, and I'm going to take time to see it right. With the lotus-eaters checked off, I'll have missed not a stitch of Ulysses' travels. I'm so happy over it. I must hold on a little longer and finish this thing properly, as you'd have me do.

[*Tunis—Thanksgiving Day, November 26, 1925.*] This is indeed Thanksgiving Day for me, for I've started home, I've completed the cycle except for one spot north of Naples (Circe) which I'll visit on my way to Rome.

I've had a satisfactory trip to Jerba and enjoyed the isle of the lotus-eaters entirely, along with a delightful friend. We reached it in a sailboat. It's quite unspoiled, all palms and olive trees and flowers. A wild lavender crocus colored the entire landscape. We were there on market days and I got my fill of Arabs and camels. I went sponge fishing all one day—searching the ocean floor through a glass-bottom barrel and spearing sponges with a twenty-foot pole. No wonder Ulysses' men had to be driven away.

We left at 3 A.M. yesterday in a motor bus. It broke down fifteen miles farther on. The guard 'phoned in to Gabès for a car to come the 30 miles out to meet us so he might get the mail to the one daily train to Tunis. We got to Tunis at twelve last night. It is lovely. I enjoyed Carthage and sent a postcard to Mr. Henry from there, as I studied Virgil with him.

[*On the boat—don't even know its name—an hour later.*] I go straight from the boat by train to Messina and change there for Taormina, where Ulysses' crew killed the Sun God's cattle with dire results, and from there to Naples, arriving Monday morning. You can imagine how eager I am to reach Naples.

I've begun to erect the skeleton of the new book in my mind. I've thought of no title better than *The Glorious Adventure,* nor can I hope to have it written before fall.

It's terribly rough. I'm the only person not flat from seasickness, and I've got to look for air.

[*Morning.*] What a ghastly night! My cabin was just below the afterdeck on which twenty cows were being transported. The ship dived and gyrated every moment and the poor beasts were catapulted back and forth, stampeding and thundering on the steel plates above my head. This morning four were stone dead from broken necks and half the rest had broken legs. You can imagine how much sleep I got. Palermo in two hours. We are three hours late and I'm going to miss the Messina express, dammit. We're passing the island where Ulysses hunted the wild goats before making the excursion to the Cyclops' cave.

Put my stockings on the Xmas Tree—I'll need it.

[*Crossing the Channel—Sunday, December 6, 1925.*] This jiggling handwriting is not my nerves, but the boat's vibrations. We're halfway across and it's cold and rough as the devil. I've not written since posting a letter to you at Palermo, ten days ago, since I've been coming north about as fast as the mails and since every minute has been packed to busting. I'm sailing Wednesday morning on the *Republic,* cabin boat, U. S. Lines, and reach New York the eighteenth or nineteenth.

The past ten days have been a fitting climax. From Palermo I hurried on to Messina and Taormina and whom should I meet at once but the English young lady I met at Naples? She already knew everybody, so the two days I stayed I had a most beautiful time. Taormina is the world's most picturesque spot and I'm going back someday for a long visit. Snow-clad Mt. Ætna seen through the roses and across the blue bay from the ruin of a classic Greek theater, I'll never forget. I rode all night to Naples and it took all next day to reach Cape Circeo (Circe's Island), where I spent three days exploring. Then on to Rome. Only one wonderful day there, but I saw everything except the Vatican Museum—closed. Thirty-six hard, cold, sleepless hours to Paris. And off for London at dawn today.

[*Rugby—Night, Later.*] All my rush was unnecessary. I didn't have an envelope to inclose this in at Dover and brought it on to London, where I had exactly ten minutes to catch the last afternoon train to Rugby, still carrying my letter. At seven I arrived, dropped my bags at this hotel, dined, dressed scrumptiously (I've one intact shirt) and at eight was seated with Mrs. Brooke before an open fire telling her all about my trip to Rupert's grave at Skyros. She is much as I expected. Sensitive poets often have such mothers, vital, dominating, strong. She seemed genuinely interested in me. I stayed two hours. She had three sons, all dead; one died in 1907 and two others were killed in the war. I learned nothing about Rupert of service in anything I may write about him, but I've met his mother, and that's next best to meeting him. I'm back at the hotel now with the porter waiting to take this to the post office. It *mustn't* miss the *Mauretania.*

CHAPTER XII

and a Rupert Brooke Pilgrimage

RICHARD sailed from England, was occupied a few days in New York and rushed home to Memphis for the holidays and as much rest and quiet as he could get.

His lectures began in Nashville. Mr. Dyer, president of the Nashville Bridge Co., who had roomed with his father during three years at Vanderbilt University, drove him out to the Hermitage, the Parthenon and through the Vanderbilt campus. He spoke at the War Memorial building before a thousand people. Richard was happy to be lecturing again, especially as he had new tales to tell from his "Glorious Adventure."

At Indianapolis he had a pleasant little visit with his editors. At Chicago he delivered several lectures and heard Mary Garden in *Louise.* At South Bend he got news that his fortieth engagement had been booked.

On this lecture gallop he had the fun of seeing Mike in Kansas City, Rod in Omaha, Paul McGrath in Chicago and Shorty in Ann Arbor. The book section at Marshall Field's gave him a reception. His publishers reported the sale of Finnish, Swedish and German rights in *The Royal Road to Romance,* which was beginning to appear in the American best-seller lists.

To Minneapolis and Dubuque. From Pittsburgh, February 26, 1926, he writes: "The last week has been *very* busy and *very* beautiful. The lectures are going fine with big, enthusiastic audiences and the bookstores are stocked sky-high with my book." Several small engagements. Back to Chicago, where he heard his pianist friend, Jo Brinkman, play at the Music Academy. "Passing Brentano's what should I see but their show window piled with our book and a great poster 'Outstanding Travel Book of the Year' and my picture? We stood aside a moment and watched a score of people stop to have a look and comment."

To Birmingham School. To Buffalo, where he had a happy meeting with his old friend, Mrs. Plimpton. To Utica, Rome and Washington. "I saw Mr. Fisher and Mr. Grosvenor, Jr. Everybody was gracious to me. I had a bang-up full house in the afternoon. The congressman from Memphis was there. The *Geographic* people were a bit shocked and startled, I was so different from their usual line." To New York, Albany, and the Ely School for Girls at Cooperstown.

The literary editor of the Chicago *Tribune* wrote him for a "confession" of three hundred words about which book he'd rather have written. He chose *Don Quixote*. To Providence to address the Men's Club; from there to Boston and back to Cleveland.

From New York, March twenty-second, he writes: "I'm rather light-hearted now with the Philadelphia Forum behind me. We had about 1500 in the audience. I had a fine introduction and never felt cooler. In retrospect, the Forum night improves. Letters keep coming with praise and approval. Huff gave six of us a little party afterward and I went to my hotel a tired and happy man."

To Washington again. "I saw Mr. Fisher of the *Geographic* and was asked back for next year." To a girls' school in Baltimore. To Princeton, "too beautiful for words. I stayed at the Graduate College and loved the place more than ever. The *Prince* is having me down in April to speak in Alexander Hall." To a girls' school at Edgewood. "I lunched with an editor of the *American Magazine*. They're giving me an article with many pictures. Wednesday I give *Physical Culture* an interview on 'The Athlete by Inspiration.' Gosh! So you see how the ball is rolling." A letter from an American Express Company friend in Constantinople said: "Our Athens agent fled to escape the outbursts of temper of one American devil customer named Richard Halliburton."

[*New York—Sunday, April 4, 1926.*] I've got an hour and want to visit with my fambly. One whole, solid, uninterrupted hour in my present life is almost a miracle—but these hurried days won't last forever. *The Royal Road* has passed the 30,000 sales mark and 40,000 printed.

This last week has been full to bursting. March 28, at Bridgeport, Connecticut, I was the big final speaker at a banquet of 600 manufacturers. We sat down at seven; at *eleven* my turn came. Everybody was so bored, so smoked out, so tired, half had gone home. I tried for half an hour to hold them and then gave up in despair. It was the depths of my lecture career. It was ghastly. I spoke the following afternoon to a lovely audience of women in Salem. Next day was a whiz! I lunched with Mr. Wickes, Mr. Alber's Boston partner. He came to hear me at the big department store in Boston where I was put on by the book department. The auditorium seats six hundred. Sixteen hundred came. The store was absolutely demoralized. Guards had to stop the elevators to the seventh floor. Wickes and his office force saw it all. I never spoke so well. I was feeling fine and looking straight at Wickes. The department was swept clean of books.

On that night to Rochester and Geneseo—huge normal school audience. Next day Buffalo. Dear Mrs. Plimpton was on the front row. At eight tomorrow I go back to Utica and home to New York tomorrow night.

Three letters came from Europe yesterday: one from Princess Murat asking me to visit her in Paris this summer. One from young Alex Thiers, the grandson of President Thiers of France. He has a villa and a car and wants me to motor for a month with him in Italy. The third from John van Druten, my English playwright friend, who wants me to go to Norway with him. Well, I deserve a little play. I'm afraid I've forgotten how.

Wow! It's eleven o'clock. I've had no supper. I'll go get one.

[*New York—Tuesday, April 27, 1926.*] At Princeton I dined with Dean Gauss and the editor of the *Prince*. I wish you could have been there. What a reception to a young alumnus! Alexander Hall was *packed,* boys seated in the aisle and standing outside, about 1500 in all, the liveliest, noisiest lot you ever saw. Frank Peabody of the *Princetonian* introduced Gauss and he in turn me. I was jolly well nervous, and who wouldn't have been? But it got over and the applause when I said good night lasted five minutes.

All's well—life is fun at times.

Richard was invited to be one of the speakers at the American Booksellers' Convention in St. Louis. His father and mother drove up for the occasion and a delegation came over from Indianapolis. When he got back to New York he found a full-column review of the English edition of *The Royal Road to Romance* from the London *Times* which he thought "noncommittal, analytical and intelligent." A Sunday afternoon spent at Long Beach resulted in a bad sunburn. "I may as well resign myself to the sun's hostility and give up my lifelong ambition of being a bathing beauty." He spoke over WJZ Tuesday, June twenty-second, and over WEAF the following Sunday afternoon.

On July ninth, he delivered his first *"American Magazine* article, 'Where Are the Romantic Corners of the World?' Last Sunday and Monday when everybody in New York was merry-making, I slaved away in the library from morn to night on it." He admits being distracted with social activities, "but I don't want to succeed bad enough to be a hermit as I was at Nantucket."

On July twentieth, Hafford and the doctor and Heinie and Dot sailed on two different ships and it kept him jumping to see them off. He spoke over the radio again, WGBS and WEAF. His first German royalties came out of a blue sky. Moiling over *The Glorious Adventure* and over his lectures and magazine stories got him in a bad temper at times. "Praying may help but cussin' helps more, and hard intelligent effort. I've got the goods; I must learn how the public wants them delivered." Explaining why he apparently had neglected the new book he writes: "I wanted to build up a magazine audience." To unleash his imagination he must "sail away from lecture management and scheming and printers and radios and a thousand other things." He strikes a minor key in closing this letter. "I'm lonely. My affections are starved. I've no time to care about people. I wish I would fall in love. It would add some sweetness and sparkle to all this brass materialism. I lead an absolutely loveless life. Friends and acquaintances—too many—all of them could disappear and I wouldn't know it."

On July twenty-eighth: "I'm writing with increasing rapidity. Chambers wants the manuscript by November first and it will take enormous industry to do it."

Richard decided to go home to do this work and stick at it till lectures called him back to the grind. When this stretch was over and the call came, he writes to Bobbs-Merrill on the train to New York September twenty-ninth:

"*The Glorious Adventure* is finished—almost. Incidentally I'm about finished too, but don't care because it's a happy death in a noble cause.... While seventeen of the chapters are safely in the ice-box, the two that remain to be *re*written are the first one and the last one, and it would not be very satisfactory either to you or to me, to submit the animal minus its head and tail.... I'll have it done and will leave it with you when I come through Indianapolis October eleventh. I want you to be absolutely brutal in your suggestions and criticism. My one fear is that you won't be harsh enough. The best asset I have is ability to appreciate, and profit by, criticism. Whatever quality I possess as a writer comes from the spirit, and not from the word; and this spirit plunges off on the wildest, and, lately, on over-exotic tangents. In this new book I've taken the brakes off. It all makes for readability—but also for incredulity. The book is a *true narrative,* with buckets of bright paint flung over it. But if the public got the idea from my style that it's fiction, I'd be done for. This is where I need help."

A few days later he writes home: "I've worked over the last chapter till I'm dizzy and I think it's satisfactory." He enjoyed the trip east because John Kidd, the Cincinnati bookseller, was on his train. "We were in the same coach and talked shop and books and writers from noon till midnight. He is as entertaining and pleasant company as ever I saw." Richard stopped off at Philadelphia to take in the dog show at the Centennial with Glenn Hunter and to see his play. In New York "tons" of letters awaited him. "I'll never answer all this 'fan' mail." A letter from Heinie Leh razzed him because he had made fun of Heinie's reading the *American Magazine* in Princeton—"and now I burst forth in it."

Just before taking the train for Indianapolis, with the manuscript under his arm, he reports (October tenth) having given two lectures. "The first one was disastrous, the other was a joy—I don't know why."

He delivered *The Glorious Adventure* to his eager publishers and then had dinner with Mr. and Mrs. Chambers. Mr. C. he had at first found "icy though practical" but now they had a fine talk and "Mrs. C. and I are great friends. She's so animated and self-possessed." He went right on the same night to Chicago for a lecture at Orchestra Hall. "It was *almost* filled—a thousand seats. Ole* and Mrs. Ole came in at 8:20 and couldn't find a seat downstairs. And then with it all I gave one of the worst talks on record—too fast, too tense, my old besetting sins." But Fort Wayne went well, and he was in great form at Godfry (Monticello Seminary) near St. Louis, and Pittsburgh was "tremendous." "Lord! Traveling!"

On October eighteenth he was again in Indianapolis, to get the editorial reaction to *The Glorious Adventure.* "Chambers wants more Halliburton and less Homer all the way through. After he finished with me last night I was sunk to the depths, but feel better today. He's absolutely right—only I'm going to have it my way." Bobbs-Merrill decided to give a big reception for him in New York on November eighteenth.

[*Bristol Hotel, New York—Monday, November 8, 1926.*] Buffalo went off beautifully. Bronxville was fun, too—we had a jolly tea party afterward. The worst bump yet was at Stamford. I took a notion not to show pictures, and just didn't. The president of the club had gone to great pains to get an operator and a screen. I had no excuse—no explanation—just didn't want to. I'm tired of them. She was simply wild with indignation and spoke so sharply to me, my fur rose. She threatened to dismiss the audience and I threatened to give my lecture in the park if she did. Well, the audience loved it, which made the president all the madder. There's never been so much excitement in history over a speaker. But I'm out my fee because of my whim. To offset all this the *National Geographic* signed me up for the evening of February eighteenth. Prince William of Sweden speaks just before me and Kermit Roosevelt just after. I'm speaking nearly every night somewhere.

The invitations for his reception went out on the twelfth. "Feeling fine. I'll be awfully glad when this party is over. Mr. Crowell, who owns the *American, Collier's* and the *Woman's Home Companion,*

---

* H. T. Olsen, then a Bobbs-Merrill salesman.

is introducing me." Then on the twentieth: "The party was perfect. All the book people were there. Mr. Crowell introduced me beautifully, and I spoke 50 minutes, better than ever before in my life. Everybody was marvelous to me."

That was indeed a "furious week" for him, including the Yale-Princeton football game and a night with Roger Baldwin at his Jersey camp—"a most amusing evening. The camp is right in the wilds. I can be as rough as anybody when need be, but when it's not needed, give me a radiator. We got along swimmingly, didn't talk socialism, and parted good friends."

His mother had written him of the death of Mr. Mooney, the editor of the Memphis *Commercial Appeal,* who had been the first to sense Richard's literary talent and had published thirty-two of his articles about the Royal Road journey. "Oh, Mother, that was bad news indeed, for no one will ever fill *his* shoes, and there's no one to whom I'll ever be so grateful."

To finish the revision of *The Glorious Adventure* he immured himself in East Orange, where he made consistent progress. "Already," he says on Friday, November twenty-sixth, "I've rewritten twelve chapters, with only eight more to do. All along the one big idea has been to cut the Ulysses story and speed up and make the most of my own experiences. . . . Thanksgiving Day I pounded the typewriter for twelve hours." His usual stint was fourteen. "Think of me as dining on a handkerchief and scribbling and typing from 10 A.M. till midnight."

This writing drive was nearly over. A week later he had a great time at "Grace Drayton's* party—about 75 people at the private showing of her 'animated babies,' the story of Antony, Caesar and Cleopatra—very original." On the lecture trek again, a long trek this time, which would take him to far western fields. His talk on Rupert Brooke at Rochester "went over beyond my best hopes. Toledo was a great success too." A fan there gave him a big fruit cake in token of his appreciation of *The Royal Road to Romance.* "And everywhere books, books, books are being sold. The University Club in Chicago was another high-water mark. I had 500 grads in my audience and gave them 'Glorious Adventure.'"

Home for a flying Christmas visit and by January 4, 1927, "back

---

* Grace Drayton was the original of "Fifi" in *The Glorious Adventure.*

in harness again with a vengeance." That day he got into St. Louis "to learn that Mike's father had fallen dead last Sunday. As yet I've learned no details. I'm in Mike's room now." He had tea with Larry's wife and saw the baby.

On the way to California he stopped off at Tucson and writes, on the eighth: "I'm sitting on Aunt Susie's back steps simply *boiling* in the hottest sunshine you ever saw. It's dry and dazzling and the air is so clean and fresh after the fog and damp of Missouri."

[*Los Angeles—January 13, 1927.*] It's sunshiny and I'm feeling fine. Everybody is kindness itself and I'm getting enough rest. Each day would make a letter. I wrote you from Tucson. *What* a perfect day Aunt Susie and I had! She's wonderful, and we get along like a coupla thieves.

San Diego was great. Nice people drove me all over the place and I had dinner with New York friends. The lecture was a whiz—1100 members of an open forum. Esther and Horace Thomson were there—had driven down from Los Angeles. Esther looks fine. I left that night by sleeper and went to Redlands. I had a lovely time there in the club president's home, and a most enthusiastic audience. In fact they got up another purse and asked me back my first free evening—so back I go on the nineteenth. *That* never happened before.

Yesterday I went out to Hollywood and lunched with Malcolm Boylan. He's an odd sort, none of his mother's peculiar sensitiveness, but *very* bright and good company. We dined with all the movie mobs and he took me over the Fox studio and introduced me around.

Esther Thomson is as full of independence and hell as ever, and has grown in grace. Her hair is bobbed, not nearly so pretty as the curls. We had dinner at her father's club.

My time is all too short here. I've had to say *No* to almost every gesture of hospitality; I've had three invitations for every meal. I'll write again before I leap north, for, as you see, there's much to write about. And may it always be that way. It's eight o'clock and I've a tired back from this chair—so I'll go out to supper by myself and enjoy being alone for once.

Richard had visited and revisited cities, towns and schools from the coast of Maine to the Continental Divide, but he had not crossed over to the Pacific side till now. It was a different world, and one to which he responded with gusto. He loved most the sunshine, and after that the colorful, vivid society. He was lecturing practically every day, sometimes twice a day. Thus, on January nineteenth, he spoke to four hundred men at the University Club at noon; then at three his cousin, Erle Halliburton, and Mrs. Halliburton motored him to Redlands, where he lectured again, and went with him to a swanky party given for him by some California ex-senator.

He writes from Seattle, January twenty-eighth: "Here I am, 'way up here, just where I was in February, 1923—in geography, but not in being." Then he was returning rather worn from his Royal Road. What tumultuous living the four years since had been! Take the week just past for example. He had spoken to a breakfast club in Los Angeles; lectured twice at Paul Elder's bookshop in San Francisco, where he was the guest of Charles Norris, the novelist; returned to Pasadena to address "a mob of an audience" and to see the "Blue Boy" in the Huntington Library; dined with Jim Tully and the Scott Fitzgeralds; gone to Colonel Fowler's party to meet famous writers and actors, and to a luncheon given by Carrie Jacobs Bond. "I left Los Angeles with a heavy heart." Passing through Portland on his way north, he had called up his old Lawrenceville friend, Don Skene, "the world's most melting personality. He was that eleven years ago, and still is."

So the exciting trip to the "coast" ended and he started east, lecturing all the way to Chicago. Rod drove him from Sioux City to Lincoln where his cousin gave Richard a supper party of sixty places at the country club. The governor of Nebraska was at his left, with General Pershing's two sisters next. At Rochester, Minnesota, he had a gala day. The whole town turned out. Dr. and Mrs. Charles Mayo gave him a luncheon at their house. "I *loved* them. Their home is too beautiful—organ—spaciousness—that calm air of incontestable honor and position."

From Chicago he jumped to New York, "only mildly glad to be back," but "free for a day [February seventeenth] to raise hell over lecture fees and to work like a Trojan with Mr. Baker on the pictures for *The Glorious Adventure*. He's all enthusiasm and we're having great fun with them." He took incredible pains with every detail in the making of his books, knew just what effects he wanted to secure and insisted on getting them.

Then "the days pile up so I lose sight of half of them. The National Geographic date was too good to be true—an audience of 4000, the auditorium packed to bursting. Mr. Gilbert Grosvenor congratulated me. Still no introduction, which angered me—but it's rather futile being angry at the Geographic."

Once more to Indianapolis. "I went out to see Chambers for a long powwow at his home and showed him my latest version of the last chapter. He thinks it splendid. It seems strange that after all the labor and struggle I've put in this chapter, I should be right back where I was in the beginning, with a very chastened viewpoint, however, which came of the intervening efforts." He was working furiously on galley proofs as he traveled to Springfield, Illinois, and from there to Cleveland on the return journey. At Cleveland he made a flying trip to see his friend, H. V. Korner, the bookseller, who mailed the proofs in for him. His last engagement before reaching New York was at Keene, February twenty-fourth, where he had an audience "suprisingly amusing—wholesome New England country people. They chartered buses and came in droves. I must be a drawing card in this rural community."

"In the bank this afternoon," he wrote on March second, "the guard said, 'You're too late, boy—get out.' Being called 'boy' when I feel 79 flattered me so I've been feeling fine ever since." A few days later, when he spoke at Temple University, there was such a mob of students they had to give over the packed auditorium and commandeer the nearest church, ice cold though it was. A few weeks later, he was apologizing for a long and most unusual silence. "I'm not dead or sick or in trouble to cause you alarm. I've been on such a mad gallop all correspondence has suffered, and for some inexplicable reason I've been in a mood where I could not force myself into writing a letter even when I had time." Perhaps it was because he was changing his lecture management. He had considered being his own manager, but realized the arguments against. "As is, it's dignified, congenial, free of detail and responsibility." So he would sign with Alber-Wickes. Maybe it was the all-consuming immediate attention that had to be given the book. "I'm free from April 9 to 26, but I'm afraid to leave New York with *The Glorious Adventure* on the press. The maps are done, the jacket ready, the pictures complete; only the captions must I still supply. The wheels are grinding surely and smoothly and the finished volume will soon be a reality."

The lectures had, for the most part, continued to go well. For example, "Bowling Green met me with a parade of buses and 300 children escorted me to the hotel. The only flop audience this year was at Exeter, New Hampshire." But the details of a new lecture agreement bothered him. "Just at present," he says, writing on April thirteenth, "I can't sleep without dreaming of fees and per-cents and railroad fares and circulars and contracts. I've a chance to worry about lectures now that I can't worry about the book. *That* is irrevocably beyond reach now. Baker hopes to have *us* a copy—you and me—by May fourth. I'll receive it with a little sadness. It's so much more amusing striving than arriving."

But when May fourth came this attitude vanished in a hurry. "I was so excited when the company handed me a copy I never realized till night I'd had no breakfast or lunch. I'm quite proud of myself for being able to be so set up. The new book excites me more than the old one, though I read through it rather impressionlessly—I've looked at it so long I can't see it. I've no idea whether it's better or duller— an improvement or a retrogression. I can only keep my ears open for public opinion, and learn that way. *G. A.* hasn't nearly so many stories that *tell* well as *R. R.* I'm eager to have your letters about it. I've decided to give a party on Sunday—have asked 40 people in for cocktails to celebrate the publication."

Here are random notes from his letters between the middle of April and the advent of *The Glorious Adventure:* "Somebody from California sent me a long, frantic wire offering me a third of $50,000 if I'd conduct a movie tropical news tour of South America. I know this is not for me—too colorless.". . . "Our breakfast at the Pen- women's Union in Washington was great fun. They themselves are a queer lot, but their guests included everybody but God. . . . I spoke on 'the care and feeding of babies,' using my baby god story. . . . I'm distressed about the river; the papers are full of flood and disaster around Memphis.". . . "Here's another check for the flood fund. My friend Mrs. Bond was so touched by my recital of the suffering in our country she gave it to me. . . . Vassar was grand and glorious. My girl turned out to be a school leader and exceedingly attractive. We led the grand march. In the afternoon it was cut-in and I danced with everybody in college. It was program that night and very formal. The next night I had 1200 people at Newton for some benefit—half of Wellesley College was there. Last night here in Northampton *all* Smith College was on hand."

He dedicated the new book to "The real heroes of this story, Nelle and Wesley Halliburton, my long enduring, ever courageous, infinitely patient parents."

With *The Glorious Adventure* launched and *The Royal Road* still going strong, "book parties" were the order of the day. "Cleveland was a whale of a day—we had a young riot—some *500* books sold that one day. The party was at Halle's—Veronica Hutchinson—but all the booksellers had a royal time. Stacks of reviews awaited me in New York. The *World's* is certainly a bump, but *G. A.* is not a critic's book. The New York reviews are never kind to 'romantic' books—but it's going to sell despite them."

"I'm having a hard time to choose between Napoleon and Richard Cœur de Lion as the peg for my next book," he wrote on June first, "or no model at all. *Royal Road* had no exemplar. After all, it's 'my own caprices,' so Harry Hansen says, that I'm interested in, that our readers are interested in. However, I'm reading up on both and all will drift satisfactorily. If I only leave my ideas alone, they always develop, but when I begin to drive them they go on the rocks."

He was conscious of the fact that his letters home in these months while regular were not often the old delightful "conversations" but had tended to become summaries of his movements reported in telegraphic style. "It seems I have no time for serious letters to you because I have to cut everything not imperatively business to the barest minimum to crowd into my day the things that must be crowded. Don't think I'm drifting away. There've been such violent evolutions and revolutions going on in your son for some years. I've built up a wall about me for self-protection and self-delusion. I'm tearing the

Richard's mother, Nelle Nance Halliburton.

Richard's father, Wesley Halliburton.

wall down slowly, and will have it all down someday. . . . If I didn't have faith in the inevitable 'drifting-out' of things for the best, I'd be frankly unhappy."

Richard, needing a complete change of air and scene and mood, decided to spend the summer in Europe and to delve into the material for a possible book about Rupert Brooke. His mother was chaperoning another group of college girls to Europe, and they arranged to sail on the same ship. He writes home to his father.

[*S.S. Melita, still at sea—June 30, 1927.*] We've just left the Belfast tender and are on our way to Glasgow. I'm honestly sorry it's over for never has a voyage been so agreeable and restful. I've slept myself silly and feel caught up nervously for the first time in years. I've read two or three books, written some 50 letters that were due last November, but generally just "wasted" the day sleeping and fooling.

[*Later*] We landed at Glasgow today, July first, and after the usual delay and inspection are all safe in a hotel. The others are going to Ayr. Ten days has been enough of the girls, sweet as they are.

A wire came to me at Montreal from John van Druten saying he'd be in the Hebrides and a letter awaited me at the boat urging me to join him at Skye. I've always wanted to visit the Hebrides—they sound so lonely and romantic—so I'm going there tomorrow and get on to London by the ninth. I'll be in and about London for a month, I expect, reading and inquiring.

I'm worried as never before about my next three years; balancing on top the ladder is harder than climbing it. A last letter from Chambers begged me to get on to another travel book, but this will not keep me from investigating my Brooke idea.

[*Isle of Skye, Hebrides, Scotland—July 5, 1927.*] Again I'm writing you from strange places. Certainly, I've never written from any place quite so strange and isolated as the Hebrides. Ever since at Lawrenceville I studied Boswell's *Journal of a Tour to the Hebrides with Samuel Johnson* made about 1773, I've wanted to go there, and here I am in a hotel built right next door to the hotel where he resided. I got Mother off Saturday morning for the Trossachs and Edinburgh and Saturday afternoon I took train for Fort William and Mallaig, on the northwestern Scottish coast just opposite the southern tip of Skye Island. I was there overnight—ferried across and motored 30 miles to John's hotel. This island is weird and wonderful—70 miles long and only 8000 people, rugged and rocky and desolate beyond belief, treeless, endless bogs, always the blue sea penetrated by the long, narrow locks and fjords. It's windy and barren and usually deluged with mist and rain—unattractive sounding I know, but there's a wild beauty to it all that grips one and removes one infinities from the moiling, dirty world.

There are about a dozen other Englishmen at this hotel—but everyone keeps his own counsel and distance. Everyone leaves in the morning, rain or not, and climbs about the pathless mountains till dark—that is, midnight. The sun sets about eleven and the twilight lasts forever. Yesterday John and I climbed a 5000-foot peak right up from the sea and the view, in the clear weather which came up just for us, was simply elegant—all the scrambled Scottish coast— Ben Nevis and the outer Hebrides and all the ragged, dour, dangerous island that has made this place a synonym for harshness for three centuries in England. We're leaving day after tomorrow for the Caledonian canal, Inverness, Stirling, Edinburgh, Melrose, Dryburgh— and London next Sunday. I'll see Abbotsford and the Forth Bridge, and still have four days with Mother in London. This tour is all familiar territory to you and unchanged. I'll think about you when I see the things you liked. Naturally, I'm enjoying this change, and feel great.

[*Hotel Victoria, London—Saturday, July 16, 1927.*] As we planned, John and I went to Dryburgh and Melrose and Abbotsford. I saw the "Haliburton" inscription on the tomb at Dryburgh and was properly thrilled. Both abbeys were beautiful, and the surrounding country. We sat up all night to get to London Sunday morning. Mother and I had fine times, going to the theater and dining together.

I wrote Mr. Marsh a note and delivered two books to him as the first move in the Brooke direction. He's the key man, Brooke's official biographer. He wrote back but as yet we've not met—and time's flying. I grow more afraid every day that nothing is coming of the idea. I shan't let it break my heart, though it's just the proper thing at this stage of my career. I must stop glorifying myself—I'm getting sick of it and so is the public. A book about somebody else with scarcely more than my name on the back of it would rescue me from all present dangers ahead. Should I do the Crusade book now I'm afraid it would be too impersonal, so reactionary have I grown to exploiting myself.

I've thought over your Oxford suggestion quite seriously, and can foresee what would happen. I'd become academic and critical and self-conscious and write refined essays that nobody would read and anybody else could write as well, and I'd lose the one thing that makes me individual—zest and illusions. Anyway, I'd be bored at a university now. I must be on my own. I see my way clearly enough, though it's been a little murky lately. I must fight an over-artistic conscience and keep my faith in the popularity and value of romanticism. Otherwise, I'm just like a thousand conventional writers. Things always adjust themselves for me in the long run. I've learned not to rush them. Once I get financial independence, I've *literary* independence too. I only hope by that time I'll still care. I miss you, Dad, especially in Scotland. Your trip there stands out so vividly in my mind, because it did in yours.

[*Hotel Victoria, London—Sunday, July 24, 1927.*] The balls are beginning, slowly, uncertainly, to roll toward a definite work. These English people won't be hurried. I've had to lose two weeks waiting to get acquainted with Marsh. I've seen him twice now, and know about the pictures and references, etc., which he's willing to lend me. My immediate job becomes clearly one of "anthologizing" old material—to include the best and finest of Brooke's poetry, to take all the material by and about him and digest it. Once I have *their* approval and material, I've got to strike out all over England to visit his contemporaries. This literary pilgrimage in itself will be interesting. Psychologically it's exactly what I need to break away from the travel rut. I'll collect for the next five weeks—and *hope* to be able to spend the succeeding five in Switzerland.

My social life here has been nil, as I've made no effort. I rather enjoy being left alone for a change. I have read several books, walked a bit and gone to an occasional theater. I've just finished *Jesting Pilate* by Aldous Huxley. It's enormously stimulating and intelligent. He makes a trip round the world and sees only the *un*romantic. It is the perfect reverse of my *Royal Road*. He goes at things with a rapier-like criticism and an icy lack of sentiment and illusion.

The clock says 2 A.M., so I must to bed and catch up for lack of sleep all my past life.

[*Rugby—August 8, 1927.*] I'm under way at last and working like the devil. I say "working"—I mean meeting people and asking questions and writing many letters. Saturday and Sunday I spent with one of Rupert's poet friends, Wilfrid Gibson. I scurried back to London this morning—washed my face and got up here by luncheon time to see Mrs. Brooke. Lord, she is the most formidable person I've ever seen—her talk was so businesslike—there's no amiability about her. "Ask your questions, young man—one—two—three—four." I didn't have any "list"; I hoped she'd just talk and suggest questions. She's very discouraging, very set, very unsympathizing. But I got a few boy pictures of Rupert, and spent the afternoon exploring the Rugby school campus and getting ideas.

Everyone gives me new ideas to expand. If I had twelve months I could do this thing perfectly. I see no hope of getting out of England till the very last boat before I have to begin lecturing. But after all I'm only running true to form. I do like resistance—it's the only thing I respond to fully—and in a perverse way I'm happiest when the resistance is greatest. When my Brooke book is done, I'll do something harder still—a dissertation on the Latin ablative case or a Persian dictionary!

I spent a week end at Cambridge—a day with Dudley Ward, who has more Brookeana than anybody else, a day in Rupert's favorite garden and house, a day with Charles Darwin's daughter, who was Rupert's friend. And I've had tea with his most serious sweetheart, now a very well-known actress. At a town near here I'm to see the sister of the man who was Rupert's companion through his last war campaign, and buried him, only to be killed the following week himself. I'm slowly getting Brooke's life in my grasp. He's becoming

Dripping and triumphant, Richard emerges from the Well of Death after his second plunge.

With Sergeant Thomas Wright as guardian at the oars Richard swims the Panama Canal the long way.

less a stranger. The mosaic is filling and shifting into a real picture.

I was a bit amused at your suggestion, Dad, that I was "satiated with success, praise, publicity." Here in England I see the proportions about myself in America and realize I'm awfully over-inflated. True, I've the second and sixth best-selling books—but there're at least 119,000,000 out of 120,000,000 people who have never even heard of me. Yes, I *am* satiated with "success in Buffalo." I don't want just "popular" audiences—I want particular ones too.

[*Hotel Victoria, London—August 19, 1927.*] I've spent the last two days engaging a secretary. I hope to be freer henceforth. I was driven to an assistant. I'd never get through without one by October first, and maybe not with. Things get more complicated every day and I realize I'm trying to write an epic before breakfast. I've plunged into such strange and unfamiliar waters. The labor is going to be enormously greater with this book than the others because I've got to learn to speak and write a new language.

I am beginning to feel the mood I want. The first half of the book must be utterly gay, vividly, strenuously alive; and the last half—the war and the circle of brilliant young men who buried Rupert only to fall themselves heroically—must be noble, gallant, lofty, spiritual, memorial. The first half all song and laughter; the last half martyrdom and immortality. The contrast will be as striking as the two Skyros Chapters in *G. A.* I'll start off with notice of his impending death; it will make the gayety so much more gripping. Rupert's friends were as gifted and as gallant as he was, and the sacrifice of these six young supermen must be brought out as one of the greatest tragedies that the lovers of Beauty and Intelligence and Idealism have ever suffered. The greatness of my occasion soars with every fresh insight. My possible inability to meet it is my only concern.

I'm doing a magazine article entitled "The Rough Road to Reality," suggesting I've traveled this as well as Romance—and prefer Romance.

[*Hotel Victoria, London—September 20, 1927.*] My inquiries and discoveries about Rupert have made me more, rather than less, enthusiastic about him. The legends, the deification have all been shattered, but a real and brilliant figure has taken their place, a vivid personality who was much more interesting than his poetry.

I am still meeting lovely people. Tea with ex-Premier Asquith's daughter. Lunch tomorrow with a Beverley Nichols who is the *enfant terrible* of England—my age—with *five* sensational books behind him. He's coming to America, on the *Majestic* with me, for a lecture tour. Today I've been working with one of Charles Darwin's granddaughters. I'm sending home a lot of books. I've collected a young library. Did I write you about my afternoon with Drinkwater? He was most gracious to me. Also I had a wonderful evening with Mr. Bles, my English publisher, and his wife. *G. A.* comes out over here on the 27th, and I'm giving them a tea party as an appropriate gesture.

[*Hotel Victoria, London—September 29, 1927.*] My last letter from London—this. I land October eleventh in the morning, I *hope,* and light out to lecture at Lancaster at four in the afternoon. If the ship is late, heaven help me!

What fun I've been having lately! I spent Thursday and Friday deep in the country with Admiral Kelly's family.

On Sunday I spent the day at Oxford, the morning with a General Hartley, turning up material, and the afternoon with John Masefield. He's interesting but hard to talk to. I've all his letters to Rupert. Monday I teaed with General Reyberg, who was one who buried Rupert, and was a celebrated English soldier of the war. Tuesday with Walter de la Mare. There's a fine fellow. He has the most charming personality I've met in England. Yesterday I dined with Maurice Brown, who is likewise doing a book on Rupert, which will help and not hinder mine. Today I teaed with the Prime Minister and his secretary.

I've seen the new Danish and Dutch editions of *R. R.* Gosh, you *should* see the Dutch! It looks like a million dollars—oil color frontispiece and as big as a house.

As the letter indicates, there was no pause for breath after his return. He almost literally stepped from the gangplank onto the lecture platform.

[*On the train, Chicago to Madison, Wisconsin—November 5, 1927.*] I had to hurry on to Greenfield, Ohio, 75 miles east of Cincinnati. A terrible night there. Dayton next day for the biggest lecture audience in its history, 2500. Youngstown was fine, 2000 teachers. Back to Cleveland and on to Indianapolis again for a long conference with Chambers.

We're having a new Christmas jacket made for *G. A.,* one like *Royal Road.* It's being done now. In fact so darned much is being done all at once, I'm absolutely dizzy.

From Indianapolis to Lexington. On to Cincinnati for the night after, two afternoon lectures, and Columbus Sunday in time for a *big* tea party Mrs. Pahlow gave me, to meet all the faculty of Ohio State University. A lovely dinner party and *the* swellest audience. Almost too good to be true. Three hundred people stood and 100 sat on the stage. Every one of the 1200 seats in the house was sold. The Pahlows are as sweet as ever. Mrs. P. has bobbed her hair—the children grow like beans—I spoke at each of their schools in the morning—simply *had* to, for the Pahlows. I left the night after for New York, arrived at two, spoke at Wanamaker's Book Fair at three. Will Durant was on the program. Back to the office for business and off to Newark to speak for a big club of 1000 at eight. I left the same night for Cleveland—the Parent-Teachers of the biggest high school—1000 of them have an annual big party. I had to re-speak to the school kids next morning—2000 of them. Off to another high school to speak to 2000 more. The same afternoon friends drove me to Canton, Ohio, and that night I spoke to 1500 of the combined University Club and College Club (Waverly) and drove back to Cleveland. That *was* a hard day. Had another whale of an audience. Shorty Seiberling drove up from Akron to be on hand, and after the lecture drove me back to Akron. I took the train from Akron to Chicago this morning in time to meet Beverley Nichols coming from New York. On his train was Will van Loon. So the photographers lined the three of us up and photographed us. I got Beverley to his address—and then went to the conference of all the affiliated lecture managers. Back to the 12:30 train, and here I am. Tonight in Madison, tomorrow a big luncheon in Chicago for Beverley, and tomorrow night back to New York state and New England. Whewww! This furious motion is stimulating, but it burns up *too* much. However, I'm never so happy as when I'm busiest and have most to worry about. . . .

I've been to Madison and back before I could finish this. I had a grand time at Nichols' luncheon. Beverley spoke for an hour, forcibly, wittily, charmingly. At the party was Sir Rennell Rodd, the English Ambassador to Italy, a famous classicist and writer on Homer. We clicked at once when I told him about my *G. A.* expedition, and I'm to see him in New York on my return.

[*On the train, St. Paul to Green Bay, Wisconsin—Wednesday morning, November 10, 1927.*] What a wonderful night Monday in Chicago! Orchestra Hall was packed to the rafters. I had no pictures to stifle me. The stage-manager had shown me where to stand for best resonance. I took a wild chance. I resolved to *think* instead of remember and walked into one of the most responsible and trying moments of my life without one word in mind. The Junior League had staked its very soul on my being worth all the noise and effort and promise they had made. My Chicago reputation was at stake. No other lecture for me has ever been like it, so much was at stake. Perhaps it was this, perhaps it was the surge of sympathy when I began to speak, but something carried me away from myself, away from grim, earthly, depressing things, back to my old enthusiasm for romance. I threw away all my old lecture and thought out a new one as I went along—and I've never been *half* so good as I was that night. The ladies were overjoyed at the success of their plunge. Stephenson was as excited as a child and pulled me through mobs of people to my taxi—we had 30 minutes to pack and check out and make my train.

Paul McGrath was there but I couldn't even see him to say hello. That evening was priceless to my spirits.

For the next four months Richard's letters read like a conglomeration of all the timetables of all the railroads in the United States, annotated with the sensations of the moment—fun, excitement, reaction, "praise and damnation, trouble and happiness."

First, New England and upstate New York. "A most difficult audience at Lawrence—husbands' night at a stiff-necked women's club. I'm having to go all around the world, the floods have torn such big holes in the rail beds. But this was only a gutter freshet compared to *our* Mississippi flood." Elmira, New Haven, Torrington, Hartford, Boston Athletic Club, Amsterdam, Schenectady (where Dr. Richmond, the president of Union College introduced him by saying that because he confessed never to have had delirium tremens he "hadn't seen *any*thing and hadn't been *any*where"), twice for Wellesley girls, Hartford again in a terrible storm.

Thanksgiving week end in New York "at the funny old Murray Hill Hotel as everything else was full up. Thanksgiving dinner with Grace Drayton, alone. We had *such* a good time. She gets more marvelous every year, quite gray hair now but painting and living better than ever. A most interesting young fellow with one leg came to see me, named Ellery Walter, with a story of *his* journey around the world. I sent him to Feakins who took him on, and three or four publishers want his book. Eugene Wright is a real rival. His *Great Horn Spoon* is dangerously like my books, but after all it's *like* and the edge has gone. I met him recently and he's very delightful. I took Dick Halliday and his very charming mother to *A Midsummer Night's Dream,* all in German but interesting."

He wrote this "on the train for a change," December fourth, Pittsburgh to Columbus. He had been again in Boston where he stayed at the Ritz "as it was Ritzites I was speaking for, the Junior Leaguers. My good friends the Bonds gave me a 'small' tea party of 250 people, everybody in Boston of interest, including the Governor and the Mayor. I worked heroically in Symphony Hall but it was only acceptably good, by no means another Chicago Orchestra Hall. Burton Holmes was on the front row. I came down from Boston with him and dined at his apartment." His last day in New York before starting west, Richard lunched with Harry Hervey, who wrote *King Cobra,* and went to a party for Glenway Wescott, "the amazing young novelist who wrote *The Grandmothers.*"

The timetable resumes: Johnstown twice, Hollidaysburg, Columbus, Greencastle, Indiana, Cleveland, Pittsburgh, Bradford, Titusville, Erie. "I'm well and full of energy. It amazes me where it comes from. My voice gets husky at times." No wonder!

He went home as usual for the holidays, caught up on his sleep, rested his voice, saw his dentist. The pure pleasure of being home always had to be impaired, he lamented, by being turned to such practical purposes! He writes next from Atlanta. "Wow, it's hot! I'm sizzling in sunshine and shirt sleeves." Atlanta, Greensboro, Charlotte, Shorter College, Atlanta again, on successive days. He thought he had never been so sumptuously entertained as in Atlanta: "lunch, book party, tea party, dinner; lunch, book party, tea party, dinner." He speaks of lunching "at the loveliest house I've ever seen," but does not specify.

Westward ho! New Orleans, San Antonio (where he was "in a most devilish mood" when the reporters called), Jacksonville, Texas, Dallas for two lectures, Muskogee, Fayetteville, "a clean and charming town," Fort Smith, and the third and biggest lecture at Dallas— the Forum. "We turned away 2000 people . . . all great fun and tremendously thrilling. I had ups and downs in Texas, but this was *such* a grand finale. . . . I've been working on an article for the *Publishers' Weekly* called 'God Bless the Book Dealers.' "

A letter of February 6, 1928, says: "It was two weeks ago I wrote last on the train going to Los Angeles, and now I'm on the train coming back, tired. I've just sat and looked blankly out the window and ossified. Lord knows I need a rest, for California was one long whirl. I raised so much hell with my lecture managers, I don't know whether it's because I've something to grumble about or because I like it. When they book me eight times in five days, I think it's the former."

Such a schedule would turn Job into a "first-class quarreler." In ten days he lectured in Sacramento, Alameda, Reno ("those who couldn't get in stood beneath the windows outside"), San Francisco ("the worst talk of my life"), San Jose ("as good as I was bad the night before"), Oakland, Long Beach, Los Angeles, Hollywood, Santa Ana, Santa Barbara, Pomona, and Pasadena twice, "and no voice left." To make his engagements he had to use an airplane four times. At San Jose he met Gertrude Atherton ("about seventy, looks fifty, is great fun") who became a lifelong friend. He devoted several Hollywood hours to trying to sell the Ulysses story to Douglas Fairbanks for a movie.

Having summarized these California doings, he takes stock of his state of mind. His father had commented on an interview of Richard's, that his start in life was really due, not to some lucky star of chance, but to persistence and constancy of purpose. Richard agrees. "I'll stop 'zaggeratin'. I do get so fed up with myself I like to poke fun at me as a relief and a change. As to my over-taut life, I find I'm no good at adjusting things immediately as one resets a clock. I've got to grow into a change. I've got to get utterly sick of the glare before I'll be happy being quiet. I find myself moving slowly toward a yearning for escape and friends and calm. I've learned that I can never decide situations, but that situations decide me. When May first comes, circumstances and instinct and the subconscious will decide my summer. I'm on the edge of literary oblivion unless I do the right thing. I have full faith that when the time comes I'll do it."

A cold sloppy February in the north. Three lectures in Chicago, one each at a Methodist college in Iowa, a church in Evanston, a little town in Wisconsin, a boys' military school outside of Milwaukee. An all-day ride to Sioux City. "I'm so fed up with this grind, I'd chuck it for two cents. It's putting me in a fine fighting mood. I'm looking forward to May, you bet." Omaha (breakfast with Rod Crane), Leavenworth (Mike Hockaday motored over from Kansas City), Cleveland, Bellefontaine, Wheeling. "Lots of 'ham and egg' engagements, but I don't intend to prepare a 'ham and egg' talk for 'hams and eggs.' "

[*Cleveland Hotel, Cleveland—Sunday night, February 26, 1928.*] What a nice, quiet day this has been! I slept till noon, and by myself went to see Charlie Chaplin's *Circus,* and by myself had dinner—and as I dined alone I had an idea for my next book that hit me like a bomb. I'm going around the world again, like *Royal Road,* and not relive *anybody's* life but my own. Reliving and retraveling set courses are too much of a strain. I'm going to start out from Paris and re-cross the Alps to Constantinople and the Holy Land, and end up somehow in South America—Peru, the Incas—and come home *via* Mexico. I'll do all I can this summer and go back and carry on next year to the completion. I'll enjoy it so much more than doing Richard the Lion-Hearted and the Crusades. I'll go semi-vagabond. I'm going to buy an atlas tomorrow and route myself.

I've shipped the originals of the Brooke letters back to England. A terrible responsibility is raised off my shoulders.

Buffalo, where he was "so terrible" they wanted his fee back; Jamestown, where they thought him the best speaker they'd ever heard; Port Huron, for a deadly night; Detroit, for the finest audience of the year; Cleveland again; a wonderful time in Huntington, West Virginia; a flop in Charleston; Pittsburgh; Akron, where he stopped with Shorty. "I'm sending 'Hands Off Homer, Hollywood' to Fairbanks," he writes en route March eighth. "I want to do a third travel book while youth predominates, and I must hurry, for spirit and outlook are changing so terribly fast."

[*Detroit—March 16, 1928.*] All my misfortunes are in the past. A new contract's signed for next year. Alber had big plans and fat fees. One minute after I left him I ran into Mr. Schuler of the *Ladies' Home Journal* by coincidence, and had a late dinner with him. I like him immensely, but he is hipped on the idea of my finding Romance in *America* and doesn't seem excited by any other idea. I'm very dubious as to our ever getting together. I may yet do Rupert Brooke this summer and postpone my trip round a year.

Before another week was over Richard was in the Methodist Hospital in Indianapolis for a sinus drainage, the result of such roaming in horrible weather and at high tension. "Mr. Chambers stayed till I was out from under the gas. Anne Johnston comes to see me, and 'Lafe' Lafollette from the office, and I've had flowers and dozens of telegrams. I feel a big cheat as I've not been sick at all. Please, Mudder, don't worry about me. . . . Chambers is coming to Philadelphia for a conference with Schuler and me on April 12. He's a lovable person and I've decided to dedicate my next book to him."

And on the twenty-sixth he was back on the job like a good trouper, headed for New England and "unusually pleasant engagements": Hartford, Waterbury, New Bedford and a Boston suburb. "A few days of sun and I'll be better than ever. A letter has come from England reporting Mrs. Brooke's objections to my biography. I believe I can overcome them when I see her again." But his objective for the summer has turned definitely to Latin America. "If we can only get together with the *Home Journal* in Philadelphia, I'm off for South America."

Fall River, for the smallest audience of the year; Atlantic City, for the biggest audience in their history; Lock Haven, Pennsylvania; home to New York on April fifth. "Chambers is seeing Schuler and I'll see him in a week when I go to Philadelphia for lectures before a teachers' association and the Shakespeare Club. I wouldn't be at all surprised if I sail from New Orleans for Mexico in May. The more I think about it, the more promising it becomes."

He spent the Easter week end in Princeton. "It was the most perfect spring day, and I walked so far I'm lame, and breathed so much sunshine I'm dizzy, but feel fresher than I have in weeks."

And so he headed south, to neglect no part of the American circuit. Raleigh; Durham; Norfolk, where he spent an hour vainly looking for "Slim," his *Gold Shell* sailor friend; Richmond; Asheville ("what a change there since our old vacation days—you'd never know it"); Atlanta; Charleston; Savannah, and back to New York. "A most happily agitated week." He met many old friends, did a deal of motoring through the riotously blooming countryside, visited the famous azalea gardens at Charleston. "How I hated to hurry away from this heavenly country!"

His contract came from the *Ladies' Home Journal,* and books, passports, banking kept him busy. He had his title ready. "I'm delighted you're happy over it, Mother. If there weren't *you* to care and love me, I wouldn't have much incentive in 'conquering this new world.' From your last letter, Dad, I know you've not lost the faculty of being able to change your diet from bread alone. It is true that I give too little time to the spiritual, 'small-voice' side of my life, but contemplation other than of timetables when you're lecturing is hopeless. The struggling, the constant squabbling with managers, the intense material effort to keep all my spreading mesh of interests and responsibilities in order give me no chance to ponder on the spiritual. One side of me has lain dormant for two years. This summer will reveal whether or not it's dead or just resting.

"I'll have many books to buy. I'm so ill-read on Latin America, and have so much to learn—for which I'm very glad."

[*On the train in Virginia—Sunday, April, 1928.*] I have to go to Mexico and South America and *like* it—and I will. The Crusade idea, after a long battle, was defeated by Schuler and Chambers. They were afraid I'd be too flippant with sacred institutions. But I'm just as satisfied with the accepted idea. It's nearer and just as pregnant with opportunity. I'll sail to Mexico from New Orleans sometime in May. Popocatepetl, Maximilian and Carlotta, Yucatan and Panama will give me my first block of stories. It will all grow as before, with time and imagination. I'll buy all the books I can get my hands on and ship them to Memphis.

A literary club in Philadelphia booked me with "exclusive right" understanding. A bookstore gave me a party contrary to this contract, and I chose to go to the party after my club lecture. I wouldn't have *spoken* at the store had not the most officious woman president said to me, "Mr. Halliburton, *one peep* out of you at a bookstore and you don't get five cents of our fee." So, as conspicuously and arrogantly as possible, I promptly marched to the store and lectured for an hour. I lost my fee but it was worth it, thumbing my nose at such a dictatorial woman.

I'll have to let the Brooke book slide a year.

[*On the train, Detroit to Lansing—Monday, April, 1928.*] Getting closer and closer home—Lansing tonight, Decatur tomorrow. Don't be alarmed by the deluge of books. Stack 'em up. There's every book on my new subject I could find in New York. I foresee a big horizon of educational and informative reading ahead for us all.

All's well—but how glad I am it's over.

CHAPTER XIII

ADVENTURING IN NEW WORLDS

SINCE it was first proposed Richard had been looking for a comrade to make the "New Worlds" trip with him. He persuaded his father to go part of the way. They sailed from New Orleans to Vera Cruz and from there went by foot to the City of Mexico, following the route Cortez took in his historic march. This led them through Jalapa, Tlaxcala, Cholula—with a side trip to Puebla and back by motor—and from Cholula they had a marvelous walk up and over the saddle between Popocatepetl and Ixtaccihuatl to Amecameca and Mexico City. Richard writes this letter home to his mother, who was preparing to chaperone a new party of girls abroad:

[*Mexico City—May, 1928.*] You got our wire yesterday and know that we're safe—so far, so good, and *what* a time we've had! It's really been one of the most original adventures I've ever had. Bad weather in spots, hot sunshine, sunburn. Dad triumphed over everything and we reached Mexico City fit and happy, having walked about 250 miles. Our last day's walking we did about 30 miles right between the two great volcanoes. I've never seen such magnificent scenery. Both mountains, one on either side, are 3000 feet higher than Mont Blanc, and we could almost touch them—a brilliant clear day. We had a young Mexican for interpreter picked up at the beginning of the trip. He was very useful and taught me no little Spanish. We took scads of photographs; will get them tomorrow and will send you copies at once. My strength and endurance have come back splendidly, and I feel ready for anything. It's been great fun having Dad along and he's enjoying it till it hurts. We both said time and again, though, that what we most wanted was to have you waiting for us here at the Regis when we arrived. Your two letters were fair substitute. It's just eighteen days now before you leave for New York, so you'll be busier than ever. I *am* so proud of you to have col-

285

lected your party and got all set to go. It won't seem right my not escorting you part way.

Yesterday we climbed the cathedral tower and tomorrow we are off for Popo, the big mountain.

[*Hotel Regis, Mexico City—June 16, 1928.*] I felt like a poor lorn widow woman after Dad's train pulled out, and it got worse all day, but I stuck by my desk and have drowned my loneliness in work. I am eager to hear about his journey home. How rusty my writing wheels are! They creak and balk, but it's to be expected, and they'll limber up with use.

I am dining tomorrow with a Mrs. Mittall who is considered the most important American in Mexico; she's quite an historian and archaeologist. I'm not going to stay by myself *too* much, but I've got to slave away if I'm to finish my three stories and get to Yucatan by July first.

I do love this high, warm air. I wish I had time to work on Spanish; I could learn so much in so little time if I *had* the time, but at that I'm learning new words every day.

[*Mexico City—June 21, 1928.*] If I guess right this letter will get to you the morning of the day Mudder leaves. You must take *this* thought with you: that I'm as safe as in our own back yard, and not going to do anything unwise.

The old pen has begun to move at last, and I'm overjoyed to find I've not forgotten how to write during the long recess. I was discouraged at first, needlessly; our new volume will be the best of all, if I'm allowed the time I need. I've got Cortez and us into Mexico City, so the worst is over. When this story is done I expect to do Maximilian next. Popo I can do anytime on boats and things without reference books.

Too bad you missed the earthquake, Dad. I've always wanted to be in one, but one's enough. It was seasickening this high up.

I spent a lovely Sunday with Mrs. Mittall.

As Mr. Schuler wants a sample of my articles right away, I may type the Cortez and send him a copy and Dad a copy and keep a copy to improve on as I travel.

[*On the train to Vera Cruz—Friday, June 29, 1928.*] Nothing very amusing has happened since you left, Dad. I climbed Popo again with an expert photographer named Hackenberger. I decided I wanted a panorama picture with me in it for my frontispiece, and the only way to get it was to climb up that damned mountain again. It was a most painful repetition. The day we rode from Amecameca to camp was perfect. We had the same guides and mules and all went beautifully. Profiting from our previous late start, we left at 12:30 A.M. so as to reach the top by dawn, but about three a most terrible and sudden blizzard struck us. The wind was so penetrating and so cold we almost froze, but we gained the top even so. I made the grade in much better form than before. The summit was one mass of fog and smoke. We couldn't see ten feet, but an hour of shivering and misery in the crater brought daylight and the sun and a fair picture. Before the storm hit us I regretted you were not along, but once the weather changed, I thanked God you weren't.

I'm all fixed for Yucatan, with letters to the governors, military commanders, *et al.,* everywhere, and easy sailing ahead. I've written Fred Healey to meet me at Progreso. He's the young fellow in New York who works at Putnam's.

This day trip to Vera Cruz is beautiful. Popo is all clear and white to my right. I leave it with mingled feelings.

I'm going to come home rugged and strong.

[*Vera Cruz—July 2, 1928.*] I've been in this damned dump three days. I wasn't allowed to sail on the American boat I came from Mexico City to make, but had to take a Mexican boat sailing today (two days later). Some coastal company regulation. V. C. hasn't changed—*much.* I am at a different hotel, but the Imperial dining room on the sidewalk, the plaza, the beach make me think of our visit together. I'm not so tongue-tied as I was a month ago; I've learned some Spanish. Also the delay has given me uninterrupted time to write and I'm deep into my second draft of Cortez, which is not so labored as the first.

[*Chichen-Itza, near Valladolid, Yucatan—July 6, 1928.*] After waiting three days in Vera Cruz for that terrible Mexican boat, I had to ride on it 48 hours across the Gulf. There were cows aboard and Mexicans. But I worked hard at my Cortez and tried not to notice the smells. I got off at Progreso, met Fred Healey, and went on to Mérida, the capital of Yucatan and quite a comfortable town. I got acquainted with the ruling American, who owned both of my books, and had a busy day inquiring about my next move. Fred got inoculated and it made him so sick he had to stay behind for a day or two. The ruins here are overwhelming. I've a good story ahead.

[*Mérida, Yucatan—Monday, July 9, 1928.*] I've had a beautiful three days. The ruins at Chichen-Itza grew on me. They're so extraordinary and so bursting with romantic history. The Mayas' form of sacrifice when they needed rain was to throw maidens into the Sacred Well to appease the rain god who dwelt at the bottom of it. It was a great ceremony. The well is still intact, 400 feet across and 70 feet from the rim to the surface of the water, with very steep sides. A little temple is still there where the priests stood to pitch the maidens in. I got the idea that it would be interesting to jump in myself, imagining that I was a warrior selected to jump as the bride was cast in, with a few gestures of farewell to earth. I jumped. It was a thrill as I was dropping down to the silent water. The only inconvenience was getting out. The Indians nearly had a fit from excitement.

I found plenty of time at the ruins to work on my Cortez story. It's going to be about 13,000 words I found Fred still inactive from his inoculations on my return tonight.

[*Belize, British Honduras—July 21, 1928.*] A boat is going *right away* from Belize to New Orleans and I must rush this along with the inclosed newspapers and pictures. In my last letter I wrote about my leap into the Sacred Well. The realization of the dramatic possibilities for a story made me go back and do it again. I must have evidence for the doubting reviewers. Mr. Arthur Rice, the dean of the foreign colony, came along, with a moving picture outfit. The second plunge in no way harmed me, except that my hand striking the water strained a muscle across my chest. The movie was shown in Mérida, the big town in Yucatan, and everybody was terribly excited.

Fred and I left Yucatan at Progreso last Saturday night on a 60-ton sailboat. It simply crept along the coast, delayed every hour by some breakdown. In 60 hours we reached the island of Cozumel. Our boat was so unspeakably filthy and crowded with dirty Mexicans we couldn't stick it and at Cozumel got off.

The island is a fascinating spot, with the most glorious swimming places beneath the palms. We just about lived in the ocean and I got sunburned as usual. We brought along our own food and bottled water, and didn't lack. Another little sailboat came along day before yesterday, loaded with a hundred giant turtles—400 pounders—en route to Belize. We climbed aboard and sat on turtles, walked on turtles, and slept on turtles 36 hours till this morning. We were both just about all in from lack of sleep and rest. We've a fair and clean hotel here and must stay till Monday night, this being Saturday afternoon—then on to Nicaragua and Panama.

I should have written a thousand words, but somehow the boat was so cramped and sunscorched I wasn't able to do much. I am rewriting Cortez one day, and cranking up Popo the next. Fred's proving almost too good company; we waste time talking. The Consul here has asked us to a dancing party at the British Club tonight. We're dressing up prepared to perspire, as it's about 110 in the shade.

[*Puerto Barrios, Guatemala—July 24, 1928.*] Belize was an awful bore for three days, but I wrote a bit and rested. We'll be in Guatemala City tonight, and there only as long as we have to before another boat takes us to Nicaragua. My writing is going slowly along, and the time is going so fast!

[*Bluefields, Nicaragua—August 7, 1928.*] Here I still am in this dismal Central America. Ever since my last note sent at Belize, Fred and I have been in furious motion trying without succeeding to get to Colon; also trying to find a little color and copy. Central America has been a most disastrous waste of time. We should have gone straight from Progreso to Panama, especially since along the way Fred was bitten by malaria mosquitoes and is now *seriously* ill. Poor fellow! With my usual luck I escaped. His illness enabled us to get transportation aboard a battleship for Colon and leave tonight. It seems like the promised land. I'll put Fred in a hospital in Colon and handle Panama by myself. If he's able to carry on with me when I'm ready to proceed, we'll continue together. If he's not, he'll have to go back to New York. You may be sure I'm eating quinine by the peck and so expect to keep well.

After Belize, we took a fruit steamer to Guatemala and spent one night and day at Guatemala City—nothing there. By luck the bi-monthly boat was leaving from the Pacific coast and we hurried to make it—then four days on the big steamer, stopping at every little port down the coast for 24 hours or so till we reached Corinto, Nicaragua. Fred and I swam every stop and had a few very slight adventures. The idle days gave me a chance to work on my Popo story. From Corinto we took the train to Managua, the capital, and hurried on to the big Nicaragua lake which we *did* find romantic and colorful. We crossed in a sailboat, climbed a volcano and canoed down the St. John's River up which the new canal will be built. The river was marvelously beautiful, with occasional rapids to make the journey varied. At the mouth is a funny little deserted village called Greytown (San Juan del Norte on the map). It had 10,000 people in 1893 when a U. S. company began a canal there, and has about 200 today, with all the old buildings still standing untouched and unoccupied for 35 years.

We had to take another dinky little sailboat to come to Bluefields, a hundred miles out of our way. We got drenched with rain in the open sea en route. Fred had had chills coming down the river and the fever began again. Malaria is no joke. But by day after tomorrow, August ninth, we'll be in Colon four days behind my original schedule.

I've always forgotten to tell you that on the little schooner from Progreso in Yucatan to Cozumel Island I had Fred take my nail scissors and whack off my hair right to the scalp, making it no hair at all. I've been looking *just* like Sing Sing; it's cool, but it looks like hell. This was over three weeks ago and it's grown back a little, just enough to stick up straight. I was to cut Fred's the same way, but I looked so tough with mine cut, he wouldn't play. It takes about three months for a full regrowth. That's been our only excitement.

From the bow of a small sailboat Richard watches the approach to the
Island of Juan Fernandez.

The combination of Niño the monkey, a hand organ and Richard prove irresistible to children of Buenos Aires.

[*Panama City, Tivoli Hotel—August 25, 1928.*] The past three weeks have been a bit overwhelming. My cable explained my long silence—the canal swim. It's over. I'm not harmed one speck, the sunburn and sore limbs are departed and I'm just where I was before beginning. It was a whale of an adventure and one not likely to be duplicated. The humor, the sport, the novelty of it seem to hit everyone. A row boat accompanied me every inch of the way, never more than six feet off. There were dirt and alligators, but neither harmed me. It was about 47 miles altogether. I was at it ten days, but in the water only some 50 hours—more on some days than others. I dived in at Colon and swam three miles without a stop. The passage through the locks was a stupendous contrast. I was locked through alone with my little boat. 27,000,000 cubic feet of water were used to lift me the 85 feet into Gatun Lake, and just as much mechanical labor, just as much expense, just as much everything, as to lift the biggest ship that ever passed through. Over a thousand people watched the unique doings. The lake was a long monotonous pull, 22 miles, and took about four days. I had to go back to Colon every night and get up at 4 A.M. to start the machinery—launch, boatmen, food and gasoline. The Gatun cut passage was wonderful. I was locked down the other side and made thirteen miles the last two days.

I'm leaving tonight (having had lunch today with the Governor of Panama and his wife) for San Miguel Bay, a hundred miles south, to find the spot where Balboa saw the Pacific first. My plans are uncertain—I may not go down the Amazon, Dad. The books I sent for have not yet arrived at Colon.

Fred is just so-so. The poor kid has had one hard time. The fever's gone but he's very weak. He's continuing, however, and we hope he'll pick up. He was in the hospital all the time I was swimming. I've got to dash off to the Navy tugboat that's taking me to San Miguel Bay.

We came from Nicaragua to Colon on a United States battleship—very grand!

[*Panama—September 6, 1928.*] Off tonight for Peru after a wonderful week in the jungles locating the Peak in Darien where Balboa saw the Pacific. I'm top hole, Fred's well again, and we're getting away in fine shape.

[*Lima—September 18, 1928.*] Whoopee! I've found the books you sent me. They'd been here three weeks, lost in the post office. It was a great relief and help to get them. I've been reading ravenously, trying to formulate my next step. *This* step has been made anyway: I've stopped rushing and decided to get as far as I can in good old Royal Road fashion and come back next May or June to the point where I leave off and carry on from there. Dad's letter helped me decide. If the book is delayed, it will be worth waiting for. This change permits me to cover more territory, collect more material and concentrate as in *R. R.* on the best.

Our voyage down from Panama was uneventful. Ambassador Alexander Moore has been especially kind, and arranged for me to see President Leguia—which I did at great length, and got a fine chapter. We've been wined and dined to death. The papers have carried so many pictures and stories I've not even tried to collect them. The President is a most extraordinary little man, weighs only 98 pounds, but, oh, my, he's absolute dictator and has been for 25 years. His life has been one long adventure. We talked for an hour and a half while ministers stormed outside. I asked him about his youth and his children, so, of course, he let go.

I've not *yet* sent anything to the *Home Journal*. With this new policy of returning later, I can afford to discard all second-class copy.

It looks as though Fred (who is quite all right again—he's been up in the mountains duck shooting while I've worked) and I will take a trip over the Andes and two days by airplane over the jungle to Iquitos, returning to Lima by air. We'll know today.

My hair is growing out a little—and my beard looks very elegant.

[*Lima—October 1, 1928.*] *Still* in Lima—over three weeks now— which doesn't necessarily mean I like the place. One blasted thing after another has held us up. I sent Fred with a party of local Americans up over the Andes to keep him occupied while I was working. The train goes almost 16,000 feet, and the altitude nearly finished him. He was unconscious for several hours, caught a bad case of dysentery and got home a total wreck. Three days in bed have repaired him somewhat. We canceled our air trip over the jungle, and have decided to skip jungles altogether this time. I know you'll be glad.

[*Lima—October 5, 1928.*] Tomorrow I get out of this blasted place and on to Cuzco. I'm having to leave Fred behind, as he's still prostrate from the results of his "high flying" in the mountains. He came *very* near dying, and but for oxygen applications would have. He's staying for two more weeks here while I go on to Cuzco and Manchu Picchu—the train goes 15,000 feet to get there—and it would be Fred's last ride if *he* went.

I've been having an amusing adventure. One of my articles is about colonial Lima legends (like *The Bridge of San Luis Rey*), told in *Arabian Nights* style by a local girl. She tells me the stories from behind her home's barred windows, while I'm outside with my guitar. Each evening one story up to the climax; then I have to come back to hear the finish, and so on, every night for three or four nights. The stories are all romantic. Today I got her photographed. She's a pretty girl.

[*Arequipa, Peru—October 10, 1928.*] On the move again. I left Lima on the sixth by boat, coasted south three days to Mollendo where the railroad strikes inland. Passenger trains run once a week. I "hopped a freight" and rode on top of a boxcar from noon till 10 P.M. Wild, desolate country. We climbed 8000 feet with 20,000-foot mountains all about. Arequipa is the most Spanish city in Latin America, and the climate unbelievable. The sun pours and floods and dazzles. It never, *never* rains, but the snow water makes a rich oasis. I've baked and soaked all day. Another train takes me on uphill to 15,000 feet tomorrow, and in one more day I reach Cuzco where I strike out for Manchu Picchu. I was loath to leave Fred behind, but there was nothing else to do. He's getting pictures, getting my script typed, and getting some iron back into his wracked body.

This place, more than any spot yet, is the one I most wish to have my fambly see with me. We're all sun worshipers, and Arequipa is one huge sun church.

[*Cuzco, Peru—October 24, 1928.*] Real action since Lima. I was painfully ill from mountain sickness all the 400 miles to Cuzco. It is 11,000 feet up, but I've become used to it. The very next morning after my arrival here I went on to Manchu Picchu, the Inca city a hundred miles north of Cuzco that was lost in the mountain tops and discovered in 1911. It's over the Andes and well down the Amazon slope, and so rather tropical. I climbed the 2500-foot cliff on top of which it's perched in the late afternoon and beheld the most spectacular panorama I've *ever* seen. It's beyond description—the white granite city protected on three sides by the bottomless canyon and backed by wave on wave of Andes until the last far-off range is all snow and 23,000 feet. When I arrived a storm was in action all about me. The black clouds raced over the tops of the distant amphitheater, the thunder bellowed among the imprisoning walls, several rainbows flung themselves across the canyon, the late sun piercing the clouds for a moment struck the granite city, and the river half a mile below on three sides roared and rumbled downhill.

I realized my photographic equipment was inadequate; so, after spending the night in one of the temples, I descended early next day and returned to Cuzco, where I saw all the marvelous ruins and prepared to return to Manchu Picchu. As my guard in the canal swim had dropped my Memphis camera overboard during an alligator scare, I'd had to buy a new one, second hand, and to be sure I knew how to use it, spent one whole day photographing the *same* picture and recording the exposure. Armed with this knowledge, I rode back to the canyon with a funny typical German professor. For four days we had to face rain—no sun—only clouds. The fifth day was clear and I dashed up the heavy two-hour climb a fifth time, for a panorama. I got it at last *fairly* well. It's in five sections, and as no two are the same shade or even-edged it's going to take a world of labor to make the mosaic look like one picture. But skilled fingers in the United States will work the trick.

There's no train out till day after tomorrow, when I go on to Lake Titicaca and La Paz, Bolivia, just to see them, as I anticipate no story but want to pay them a visit on my own.

[*Santiago, Chile—November 6, 1928.*] I reached Santiago last night. From Cuzco I crossed the famous Lake Titicaca and visited Bolivia. The lake is 12,500 feet high, big as Lake Erie, and the scenery perfectly gorgeous—20,000-foot mountains strewn all around. I reached La Paz, the capital of Bolivia, at midnight and saw another scenic drama by the full moon. The city is in an abrupt gulch 1500 feet sheer below the 13,000-foot plain, with the snowy Andes encircling it. In the moonlight, to look down at the city and up at the mountains took my breath away. La Paz is as colorful and foreign as anything in India. I was there three days and took train to Antofagasta in Chile and boat three days south to Valparaiso. Fred had wisely come on ahead and I found him quite recuperated. We're to be here a week waiting for the little lobster boat that takes us to Juan Fernandez. Four days there and four back, so it will be about December first when we start moving again—where I don't know; I've given up trying to make plans.

I still have my beard, and my hair has grown out normal.

The spring sunshine is glorious here. In fact Chile is very, very beautiful, with myriads of flowers, and unbelievably *cheap*. I'll probably freeze when I get back to North America.

[*Valparaiso—November 30, 1928.*] My usual luck of just *catching* things has turned lately to just *missing* 'em. We had to wait ten days in Santiago for the Juan Fernandez boatlet which runs twice a month, and on getting back at last after delays on the island find the trans-Andean railroad to Buenos Aires washed away by a cloudburst and all traffic suspended for a week. Fred and I nearly die from chagrin. My lectures begin at New York on January eleventh. The trip from Rio takes twelve days, leaving twenty-five. Now if I find I can buy a monkey and an organ and get to Rio overland in twenty-five days, I shall do it, since with that checked off I needn't come back to this far-off part of South America any more.

Juan Fernandez was *some* trip in our ridiculous little schooner. The weather was vile, the waves were mountainous—we dived and rolled and tossed. For three days and three nights I was absolutely prostrate with seasickness, after all my sailing. Fred was just as ill. We couldn't even retain a glass of water, and so landed on the island in very sad plight, too weak to stir for twenty-four hours. We found comfortable quarters, however, and enough food, and the second day began to look about. The island is striking in a stern, rugged way, wild and precipitous. We spent a day in and about Selkirk's cave, climbed over the mountains, fished, swam and boated for a week. The fishing was extraordinary, bringing up the famous lobsters, and cod and sea bass weighing 100 pounds, big as we were. The return was just about as bad as the out voyage. Valpo certainly looked good to us.

My Crusoe story will include Juan Fernandez but I'll do my "reliving his life" at Tobago next summer.

[*Buenos Aires—December 12, 1928.*] Fred and I reached here from Valparaiso on the fifth. In coming over the Andes by train, 11,000 feet, the heart strain he received 'way back in Peru returned with a bang. He passed out, and reached Buenos Aires prostrate. Now the only thing to do is let him recuperate here in the hospital, and I'll catch a boat at Rio on January second. The *Vestris* which sank *would* have been our boat, due in New York January ninth. Now the next one arrives there the fifteenth. I've wired Wickes already to cancel or postpone the 11th, 12th, 13th, 14th, 15th dates. He'll have seventy fits, but that can't be helped—there's no boat and it's too far to swim—and I was determined at all cost to clean up down here before leaving.

Well, sir, I'm having the craziest adventure ever. After seven days of grim effort I *did* find and buy a monkey and a hand organ. Both are prohibited in Buenos Aires for some silly reason, and are scarce as diamonds. But yesterday, dressed to fit, I sallied forth, made three pesos, $1.40, by playing and passing the hat. Also a photographer took a dozen pichers—lots of children, of course—and all in all a very amusing day. I'll see the plates this afternoon. The monkey is gentle and knows his begging tricks. I'm taking him with me to Rio.

Buenos Aires is big and rather grand, but Latin American—that is, lazy and incredibly inefficient. People have been very hospitable.

[*At Sea, Pan-American—January 14, 1929.*] Whoopee—almost home! Tomorrow afternoon we land. I'm sorry in a way, it's been such a sunny, busy voyage. I never enjoyed one so much, thirteen full days of tropical seas. It seems impossible that in 24 hours we'll be in ice and snow. There's been a canvas pool on deck, and Fred and I have swum in it every day, even this morning, and I'm now lying half-dressed on the top deck getting my last sunburn. On January ninth your birthday radio came to me at dinner just when I was feeling particularly lonely. It made me feel like a king.

I dread having to plunge in, but I've had a fine rest on the boat and need activity. I'll be busy buying an overcoat, getting a new suit, hat, shoes, and on to my lecture date. My wardrobe is all white, and in rags.

What a time I've had since my last letter! The monkey business gave me what I wanted, a good story. We left B. A. and played the part, traveling second class, 36 hours by train to a point on the Paraná River (Posadas) and 36 hours by river boat. Everywhere Niño the monk stopped traffic. I never saw such an irresistible pet. He was fed to death, of course, but was always able to dance when I played the hand organ. We attracted children by swarms—the Pied Piper had no more lure than our monkey. We saw the marvelous Iguassú Falls together, greater than Niagara, and the La Guayra Falls, three times as big as Iguassú, 125 miles deeper into the interior. It certainly was the wilds, the very heart of Brazil. We started up the Paraná on a tiny river boat but 36 hours out a passenger died and we had to turn back to bury him at the home port—then four more days and nights back up the river. We reached a railroad at last and traveled 36 hours to São Paulo where I sent you the cable. Christmas Day was spent on the train. It was desperately hot and insecty—mosquitoes and flies, and dust. We got to Rio in one night's ride. The distance from Buenos to Rio is as far as from Boston to New Orleans.

Fred had arrived by water two days before me. We found a small hotel outside of town on a beach and proceeded to live in the surf. Niño and I, however, saw Rio right, and played our hand organ on all the principal corners. Rio is indescribably beautiful, by far the gem among the cities of South America, of the world for that matter—a thousand times more charming than B. A.

I brought the monkey aboard to give him to Ammudder's kindergarten but it died on the boat.

[*New York—Sunday, January 20, 1929.*] I'm still faint and dazed a bit from the past four or five days. On landing I taxied to the Bobbs-Merrill office where I collected three tons of mail, which I'm *still* reading. Between no clothes and lecture pressure and torrents of upsetting news, good and bad, I was about ready to pass out. But things are adjusting themselves. My lecturing is straightened out, though I sputtered and groped at first.

I had a busy time speaking in Boston and Danbury and got home to sleep for the first good rest since I left the boat.

[*On the train—January 23, 1929.*] This morning the first check from Schuler came, $2500, and I saw the layout for our first *L. H. J.* story, a beautiful decorative map and *three* full pages. He thinks Cortez is swell.

I'm back in New York Saturday to see the *Times*. They're giving me a double spread of rotogravure pictures.

The letters that follow resume the kaleidoscopic time card. To rehearse its details would serve no purpose but to create astonishment at the energy which saw the schedule through, all the "fixed and steady motion." The geographical hurlyburly, the hours of arrival and departure, are therefore omitted, and only occasional comments selected.

"I had a long talk with Wickes in Boston and am going to ask $900 per week next year. I've found a secretary named Shattuck, made to order, a recent Harvard graduate. . . . I didn't object to Beverley Nichols' opinions of me, but most violently to the invented words he puts in my mouth."

At Notre Dame University, February 8, 1929: "Two thousand boys, from seventeen to twenty-two years old, were in my audience, and we had a regular riot. I don't think I ever had a more intent audience. I talked about Rupert Brooke and you could have heard a pin drop. When I ended they cheered so long I went back and told the Panama swim story. The Catholic Fathers who ran the engagement did it with rare distinction. . . . I can use Shattuck only in spurts, but he's *very* useful then."

In Chicago after a trip to the northern peninsula of Michigan: "Schuler was in town, incidentally to see me, mainly to take part in a big annual Curtis Publishing Company conference of advertising men and sub-managers. He asked me if I'd speak. I certainly would, and did, for half an hour. It was a fine chance to get to know my new family."

Finding that he is to be in Springfield, Missouri, on February twenty-third, Richard insists his mother and father and Ammudder meet him there. At Boise, Idaho, March first: "Our day together worked out beautifully, didn't it?—except for the nervous prostration I gave everybody by being so late. You mustn't ever worry about my being late. I went on my way with a light heart. . . . Of course, Dad, there'll always be new and alluring adventures awaiting me. I told the Panama yarn at Springfield just for you. All through it is the theme:

> 'It is the things we have that go.
> The things we cannot have, remain,'

with the idea that I'd never have been happy unless I did the canal. It would always have 'remained,' but once I'd swum it, all interest departed. I forgot it in yearning for the Hesperides. Next year, by way of resting, I may do the Crusades after all. It's too good not to. *Off to the Crusades* would make a fine title. . . .

"Mike brought Chan Sweet to the Kansas City station and we had a grand reunion. . . . I had a dumb audience of cowboys at Pueblo."

On the train in California, March twelfth: "I'm more than usual living by a machinery that doesn't permit any *would-like-to's,* only *must-to's.* Every seizable minute for five weeks I've put on my Panama story and at last got it off yesterday to Philadelphia, 9000 words. It's a week late, but maybe Schuler can squeeze it in beside President Coolidge's third story. Think of my being featured along with the President!

"Judge Ben Lindsey stayed over for my lecture at Eugene, Oregon. We breakfasted and lunched together. He sees social problems straight and true."

On the train from Denver to Colorado Springs, March eighteenth: "I had airmailed my Panama story and the mail plane *crashed.* It was, as I've said, already late for Schuler, and he and I were both going gray-headed from worry. Finally he telephoned me to get him a carbon copy. I didn't have one. So I had to sit at a desk from five yesterday afternoon till eleven this morning—seventeen hours—to rewrite the entire 9000 words from my notes. Schuler probably heard my howls in Philadelphia."

At Arkadelphia, Arkansas, March twenty-eighth: "I had a funny adventure in Lafayette, Louisiana. My impersonator had been to town last fall—said he was there incognito collecting copy for stories. He was entertained by the college I spoke for and the people who met him would not believe me when I vowed I had never been in their town before. My double must be a good one. I would like to meet him."

After engagements in the Southeast which he always especially enjoyed, a friend motored him through the Shenandoah Valley. "It was apple-blossom time and all the orchards in bloom." He heard Roland Hayes' "wonderful and moving voice" in New York.

In Indiana, April thirtieth: "Bobbs-Merrill wants my new manuscript by October first. They're starting the pictures already. A very good book or nothing. I've told Alber nothing doing next year. . . . Last night I spoke at the big Catholic girls' college at St. Mary's of the Woods—about a thousand girls and several hundred Sisters. The entire school escorted me across the campus to my taxi. I'll probably miss such evenings next year, but I'm quite resolved on taking a vacation. Dad is right about my nerves needing a change. They'll get it."

Richard breathed a great sigh of relief when he had filled his last speaking date, and could hurry home for a little rest. Soon he must adventure forth again, for to complete *New Worlds to Conquer* he had still those Devil's Island and Robinson Crusoe stories to develop.

[*S. S. Matura nearing Barbados—June 20, 1929.*] I stopped in Philadelphia. There I found notification to call Bobbs-Merrill and learned the *Matura's* sailing had been postponed at the last minute from June seventh to twelfth. Naturally I was wild—days are so precious—but I resolved to make the best of it, and since I'd been cheated out of five days more with you I'd see to it that my monkey story profited anyway. So I went to the hotel in Philadelphia, locked myself in, worked like everything, and got it delivered. Schuler was very pleased. But I didn't get to New York till 24 hours before sailing, for I was determined to finish the story or bust. Then in New York I simply dashed. The boat sailed at noon next day from Brooklyn. I nearly had heart failure taxi-ing to it. As we turned a corner a bag I'd stowed up front rolled out. I didn't discover the loss for two blocks. We went back and found it on the sidewalk. It contained everything of value. I was weak for hours.

The boat is the most awful tub I've ever sailed on, dirty and old and chiefly for freight. But even so I've enjoyed it. Not a soul on board knows me. I've lived quite alone and already written half my Central American episodes. I'll finish the other half soon.

The sea has been like glass—nice breeze. I saw a whole *school* of *whales,* six or more all at once. Before, I'd seen only one at a time.

[*Queen's Park Hotel, Trinidad—June 22, 1929.*] I'm expecting a most curious and successful adventure, Crusoe on Tobago, though I will have to build it up. I missed the weekly steamer and couldn't wait six days for it. So I engaged a big launch. At the last minute it couldn't go, but I *had* to go. I took a motor to Toco hoping to find a sailboat. No luck. But at Bolinda I did find a tiny sloop willing to go for $50. So I'll be leaving tomorrow. I must get my wares together.

[*On the train to Miami—August 20, 1929.*] Believe it or not, you *have* a son who is still very much intact, though this is the first letter I've written since the last of June. Here's why:

I got away on my sailboat for Tobago and it was a wild adventurous voyage, stormy and wet. She carried a small cargo of week-old fish that made us all seasick, and took 24 hours to sail 40 miles. I found Tobago a most heavenly island. I could have stayed there indefinitely, but not with the family I had accumulated. It was all just play, and it was fun doing it. The pictures came out fine. And I finished my two Central American stories and caught up to date.

Back to Trinidad on the regular steamer. The airplane for French Guiana was leaving the same day.

The trip to Devil's Island was unquestionably the most successful I've yet enjoyed. I had the luck of the Devil at every turn and brought back a story which in itself will make our book a success. I've returned entirely satisfied with results; my pictures turned out superbly; and the story—16,000 words—has been delivered to Schuler and forgot about. I worked furiously on the boat coming back and buried myself in my New York hotel room to finish it.

Yesterday I caught the night train for Miami. My seaplane is waiting for me. It's going to be thrilling to fly to Columbus' island, the first time anyone's done it. Back to Miami Friday to catch the night train for Memphis. I should arrive Saturday night and can stay till the next Saturday night. Then I must go to New York again for two weeks. I'll not begin my Crusoe story till everything else is on the press.

This pressure of work against dead-line dates is terrible, but I love it. If I only had my Crusoe written the rest would be too easy.

CHAPTER XIV

SELLING TO THE MOVIES AND BUYING A PLANE

[*Atlantic City—Sunday, September 8, 1929.*] See where I am. I fled down here to write Crusoe, which I'd not yet begun. I was getting desperate. I finished the rough draft last night and will type it today, and on Monday morning I'll go to Philadelphia to deliver it to Schuler and talk about our future plans, if any.

[*New York—September 15, 1929.*] The contract with the Garden City Publishing Company for popular editions of my books *guarantees* us 250,000 sales. I'm told it's the biggest guarantee they have given up to this time.

I turned in the Crusoe story to Schuler and Chambers Sunday. Schuler telephones that he is enthusiastic. Trying to write in an assumed, archaic style nearly drove me crazy. Now I'll be full of nothing to do.

[*Monday, October 7, 1929.*] Tomorrow I'm spending three hours with Schuler in Philadelphia. I want to do another Devil's Island story, using the manuscript and the letters that I've received. A flock of them came yesterday, some informing me that the kindly old commandant of the islands had been court-martialed because of my visit. He'll probably be shot when my book appears! I'm distressed. The letters from his sister and daughter are pathetic.

We are planning a series of book parties, one each day in a succession of big cities, starting November thirtieth in Chicago. They will last through December seventh.

[*New York—Tuesday, October 22, 1929.*] Yesterday I went to see the *Times* rotogravure man with my pictures. He's taking twelve for a full page on Sunday, December first, the same day Bobbs-Merrill burst forth with a full-page ad in the book section, and *simultaneously*

303

in many other newspapers in the country. We're going to have a party here on November 26, two days before Thanksgiving and one day before publication date. We're asking about 100 and planning for about 80 to come. I don't like the idea, but it seems a shame, having worked so hard to produce, to let down now and not help make the product a popular success.

His mother went to New York for the reception and accompanied him to Chicago, Indianapolis and Cincinnati where other parties were given to launch *New Worlds to Conquer*. In January the weary traveler took a busman's holiday in Bermuda, without thought of copy, but only of sun—sun—sun. On his return he had an excellent radio opportunity if his voice was right for it. But the judges at the audition didn't think he could get close enough to the "vast unseen audience."

Once more he started on the "terrific motion" of a lecture tour. Notable was an address on Devil's Island to the American Educational Association at Atlantic City. He was working on a short article for the *Junior League Magazine,* called "Where I'll Spend My Honeymoon." In the course of a long swing he saw John D. playing golf on a very cold day in Florida; addressed an audience of 2200 at his beloved Philadelphia Forum, with Heinie and Dot on hand; traveled west in a furious snowstorm; passed a sunny Sunday with his friend Noel Sullivan at the estate near San Francisco of Noel's uncle, ex-Senator Phelan. "This is the perfect week for flowers and the sixty-mile drive through the orchards was bewilderingly beautiful."

[*Tucson—April, 1930.*] *New Worlds* is not going so well as I had hoped for. The difficulty is this general nationwide depression in business. Bookstores are experiencing the worst slump in twenty years and are not daring to buy five-dollar books by *anybody.*

Yesterday I had a busy time in Los Angeles with the Fox Film people. We just got acquainted. They were most cordial. They want me to do an "adventure story" and I want to do my own books.

[*Roosevelt Hotel, Hollywood—Easter Sunday, 1930.*] Last week end a friend of Noel's and I motored to Yosemite Park. Wonderful roads, wonderful country. The falls are thrilling beyond expression. Monday we went to San Quentin prison for the day. It was most depressing—packed to bursting and unspeakably miserable. The warden invited me to attend a hanging and stay a week as his guest to do a story about the place!

The money figures people fling around out here are dumfounding. The Fox Company keep urging me to do an original. Nothing may come of it. Perhaps my books are really not suitable for movies. They may buy a title and my name, I suppose.

As I wired you the flying business is much exaggerated. Last February one Captain Pat McCarthy (British) called and said, "I'm flying the Atlantic. Want to go?" I said, "Sure." We had lunch. There was no plane, no money, no backing. I haven't heard from him in a month, and had forgotten all about it. My health is all right. I weigh 152, more than ever before in my life.

Maybe you're right about publicity, Dad. I'm tired of it myself, but it's sold books and may sell movie rights. Phil Kubel at Robinson's had a nice book party for me.

This is the most demoralizing place in the world.

[*Roosevelt Hotel, Hollywood—Wednesday, May 14, 1930.*] Your phantom son has been doing a Job lately, with a capital J. Not having been ill for some years, I seem to be making up for lost time. Last Friday I went to the beach for a swim, lay on the sand with friends for half an hour, knew better than to risk the sun with salt on me and didn't go in the sea, but even so I got the worst burn in my life. I've *never* been so uncomfortable for three days.

Friday night, fried though I'd been that day, I went out to dinner at Eleanor Wilson McAdoo's, President Wilson's daughter. She took me to the theater and *dancing,* imagine! She's enormously charming and intelligent.

Still nothing has happened to our books with the movies. But it takes time. We must remember the agonizing struggle we had to get a lecture manager; and then it took two years to find a publisher. I can't expect to walk into the movies without more battles.

Except for being darned ugly from peeling skin, I can't think of anything wrong with me this morning.

[*Roosevelt Hotel, Hollywood—Saturday, May 17, 1930.*] Things seem to be moving a bit. Two days ago the Fox Company called and asked how much I wanted for *Royal Road*. I talked with Mr. Curtis* and yesterday made a proposition at a conference. The figures will be presented to the highest-ups, and I'll hear again next week. A hundred projects collapse out here to one that succeeds.

[*Roosevelt Hotel, Hollywood—May 27, 1930.*] The Fox Company made me an offer and I wouldn't accept! I'd asked more. There it stands. I may not hear for another week.

The money thrown around out here still appalls me. People of the commonest, stupidest type get $5000, $7000, $10,000 a *week*. Any actor or director or writer receiving less than $1000 feels ready to join a revolution. At the same time other people are starving by the thousand. There's the worst depression in history here.

Tomorrow night I'm having Mr. and Mrs. McAdoo to dinner and the theater. I had tea with them Monday to meet Wei San Fang, the Chinese actor. He is a graduate of the University of Tennessee, by the way.

[*Hollywood—Thursday, June 5, 1930.*] Last Sunday I spoke at a boys reformatory school—500 misfit boys. We had a great time. Thursday morning I spoke at a breakfast for the benefit of the Hollywood Bowl. Tomorrow morning I'm speaking for 4000 kids at the Hollywood High School. June 26 I'm speaker for the banquet of the convention of the American Library Association. So you see I'm busy, even if I'm not working for the movies. The Fox people haven't peeped.

I have been taking a balance of my affairs, trying to stand off and look at myself objectively. By no means do I intend to give up writing books to devote myself to the movies, but I do not see that collecting a fat fee for the movie-izing of a book already done should hurt. A certain money consciousness has been developed in me from my own past experience. I must have security. I can no longer enjoy the rewards of creative work enough to accept economic pressure along

---

* John J. Curtis, then President of the Bobbs-Merrill Company, who had been working to advance Richard's movie cause.

To show its vast size Richard poses on top this huge monolith quarried by the ancient builders of Palmyra.

Before swimming the Sea of Galilee, Richard is photographed with two fishermen.

with it. Don't worry about Hollywood demoralizing me. It's no worse than any other place, but I must admit I'd rather be writing a nice book than messing with these lousy movies.

[*Hollywood—June 30, 1930.*] My wire informed you that at last we sold *Royal Road*. I'm dead tired from the struggle and am going down to the beach now (Friday afternoon) and stay till Sunday night.

Richard's reaction to this battle of selling movie rights and to the artificial life in which he had been whirling was an impelling desire to get away from Hollywood and out again into the wide fields of adventure. The idea of a trip around the world in his own airplane struck his imagination. Such a journey offered, he thought, un-limited possibilities for the adventurous variety which he craved, and for a new book. He determined on it immediately.

He wired his parents urgently to come to Hollywood, not di-vulging what was in his mind. They left Memphis at once and when they reached California Richard told them about it. After several days' discussion and analysis, they agreed that they would not oppose such an unusual enterprise.

Acting with his usual impulsiveness, he straightway began the the search for plane and pilot. This proved a greater undertaking than he had anticipated.

[*Chicago—Wednesday night, September 10, 1930.*] I left, not the morning after you left, but the next. I flew on to Wichita and then learned of a grand big Stearman plane with a 500-horse-power motor for sale by Cliff Durant of Detroit. I sped on to Detroit and saw the plane and Durant. He liked my idea and offered me the plane *free* if I'd take his own pilot, but the engine burns 30 gallons of gas an *hour* and abroad gas costs 75c. I got a wire from Schuler today saying, "When do you start? I want Foreign Legion first." So all is coming out O. K.

[*The Stevens, Chicago—Friday night, September, 1930.*] It's been just about the most unpleasant ten days I can remember, and not over airplanes or gasoline but a wisdom tooth. It had been sensitive for several days and the day I arrived it blew up. A dentist finally had a look, gave me gas, and out she came, but I've been absolutely prostrate ever since. I've forgotten airplanes, gasoline, Schuler, Hollywood—everything except the pain. But it's better for it to have happened in Chicago than in Morocco.

The Durant ship was just too good to be true and too big. I'm going on to St. Louis tonight, to Wichita and back to Hollywood with only one resolve—to get Moye Stephens, who has been so enthusiastically recommended to me, and a satisfactory ship and get going. I've had no end of alarms and warnings and *can't-be-done's,* but so have I always had.

Chicago swarms with bums and beggars. There are 400,000 men out of work here.

I am so eager to begin producing again. This delay has given me a chance to look over a few books on Morocco. It grows in interest. I'll go there first.

[*Los Angeles—Tuesday night, September 23, 1930.*] I got to Wichita again Sunday night and saw the Stearman people on Monday. Talk! Talk! Talk! Bids and bargaining, engines and instruments, gas and oil—Lord, the things I'm learning! Nothing definite was settled. I left Wichita for Los Angeles Wednesday by air. It was a long, heavy trip—strong headwind—we were three hours late—flew from 6:30 to 11:30 P.M. in absolute darkness and fog. It was no fun, but we landed quite safely.

[*Los Angeles—Monday, October 6, 1930.*] Fortunately these delays have given us time to have plenty of actions and reactions, and have left the idea of my world flight stripped of all the clothes that cover the facts. I've never swerved from a tremendous enthusiasm for this idea—*for me.* I've tried to reason out some substitute that would be reasonably acceptable, but always I come back to the Flying Carpet as the best program. If I'm to keep my position in my own field I must continue to pioneer where others may follow. Our imitators and my own repetitions have exhausted the soil of the once rich romantic travel form. We must up stakes and strike out for fresh fields. This flying idea will hit a new note of adventure. It has been attacked from every side. It continues to stand unshaken.

The practical facts to be faced have reduced themselves to this: I am not going to start out in a feeble plane. It must have all possible power that can be carried by a plane of small enough dimensions to be handled by one pilot, carried on boats and landed in ordinary rough fields. I find there are landing fields very nearly everywhere I want to go. The plane will be used where it can safely be used, and I'll radiate out from its stable.

[*Hollywood—Friday, October 10, 1930.*] There's light amid the encircling gloom. The Shell people have written they will sell me gas wholesale and return to me the price paid, as a bonus, on my *return*.

[*Hollywood—Sunday, October 26, 1930.*] I went to Erle Halliburton's ranch Saturday morning and didn't come back till Monday night. We had a *grand* time. He said he "thought it could be fixed to get me a plane *free.*" And after a week's time, he did get me one—his own Lockheed. It's the plane he and his pilot have flown all over America in. He has bought him a new tri-motored Ford for his own use, and no longer needs the Lockheed, which he insists is the best, fastest and safest plane I can get—and he's *giving* it to me with no strings whatsoever. I've told Moye Stephens about my new plans. He doesn't want to go in anything but an open Stearman, thinks the Lockheed too big.

I'm not letting myself be elated over this new turn—I've had too many last-minute disappointments.

[*Hollywood—November 19, 1930.*] My wire two weeks ago told you the good news—that I had definitely chosen a small Stearman plane, and once my mind was made up, I went forward with concentration of purpose. Immediately after I closed the deal for the plane, I went to the mat with Moye Stephens and won him over as my pilot. I am quite sure he is the best qualified pilot on my horizon for this particular trip. I have turned over to him the entire equipping of the ship.

The engine, the "J-5"—225 H. P., is the same engine that Lindbergh used to fly the Atlantic. I am leaving the wings as they are but painting the body a bright scarlet, with black struts. I think it will be very beautiful. Moye and the mechanics all agree it is going to be a flawlessly equipped ship and the sturdiest and the safest. Yesterday, Moye and I acquired fur-lined flying suits, since, because of the late date of our departure, we will have cold flying from here to New York, and from London to Morocco. The mechanics and Moye are working day and night, and we expect to be in the air in about ten days.

Mrs. Stephens, who is a most wise and charming woman, wanted us to stay for Thanksgiving Day, that she might give us a farewell party. I had hoped to be home for Thanksgiving, myself, but couldn't make it, and to be with the Stephens, to whom I have become truly devoted, is the next best thing. They have not the slightest uneasiness over the hazards of our expedition; they have seen Moye flying almost daily for eight years, and think no more of it than they do over his driving their motor car. Time and again, he has demonstrated his clear and cautious head as a flyer, and they know that he will not take the slightest chance.

I have been speaking at banquets, at schools and over the radio two and three times a week. This morning, for example, I spoke for the famous Breakfast Club to a thousand men, and my speech was broadcast over the radio. An hour later, I had a high-school audience of 3000 students, and tonight, I'm to speak at the University of Southern California. I love the excitement and, as you know, I'm never so alive as when I have too much to do.

[*Hollywood—November 30, 1930.*] Our paint job is complete, the gas tanks installed, and the engine attached. The mechanics are working overtime, and I stand by to superintend. "The Flying Carpet" has been painted on the gold stripe along the side. We have had our first inoculations for typhoid and our vaccinations, and we're both sick as dogs.

I'm not the least worried over my neck, with Moye as a pilot, or over my safety with myself as captain. I've always had a gift for taking care of Riffs and Berbers and Arabs. However, I'm having two big American flags painted on my ship.

[*Hollywood—December 13, 1930.*] Each adjustment for the Flying Carpet takes hours. Moye is leaning over backward to have everything running mechanically perfect. We have had several short flights, so that already I feel at home in my own airplane.

Four days ago, I flew with five friends of mine 300 miles south into Mexico and spent a day and night. We flew all along the coast and had a very beautiful journey. The days continue to be packed to bursting, and with life so exciting and so full, the strain is beginning to tell.

Richard and Moye took to the air on December twenty-second and headed for Memphis, where they expected to arrive in time for Christmas dinner. Out of Wichita Christmas morning they ran into fog and were forced down at Fort Smith. It was the twenty-sixth when they got in.

The morning they left Memphis for New York was cold and gray, but the gaily painted plane made a gallant sight. The family and a score or more of Richard's friends braved the chill wind to wave them farewell.

[*Philadelphia—January 14, 1931.*] Our journey to St. Louis was uneventful. We had dinner with the Shell official, and were up long before dawn next morning, hoping to lunch in Indianapolis and sleep in Columbus. But the ground fog was impenetrable, we had to wait till after five o'clock to take off, and made Indianapolis before dark and no more. I had a good visit with Chambers before dinner and took Moye out to his home after dinner.

Wheeling the next night, and the morning after the weather was terrible. We got to Pittsburgh and started out for Washington, but the fog came along and we found a small landing field some twenty miles east and lay over. The following day was beautiful and we simply raced into Philadelphia. Schuler had a number of nice people in for Moye and me to meet Sunday afternoon. He is much taken with Moye and our ship, but he still shows little enthusiasm for our expedition—feels it will never produce stories right for him. I asked him the direct question, "If I produce, will you publish?" And he answered directly, "Yes." So that's that. It's up to me.

Moye and I went to Washington and yesterday saw the Department of Commerce and the State Department. They are helping us in every way they can.

The experiences we had on here from Memphis—fog, rain, mountains, strange country—have been a good test for Moye, and he continues to give me a feeling of the utmost confidence. His ability and steadiness as a flyer continue to amaze and delight me.

[*New York—Tuesday, January 27, 1931.*] I've been on the job day and night, getting things done. Thursday we take the wings off and stow her aboard the *Majestic* which docked today. Then Friday *we* go aboard and sail at five o'clock. And *what* a relief that will be! I'm pretty tired and will enjoy resting and reading. Max Aley is going along on the same boat.

I went last Friday to dinner and theater with Mary Pickford—had tea with the Norrises—met Odd McIntyre and Irvin Cobb, and Fanny Hurst, and Edna Ferber, and no end of others. Tomorrow Moye and I dine with Haff and Aunt Susie to say goodbye.

I have found pontoons, and am having them sent to Calcutta. The White Star line is charging me $450 to ship my plane and $270 each for us, but watch me *get it back*.

[*The Duane, New York—January 30, 1931.*] All went well yesterday when we loaded the Flying Carpet aboard the *Majestic*. I just about had nervous prostration during the few tense minutes when our ship was suspended in the air.

I'm leaving in the best of spirits, and happy that you are so wholly with me. That is such a *big* help.

CHAPTER XV

[*On board S.S. Majestic—February 5, 1931.*] We are five days out
and land tomorrow night, but I am staying aboard to help unload the
airplane and get it safely on its way to the flying field where we can
reassemble. The plane was beautifully tied down and covered up,
so Moye and I have never given it a thought. I will hurry on to
London with the baggage and get our British permission to fly.

At our table on the boat are Max Aley and the editor of *Collier's*.
We've had a very happy time, and the trip has gone all too quickly,
since I am just beginning to get rested and relaxed.

Dad's letter was a masterpiece. I am going to send it back home
to be put away for his grandchildren to read.

[*London—February 21, 1931.*] We leave tomorrow morning for
Paris. Every day we've made the rounds of map-makers, insurance
agents, consuls, flying offices—endless red tape and silly regulations.
But tonight we seem ready. Our books and baggage have been
shipped ahead, our insurance is settled, our maps glitter before us (to
Morocco and back to Paris and over the Alps to Italy)—they are perfect and we can't *possibly* get lost. We have a stack of official papers
a foot thick.

We got ashore from the *Majestic* with considerable difficulty.
It was cold and raining, and the plane was banged about no end by
the wind. We spent three days repairing and reassembling. The
fourth day was storming, but on the fifth we were able to make a London landing field easily over the lovely country of rural England. The
airdrome was most efficient and accommodating. Moye has continued to test, our 'chutes have been repacked, our complicated contracts with the Shell Oil Company made satisfactorily. This maze
of custom deposits and military restrictions, etc., is all being ironed
out here at the beginning, and once we're under way and get into our
stride we'll shed these worries and these burdens.

Here in London Moye and I have divided our duties. He goes to the flying field, and I to the offices. We get along beautifully, with perfect understanding and mutual respect. I nearly blow up from impatience at times over his slow gear, but never have I felt so certain that I am in safe hands.

The most wonderful thing in London is the Persian art exhibit—rugs, jewels, bronzes. I saw Eddie Marsh about the Brooke situation. Mrs. Brooke died recently. But I'll have no chance to look that way for another two years at least.

[*Paris—Wednesday, March 4, 1931.*] We arrived safely from London on schedule. The sun broke through the perpetual gloom and we enjoyed clear sailing. Everything was checking smoothly, and Moye, with his unerring eye, hit Paris right on the head. We seemed to cross the Channel in no time. We've been here ten days, terribly impatient to be off. For some reason Washington failed to include Spain in its flying permit requests; so we sit until Madrid obliges us. Also the American government has never recognized the French occupation of Morocco, and that has complicated things.

On Saturday I went to St.-Malo and Mont-St.-Michel, on the Brittany coast; away three days.

[*Paris—March 12, 1931.*] We have our passports in order, and diplomatically are all set and ready to begin getting somewhere. Moye is still having trouble with his ailerons (the rods that control the elevation) and we may be delayed again from mis-mechanics. I'll about burst if we *are* delayed.

I've frozen for two months. It snows here all the time. I've wet feet and a blue nose. Thank God for Morocco!

[*Paris—March 20, 1931.*] We *were* delayed. Fortunately a Wright expert came to Paris, and to our rescue, a master mechanic who found the vibration of our ailerons was caused by their having been installed upside down when the ship was assembled in California. This was corrected. I hope we can truly be off tomorrow. Some years ago I'd have accepted this delay with ill grace, but I've learned patience better by now. But my God, won't I be happy to work again!

The more I read about the Foreign Legion the more interesting it becomes. I'm going to enjoy my job there.

[*British Post Office, Fez—March 31, 1931.*] When we finally left Paris all was in perfect order. The ailerons were finally cured, the engine hummed, our passports were in order. We stopped for fuel at Lyons, where I spent Xmas day in 1919, and moved on down the Rhone valley, all green and blue in the spring. Evening found us at Avignon. I'd always wanted to see this town, so we called it a day. Avignon was lovely—all sunny (at last) and romantic. We spent the morning there, flew over the Roman Pont du Gard, had a look at Vimes and stopped at Perpignan near the Spanish border for fuel and customs. Between them, we were held up so late we got no farther than Barcelona.

Barcelona was familiar, too. I'd stopped there two weeks after Andorra to write my Andorra story, and to meet Paul McGrath. No time to tarry now. All the next day we flew down the beach, nearly 600 miles, over Valencia, Alicante and Cartagena. Bright sun— stormy mountains inland—clear skies over the Mediterranean. It was movingly beautiful, and compensated in one day for all the tears we'd shed to achieve it. That night at Malaga, with vineyards for miles on every side. Two French civilian fliers accompanied us that far from Barcelona, but we were too fast and efficient, and we lost them there.

And next day Gibraltar! I've not experienced any emotion in ten years that set me to thinking about time and tide so much as the re-vision of this old Rock. I'd had such memorable adventures there in 1922, the ecstasies and escapades. The Rock had not changed by so much as a tree or bush, but I'd changed into a different person. I seemed not ten but a hundred years older. Gibraltar typified my youth. That's gone, but the fact that I should again visit it in so adventurous a vehicle as an airplane, and that my own, assured me I had not yet begun to fossilize. Had I looked ahead, that famous night, from Rock Gun Point to March in 1931, I should certainly not have believed so full and violent a career could possibly result from the leap I was taking off the Gibraltar springboard.

But I couldn't day-dream long. The Straits of Gibraltar were beneath us, and exceedingly rough. We circled over the Rock, and fled straight south down the African coast. I piloted all that morning as the course was straight. We landed at Rabât in French Morocco and had a fine welcome (as everywhere else). Our plane caused a sensation with its lines and color. We had to get more documents—and came on across country to Fez. Moye has never missed a destination by one inch. We fly with absolute precision. And we reached *this* destination as safely and casually as you please.

The Legion is all about. I've talked and read and observed, but I've been too occupied seeing and getting organized to concentrate on it yet. We spent a day and night visiting a Lieutenant Hamilton who is the only American officer in the Legion. He was *very* helpful. I've engaged a house to live in on my return. I'm writing in it now. It's a typical Moorish house—a garden and pool surrounded by a court. I'll not be in it much, but need some place to store and to invite. Fez is marvelous. I'm going to get a good story out of it, I'm sure. This morning Moye and I are leaving for Timbuctoo.

[*Colomb Bechar, Algiers—April 6, 1931.*] I wrote you only a few days ago but unexpectedly find a chance to continue. We left Fez and flew over the Atlas Mountains to Colomb Bechar. We ran into a sand storm after getting over the mountains and had some difficulty finding it. It was quite exciting, but we landed and the noise of the Flying Carpet brought out French soldiers who aided us in getting the plane into a hangar.

Now we plunge into the Sahara. It's 1300 miles to Gao, and not one tree or house or human being.

[*Timbuctoo—April 25, 1931.*] It's been a wonderful experience, getting here, trying our endurance. We ran into more trouble at Colomb Bechar, waiting for permission to cross the Sahara, the idea being that in case we failed to reach the other side, the French air force must search for us. Finally we got the word.

From Colomb Bechar, on the north, to Gao, on the south edge, was 1300 miles. There was one oasis at 400 miles, and a gas tank at 400 more. We had only the very faint automobile track to follow, and it was often obliterated by the shifting sand. We must follow this track, otherwise we would never find the gas station. And follow it we did. Moye's eyes and mine were fixed desperately on it. It took intense attention to observe it at times, on hard ground.

The first 400 miles, we saw several oases to break the monotony of wilderness. But the next 800 miles were real blankness—not a rise of 100 feet, not a blade of grass, not a human being. This part of the Sahara is hard ground, a burned crust of gravel without a dip or a crack. The calm sea is no flatter.

I had no time to philosophize about life, though it took us eight hours. We had to fight a heavy head wind to reach the gas station—just a tank left for passing trucks and airplanes. At 500 feet it looked like any one of a thousand rocks, but Moye saw it. The heat and sun were incredible. The horizon was a straight line. What with head winds and filling our gas tank by hand in the blistering sun, we could not make our destination and had to come down and sleep on the desert. We had all north Africa for a landing field. We slept on our parachutes and almost froze, whereas four hours before to breathe had burned our lungs.

Next morning we flew on to Gao, arriving at seven. It's just a military station on the Niger River. Three days to clean our engine of sand, then 300 miles up the river to Timbuctoo. An odd place this, terribly decayed, interesting for its memories. About 5000 people, 4500 of them Moslem Negroes—a great market still—built of mud houses—300 years old—right in the desert.

We found a possible landing field, and are eating with six French officers. Our sleeping quarters are dirty and thick with flies, but we will endure it till we are ready to fly back to Gao and back across that terrible desert to Colomb Bechar.

If Schuler approves my first two stories, Timbuctoo and the Legion, it will help both materially and spiritually. I've done about 4000 words roughly on the first chapter and like it. The heat and flies and thirst make writing difficult.

Our plane continues to run like a clock. It heated up very little, even on the Sahara. I'm piloting more and more, though I've not landed yet.

[*Sidi-bel-Abbes, Algeria—May 11, 1931.*] Your cable was a blast of fresh air on my two months of ignorance of things at home. It relieved all anxiety.

My letter from Timbuctoo has told you about our flight across the desert. It was deadly monotonous and tormentingly hot, but a great adventure just the same. We flew back along the river to Gao and once more followed the elusive motor track across the Sahara to Colomb Bechar and Oran.

I've been working with my first story and have finished the first draft. It's 10,000 words and must be cut to 6000—and it's got to be good. I'm calling it "The Flying Carpet" and it's mostly about my acquisition of the idea and the airplane—the release I sought from stagnation and the splendid means the plane provided, an idealistic rather than a practical vehicle. I get to Fez rather in a hurry, with remarks about Gibraltar, and use my big guns on the Sahara.

Meanwhile I'm deep into the Foreign Legion. It won't be nearly the story Devil's Island was, because the Legion has been done so well so often and is scattered over the world instead of concentrated in one handful as was D. I. Also I've not been nearly so able to act quickly and boldly.

This town, Sidi-bel-Abbes, is the great headquarters and training school for the Legion. All the new recruits come here. So we came too and have remained several days, looking around and talking to Legionnaires. They're mostly German, and a rather low lot generally. I'll go post this, and then chase into the country to watch the Legion maneuvers.

[*Fez, again—May 17, 1931.*] Our flight back to Fez was uneventful. I wanted to work here, *had* to work. I'm installed in my house again, and so happy. The garden is blazing with spring flowers. I'm having friends in tonight—an Englishman and two Swiss. I love Fez. Its variety and color are endless.

Bad news awaited me—word from Russia that I would not be allowed to fly there. I do hope that Russia will relent. I'd hate to miss Samarkand. I'll stop now and have lunch here in the sunshine among my geraniums.

[*Wagram Hotel, Paris—June 9, 1931.*] Well, to go back. It just about killed me to leave Fez. Rarely have I been so in love with a city. A number of Foreign Legion camps were in the mountains south of Fez, so Moye and I, refused permission to fly, took a bus and spent five days visiting these posts. They were fascinating, right in the heart of the enemy country. We could hear the bombs. And every now and then (though not during our stay) a Legionnaire, fetching water, had been shot. We got filled with stories and copy, and lots of good pictures. It was a *very* successful excursion.

We flew on to Casablanca from Meknez and to Marakesh. This last is as fascinating as Fez. In the big native square 10,000 people every afternoon gather around every form of entertainer—snake charmers, exhorters, dancers, trained animals. It was dirt and color and *Morocco* to the last degree. But it had no relationship to my stories—so four days just seeing and absorbing and we flew back to Rabât.

It was repeat flying from Rabât to Gibraltar, but instead of turning north to Malaga, as we had come, we turned west to Seville, had lunch there, and on to Lisbon. We hadn't thought of Lisbon till the day before—we had no flying permits. The American Minister got us clear—the very first American plane to visit Portugal. Our visit to Lisbon was a joy. I'd never dreamed it was so full of interest and beauty.

The day we took off for Madrid was beastly weather. We dodged storms and fog all the way. But Moye saw it through bravely. We had no reason to stop at Madrid for more than lunch. I'd seen it before, and the skies had cleared and we were eager to make Toulouse, across the Pyrenees. But what a mess we ran into! The Pyrenees, despite our weather reports to the contrary, were hidden in storms. The higher we climbed the worse it got, the wind was frightful, and in time it became evident that we simply couldn't make the grade without danger. So we turned tail and were catapulted backward the way we'd come. We tried outflanking the storm and the mountains, and finally got around at Biarritz, on the Bay of Biscay. The battle was grand and beautiful beyond words, for me, but Moye was too busy holding on and keeping control to enjoy it. That was the first and only really dangerous storm we've encountered—and one is quite enough.

We spent the night at Biarritz and fled on to Paris next day, stopping at Poitiers for lunch. The entire afternoon was over the garden of France and the châteaux of the Loire that I'd visited in 1921. They seemed lovely in their fresh June dress. We flew over Versailles and Paris, in a burst of sunshine, and landed at our old field, Le Bourget, sunburned and content.

Paris is a June bride, but I refuse to look. I'm a working man.

[*Paris—June 21, 1931.*] It seems to me I've addressed more letters to you from Paris than all other places together. We've been here two weeks yesterday, and I'm not finished. On Sunday I'm going to a farm on the coast near Le Havre to work.

Last night Moye and I dined with Captain and Mrs. Richmond Pearson Hobson. I had lunch yesterday with Robert Nathan (*The Bishop's Wife,* etc.) and his wife. Tomorrow I'm dining with Katy Seabrook, William Seabrook's wife, who was with him on his African book. But don't think I'm just playing. We were given our permit to fly over Jugo-Slavia, *provided* I would lecture at the University of Belgrade, en route. I said sure.

[*Villers-sur-Mer—July 15, 1931.*] If you'll get out the Atlas, and find Le Havre on the Normandy coast, and look across the bay, you'll see Deauville. Then go west a half-dozen miles, and you'll see Villers-sur-Mer. That's where I am now, about two miles outside of town. I've been here six days, working furiously on the Legion story. In fact, it's finished—the first draft, and I'm starting in this morning to type it.

I'm very comfortable. We're a mile from the beach. Lots of trees. I've walked into Villers twice.

[*Villers-sur-Mer—July 18, 1931.*] I'm going back to Paris tomorrow, with my Legion story under my arm. After the delicious dry heat of Africa, this damp weather is doubly unpleasant. I'm looking forward to Palestine and Persia, where there'll be sun again.

I don't seem to be able to capture the gaiety of *Royal Road* any more, but perhaps neither the grim Sahara crossing nor the blood-stained Foreign Legion has given me the chance.

[*Paris—July 31, 1931.*] We are all set to fly away tomorrow. We'll take off about nine and be in Geneva for lunch. I'm so impatient to be in the air again, I'm about to bust.

A wire came from Schuler: "Cannot commit myself until I see Foreign Legion stories." That was leaning to the side of good news, though not far! I can't hear again for at least two weeks.

I'm all packed. The propeller and cylinder which we ship ahead have gone on to Cairo, two tin auto trunks to Jerusalem, and books to Bagdad and Memphis.

[*Geneva—August 4, 1931.*] At least we're not still in Paris! Geneva isn't so far along as I'd like—but it's good to be on the move again. Our flight was through more fog and rain, but as we sighted the lake the sun burst forth.

We dined at once. Then for the great moment! We flew right smack over the Matterhorn! We left behind every ounce of removable weight, and climbed to 16,000 feet. It was a bright day with great masses of fleecy white clouds, so we could see and yet had variety. It was fiendishly cold, but so beautiful and dazzling I didn't mind. We got a few bad pictures, and fled back to the Rhone Valley and along this lovely, lovely lake, over the Castle of Chillon. On the home trip we went over Mont Blanc, higher than the Matterhorn, but much less interesting. The whole flight took only two hours. In the afternoon I had a sunbath and a swim and was really warm for once.

This morning we started to cross the Simplon Pass. But the clouds caught us. With our baggage we couldn't rise above them, and had to return. But it was another thrilling flight. Tomorrow we'll try once more to climb over. We'll have lunch in Milan and dinner in Venice.

[*Hotel Metropole, Vienna—August 17, 1931.*] We tried again to cross the Simplon Pass, and though we climbed to 15,000 feet the clouds climbed higher, and we had to give up. It stormed the next day, so we tried another route—southward over Aix-les-Bains and Grenoble, and then over the mountains to Turin. Moye did some masterful piloting to get us over those terrible Alps.

The day we left Geneva we landed at Milan. The Italians gave us no end of bother but we finally prevailed. We had only half a day in Milan, took a sight-seeing bus; I loved the Cathedral. I climbed up the spire and wandered around. We left in the afternoon and reached Venice in no time. That was almost as big a thrill as flying over the Matterhorn. I had fallen in love with Venice from afar, and it got worse every day I was there. I just couldn't pull away. We had happy, well-informed friends who showed us everything. With one of them, "Whoopee" Jimmy Lownes, I started to swim the Grand Canal at the upper end, and intended going all the way to St. Mark's square at the lower end, two and a half miles away. Moye was alongside in a gondola. Whoopee and I got halfway, to the Rialto Bridge, and were stopped by the police and fined ten lire (fifty cents) apiece. We had swum right past the police station. Swimming in the Grand Canal is *prohibito*. The police were very pleasant. We all laughed over it and had a beer together.

The mountains between Venice and Vienna are 10,000 feet high and we had *more* storms, but once over them the sun came out and we found Vienna easily. We've been here two days and leave tomorrow—and have loved it. I took a rubberneck bus yesterday and went swimming in the afternoon. This morning, alone, I took a train to Dürnstein Castle, where Richard Cœur de Lion was imprisoned and found by his minstrel Blondel. It was lovely—1000 feet above the Danube, 40 miles west of Vienna.

[*Bucharest, Roumania—August 24, 1931.*] By the address you'll see we're still moving along. It took three easy hops from Vienna. The first was to Budapest, right down the Danube. Budapest is beautiful. We remained three days, waiting for Schuler's wire. Alas, it came! I'd been afraid that whatever I sent would not please him on account of high price and hard times. The telegram is still noncommittal, but it indicates the wind very clearly. But suppose Schuler *doesn't* take them, what then? Well, we'll see. Let's not be blue. Things are going smoothly. I'm safe and sound, with a fine grip on the reins.

Out of Budapest we were forced to land at Belgrade by dangerous-looking weather ahead, but next day sped on here. I was hopeful I'd be able to meet King Carol and his young son, and take them, or the

Near Bagdad the Flying Carpet, escorted by two British planes, gives Prince Ghazi, later King of Iraq, his first glimpse of his domain from the air.

This symbolic lion, on which Moye and Richard are seated, was carved in Babylon almost six thousand years ago.

boy at least, for a ride. But I find they've moved to their summer residence in the mountains with no landing field in the neighborhood. So I've had to abandon the idea and go on to Stamboul.

[*Damascus—September 1, 1931.*] Since I wrote you last from Bucharest, we've flown another thousand miles farther east, and today are in Damascus. I enjoyed Constantinople *much* more this time than before. I knew more about it and had a keener interest in it. Santa Sophia was as stupendous and moving as ever. I spent another moonlight night inside, as in 1925, and at dawn stood beside the muezzin in the minaret when he made his morning call to prayer. He was wearing sleeve garters, a vest, no collar—and a *derby*. Modern Turkey!

We had lunch with the American Ambassador and his family and would have taken them riding but felt pushed for time. I made the most of my four days in Constantinople, doing and seeing every minute. It still remains, next to Rio, just about the most beautifully situated city in the world. The city itself is only junk, but full of such romantic history. The day we left was perfect. We flew up the Bosporus to the Black Sea and 50 miles along the southern shore; then inland to Konich, on the railroad halfway to Aleppo, for lunch. It was about 700 miles to Aleppo, the longest stretch since the Sahara. All barren mountainous country with lots of glorious scenery.

The Flying Carpet seems to run better every minute.

We spent the night at Aleppo—after Fez no Arab city amuses us much—and flew on to Homs. From here we took a car and visited two of the most wonderful twelfth-century castles built by the Crusaders, Margab and Kalat-el-Husein. Next we flew directly east to Palmyra, the ruined Greek city with marble temples almost as beautiful as Athens, right in the middle of the desert. The way this whole part of the world has dried up is amazing. Palmyra must have had a million people 2000 years ago. It's only a sandpile now without a tree. I've rarely so enjoyed an archaeological site.

We flew on across more desert directly to Damascus. Here last night. I walked down the "Street called Straight," this morning and watched the workmen making Damascus blades. We're motoring to Baalbek this afternoon, then to Bairut, down the coast to Sidon,

Tyre and Acre, and over to Nazareth and the Sea of Galilee, which I'm going to try to swim. Galilee is about six miles across. We'll leave the Carpet here in Damascus and come back for it before flying to Jerusalem.

It's appallingly hot but I really like it. We're both very brown from the sun and wind. Here's a page from the Constantinople papers.

[*Amexco, Jerusalem—September 9, 1931.*] At last—at *long* last—your son has put his feet squarely on the earth again, at a place where you can find him and reach him and put your finger on him, and is not up in the air, at some vague where. I think the hour I reached Jerusalem was about the lowest my spirits have been in for many a year. Now, with your letters, they're up again—'*way* up!

I got sunburned swimming the Sea of Galilee—600 feet below sea level—the worst burn I've ever had, worse than the one I had in California. For two days I lay prostrate in Tiberias, for two more in Damascus, with high fever and tormented body. Finally I got into the Carpet and flew to Gaza, 60 miles from Jerusalem. There I 'phoned the Amexco to stay open till I could arrive. A motor drove me the 60 miles along a dried-up stream. Every bump was agony. It took four hours. I'd had no food and no sleep for five nights. I didn't have spirit enough to face the mail. But next morning a doctor and nurse made me comfortable—and your letters did the rest. That was four days ago. Tonight I'm sitting up, in the scaly, flaky stage, and expect to put my clothes on tomorrow.

A wire came from Aley: "Second conference with Schuler—hopeful—send me stories direct." I'll have to be in Jerusalem at least three weeks, so we'll soon find out. At worst this is all only a bump, not a break. So for ten days more I'm going to enjoy Jerusalem and work and not worry. Moye took the plane straight on to Cairo to begin overhauling the engine.

I wrote you last from Damascus. From there we took a car and drove to Baalbek. The ruins are glorious but not so moving as Palmyra, lost in the desert. There's one block of granite left in the quarry that's fifteen feet square and *seventy* feet long—*one block*. There are three others actually in the temple walls 15x15x65. They weigh 800 tons apiece and were moved ten miles, and raised fifty feet, no one knows how! Between earthquakes and Arabs, the most huge and splendid Grecian temple in the world has been tumbled into dust.

Next day we crossed the Lebanon mountains through the famous cedars to visit Beirut and Sidon and Tyre. Tyre and Sidon! I'd always wanted to go there. They now are only two miserable villages, but what glories they have seen. Acre was in perfect preservation— just as Richard Cœur de Lion left it. I spent a whole day dreaming and swimming beneath its sea walls. We went to Nazareth. Not a relic of the past there—just a Jewish town full of new churches and convents. The city in which Jesus lived lies buried many feet below the present town. On through Cana and Capernaum to Tiberias, beside the Sea of Galilee.

I'd been wanting to swim it from the start of this trip and knew I was going to have a try. The first afternoon I sneaked off from Moye, hired a boat and saw if I *could* swim. To my astonishment and delight I found I could, and did, over a mile along the shore. The Sea is a deep, clear blue and surrounded by steep olive-green mountains. One of them is the Horns of Hattin where Christ preached the Sermon on the Mount.

Next morning at nine, with two fishermen and their boat, I started out from Tiberias. I didn't put on any oil as I was under water and didn't intend to get out, nor did I. I swam seven miles in five hours, non-stop—and, except for the day before, I hadn't been in the water for a swim since Panama. The seventh mile I was going stronger than the first. I honestly believe I could have swum the seven miles back again had the wind not been against us and the sun shooting flames into me. The wind was so strong we couldn't get directly back, but had to rest on the eastern shore till the sun went down at six, and then tack back and forth half the night with our sail. We were pitched about, and I could well believe the Bible story of Christ's having to calm the water when his fishermen disciples became frightened. I got home at midnight in a terrible state and realized then for the first time how seriously burned I was, though not the least tired. I've told you the rest.

[*Next morning.*] I'm *much* better—have put my clothes on and shaved for the first time in a week. Tomorrow I'll go out and see

Jerusalem, and then get busy on my stories, one on the Crusades and one on Galilee and Jerusalem. I'm in a pension here, very comfortable.

It is going to be so easy to write quantities of half-good copy, but so hard to make it exceptional. I've never had such opportunities—and such handicaps. As for the Carpet I've ceased to think of it as an element of danger, and so must you. The only mishap I've had has been too much sunshine.

[*Amexco, Jerusalem—September 25, 1931.*] Moye and the F. C. are still in Cairo. I'm here, working hard. It took me over a week to recover from my burns, care for my mail and read the books I needed to before beginning to write.

Jerusalem is best at long range, very dull at close. That's why I'm staying on here—I can work. I went swimming in the Dead Sea, 1300 feet below sea level, but not till the *sun had set*. It was a strange experience—like Salt Lake only *much* more so. I've walked at night no end. The Mount of Olives is my favorite excursion. It's been full moon lately and Jerusalem *is* lovely from the top of the Mount. The flower I'm inclosing came from Gethsemane. Last night I walked to Bethlehem, and today I'm going out to the hill where King Richard saw Jerusalem—to get no closer. This country is overwhelming if one loves history. If one is religious but not sectarian, one should keep away. The hatred, the fighting, the fanatic fools, sicken one away from any Christian feeling about it.

[*Amexco, Cairo—October 6, 1931.*] In crossing the Suez Canal, yesterday, on my train trip from Jerusalem I looked for the *Gold Shell* and had many memories.

I was in Jerusalem more than a month, enjoying every day of it and working. The last night I had a good adventure. There's an ancient tunnel built under the original City of David by the earliest citizens of Jerusalem, to convey water from one side of the city to the other. It goes in a most serpentine manner, and yet there is an inscription halfway through the tunnel (which is 1700 feet long) saying two gangs of miners began at opposite ends and met in the middle—maybe that's why it zigzags—and of the rejoicing when they heard each other through the remaining rock. This was in 1500 B. C. The tunnel is still there and still brings water underneath the City of David to the pool of Siloam. Part way along the tunnel is a shaft going up to the top of the mountain. Up this one of David's soldiers, Joab, during his first attack on Jerusalem, climbed with a few men and so surprised the defenders that they were overcome. The shaft is about 60 feet high.

Well, Moye and I took candles and explored the entire tunnel, with the water flowing past up to our waists. Every chisel mark—3500 years old—was still there. How the two gangs ever met is a mystery, for the tunnel winds and writhes. It is three feet wide and about six high. We found the shaft, and I climbed up it. Débris has accumulated over the upper opening, so I couldn't emerge as Joab did. It was a fascinating night and will make a fine story.

The train trip to Cairo was long and dull. The plane is O. K., a few adjustments made. I'm having pontoons shipped to Singapore. I want to go round the world, stories or no stories. I'll be home in the spring.

I'll not be able to write again until after we return from Abyssinia.

[*Cairo—October 23, 1931.*] We've given up our Abyssinia dream, and are leaving on Monday (today is Friday) for Bagdad. The other excursion became too costly in time. I'm going on east.

Moye is down with a cold. Poor fellow, he's had seven weeks of stagnation while I've been working. We went last Sunday to the Near East Relief Club here—1000 Armenian boy and girl refugees—and I spoke for them, with an interpreter. I've had tea twice with the American Minister and his wife, but haven't let myself be social as I had no time. Our airplane is in first-class order for our departure Monday. I'll be 2500 miles nearer you when you get this. Ten months down—seven to go.

[*Bagdad—November 10, 1931.*] We got away from Cairo in the presence of quite a crowd of Americans, including the Minister and his wife. We flew over the Suez Canal and back up the coast to and over Jerusalem, then straight and low over the Dead Sea. We landed at Amman, on the railroad from Damascus to Medina, a big British flying post. From here we flew south next day about 150 miles down the railroad to Maan, the jumping-off place for Petra.

Starting early in the morning, we motored thirty miles and rode mules five to reach that extraordinary dead city. To see it was one of the great moments of my life. It was as astonishing as Angkor. You enter it along a canyon, a thousand feet deep and twenty feet broad. Twilight gloom! And suddenly you break forth at the end upon a pool of light that floods one of the most beautiful buildings ever built, a temple 150 feet high and 100 feet broad cut out of a glowing red sandstone cliff—columns, cornices, statues, etc., all a part of the solid rock. It takes two looks to believe it.

After this introduction the city spreads open in a vast amphi-theater surrounded by cliffs all the walls of which are covered with these rock-carved temples and mausoleums. There's hardly a piece of masonry in the entire city. I roamed and climbed about all day—and spent the night in one of the temples. It was full moon and glorious. Moye chose to go back to his hotel and bath—so I was alone but for a guard.

Flying back to Amman we motored to Gerasa or Jerash, a ruined Roman city that's been uncovered, and next day motored back to Jerusalem. We passed the Dead Sea again and had lunch at Jericho.

We flew from Amman to Bagdad across 600 miles of Sahara-like desert, stopping once for fuel at Rutbar Wells—300 miles from no-where, and the only wells in Northern Arabia. Thousands of sheep and camels flock here daily for water. It was a wonderful picture.

We crossed the Euphrates at sunset and approached the Tigris and Bagdad just in time to see the sun shining against the golden domes—beautiful and appropriate. Bagdad needs lots of imagination. It's tumble-down and new—but I'll see in it the *Arabian Nights* city. The Consul here is Princeton, 1907, so I've entré everywhere. Tomor-row I'm having tea with the Crown Prince to persuade him to go flying in our plane. I'm having to speak at the American School on Armistice Day. Next day we go to Samarra, and next after that to Babylon. I love it here.

[*Bagdad—November 20, 1931.*] This is Friday night. We plan to fly to Teheran on Sunday or Monday. Our ship is in order and we are impatient to be on our way. We've had a happy, fairly active three weeks here. It was one of our big goals, so I do not regret the 21 days. Thorough scrutiny has not revealed much in the way of atmosphere and copy, but I've enough to give me a good story. I've been working on a plan to take the Crown Prince of Iraq for a ride in our airplane. "The Prince of Bagdad Goes Riding on the Flying Carpet." It's all arranged for tomorrow. We're flying him—he's seventeen—to Samarra, to land and have lunch. Samarra is 75 miles up the Tigris River. Two British planes are escorting us, one bearing the Prince's uncle, the Queen's brother; the other, a photographer.

Since writing you last we had three wonderful days down country by motor car. Nejf and Kerbela are the Holy Cities of Iraq as Mecca is of Arabia. Pilgrims gather from all over the Moslem world. Only recently have foreigners been able to go there. Our escort was the son of the rich local sheik in whose house we visited. We were entertained lavishly in true Arabic fashion, and saw everything. The two towns are fascinating, built right in the desert and surrounded by the countless graves of those who have come there to die. The mosque in each city is a dream of beauty, its domes and minarets plated with pure gold that glitters brilliantly and can be seen for miles across the desert.

On our way home we spent an afternoon at Babylon. That *is* a sight, and only a part of it has been uncovered. The entire city was made of brick, so that only fragments of walls, here and there, still exist. I sat on the highest ruin—maybe the Hanging Gardens—and watched the shadows creep over Nebuchadnezzar's throne room, and over the hall where Alexander died. Persia is Mohammedan—mosques, veils, decay, etc.—and I've had much of that all the way from Morocco.

It's bitterly cold in Persia, so we won't tarry long there. I've spent some time getting fitted for sheepskin coats and boots, and ready to face it. Moye will not stay in Teheran but will fly on south to the Persian Gulf and wait for me, as I'm going overland. There's so much I want to see.

We've been beautifully entertained. Today the Commander-in-Chief gave us a luncheon party, and yesterday the Chief Flying Officer. One night we dined at the British Governor's, and took his wife riding in our ship next day. It was her first time up. In return she gave me a little jar dug up from Babylon and dated about 3000 B. C.! I've spoken twice to schools. A student body gave me two tiny Oriental rugs for mascots, "Flying Carpets from Bagdad." I'm sending one home with another pile of books, and keeping the other in my plane. I've been reading tons of books, all the *Arabian Nights* again and books on Alexander. I'm sure I've never enjoyed a journey so much as this one.

[*Teheran, Persia—December 4, 1931.*] We had a beautiful flight from Bagdad, crystal clear and sunny and cold. We were wrapped in our sheepskin overcoats and kept warm. Persia is wild and arid, the mountains in our path rising 12,000 feet. We could see Mt. Demavend, 19,000 feet, hanging over Teheran, from a hundred miles away—a great white iceberg. The flight took five hours. It takes three full days by automobile. We are crazy about Teheran.

The bazaars are marvelous—carpets all over the place—and I'd like to buy everything I see. What with the economy problem, and the shipping problem, and the baggage problem, I've not bought anything. But we've been busy absorbing and looking. I spent an afternoon in the nightingale bazaar, and bought me a nightingale! He's hanging in his cage in my hotel room, and has bursts of song when he's warm and well fed. When we fly on south I'm taking him aboard, the first nightingale ever to ride on an airplane, I'm sure. There is an entire shop dealing only in nightingales, all prices. They are small, modest-looking birds, but with a voice that can be heard extraordinary distances. The chain-armor shop was almost as interesting and the Persian gymnasiums, too.

We dined one night at a Persian merchant's house, ate a typical meal and enjoyed private theatricals and dancing and music afterward. I found here Dr. William McGovern, the man who wrote *To Lhasa in Disguise*. We've had a busy time together. We spent 24 hours in the local prize prison, wearing the stripes and eating the food. The American Minister's wife called at tea time to feed us peanuts through the bars—and the General-in-Chief of the Army called next morning to escort us about. It was a comic picture, the General and his staff escorting two "prisoners" in stripes all over the

Bas-reliefs cunningly cast in brick adorn the ruined walls of ancient Babylon.

Two robust Persian princesses are given a ride in the Flying Carpet near Teheran.

place. He emptied the entire prison out into a compound where we could see them—some 600. It was a curious and vastly interesting adventure.

But most of my time has been spent chasing down Persian princesses in order to take them aboard our Flying Carpet. I've forgotten whether I wrote you about the luck we had with the King of Iraq's son. We flew him all over Mesopotamia, and he loved it. He's a most likable youngster. The idea worked out so well I went after a princess here. The present Shah is not of royal birth—a sort of self-imposed Mussolini. He would not allow his daughter to fly with us. But we prevailed upon two nieces of the deposed royal Shah, and took them up, and also the wife of the pretender—the legal heir, who, were the present usurper not on hand, would be queen of Persia. She is the daughter and granddaughter of Shahs—and charming. She went riding, too.

So I'm all ready now to write my Arabian Night story—Bagdad— Persia—princes and princesses—and nightingales.

Tomorrow or next day I'm leaving for Isfahan, Shiraz and Bushire by mail truck and otherwise. I want to see Persia. It's too good to waste flying over it. It will take me from ten to fourteen days.

What a year it has been. If only the book will be worthy of the year!

[*Bushire, Persia—December 20, 1931.*] Tomorrow morning at 3 A.M. we are off to India. Bushire is Persia's main port.

A year ago today we left California on our journey. As far as seeing things and doing things goes, we've been successful. Our writing arrangements to date have gone badly, but that is not disastrous, and everything may come out for the best. I asked myself the day we took off, "Where will you be this morning one year hence?" Flying was such a new idea—our plans were so vague—all such a truly new world. And here we are, 25,000 miles flown and not a bump. I've never passed a year of such excellent health, the sunburn in Galilee being my only indisposition. I will make the output back on the book, and I will have had one of the most beautiful adventures in history.

My journey across Persia south from Teheran has gone well. It is a most enormous country when you start motoring. Teheran to Bushire is 800 miles—it's 900 by train from New York to Chicago. I was thirteen days en route overland. Moye made it in one day by plane. From Teheran to Isfahan I was in a private car with the Bishop of Persia, a big gun in the missionary world, and the headmaster of the English boys' school in Isfahan. It took us from five in the morning till nine at night—280 miles. It was desperately cold, but I had my Persian sheepskin coat and so was comfortable. One pass reached 10,000 feet. All wild, barren country, but curious and Persia. We stopped along the way at the ancient caravansaries, where the caravan drivers spent the night and rested their camels.

Isfahan, next to Fez, is the place I like best on this journey. It is the center of all the Persian arts, and has a turquoise mosque that is *almost* as beautiful as the Taj. In fact, I've decided to include it in my book on the Taj—one so pure white, the other so dazzlingly blue-green. It's covered with enameled tiles, 300 years old, but fresh as if they were laid this morning. This mosque faces the most imposing plaza in the world—half a mile long and a quarter of a mile wide. All the beautiful and romantic things one associates with Persia, one finds in Isfahan. I bought you and Haff each a present there. Rugs, of course, there were in mountain loads, but the problem of shipping and customs discouraged me. So I got something more useful and simple—silver cocktail shakers that will delight you, I'm sure, ordered moulded and engraved by the Isfahan silversmiths who are famous for their art. The engraving is marvelous. An agent will send them to the Legation at Teheran to be entrusted to some diplomat homeward bound.

After Isfahan I took a truck seat to Shiraz. Along the way I stopped to see the Tomb of Cyrus the Great before which Alexander stood in considerable respect 150 years after Cyrus' death. Then to Persepolis. It was the wonderful winter palace of the classic Persian kings, Cyrus, Xerxes, Darius. One hill contained 100 fluted columns, 65 feet high. Alexander burned it to the ground in revenge for Xerxes' destructions at the time of his invasion of Greece, but much of the place still remains, and is still one of the ancient marvels. I spent two days there. Shiraz is the home of the famous Persian poets, and famous in Persian poetry as the headquarters of wine, love and song. The best Persian gardens are there, and the most pleasure-loving people. The road from Shiraz to Bushire is 70 miles by air, and 190 by road—a violent, struggling affair. It took us two long days. I spent one day between at Shupur to see the famous rock carvings of ancient kings, reproductions of which are found in decorations all over Persia.

My nightingale I turned loose in Shiraz, at the tomb of Hafiz. It was a rough journey for him. I attended an all-night celebration in memory of Hafiz, the like of which I had never seen before.

And so Persia is over, and it's been splendid. My capacity for enjoying new and lovely things has not faded. India will be beautiful all over again.

The Carpet still flies perfectly. Tomorrow will be one of our longest stretches. I don't like such an endurance test—thirteen hours in the air—but I'm impatient to be on.

[*Delhi—December 27, 1931.*] The stretch from Bushire to Delhi we made at a fast pace. The first day we followed the coast to an airport called Jask, about 700 miles. This is just a station for the airlines to India. The next day 750 more to Karachi. We spent one day in Karachi, and hurried on to Delhi, 800 miles more, to arrive on December 24.

This town has changed greatly since nine years ago. There are unrest and "sedition" everywhere, and a feeling for independence. The Viceroy doesn't dare leave his new ten-million-dollar palace without a tremendous bodyguard lining the streets, for fear of being shot.

I bought us something yesterday—a herd of elephants, *twenty* elephants of ebony wood to march across the mantelpiece. All my life I've wanted a herd of elephants. I saw just the thing, in a wood-carving shop, and fell. You'll love them—eight big fellows, no two in the same position but alike in size—five smaller ones, half-grown—three babies—and four off-size children. I played with them myself for hours yesterday. They'll make everybody who sees them covetous, and we'll have to *nail* them to the mantelpiece.

Tuesday we're going on to Agra to see the Taj from the air.

[*Calcutta—January 6, 1932.*] It's 4:30 A.M. and we're leaving at six for Darjeeling to fly around or near Mt. Everest. This is just a word to make the next boat. We're tip top.

[*Calcutta—January 15, 1932.*] Today I sent you off a whopping big package of pictures and clippings. The clippings tell a grand story—our call upon Mt. Everest. It *was* beautiful!

We're off tomorrow for Rangoon. I must be up at 4 A.M. This is a good-night line—to help fill the gaps.

I spent my birthday on the Everest flight. Well spent, say I.

[*Singapore—January 23, 1932.*] I have engaged a stenographer to take care of the rush of correspondence here in Singapore, in order that I may get to work on my stories as quickly as possible. My cable to Chambers asked him to notify you of my arrival here, and I know it was welcome news to you. I was delighted to reach Singapore myself, not that Singapore is anything, but it marks the successful completion of the major part of our flight.

We arrived here from Calcutta, where I wrote you last, without any mishap whatsoever. From Calcutta, we skirted the coast of the Bay of Bengal and, in about seven hours' flying, reached Rangoon, following the beach all the way. One day in Rangoon was enough, as I had been there before. Next day we had a very dramatic and beautiful, but dangerous, flight to Bangkok, over 400 miles of impenetrable jungle. We could not so much as see the ground. I think I was more nervous over that stretch than over any place we have flown, but the engine functioned perfectly, and we reached the Bangkok port on schedule. Moye continues to be the world's best pilot. Once we are in the air, no matter where, everything goes like clock-work.

Again Bangkok was nothing new to me, and I was impatient to get on. As on my previous visit, I was the guest of the American Minister, and enjoyed a pleasant party or two in the legation. It took us two days, flying down the peninsula, to reach Singapore, as it is over 1200 miles long. I noted the path leading across the Isthmus, where I crossed ten years ago, and looked down upon Chumpon, so familiar to us from *Royal Road.*

The air base in Singapore is first class. Immediately on landing,

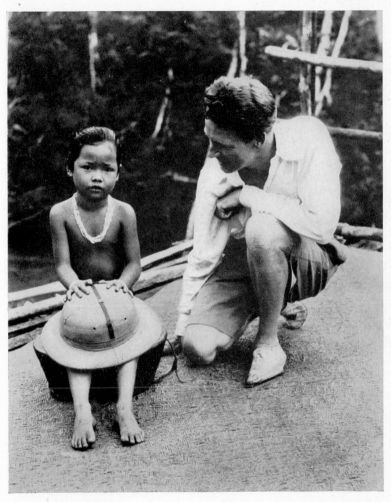

While she explores his helmet, Richard interviews a young lady of Borneo.

In Borneo Richard and Moye are entertained by the Ranee Sylvia, wife of the white Rajah Brooke, and her daughters, the Princesses Valery and Elizabeth.

we began to arrange for the fitting of our pontoons. They had arrived on schedule. The crate was twenty feet long, and we had great difficulty in finding a truck big enough to carry it. It took twenty coolies to push the box into the hangar. Now an engineering company is busy removing the under-carriage of the Flying Carpet, designing the struts, and attaching the floats. The work, from first to last, will take between two and three weeks. In the meanwhile, Moye will be taking lessons in pontoon flying, and once I get out from this huge pile of correspondence, I'll get busy with my notebook.

We are for the moment at Raffles Hotel, but, in a day or two, I am going out to a beach boarding-house and retire from the world. Singapore is dreadfully hot, and I am having to find me lighter clothes. But, as always, I have thrived upon the heat.

Our airplane, for the first time, has begun to show unmistakable signs of age and hard usage. The paint is peeling off the top wing, and most of the gloss has disappeared. The engine too is running rough, but we will make Manila safely, and there have the Wright experts give us the proper overhaul.

[*Singapore—February 4, 1932.*] The last two weeks have been dull enough, spent mostly in writing letters. I'd been carrying ten pounds of unanswered mail all over the world, and at last drove myself into it and swept away every blasted one. A new batch came yesterday, but only a few.

Our pontoon fittings are moving at a snail's pace. But I'm helpless to hurry them, knowing nothing about it. The fitters have been working sixteen days, and say they'll take fourteen more. I'd be consumed with impatience were I not able to retire to my desk. With correspondence clear, I've been plunging into my notebook. I have already done two neat little chapters on Jerusalem and tonight will move on to Petra and Bagdad. Once under way the writing flows easily. I'd like to have everything drafted up to India by the time I get home.

Moye's brother came by on a round-the-world cruise, for a day— and we entertained him a day and night. I spoke for the Rotary Club and at yesterday's meeting introduced Elly Beinhorn, the German girl flyer, who has paralleled our course since Persia.

[*Singapore, dammit—March 8, 1932.*] I can hear you groan to read I'm *still* in this town—almost two months, now. If I hadn't had my book to write I'd long since been a maniac from impatience. The pontoons are only today being attached to the ship. Never in my life have I felt so helpless and so caught. All I've been able to do has been to console myself with work at my typewriter, and as the precious weeks have passed, so have the new chapters.

Being a flying boat is going to be fun. We've bought bathing suits to fly in, and *sunburn cream*. We're shipping our wheels and parachutes straight to San Francisco. I've had all the social activities I wanted. My obligations mounted up so, I had 35 of my friends in for cocktails.

Last week, feeling desperately in need of relief from the pressure, I got aboard a Dollar Line boat and sailed 24 hours up the coast to Penang, a most beautiful place, and came back on another boat two days later. I took my work with me, and got some fresh air into my lungs.

I'm speaking for the Rotary Club again tomorrow. Moye spoke last week and I five weeks ago. They're announcing me as giving a "Farewell Address." I hope to heaven they're right. Mr. Catlin, my host in Kashmir ten years ago, has been here, and giving parties right and left.

This time last year, I was in Oran, on my way to Timbuctoo. This date next year I hope a successful book and lecture tour will be well behind us. And then I'm going to rest.

[*Singapore—March 23, 1932.*] Moye has been up several times on the pontoons. They work satisfactorily, but anchors, and landing wheels, and anchorage lights, etc., etc.—our needs seem endless. Water flying is so different from land flying, it requires a completely new organization and equipment. This helplessness to control my own movements is maddening. However, I'll forget this period, once we're under way. We'll take ship home from Manila. That's definite. We'll have about four weeks to drift up Borneo and the southern Philippines, where the color is.

[*Manila—May 2, 1932.*] Believe me, I'm relieved that our flying is almost over, and our long journey ended without mishap. The strain was becoming a bit too much. I feel like a man let out of jail. Our reception in Manila was wonderful. We've been here six days, and this is the first minute I've had to write you. The *President McKinley* leaves next Saturday. So we'll be here five days more, and land at San Francisco May 31.

Our adventures from Singapore to Manila are too varied and extensive to report in this hurried letter. I'll wait till we're aboard ship. We certainly saw Borneo and I've two *good* stories out of it. We got right into the heart of things—took our plane up to the head-hunters and caused the greatest excitement imaginable with them. We cut short our tour of the Philippines, since it seemed anticlimactic after Borneo.

Manila is nice, I suppose; we really haven't had a chance to look at it. Governor and Mrs. Roosevelt have had us twice to lunch and the Navy flyers have given us no end of parties.

[*S. S. President McKinley—May 10, 1932.*] It's all such ancient history now that the telling of our adventures from Singapore to Manila seems flat. They were trying at times, and the nearest thing to danger we've met. Our first day out we met a fearful rainstorm and had trouble finding our island, Banca, south of Singapore, near Sumatra. But, trust Moye. He wasn't lost long. The pontoons worked perfectly. From Banca we followed islands in a curve south and east to Pontianak on the west coast of Dutch Borneo. There we had our first accident. In pulling up the anchor rope it caught in the propeller and nearly wrecked us. The propeller was bent double and the rope torn in shreds. It looked as if our flight was over as I'd shipped the spare prop. on home. But a local blacksmith straightened it again—or straightened it enough. Landing and taking off in the tidal rivers, with the current rushing past, and logs everywhere, was no fun.

From Pontianak we flew via the coast to Kuching. This is the capital of Sarawak, an independent country under British protection. It has a British Rajah and Ranee. The Rajah was in England, but the Ranee and her two daughters took care of us at the palace. We took her for a flight—the first woman to fly in Borneo. From Kuching we went to Sibu, 100 miles up the coast, and inland. From here by plane we followed the river into the very heart of Borneo, and lived ten days with the head-hunting Dyaks. It was one of the very best adventures. Brunei—Sandakan—Jolo. There we missed a typhoon by 48 hours. Over 100 people were killed, and every house demolished. From Jolo we flew to Zamboanga and then east to Cotabato, and up the river to a lake 60 miles inland, where we hunted ducks and crocodiles (with harpoons) for three days—got 25 crocks—4800 have been taken out for their hides in recent months, and thousands are left still. We tried shooting ducks from the plane, but it didn't work. There were millions and millions of them. Then Gebú, where I visited Magellan's grave, and Manila.

I had one happy adventure in Luzon. There is a crater lake about fifty miles from Manila, which is some fifteen miles wide. In the middle is a conical island five miles across, and in this crater cone is another lake one mile across, and in this lake is another island. So I swam from shore out around the little crater lake island, and back to shore. The complete story is in the newspaper clippings, so I won't repeat, only I nearly had the hide taken off me by the acid in the water.

Getting the Flying Carpet crated and on the *President McKinley* was a job. We were eager to see the ship in motion.

We had a fine day in Hongkong yesterday. We went for a swim, and slept last night on shore, the heat was so intense on the boat. Here I had the further job of getting our under-carriage (wheels) crate aboard, which we had shipped from Singapore to Hongkong.

[*One day out from San Francisco—May 30, 1932.*] Tomorrow we land. It's been a happy voyage. We spent a day in Shanghai but didn't get to see much of the war zone. Another day in Kobe, and a fine day in Yokohama—spent mostly in Tokyo! Having seen Tokyo before the earthquake, I was interested in its wonderful reconstruction. I should like to have spent more time there.

Eight days in Honolulu. Duke Kahanamoku, the famous Hawaiian swimmer, interested me. A big luncheon was given for me. I spoke at the main high school to three Americans and about

After 1932 this white brick cottage in Memphis was home to Richard.

On the steps of his home in Caucasia, Richard interviews the oldest man in the world, Zapara Kiut, who, Soviet scientists claim, was born in 1782.

2000 Japs and Filipinos—very curious. Then I spent all afternoon on the beach. It was great fun.

I will truck the airplane straightaway to Alameda, across the bay from San Francisco, and get busy. I've a luncheon club talk scheduled, to be broadcast, next noon. What busy, busy days these next 90 are going to be!

[*San Francisco*—6 P. M., *May 31, 1932.*] Your welcome telegrams to me and to Moye met us at the boat, and I wired you back this afternoon, when I had a chance to breathe. It took hours to clear the airplane, and get it onto the trucks. Already the mechanics are at work, and we hope to fly away again Thursday noon for Hollywood. It takes four hours' flying. We had a nice reception this morning. My California friends are all waiting for us—many letters came.

"Rid of the pontoons and equipped with wheels again," Richard was to write at the end of his book about this spectacular journey, "the Flying Carpet soared high into the sky of California, turned toward the south and arrived at last above the familiar hills. Like a homing pigeon, the plane spiraled down to the airport from which, one morning some forty thousand miles before, we had set out to see the world.

"Moye and I wheeled the old Carpet into the hangar ... and there, for the first time, we realized how much it showed the marks of battle with the elements in a hundred lands.... Through desert and jungle, Africa and Arabia, Himalaya and the islands of the sea . . . these brave and sturdy wings, these willing and fleet wings, had brought us safely home.

"Now they could rest."

CHAPTER XVI

INDIA SPEAKS

and the Seven League Boots Start Traveling

A STURDIER and fleeter plane brought Richard to Memphis for a visit with his parents, a visit necessarily brief. There was much to be done—magazine and lecture people to see, radio possibilities to investigate, above all the new book. That "was not going to wait on any man." He consulted with his publishers in Indianapolis, hurried to New York, got out of New York as soon as he could pick up loose ends. He had planned to rush back home to write in peace and quiet, but that idea had to be abandoned; he needed to keep in closer touch with New York, since a radio scheme seemed near going over. Instead, he went to Alexandria, Virginia, where he would not be distracted and would have the Library of Congress at hand.

His first letter from Alexandria is dated July 3, 1932. His mother and father drove up, at his urgence, to spend two weeks but saw very little of him except at meals. Then and later he got ahead rapidly with the writing. "It is proving much easier than I expected. I am working like a fiend." On August twenty-seventh after a flying visit to New York: "Am I busy! But it's fun. I saw our jacket and it's fine."

On September fifth, with the writing well along, he says that he has decided to go back to New York to stay, so that he may oversee the mechanical details of *The Flying Carpet*. He put up with his friend Maxwell Aley for a week or so and then took rooms at the Standish Arms in Brooklyn, where "the view is indescribable— straight across the harbor to lower New York. I've worked two days and nights on pictures. What a job to reduce 1000 to 64!" *Red Book* wanted his Legion story but couldn't get it in before the book would be out. More radio negotiations, "but I've learned not to count the eggs until they hatch—or is it the chickens? Somehow I can't visualize myself playing to the public advertising baked beans. The lec-

340

ture dates keep coming in. Moye announced his engagement to an old sweetheart 24 days after we got home." He was dedicating *The Flying Carpet* to its pilot.

On October twelfth: "The captions, pictures, etc., are finished. The book goes on press tomorrow. I still have the maps to do. Of course I'm tired but it's worth it. I'll be in Greensboro, North Carolina, Monday night for my first lecture."

[*Baltimore to Atlanta—October 18, 1932.*] Believe it or not I'm still alive, though pretty weary I'll admit. This morning in Atlanta is the first breath of freedom and peace I've had in long weeks. The last fortnight has been so hectic, with such astonishing things happening, I know you'll forgive me for waiting so long to write. Our book is going to be by far the most beautiful of all. I hope to have a copy in your hands by next Tuesday or Wednesday.

That Taj chapter almost ran me crazy. I spent days of despair, and nights of sleeplessness, over it. It was *the* most important chapter. My standing as a writer, as a person, has been damaged by the persistent legend that the Taj pool is only three inches deep, too shallow for me to bathe in—a petty, ridiculous story! I went back to Agra on purpose to meet the attack. I wanted to tell them, and have them remember, that the pool is five feet deep.

I spoke to 2000 students last night at Greensboro. I told all my new stories and had a grand time. They wouldn't let me quit, so I spoke another twenty minutes after saying good night once. I'd forgotten how much fun speaking to a responsive audience can be. Three more dates in the next three days, and the management had half a dozen others for me, but I couldn't accept them. I must be in New York on Friday, and this is why:

I've agreed to accept $10,000 for six weeks' acting in a United Artist picture! I go to Hollywood on November third. I'm just as flabbergasted as you are. Every agreement has been reached. The contract was ready Monday morning for me to sign. The picture is called *India Speaks*. It's being made by the same producers that did *Africa Speaks*. It's a travel picture, to be released in February. The film has been collected for years—India, Tibet, the Himalayas. The camera begins to grind on November seventh.

[*Back at Standish Arms, Brooklyn—October 21, 1932.*] Good news! I'll be home Sunday, October 30, at 5 P.M., from Atlanta! Isn't that elegant? But I can stay only two days, having to leave in time to be in Durant, Oklahoma, Wednesday at 9 A.M. Also tomorrow I actually send you a book called *The Flying Carpet*. By the way, I told the radio people to "cease firing."

My last two lecture dates, at small colleges, were great fun, even though I had to flag my own New York train at 3 A.M. with a burning newspaper.

[*Durant—November 1, 1932.*] I got into Durant at 2 A.M. pretty tired. But I had a good night's rest and spoke at ten this morning. I'll sleep this afternoon and go on again tonight.

All day yesterday on the train I worked over my address book. The old one was played out. I'm sending it to you for safe keeping. It made the trip to Greece with me, to South America, and the Flying Carpet, and was never lost once.

Of course, our new house pleases me to pieces. It's going to be exactly what we want. A new house, a new book, a new movie, and all four of us in good health and high spirits—I think we've lots to be thankful for!

I'll wire you Saturday night from Hollywood and keep you informed of all I do.

[*En route to Hollywood by air—November 5, 1932.*] The air has been very rough today, and I've been *sick,* after all the Flying Carpet. The four speaking dates in two days were terrors. We'll reach Los Angeles about eleven o'clock tonight—and won't I be glad! I'll sleep tomorrow and see Futter—the movie man—in the afternoon.

Bebe Daniels, the movie actress is across from me, but we're both too sick to care.

[*2029 Pinehurst Road, Hollywood—November 13, 1932.*] After waiting a week to write you, it can be only a slap-and-a-dash. Things are going smoothly. I have a *grand* little house not a stone's throw from where you had your apartment in 1930. A rose garden and patio and a rented Ford roadster and a Negro man cook—all in a week.

The picture is coming on splendidly. I've had all my tests and seen the first sequences. I photograph not too badly. It's great fun and I'm relishing every minute of it. Some of the background pictures are magnificent. The voice tests came out well too. Walter Futter does get things done and certainly knows his business.

I had dinner with Moye and his family. They are all overjoyed about the book. I met Moye's gal; she's lovely. The sun is beautiful. It's warm and dry, and I'm delighted to be here. Off to bed. I must get nine hours' sleep if I'm to look fresh for the camera—we movie stars!

[*Hollywood—Tuesday night, November 29, 1932.*] The picture rushes on—good and bad. I've become quite accustomed to the camera and have no more shyness.

I'm delighted to have Dad's fine report on the house. I know how interested he is. So you think we'll be in it February first?

[*Hollywood—December 8, 1932.*] We leave Tuesday, a whole caravan of motors and trucks, for the Yosemite Valley for more scenes. One day to go, three days there, and one back—almost a week.

Of course, I had to get sick and miss Moye's wedding, and it was an especially fine affair, I hear.

No, there is no "leading lady" in my picture. It's in chapters, like *Royal Road*. Only one chapter has a love-girl in it—and she's sweet, too—named Rosie Brown. She's dressed up like a Kashmir girl, and I have a romantic scene with her in a garden, when the rain comes and puts an end to my courtship. The "rain" was a fire hose. We got sopping wet and I caught this case of flu . . . but it was incubating already . . . the dousing was just the final push. Rosie Brown has called up to ask after me every day.

[*Hollywood—Thursday, December 15, 1932.*] I've just sent you a wire saying, "Back from the mountains after four days—flu all gone—feeling fine," and it's all true. On Monday last I felt quite up to moving again. Walter came by in a closed car, I bundled up in sweaters, and away we went—400 miles, up past Yosemite Park, right into the wildest of the wilds—deep snow, and ten below zero for four days. We had no form of heat whatsoever, but I piled on more sweaters and kept comfortable. The sun was bright, the air dry, and the snow three feet deep. It was an interesting interlude after the hospital.

Next Monday, Hal Horn, the man who will promote and distribute our movie, arrives from New York. We'll discuss my personal appearances, etc. They believe the picture will open March first, the same day twenty lecture dates begin on the Pacific coast. I'm seeing my lecture manager tomorrow. It's all most difficult and complicated.

With the novelty of *India Speaks* behind him Richard resumed his accustomed lecturing. The season was more than usually full, but it was merely another arrangement of the crystals in the kaleidoscope.

He passed through Memphis, was pleased with the progress on the new house on Court Avenue, liked the white brick and green blinds. "I congratulate you both on your creation." At Chattanooga his introducer "announced President Coolidge's death, by way of cheering up the audience, just before I spoke." From a series of lectures in his beloved Southeast he jumped to Canada for an address in Toronto on Rupert Brooke to "a fine audience in a beautiful auditorium."

In New York: "Lowell Thomas took me to supper and to a preview of *his* movie, *Mussolini Speaks*.... Fox Movietone are interested in my producing shorts based on travel actually taken on the spot, not less than five and not more than twelve, but I'm not much attracted. ... Some Russian princess interviewed me today [January 22, 1933] for *Liberty*. Last night I had supper with Corey Ford, who has been a pungent critic. I had written him a hot letter a week ago. We got along famously. ... We've sold scads of books. We've reached a total of 490,000, all titles.... Did you see *Ballyhoo's* parody of *The Flying Carpet?*"

Out of Boston, February eighth, in a blinding snowstorm: "The book party at Jordan Marsh's was the wildest mob scene you ever saw—over a thousand people." Other book parties at Nashville, at Indianapolis, and at Cincinnati with his old friend John Kidd. "Give my room in the new house a pat for me."

February twenty-sixth: "I had a full day in Washington . . . was taken to President Hoover's office and had a chat with him, surrounded by six bodyguards . . . lunched with Huey Long, of all people, at the Capitol. . . . I've found that our movie can't open till after April first, so I'm going to California to fill my all but canceled dates. I'll take the train to Cleveland, the plane from Cleveland to Memphis, the same plane next day from Memphis to L. A."

[*Laguna Beach, California—March 10, 1933.*] That night, after seeing you in Memphis, was long and cold, but the sunrise, high above the California hills, made up for it.

I saw a preview of *India Speaks* in San Diego. I was a little weak afterward from trying to note so much at once. It's all right. The lion and tiger fight is a hair-raiser. My voice sounds strange to me.

Moye and his wife and Walter Futter were on hand when I spoke to the Breakfast Club. They made me an honorary life member.

I must go for a swim.

[*Laguna Beach, California—Sunday, March 12, 1933.*] Knowing you'd read about the earthquake I sent you a wire saying I was unhurt—just scared to death. It was a first-class quake, though our town was off to one side of the worst area. I was buying fruit in a grocery shop. I was flung off my feet, with apples and canned beans and bread on top of me. I was diving out the door when the roof came down. It was the worst pandemonium I've ever heard—the deep ominous roar from the earth and the smashing of plate glass, roofs, chimneys. Up the line at Long Beach, 200 people were killed. I got to see it today. The big buildings stood—the little ones crashed. Most of the people were killed by bricks and stones falling on them as they stood on the sidewalk. People seated in cars parked in gutters suffered worst, when brick cornices came showering down. This house in which I've been living lost its chimney.

Yesterday I motored to Hollywood to see Walter and rehearse a radio talk for tomorrow. Traffic was so congested, and so many bridges were down from the quake, I stayed in town for the night. It took all today to get the 50 miles home in the Ford, as I plowed through Long Beach to see the wreckage.

[*Roosevelt Hotel, Hollywood—March 24, 1933.*] Hooray, I'm starting home tomorrow. Things are cleared up out here, and beginning to come to life in New York. I'm going to the Grand Canyon first. I'll keep you informed.

My trip north was a great success—two days in the Yosemite, two with Noel Sullivan in San Francisco, a nice visit with Kathleen and Charles Norris in Palo Alto, and a night in Santa Barbara. I needed the vacation and am enjoying every minute.

Walter writes our movie is having a fine reception—previews— in New York.

After two days in Memphis he drove on east in the Ford. "I never realized before how beautiful Middle Tennessee is. I put in an afternoon at the Natural Bridge, where everything was fresh and green." He spoke at the annual Boy Scout dinner at Middletown, New York, in Lowell Thomas's place. Grosset and Dunlap were making a large book, quarto size, of still pictures from *India Speaks,* with the long dramatic captions at which Richard was so adept. The Flying Carpet airplane, which had been sold to an army officer in Honolulu, crashed with the pilot and two passengers and was completely demolished.

[*New Roxy Theater, New York—Sunday night, May 7, 1933.*] Am I tired! This five-a-day personal-appearance business is the hardest work I've ever done. Our theater today has been only moderately filled, about 2000 people at each of the five performances. I speak about two and a half minutes and say, among other things, that "not all the adventures in which I take part on the screen happened to me personally. I am chiefly an actor playing a part." I'm still in a terribly nervous strain over this new role, having to recite a set speech in the face of blinding lights. But as I've got things fixed now, the picture is good general publicity for our books. I must wear make-up, so I can't go out between shows, but I've a fine, big dressing room to myself, where I can read and write letters. I don't get much relaxation!

The summer of 1933 was sorely trying to a restless spirit. The flight around the world in the Flying Carpet, the tense months of preparing the manuscript for publication, the turmoil and excitement of the most exacting of all his lecture seasons had left Richard Halliburton in no frame of mind to meet the stagnation of depression that had settled on America. His motto was: action, action, action; and now he met with delay, procrastination and indifference. He could not slow down, he had to slow down. His letters reflect his impatience. He went from the radios to the movies to the magazine editors and back again. He returned to Alexandria to work on various articles; he sold one called "The World Is Still Wide" to the *Cosmopolitan* and one or two to smaller magazines. He took a motor trip through the show places of Virginia—Williamsburg, Yorktown, Charlottesville. He went to White Mountain, Virginia, for the Mountain Music Festival. He saw the World's Fair in Chicago with his mother and father. These things helped him to keep his feet more or less on the ground till lecturing began again in October.

[*The Bobbs-Merrill Office, New York—November 12, 1933.*] What a two-weeks these two have been! Today is my first breath of tranquillity since getting back, and I had to use manhandling to get it. I've written 75 letters today and the table is clear.

I spoke for the Baltimore Blind School—200 blind children. It was a most heartbreaking experience. I haven't got over it yet. They all knew my stories from braille.

Don't be so downcast about your lack of grandchildren, Dad. There's lots of time. As I grow more weary of this headlong life I'll grow more hungry for domesticity. The current gets stronger that way every year. In any case, I'll have two good weeks Xmas to think and talk away from the battle line.

[*On the train to Boston—November 24, 1933.*] I'm on the move again, and not minding much. It's quite like old times, the relentless march of appointments and engagements. I admit it's nice to be in demand, though I'd like to be accomplishing something more important than is represented by this flow, however steady, of pleasant contacts and responsive audiences. The dollar books have certainly made me friends. My audiences get increasingly larger, there's that consolation. Speaking dates come and go so fast I can hardly remember them.

I spoke one noon in New York for 500 Jewish women, probably the richest group of women on earth. The officers were brilliant people. The next two days I was at Dannemora Prison near Plattsburg. The prison had no distinction except that it was cold. I met the Prison Commissioners and hope to get into Sing Sing—to see, not to stay! But the visit will have to be in January as I'm booked solid for December. Back in New York I heard Commodore Fellowes lecture on his Mt. Everest flight. He was kind enough to mention me. I attended a big book fair at Abraham & Straus in Brooklyn. Shall I break away and do my American book? Schuler wants the serial.

Tonight I speak in a Boston suburb. There's a date every day until the eighteenth and three dates on two days. I'll have a visit with you from the eighteenth to the twenty-ninth. I have to be back in New York for the thirtieth, when the Women's Press Club, reporters, reviewers and so on, have their annual banquet.

I go to the gym every possible chance.

[*The Bobbs-Merrill Office, New York—November 28, 1933.*] A mild disaster in Boston. Monica Grey, Mr. Wickes's assistant, planned to take me out to my suburban date. She didn't know the way. We were exactly 45 minutes late. All the apologies in the world didn't help. I'll never again leave it to a woman to escort me to my dates. Monica is a dear, but—

[*New York—Tuesday night, January 2, 1934.*] A happy, if belated, New Year to you all! Let's hope it's the best and most prosperous year of our lives. I have a feeling it's going to be.

I came to New York for that Saturday night engagement at the Women's Press Club. My train was four hours late because of a blizzard, but, even so, I got into the depot about 4:30—to find Jo Reynolds from the office simply *wild*. My date was for the *afternoon,* and 500 press women had been killing time two hours waiting for me. Jo rushed me over to the auditorium and on to the platform, dirty and unshaven, right off the train. But somehow I got away with it. When under pressure I tell my fat princess story and all is saved.

The radio deal is sizzling. It's like Banquo's ghost, and getting to be about as popular. But we can plan so much with this radio contract before us—capital for Dad to buy bargain lands with, a splendid trip to Europe for Mother, a diamond tiara for Ammudder—and for me *two undershirts.*

[*On the train to Boston—January 4, 1934.*] I went to a bang-up party last night—a group of fabulously rich people, Huttons and Woolworths and Biddles and the like. About 40 to dinner at the Plaza—gold plates and six wines. The hostess hired sixteen Packards to take us in a parade to the Russian Ballet where we had the first three front rows of solid seats. The ballet was marvelous; you know how I've always loved it. Then our parade drove to the Casino in Central Park, the most expensive night club in New York, for more champagne and dancing. Each of the twenty women had enough orchids on to hide her. And $500 worth of orchids were dumped on the tables when we left. They had everything money can buy—and nothing else.

[*The Bobbs-Merrill Office—February 7, 1934.*] Chambers is in New York, demanding a new book, and I mean for him to have one. He tells me we have sold over 530,000 grand total, so I must get my eye ready for 600,000. It will be a million some day.

[*On the train to southern Georgia—March 1, 1934.*] I've good news at last about a job. The Bell Newspaper Syndicate is keen about my Sunday syndicated story idea, and they and I are launched forth in preparation of a prospectus to be sent as sales talk to all their 40 newspaper clients. I propose to do about 50 Sunday articles with pictures. I told them I couldn't afford to go on a year's quest for copy for less than so much insured capital. They seemed to think we'd have no trouble at all raising it. I'm going at this idea with vigor.

Indeed both he and the Bell people attacked it with vigor. He found it difficult to get the prospectus quite to his satisfaction, but was comforted to have the assurance that no newspaper buyer would look at it for more than forty-five seconds anyway, as the real selling was done by the agents in person.

As part of the prospectus he had to prepare the detailed list of subjects he would treat and write a sample story. He dashed off the list in no time but the interruptions of lecturing and traveling held him up on the story. What should be his first article? He thought of Boulder Dam which he saw late in May, and he considered going back as a workman to do it; but Bell rejected this suggestion. So he decided on the Gulf of Lower California, and talked with people familiar with its primitive Indians. His chief concern was to "get to the Alps with his elephant before cold weather." Long before this the idea of emulating Hannibal had appealed to his imagination and his sense of humor as something "gay and ridiculous and outrageous," and he had mentioned it to his parents and his friends. Now it would fit into the trip abroad which the syndicate project would make possible.

These are random jottings from his letters, which are mainly concerned with aspects of the syndicate problem and program: "[*March 17.*] At Cambridge, Ohio, the other night, who should be sitting on the front row but Jimmy Lownes, the 'Whoopee' of the Venice swim. . . . [*Easter Sunday.*] A radio company offered me $500 a week for 26 weeks to speak on a beer program. I declined. . . . [*April 12.*] I've bought a used Ford roadster. A friend and I drove northwest from San Francisco 200 miles deep into the '49 country. The mountains were glorious, with giant dogwood in the valleys and snow on the summits. The whole country is fascinating—abandoned towns, wonderful redwoods, and fortunes being made by the turn of a spade. Lake Tahoe at this season is indescribably beautiful. . . . [*May 6.*] I went to Palo Alto to the Norris party—400 guests, 400 bottles of champagne. . . . [*May 9.*] I laughed aloud over Dad's admonitions about my drinking. I think twenty cents for two glasses of beer about covers my liquor expenditures for the past two months. . . . [*June 1.*] Death Valley didn't seem so grand after the Dead Sea—300 feet below sea level as against 1200. But my little vacation was a great success. Harry Catlin, my houseboat friend in Kashmir, is in Hollywood. . . . [*June 19.*] I had a beautiful speaking date, for a local society called Ephebians, the honor students of the graduating class of ten Los Angeles high schools and the alumni. The meeting was held in a Greek amphitheater in a park, very serene in the twilight. I spoke for forty minutes on Greece—the Acropolis, Olympus, Brooke on Skyros. I've a fine string of speaking dates for next year, all of which I must cancel. . . . [*June 23.*] You remember that unbalanced girl who sent me *sausage* for Christmas, and her box of love letters—a letter a week for five years—and who threatened to commit suicide unless I answered? Well, she is here. Woe is me."

Meanwhile, his Bell friends were lining up the newspapers. He records their first contract—with the Boston *Globe*—on May fourteenth. From then on each letter reports new takers. The sales campaign had for him all the excitement of a contest and he greeted its success with jubilation. By June eighth Bell were ready to guarantee him $8,000, which he felt sufficient encouragement to strike out.

But there were things to cause delay. United Artists, who were doing a movie on the life of Cellini, asked him to write a thousand-word newspaper story elaborating on one of Benvenuto's love affairs. He had to read two long books in preparation. His typhoid shots knocked him down, and vaccination took half way. Then, "there's dynamite in the air. The movie-short situation has flamed into a bonfire. All my plans may be violently changed if this is to be added to syndicate and book, but I doubt anything can develop in time."

The Bell Syndicate were getting impatient for him to be off, and he was just as impatient. The movie-short situation looked "hot," but if it couldn't be settled at once on his return from Lower California, he'd move right on to Cuba, as planned in the prospectus.

[*6626 Franklin Street, Hollywood—July 13, 1934.*] My dip into Mexico was a great success. I got back by air yesterday and am rushing to Laguna tonight to do the story while I'm full of it. I flew for four hours to Hermosillo, found a good guide who knew the Seri Indians, and motored 100 miles right across the open desert. Half the Indians live on the mainland and half on Tiburon Island. I visited both, and got lots of pictures. The Seri are no longer dangerous, just dirty and slovenly. But it's still extraordinary that such a primitive race should live so close to Hollywood. They have no houses, no arts and crafts, no religion, no villages—are just gypsies and scavengers, living on raw fish, and always in motion. The marine and seabird life was extraordinary—clouds of aigrettes and pelicans and pink flamingoes—sharks, porpoises and whales. We hunted turtles one morning and pelicans, with a club, one night. I won't go into more details as you'll read it all next week when I send you the carbon copy of the story I'll hurry to Bell.

I'm planning to move on to Havana the moment I mail it. I expect to do Cuba, Haiti and Martinique in two weeks, and be in Memphis August 15 to 20. I can't wait on the movie thing.

Goeffrey Bles, my London publisher, has asked me to do an introduction for the English edition of Elly Beinhorn's book. I'd like to.

[*Hollywood—July 18, 1934.*] I'm sending you my Tiburon story. Tomorrow I get the pictures to illustrate it. I'll rush everything east, and come rushing behind it. It's hard to convey interest when the 2000-word deadline faces you. It's going to be a problem every week, saying all I want to say in the way I want to say it—in 2000 words.

[*On the train approaching Miami, Florida—July 30, 1934.*] I picked up a magazine yesterday, and there was a story about the Dry Tortugas. My interest was aroused, and I'm definitely going there. I will be in Miami just 24 hours; then to Key West, Tortugas, Havana. You all looked so wistful, on the station platform, as my train pulled out. Don't be depressed over my going—this trip is going to give all of us fresh interests and occupations. I'll be shooting manuscripts and pictures at you as never before.

[*Key West—Tuesday, July 31, 1934.*] I'm busy today making arrangements to get to Tortugas. It's 65 miles west of Key West—and I must hire a launch.

[*Havana—August 9, 1934.*] Have I been busy! My new story, Fort Jefferson and Dr. Mudd's imprisonment there and Dry Tortugas, is coming in a separate package. I'll not tell about my marvelous trip out to the last Florida key to see the Fort, as it's all in the story. I've been in Havana a week, working on script and pictures and sightseeing. Havana is grand. I spoke over the radio. Everybody has been kind to me. I'm leaving today for a 500-mile bus ride to Santiago.

[*Santiago de Cuba—August 16, 1934.*] My "rush" through the West Indies has been held up for lack of transportation. But I'm off at last today by plane for Port-au-Prince, Haiti.

I've enjoyed this place. The first day I hired a launch, and sailed east along the marvelous south coast of Cuba, to visit the wrecked battleships of the Spanish War. Of the six that were sunk in the Battle of Santiago, only two are visible above water, just gun turrets. I got good photos of them with my little Leica, and will have a fine story. Hobson's *Merrimac* is still here, faintly visible in 40 feet of water to one side of the channel. The hull is split in two. I'll not write this story till I see Admiral Hobson in New York.

The long bus ride from Havana nearly finished me, but the east half of Cuba is gloriously beautiful and I enjoyed the scenery. I've a room overlooking the bay, and can see the narrow entrance where the *Merrimac* lies. I persuaded the air company to lend me their big Ford plane and went photographing from the air. Two English fellows followed me down from Havana, for a holiday. They run the radio station where I spoke. We explored around San Juan Hill and swam. So all in all the six days have passed pleasantly.

[*Santo Domingo—Friday, August 23, 1934.*] I'm starting Americaward again. The next plane out reaches Miami Tuesday night. I must stop at Washington and Philadelphia for photographs and references, and will be in New York about a week from today.

I've been busy since Santiago. My week in Haiti gave me grand copy. The Christophe citadel is the *most* thrilling thing I've seen in a long, long time. It was built by a Negro slave who couldn't read or write. Friends took me 200 miles north from Port-au-Prince to Cape Haitien where Christophe ruled. There is his palace, Sans Souci, and, 300 feet above, the citadel. I'm writing furiously about it.

Tomorrow morning I am to hold the bones of Christopher Columbus in my hands. The Governor is interested in my ability to publicize the country and the new Pan-American Columbus lighthouse proposal, and is uncovering the lead casket containing the bones, for the first time since 1891. I'll have a photographer ready. I'll have the two articles on Christophe and one on Columbus finished when I reach New York. Bell will then have six. I'll see Hobson for two more, on Santiago. Two on Devil's Island, one on Crusoe, and one on the Veiled Empress—a marvelous story.

[*New Weston Hotel—Saturday night, September 1, 1934.*] I left Miami Wednesday night by train for Washington, to see the Navy about a photograph and to do a little research at the Library of Congress, and came on to New York last night—and here I am.

I had a fine conference with the Bell people today—and good news. Milwaukee, Kansas City, Columbus and Toronto have joined up. Bell seem *very* well satisfied. They're running the Seri story September ninth. I wish they'd waited one more week. Still, I'm glad the fight is on. If I work day and night I might get away in eight days. I must see Hobson next.

[*New York—Tuesday, September 11, 1934.*] The series is under way, three weeks sooner than I wanted. The papers had all advertised it to start the ninth and I had to submit.

I spent all yesterday at Asbury Park watching the *Morro Castle* burn. No one in New York has talked of anything else, nor have the newspapers printed anything else. The ship is right up on the board-walk, and, after three days and nights since the disaster, was still red hot, and burning furiously. It's the most terrible sight I've ever seen—the steel plates buckled, the superstructure twisted and consumed. There were still 50 bodies in the staterooms which were too hot to be entered. There seems to have been criminal neglect on the part of everybody, and as much panic on the part of the crew as the passengers.

I haven't the faintest idea where I'm going from New York. Anyway I must go *soon*. I'll do Santiago on the boat. Hobson returns tomorrow.

[*New York—Friday night, September 21, 1934.*] It's 2 A.M. I'm packed and all ready to sail away. As always the last day is

A study in contrast: Richard, as an involuntary monk, with a brother of a Grecian monastery at Mount Athos.

While collecting material about Lord Byron, Richard visits his tomb at
Missolonghi, Greece.

bursting with details—goodbyes, money, baggage. I'm dizzy from the complications, but remember getting off in 1931 with the airplane, and rejoice that I've so little to do *this* time.

I delivered stories No. 7 and 8 Wednesday. The next boat was tomorrow, the *Champlain,* so I'm sailing on it. I'll reach France October first and start looking for elephants *at once.* As soon as I'm over the Alps with Jumbo, I can relax. I've my Russian visé applied for. If there's no elephant there's Russia.

I had dinner with the Hobsons last night and lunch today. He loaded me up with books and notes. You'll see my stories from Hobson as they appear in the *Commercial.* He and I were photographed in his office.

It's now 3 A.M. I must be up at seven. So good night and goodbye.

CHAPTER XVII

[*Almost landing—September 30, 1934.*] Hello from France. I've not even seen the ocean, just stuck to my cabin and worked like mad on "Seven Volunteers for Death"—about Hobson and the *Merrimac*. I got so interested, the story ran away with me, and after ruthless cutting it's still 3000 words, or 500 too long. But I'm sending it in. A few papers will take all of it. And, as it is, I can use it in the book.

I'd planned to do at least two stories on board. But I finished only the one. So tonight, instead of going on to Paris, I'm staying two days in Havre, to write the second. I've heavy books on the Battle of Santiago and want to be rid of them before I move.

This trip is going to be mostly work, but the harder I work, the sooner I'll have my 50 stories delivered.

[*Paris—October 13, 1934.*] By next Tuesday night Dally and I expect to leave for Switzerland. Dally is not my new girl. She's my new elephant. We will relive Hannibal's march over the Alps with his elephants. I've had to labor ten hours a day for two weeks to get her, as such a project as mine is unheard of, without precedent, and so I've made terribly slow progress. The owners of three other elephants strung me along, asked too much money, changed their minds, lost their nerve. At last I found a small zoo, where the director took definite action. Everybody is intensely interested and amused. The Fox movietone people will cover the story for the movies, and the Associated Press. I hope to start walking (and riding) at Montreux, at the eastern end of Lake Geneva. The summit of the Great St. Bernard Pass is about 45 miles from Montreux. It will take two days to reach the summit. Then we'll rest a night with the St. Bernard dogs and monks. I want to see the St. Bernard hospice.

Yesterday I spoke for the American Women's Club here in a lovely ex-palace. A new students' building for English and Americans is being dedicated tomorrow and I've agreed to be the speaker.

Mother writes, "I know you are free without the burden of the plane"—and then I take on an *elephant!* I must like trouble. But it's only for a month.

Paris is ever beautiful. I've sandwiched in miles of walking— went to the top of the Eiffel Tower, to Napoleon's Tomb, and the Louvre; to a night club, looking for gypsies, with George Vanderbilt's daughter, who is now married to an Englishman. She was born at "Biltmore," the Vanderbilt estate in Asheville, N. C.

Bles sent me Elly Beinhorn's book, for my preface. She speaks of Moye and me most affectionately. There's so much more I'd like to say, but I must say it to Bell, instead.

[*Berlin—October 24, 1934.*] Don't be surprised, hearing from me from Berlin, and not Rome. The elephant did *not* come to pass. After writing you all about my departure, I went to the zoo, and all seemed well. I paid my money and away we went—as far as the street. Here Dally was honked at by automobiles and became so terrified she fled in a panic down the boulevard for half a mile. Fortunately nobody but the mahout was aboard. I saw Dally would not do in the Alpine passes. She was accustomed to being ridden in the park but not on main roads. So that same night, desperately rushed for time, I hurried on to Hanover, where I knew there was another elephant. But meanwhile she had been leased to a circus. There was one in Berlin. I dashed here. This one was about to have a baby! I collapsed. And anyway, the passes in the Alps are snowbound. It would have been pretty desperate. Now I'll wait and go next May. I've a Sunday story out of it, "How to Buy an Elephant." This morning I got off No. 12—"The Girl from Martinique Who Wrecked Napoleon."

Even with a story to do, I've managed to see Berlin, superficially. It's much as it was in 1921. Uniforms are everywhere. The older people seem very cool about Hitler, but the kids are all maniacs on the subject—and they will be in command in a few years.

I'm having a Hitler problem of my own. I came into Germany with $1500 cash, in marks, for my elephant. No elephant. Now I've still got the marks and can't exchange them or *get them out.*

I've spent two full days fighting over it. And even now it's not settled. I'm taking a plane at 7 A.M. tomorrow for Leningrad, expecting to get through with the money—but if *not,* I'll just have to hire a lockbox and leave it here till I come back in May. It doesn't make me like the country any better.

[*Moscow—November 7, 1934.*] Thank heaven for the Sunday stories. Otherwise you never *would* hear from me. The grind is *awful*—perpetual motion. Never once am I free from consciousness of the weekly deadline.

Russia is certainly exciting, an explosion of energy that bewilders. Factories, construction, street paving run 24 hours a day. There is no unemployment. A hundred and sixty million people suddenly have to be supplied with *everything.* It's this terrific demand that keeps industry booming. But it's thrilling to see the country almost blowing up from steam pressure. At the same time the people are the dirtiest and most poorly dressed I've seen anywhere. Good clothes, shoes, etc., are impossible to buy. They live jammed helplessly into living quarters that would be unendurable to Americans. They cannot leave Russia. Their newspapers, books, movies are nothing but Soviet propaganda, extolling Communism and spitting on all other systems. All refined, cultivated classes, all money classes, all rich farmers, factory owners, merchants—*everybody* in fact except peasants and factory workers have been killed or exiled. The "toilers" have taken possession. Now nobody has anything, but nobody is hungry (theoretically) or shelterless.

For one used to, and requiring, personal freedom to travel, to read, to enjoy the fine things that make life worth living, Russia is a hateful, tyrannical prison cell. None of these things can one enjoy privately, for one's self. But on the other hand Russia has achieved reforms that we must inevitably follow. She has abolished crime and closed her prisons (except for political offenders who get ruthless punishment). She has increased literacy from nine to ninety per cent. Women have absolutely equal rights with men. A wife can divorce her husband by sending him a postcard. A woman is expected to work like a man. She receives the same salary, is distinguished in no way from a man. Women shovel gravel, run steam rollers, build houses, wear overalls. They marry and divorce with a wave of their hand—or don't marry. There's no such thing as illegitimacy. Prostitution is ended.

The dictators here sit on high with half-closed eyes and consider the 160,000,000 Russians as guinea pigs. Their pigs are injected with this, deprived of that. Millions may die from a bad experiment— the dictators are not even conscious of it. Next generation we'll see how enduring their equality theories are, how their tests have worked. Meanwhile the "specimens" are fed what's good for them, denied all knowledge of the outside world, killed off. To watch from the sidelines is one of the great privileges of the day, but to be subjected to it would be fatal for a liberty-lover like me.

Today Moscow is full of American Reds, shouting their heads off for the Soviets. But you may be sure they are getting back to America by the first boat. Today was the seventeenth anniversary of the Communist Revolution. I stood in Red Square and watched 100,000 soldiers, 1000 tanks, 2000 airplanes and 1,000,000 workers march past Stalin's review stand. It was probably the greatest military show in history. But I firmly believe such gigantic armament is to defend their Soviet system. They claim to abhor war, and I do believe that Russia has no thought—no more than America—of taking her army across her borders.

My plans, as always, are subject to impulse. In a few days I'm flying to Sverdlovsk, the first big city on the Trans-Siberian on the Siberian side of the Urals. Here the Royal Family were murdered in 1917. The house is still there, and two of the men who acted as executioners. I want to interview them for a story. I'm also seeing Mrs. Lenin for a story about Russian women. And I'm trying to get to Samarkand.

Oh, I almost forgot to say that I got out of Germany with my marks. Alas, I still have them, in cash.

[*Moscow, dammit—December 2, 1934.*] The Sverdlovsk expedition was a grand and glorious success, beyond my wildest hopes. The man who murdered the Czar and all his family, the actual assassin who was jailor, executioner, undertaker, cremator, has kept silent for seventeen years. I got him on his sick bed, and heard his story poured out—unguarded, complete and terrifically vivid. I happened, by this good break, to be his confessor. He's never spoken to any other person. I'm still a little weak over the melodramatics of the thing. This interview should insure the success of our book. It was *history* he told me.

The story is so tremendous I'm writing it for *Liberty* or *Cosmopolitan*. The pictures are excellent, though the collecting of them is holding me up another week in this freezing, snowbound city. Winter has descended on us with a vengeance. I've run out of copy about Moscow, and am hell-bent to get to new, and warmer, fields. But I must hang on for the pictures.

The nineteenth story went off yesterday. It's called "The Hundred Happiest Children in the World"—all about circus schools.

Twice I've been to the theater. Russian theater and ballet are superlatively good, the best in the world. I'd go every night if I had the time. Front row at the opera house costs sixty cents. Russia continues to infuriate and astound me.

I have had good news about our Syndicate. More papers are joining the fold right along.

On December fifth I leave for Tiflis, Armenia, Baku, Samarkand. A young German moving-picture cameraman will go with me. He speaks no English but perfect Russian. My German is being forced. I'm remembering lots of it, and this trip will be of great help.

I finally got off to Bles a 1500-word preface for Elly Beinhorn's book.

Inclosed is a lot of this and that—but mostly love from Comrade Richard.

[*Athens—January 2, 1935.*] You must blame Russia for a month's silence. I left Moscow after the most trying and irritating week I've ever known. I was worn out trying to get around and see things, in the face of the mountainous obstacles put in the path of every journalist. I was generally so fed up with the arctic weather and the filth and the food, that I looked forward eagerly to my journey south. Also I began to feel desperate about the mails. Every word I wrote was opened. My letters to you telling the truth about conditions were considered "unfair." My interpreter turned out to be a spy.

A Russian friend who came to see me was arrested and pumped. My movements were watched day and night. Innocent packages of Soviet official photographs never reached New York. If groups of people collected in my room, or anyone remained later than twelve o'clock, my 'phone rang, and the manager curtly ordered me to send them out.

Then came the Kiroff assassination just the day I was prepared to escape. He was killed by one of his own associates, but the Soviets, seeing a chance to beat the tom-toms, declared he was killed by "class enemies," counter-revolutionaries. For three days Moscow, by order, was given over to mechanical grief. All life stopped, except the three day and night procession that crept through the snowy, ice-covered streets. I wondered how many people died of pneumonia, since good shoes are non-existent.

Later Kiroff's body was placed in state opposite my hotel. All streets leading to the square were cut off—no exit—no entrance. And so for three days and nights I could not leave my lodging. Every guest in the hotel was a prisoner. On the fourth day in desperation I broke through, as a filling had fallen out of a tooth and I was miserable from toothache. And then I couldn't get back, and had to sleep at the embassy. On the fifth day I reached the bank. It took two hours to get to the window—and *then* I didn't get my account because I didn't have my book of blank checks to turn in. By the time I rushed home and back the bank had closed (one o'clock) and the next day *everything* was closed. Then my passport was held up, and when it came I was given ten days to get out of the country, and two of those ten were spent trying to get a seat in a train.

Perhaps it was the strain—anyhow, when I got aboard I had fever and a grand case of flu. The Black Sea was as cold as Moscow. I had to ride in open-top busses. Even so, I managed to get a story on the coast about the Oldest Man in the World, 152 years old. He was herding sheep during the French Revolution and fought against the Turks in the Napoleonic wars of 1812. Finally I reached Tiflis. From there I forced myself into the mountains to see the Crusaders—mountaineers who still wear armor handed down from the twelfth century Crusades—and got to Batum on the day my visé expired. There was no boat for two days, and the police kept me in my "hotel," the foulest hole you can imagine. The guests, all first-class Russian Communists, had so befouled the toilet that they were using the floor. I had no heat and only a candle and was charged six dollars a day for the "apartment" alone.

But at last I got aboard the boat, and went to bed with high fever. One hour before sailing the steward reported to the captain (I was the only passenger) that I was sick and shouldn't be allowed to sail. The captain called the Soviet doctor who said he didn't know what I had and they'd better not take a chance in letting me stay on the boat. I was put off and back to the hotel I went. The Soviet doctor was so incredibly dirty I wouldn't allow him to touch me again. Two days later there was another boat. I went aboard a second time, and sat in the salon pretending I was exuberantly well—until we sailed. Then I went to bed and stayed there for three days till we got to Constantinople. I'm quite all right now. It was just Russia.

I had four days in Constantinople, in which I turned out two stories. I took a steamer and sailed through the Hellespont at midnight on December 31, with the whistle blowing. I couldn't even see the shores.

Of course, I was lonely to be away from home Xmas. It was spent in bed on the Black Sea steamer, working on my stories—quite the dullest Xmas I've *ever* spent. But I was so happy to be out of Russia, it seemed a *beautiful* day.

I had a wad of cables from Bell, calling for more copy, faster, faster. I've sent in twenty-three stories and mailing one more tonight, on Constantinople. The *Readers Digest* has taken one article— I don't know which.

Mount Ararat was closed—and too cold anyway. Tomorrow night I'm going to Saloniki to visit Mount Athos and the monasteries there. They'll make a good story. After that?

[*Athens—January 21, 1935.*] Every Sunday morning you read that I'm still alive and getting around. Otherwise maybe you wouldn't believe it. Since writing last I've been plunged into the Mount Athos stories, trying to pick up the schedule I lost while trying to get out of Russia. The Athos adventure was all I had hoped for, a marvelous place. No female has been in it for a thousand years—not

In the days of its glory Alexander consulted the oracle at the oasis of Siwa.
Richard and two of its young inhabitants before the ruins.

With a guard of honor of native Ethiopian warriors Richard stands before
a sculptured figure of the king of beasts, at the court of the King of Kings,
Addis Ababa.

even a hen or a cow. At the isthmus where the peninsula joins the mainland, a body of monastic police are stationed "to prevent wolves and women from approaching the monastery."

Athos was good for two stories, "No-Woman's Land" and "The Involuntary Monk"—meaning me; snow had blocked the trails and a storm lashed the sea. The moment No. 2 was mailed I rushed off to Missolonghi, across from Patras, to get atmosphere for a story on Byron. I'm trying to get ahead a little, so I can work on the Romanoff yarn. The Missolonghi trip would have been lovely in summer, but in January it was terrible—freezing rain, bottomless mud. Byron was in this swampy town from January to his death in April, 1824. I'm surprised he endured that long.

I've Maurois' *Byron,* the best biography I know. I'm eager to get on to Egypt, but more eager to do my Czar story. *Cosmopolitan* writes me again for a short contribution, 600 words, on my favorite spot in the world. As if I had nothing else to do!

Twenty-six stories have been sent in—twenty-four to go.

[*Athens—January 31, 1935.*] The same day the Byron story got off I went to Crete with the New York *Times* correspondent, one night's ride by boat. We spent the day at Canea, had lunch· with Venizelos and his wife. He's been in world politics for twenty years and is an amazing man. Twelve assassins tried to murder him and his wife recently. She was wounded badly four times. He escaped. They're living now, carefully guarded, in Crete. I've just mailed off "Experiments in Assassination"—No. 28—all about my interview. Next day we motored 150 miles down that beautiful island to Candia. Near by are the marvelous ruins of Knossos where King Minos had the labyrinth in· which he kept the Minotaur that Theseus slew, and escaped by a thread, etc. This will make story No. 29. Next day we visited a lonely leper colony—300 Greek lepers herded together in a twelfth-century Venetian fortress on an island. It was horrible, but so interesting as to make No. 30. So I got three weeks of stories unexpectedly on this island. This, I hope, will give me a chance to work on the Romanoffs.

Yesterday I got a photographer to take a picture of the Acropolis and me to illustrate the short article I'm doing for *Cosmo,* "Athens—

My Favorite Place in All the World." Tomorrow, I'm taking 24 hours off with the American Consul to visit friends who live on an island *I* might live on some day.

I've lost taste for the title I had had in mind for the new book. *The Islands of Desire* sounds like a belated South-Sea book. I'm trying to fit in the word *map—My Magical Map*, or *The Magic Map*, or *Map Magic*. Put your minds on it.

I'm a little weary of this grind, but would be lost without it.

[*Athens—February 12, 1935.*] It's full spring here. The fruit trees are in bloom, and the whole country smells of perfume. I hate to think of leaving.

I'm less and less satisfied with *The Islands of Desire* for our next title and I've come to the conclusion that *Map Magic* is no better. They haven't enough vitality. I've a new enthusiasm (for the moment) *My Seven League Boots,* or just *Seven League Boots.* It covers the wild shifts in geography—Cuba—to Russia—to Greece—to Arabia. It indicates action. It's short and snappy. What do *you* think?

My stories roll on. No. 29 was on one of the famous ruined cities in Crete; 30 on the sports of 4000 years ago, in ancient Crete; and 31 on leprosy. This last is a terror, and may be thrown out by some of the editors as likely to spoil too many Sunday dinners. I've been working harder than ever to get ahead of schedule, so that I may write on Romanoff. With thirty-one down, I've nineteen to go. We're on the home stretch. No. 32 will be "The Wonders of the World I Want My Son to See." But for the next seven days—come what may—I'm writing my murder story, the biggest story I've ever encountered.

All my Sunday stories are letters to you. As I write each one I begin it mentally: "Dear Family."

[*Athens—February 26, 1935.*] During the past two weeks your son and heir has been working grimly here in his little hotel room from twelve to fourteen hours a day on "The Massacre of the Romanoffs." I've let everything else drop, haven't seen anybody, been any place, and, worst of all, I haven't written my family, or any stories for Bell. It's finished now, all but the final typing—about 18,000 words, in three chapters. I'm sending one copy and set of photos to New York, and one to London. In any case—even if it doesn't sell—it's 18,000 words ahead on the book. I've become so excited over it I've forgotten to eat or sleep. It's one of the most moving, tragic and shocking chapters in the world's history. Is it too old?—that's the catch. *If* it isn't, we go places. I'm going to buy myself some new socks; I've holes in every one.

Seven League Boots doesn't apply to the eight weeks I've been stuck in Athens. Spring has burst upon us. It's intoxicating, just to go outdoors onto the sidewalk. There are flowers everywhere.

[*Jerusalem—March 22, 1935.*] In 1931 I was bothered with Flying Carpets and couldn't relax to the wonders I was seeing. This time my worry is that I'm too busy with Bell to get around all I'd like to, and must leave before I'm half ready. But I must keep *Seven League Boots* in mind. I can't write chapters for that, sitting here.

My boat trip from Greece to Palestine was geographically beautiful. I spent a day at Rhodes, a lovely, lovely island, about which I'd read a lot in preparing my story about the Colossus. Venizelos was seeking a refuge there. I saw him and spoke with him again. He looked terribly sad, as his revolt had failed, and he had lost everything. He is over 71. We spent another day at Cyprus, dull after Rhodes, but there's a glorious twelfth century French Gothic church still standing at Famagusta. My chauffeur, a native, took me around and, reaching the church, said, "Here's the mosque"—and so it was. The lace-like Gothic tower had been used as a minaret for centuries.

We landed at Haifa and motored on straight to Jerusalem. It hasn't changed one brick. The Holy Sepulcher Church is being strengthened with a lot of ugly steel. The Garden of Gethsemane—now that it's spring—is more beautiful than ever. I was in it in the moonlight three nights ago.

Dad says "If Communism Comes to America" caused comment. It brought out several blistering replies from Reds and Bolsheviks in America. The *Daily Worker,* a Communist labor paper, published an editorial entitled "Liar!" But I've no time to fight about Russia now. I'm too busy getting ready to fight about Arabia.

I'll find a nice birthday present in Egypt for my mother—maybe one of the pyramids.

[*Jerusalem—April 4, 1935.*] I leave tonight for Cairo, at last, after three weeks here. I've done four stories in three weeks, and so have caught up a little. The last one is about the ruined citadel overlooking the Dead Sea where Salome danced for the head of John the Baptist. It's a *good* one. The pictures for it were taken in a wonderful canyon near the Dead Sea. The waterfall is boiling hot sulphur water. I was gone three days, and had lots of climbing and riding and fresh air which I needed. I went swimming in the hot sulphur river and cured my insect bites. This last story was No. 37, so I'm moving along.

The American Consul and his wife, Mr. and Mrs. Palmer, have been especially pleasant. She drove me up to Samaria—Jacob's Well, etc. The little double picture she took of me standing in the tower from which Jezebel was thrown down. I spoke at the local Y. M. C. A. two days ago. I like to keep my speaking in practice.

[*Cairo—April 24, 1935.*] During the last ten days I've been out in the desert 350 miles west of Cairo, to an oasis called Siwa, three days each way, four days there. The resulting story is a peach, such a wonderful place historically and scenically that I didn't mind the hard trip. You'll read it before long—"The Oasis of the Oracle." It was to Siwa that Alexander the Great marched to consult the oracle, which in his day brought pilgrims from all over the world. He wanted to ask if he really were the son of Zeus. The ruins of the oracle's temple are still there. On coming back to Cairo I worked 24 hours non-stop, mailed my story yesterday, and am dashing for a boat.

[*Red Sea, Suez to Jedda—April 25, 1935.*] My ship is only 700 tons, a freighter, and goes so slow we'll stop if we hit a head wind. The water is gloriously blue. Just across the way is the coast of Sinai. Had I had more time I'd make the trip to and up the Mountain. I had to choose Jedda and Abyssinia. The story about Cairo wouldn't flow. I couldn't get interested. I'd heard about a eunuchs' club and was determined to find it. I did. It fitted into a discussion of Cairo's morals. I decided I might have *one* sex-sensation story out of the 50.

[*Jedda, Arabia—May 8, 1935.*] I'm getting story No. 41 off on the weekly boat—"The Road to Mecca." Only the *Road to*—not Mecca. As I feared, my time wasn't sufficient to get organized for a grand invasion. But the story is unusually good, I think, and I'm not too disappointed. I got dressed up and photographed, umbrella and all. It makes a fine illustration. It will show you how *fat* I'm getting.

There are about twenty Europeans here. They had a nice party to celebrate King George V's twenty-fifth anniversary, and I was invited. I'll be glad to move on, near Abyssinia, nearer Egypt, nearer *home*.

[*Port Sudan—May 15, 1935.*] I've moved again—across the Red Sea from Jedda. In Jedda I was told I could find a ship for Aden every day, but it's every *week,* and I'm stuck here, bursting with impatience. It's the dullest place in the world.

My last week in Jedda was exciting. The King of Arabia came out from Mecca eight miles to see me, to the deadline of the Holy Area into which non-Moslems cannot go. He's a magnificent figure—six feet six inches tall—55 years old, married 160 times, and has 54 children. He had his royal pavilion, a huge purple tent, set up in advance and sent a military escort for me. I rode again over the familiar road to Mecca for 37 miles. He brought an enormous entourage with him, his six oldest sons, slaves, secretaries and a bodyguard of 200 soldiers. I was certainly impressed. I first asked conventional questions, leading up to more intimate ones as we went along. At six o'clock, being very religious—his whole dictatorship is based on Koran law and regulations—he spread carpets on the sand outside our tent, and said his prayers, with his six sons lined up behind him, and the 200 soldiers behind them in lines, all kneeling and bowing toward Mecca, eight miles away. The King acted as leader and quoted from the Koran, and all the sons and soldiers responded *Amen*—our own word taken from Arabic. This desert prayer meeting made a fine climax to my story. I rushed home to work on it, but as always had so much to tell that the length became unreasonable—7000 words—and Bell beg me *never* to go over 3000. By desperate sacrifices I cut it down to 4000. It's the longest story I've sent in, but just about the best. It was No. 42. My Hejaz visit will add some 7000 words to the book. From Jedda I sent off "Where I'll Spend My

Honeymoon," "The Road to Mecca" and "The Giant," that is, the King.

I'm just on the brink of the deadline, as usual. This is the first time I've been absolutely empty of ideas. We may have to skip a week till I can get to Abyssinia.

My plans, for months, have been to be in Constantinople May fifteenth. It's May fifteenth today, and I'm not even to Abyssinia. I spend most of my time just sitting and waiting for a boat. It may be another month before I get back to Cairo, but I've no intention of failing to have a book for fall publication just because of a few weeks lost in the Red Sea. My stories lack humor, and conversation, and comrades. I've had plenty of acquaintances, but no friends who might become part of the story, no characters for the reader to like or dislike.

It's almost certain now that I'll not be back till August first. The elephant expedition must come off. With Samarkand, Mecca and the Queen of Sheba's city all lost to me, through lack of time to promote them, I'm going to make a special effort to put the elephant over.

This isn't a very amusing letter, but I feel dull and hot and angry at the flying calendar.

[*Djibouti, French Somaliland—May 24, 1935.*] Having spent four days here in Djibouti waiting for the Addis Ababa train, I'm on the move again. I'm away this morning, *three days'* trip to go 900 miles.

I got off No. 44 this morning, "Three Queens and a Reporter"— about Mary Pickford, Elly Beinhorn, Ranee Sylvia. I'll be back here soon for Aden and Egypt. My train is whistling.

[*Addis Ababa—May 31, 1935.*] I've finished story No. 45, and it's five o'clock in the morning, and I'm dead tired and cold. Addis Ababa is 8000 feet high, and it turns very cold after sundown.

The Emperor whom I've come to see has been away, and I must hold on till he comes back, in three or four days more. Abyssinia will have to provide three stories, as I'll be here—Djibouti to Djibouti—nearly three weeks. It's an amazing country, this, and I'd like to stay much longer.

Two young Swiss boys have thumbed a ride atop Elysabethe Dalrymple, on the trip up the Great St. Bernard Pass.

On a craggy point six hundred feet above the waters of the Pacific at
South Laguna, Richard built Hangover House. An S-shaped road with
two hairpin turns leads into it from the highway. Immediately behind is
a canyon lost in deep shadow.

People have been extremely hospitable—parties among the Europeans everyday—but I've done my story on schedule. It's called "Journey to the Land of the Moon."

The three-day train trip up on the "Rhinoceros Express" was great fun. I never saw so many wild animals. I had my portrait painted for you by a native Ethiopian—I'm seated on a white horse spearing lions!

[*At sea, Egypt to Greece—June 19, 1935.*] I'm homeward bound. Not that I'm in sight of New York, but it's that general direction.

I wrote you last, weeks ago it seems, in Addis Ababa. His dusky Majesty refused to come to Addis to see me, and ten days had passed, so in impatience I went in pursuit of him. I hated to say goodbye to Addis. Except for the pressure behind me I'd have liked to stay on several weeks. The United States Minister had invited a hundred people in to meet me, and I had to leave the morning of the party, in order to catch the King. He was in a smaller city on the railroad line. Two days' riding to get there. You'll read all about that crazy railroad on Sunday, July fourteenth. I lost a week on my stories again, as Bell wouldn't distribute "Cairo, Capital of Sin." They say it is shocking, and, even censored to death, still indiscreet. They're saving it to use only in an emergency—and I spent two weeks writing it!

When I got off the train at the King's town, he had sent a messenger to invite me to dinner that night. I was the only foreign guest—the King, the Queen, a grown daughter and a half-grown son, and a general. Everybody spoke French except the Queen. I had only my dark double-breasted suit, but went ahead and made the best of it—and I had a good time. The King is a real charmer—forty-two years old, light brown in color, but in no sense negroid. The high-cast Abyssinians consider themselves a "white" race, and they *are* fine-featured and thin-lipped. I sat next to the King, who was dressed in a white satin cape, and I asked questions to my heart's content. He answered intelligently and amiably. At coffee in the living room we talked for another hour.

I'd planned to stay over till next train, four days later, in order to have a second audience, but as I'd asked all the questions I could think of there was no need. I was able to make a boat by continuing on next morning and so get to Egypt four days earlier. Also I was broke, had just enough to get to Egypt on. A terrible trip; the staterooms were like furnaces. Dozens of sick, miserable, squalling children and bad food. The ship was fast—only four days and nights. I did my second and third Abyssinian stories, "War Next September" and "The King of Ethiopia," somehow—Nos. 46 and 47. I got to Suez without a penny and had to borrow money from a taxi driver to take me across the desert to Cairo. There I cabled Bell at once.

We get to Piræus day after tomorrow morning. I change boats straightway for Stamboul, and catch the next plane east again toward Ararat. I'll leave most of my baggage in Stamboul, as I'll be returning in a week. I may have to go to Angora for permits, etc., and if so will try to see Mustafa Kemal, the dictator. I fly two days and motor two days, each way.

In Cairo I had news that my Hanover elephant had had a baby, which was attracting so many customers to the zoo that the manager wouldn't release the mother. So that elephant was out. I wired to Paris about Dally who ran away with me in October and instructed the zoo-keeper to start traffic-training her *now,* so that when I reach Paris we could depart at once. He wired back he would. I'll go on straight to Paris from Stamboul.

There was a ton of mail at Cairo, eight weeks of it. Jean Wick, my New York agent, accepted *Liberty's* offer for Romanoff. Not a word from London, which is curious. Apparently they've not made a sale there.

From Cairo I sent two boxes of books and pictures and two oil paintings done by Abyssinian artists. One is the story in strip pictures of the Queen of Sheba and Solomon. The other is a battle scene between Abyssinians and Italians. The portrait I wrote you about is a scream. It might do for our frontispiece. I'm bringing it myself.

The sea has become very rough, and I'm being pitched about. I'll tune off.

[*Paris—July 6, 1935.*] I'm out of breath from traveling so fast. I spent a day at Athens and rushed on to Stamboul and to Ankara. If I was going to climb Ararat I had to get permission from the military authorities. This they said I must wait for ten days at least, and the

Close-up of Hangover House. Modern in design, of steel and concrete, it becomes a part of its rugged and lofty setting.

In Hongkong Richard made the acquaintance of an amiable giant-panda whom he considers as a prospective mascot for the *Sea Dragon*. Photograph by his friend, Arthur Read.

answer might be negative. I delayed two days only trying, vainly, to
see Mustafa Kemal, and went back to Stamboul completely empty-
handed, with a precious week lost. I took an airplane to Vienna, a
day there, and on by train to Paris.

Right away I rushed to the zoo. No progress at all had been made
training Dally! It was soon found she would *follow* something, especially a truck. I put in two days, in vain, fighting with the police,
trying to get permission to take Dally on the Paris streets. But they
remembered my adventure last fall, and refused. The complications
of this idea are beyond belief—insurance, contracts, permissions, se-
curities. Of course, it's the first time such a thing ever happened,
which makes all negotiations slow. But I'm all set to go, waiting only
on permission from Italy to use her highways.

Day before yesterday I took the night train to Lausanne to hire
a truck to accompany me over the Alps. By good luck I found a
second-hand one, a Chevy which the owner wanted to sell in a
hurry for a hundred dollars. It looked all right to me, but I wanted
to test it. So I had him drive me 95 miles up the Great St. Bernard
Pass, over the very route I'm to follow, right to the summit 9500 feet
high. If the truck could climb once, it could climb again. We got
there easily. I had tea with the St. Bernard hospice priests and their
famous dogs, found a garage where Dally can sleep and keep warm
overnight, talked to the Italian customs, and so on. It was a most
sensible trip, all in all. Of course, the priests at the hospice were
flabbergasted and fascinated at my elephant idea.

I got back to Lausanne with the truck, which I've agreed to buy,
if my Italian papers come. I'm hiring a chauffeur and giving him the
truck as salary. The elephant keeper and trainer who will go along is
first class, a pleasant companion, and very capable. So there'll be the
chauffeur, the trainer and I. I'm badly worried over my Abyssinian
anti-Italian stories breaking right when I'm in the middle of Italy,
the Italians are so touchy. I've stopped writing stories. I have a
rough, dull draft of one on New Turkey (instead of Ararat) but can't
find time even to type it. I've gone terribly stale. It's well I've so few
more to do.

Bles says they expect to sell Romanoff to *The People,* a weekly
with a 2,000,000 circulation.

[*Paris—July 12, 1935.*] I'm just back from Rome, a hurried but successful trip. I have all my elephant papers in order both for Italy and Switzerland. I accomplished in two and half days, in person, what would have taken as many months by correspondence. I'll sign my elephant contract today and hope to have her on the train in two or three days more. Rome is already excited about my arrival. If only my Abyssinian stories do not cause trouble! I hardly saw Rome, I was so busy going to bureaus and seeing officials, but the trip back through the Alps to Berne was glorious. Unless I encounter *too* much grief with the elephant, the expedition is going to be a grand outing. I'll walk probably half the time. The sun is hot and healing, and the fresh air and exercise will harden me, after all these weeks of sitting on trains and boats.

[*Paris—Monday, July 15, 1935.*] Things are moving. I've bought my ticket for Switzerland, for Wednesday night. The elephant leaves tomorrow night. I get to Lausanne Thursday, pick up my truck, drive back to the border to meet the elephant's freight train and assist in customs regulations, and go on to Martigny. The road starts to climb there up the St. Bernard Pass. This morning I had my first ride on the elephant—not at all bad. I "drove" about a mile.

Richard did no better than Hannibal. Neither reached Rome, though both got over the Alps. Elysabethe Dalrymple with Richard on her back climbed stolidly up the Great St. Bernard Pass, spent the night at the hospice, entertained the monks and their famous dogs, went on a stampede when a company of mountain soldiers fired a volley of cannon too near her, and descended to the plain of Italy. An elephant was a sight for the Italian children. Nothing since the passing of Hannibal and his Carthaginian army had created so much excitement. But alas, not being accustomed to such long marches about the zoo in Paris, Dally's feet grew tender and she began to limp. The keeper decided she must rest for a week or ten days, and then her daily marches toward Rome would have to be shortened. This was too costly in time; so Elysabethe was put in a freight car at Turin and sent back to her quiet life in the zoo.

This adventure was told in the last of Richard's syndicated articles and, as all his readers know, in the last chapters of his *Seven League Boots*.

After squaring accounts with the zoo authorities in Paris, he took the first available ship for New York, where he arrived on Friday, August ninth. His parents and Hafford were at the dock. Four days later he took plane to Memphis, and his mother and father followed in their automobile. Richard worked furiously on his book at home till early September, when he started back east to the lecture front. Now for the first time he was to confront that terror of the public speaker—serious trouble with his voice.

CHAPTER XVIII

WONDERS OF WEST AND EAST

Hangover House

ON THE train east September seventh Richard wrote: "The little Welles boy who was named after me, I hear has been struck by an automobile, had both hips broken and is in the hospital. I must write him and send him a toy." Arrived in New York, he was glad to find *Seven League Boots* coming along satisfactorily, with the pictures reproduced and a "gorgeous" jacket—the elephant and the Alps. He was dedicating the new book to Miss Hutchison, Ammudder, "who with patience and understanding first taught a small boy to love ages that have passed and places that are far away."

In Montgomery for a lecture late in October he wrote a story for the *Cosmopolitan* and the editors called him on the telephone to express their pleasure. En route to Winston-Salem he hammered out a 2,000-word article for the Yale-Princeton football program, which he had promised weeks before.

The lectures were proving increasingly successful but when he went on in Birmingham the first of November he could hardly speak, he was so hoarse. There was nothing to do but give his raw voice a rest. He canceled two engagements, but was in motion again, headed for Texas, on the sixth. Nine days later, in Oklahoma, he wrote that his throat was still troubling him. "If it isn't healed soon, I'll have to start canceling dates again. Half my time is taken avoiding and escaping people. In Oklahoma City so many came to my hotel door without being announced that I had to get a house detective to stand guard. Perforce I'm getting hard-boiled. Henceforth I'll sign a false name at my hotel and stay in hiding till the hour I speak. I *must* spare myself. . . . The new book goes on sale today."

He went through with a fine book party at Scruggs, Vandervoort and Barney's in St. Louis the next day, and then for three days at

Indianapolis gave himself to complete rest (except for inscribing copies of *Seven League Boots* for fifty of his friends) under the care of the doctor who had treated his sinus trouble in 1928. Then he went on with the grind, the hoarseness still plaguing him. In Hamilton, Ontario, for Thanksgiving Day he forgot it was Thanksgiving because that holiday is not observed in Ontario. In spite of the raw voice, he enjoyed lecturing at several colleges—college audiences he always found particularly responsive—and book parties at Hudson's in Detroit and at Jordan Marsh's in Boston. He was longing to get home "and I don't want anything for Christmas except a *bed* and the *house telephone muffled.* . . . But go ahead, Dad, and send out your invitations for our stag party."

This party was a dinner for fifty of his father's friends. Although Richard called Memphis his home he had been there so little during the past twenty years that many of these men had never met him. It was a happy evening. Immediately after the dinner Richard, ever the sun-worshiper, flew down to Miami to bake in the sunshine and recover his voice. He could be there only four days, but they worked, he thought, a partial cure.

[*On the train to Chicago—January 15, 1936.*] Well, so far nothing has gone wrong in 1936. Ammudder sent me five dollars for A. B. D. vitamin tablets. I'm going to buy a bottle, and I'm going to eat Mother's yeast tablets, and take cod-liver oil. Then I won't need to eat meals at all.

I connected with Mike Hockaday in Kansas City on the eleventh. He's been made a partner in his brokerage firm and his marriage is *very* happy. I saw also Paul Gardner, my old friend from Washington. He's now the Director of the Museum of Art, with a billion dollars a year to spend on pictures.

The next afternoon Marcella Hahner of Marshall Field's gave a swell party for me in Chicago.

[*On the train to New York—January 20, 1936.*] My schedule has continued to be fierce—but fun. In Lansing on the sixteenth I had to speak twice, as the auditorium seats only 1500 and 3000 had tickets. So I went on at seven and again at half-past eight. I hated to do it because of my hoarseness, but the kids were so responsive I enjoyed it, too.

In Indianapolis Friday afternoon for a teachers' conference. Chambers had good news and bad. *7-L-B* had not sold quite so well as I'd hoped. The dollar books sail on.

I have three lectures for tomorrow. I canceled one. My voice grows slowly better, and I mustn't set it back by further strain.

[*Atlantic City—January 26, 1936.*] I'm about to have a new job, if I want it. I'm to agree to do a daily "strip" for the Bell Syndicate of adventure drawings for newspapers, like Tarzan of the Apes, the Gumps, etc., and a full page in color on Sunday. I'm looking into it, but with little enthusiasm.

My mail is overwhelming me. I've hired a traveling secretary, but find I still can't keep up.

At Reading, Pennsylvania, he sent out to be pressed the only suit he had with him. It failed to come back in time and, much amused, he had to go to an afternoon lecture in evening clothes. He decided, in order to spare his voice, to cancel all "two-a-days." The newspaper strip serial was exciting more of his interest. He thought it "fun, and a brief respite from the grind," when he could find time to work on it in New York or on the train, "and a grand opportunity for the imagination if one wishes to use it that way." His lectures took him to Allentown where he had a happy time with Heinie and Dot— "Dot *is* a charmer"—and to Cleveland. There Shorty Seiberling met him with his car, took him to Akron for a cheerful little reunion and drove him to his date at Ashland. At a book party at Rike-Kumler's in Dayton 2,000 pushed in, "and more were prevented by the fire department!" All was as well with him as it could be at five below zero. "I'm so fed up with this agonizing cold weather I could die. But in two weeks I'll be headed south"—this on February 13, 1936.

[*Indianapolis—March 1, 1936.*] The last of the worst of the winter's grind is over. I've only sixteen lecture dates in March, one every other day. My voice is definitely on the mend, though still troublesome, and I foresee no more anxiety this year.

I hate to go back to New York, but the newspaper strip needs me, and this is the last chance for six weeks to work on it. The sales campaign starts April twentieth. Chambers is worried for fear I'll get too engrossed in this new project and neglect books. But I shan't. I'll get at the book for children in May.

[*Miami—Saturday, March 7, 1936.*] I reached Charlotte for the fourth. Never have I been so besieged by reporters and photographers. By lecture time I had the jitters. I had hardly started to speak when the woman president of the Travel Guild, having just introduced me, fell down the steps with a fearful crash. She wasn't hurt, fortunately, but you can imagine what *that* did to me. I've never talked so badly. But I've relaxed again and am all ready for the big Biltmore date tomorrow.

I've had two days of sun, and my voice has responded.

On March thirteenth he was booked for Corinth, Mississippi. His parents motored there, fetched him back to Memphis to sleep, and next day, after he had spoken to Ammudder's school, saw him off on a plane to Jackson, where he had an evening engagement.

[*Temple, Texas—March 19, 1936.*] I talked just as well at Jackson, Dad, as I talked badly in Corinth. Sometimes, for no reason, as in Corinth, I get so tense my tongue goes completely out of control. Sunday friends took me over to Vicksburg. We wandered all over the battlefield. I want to do a chapter on it for our American book. On to Ruston [Louisiana] for Monday morning. I had to speak in an old gymnasium with a huge tin roof, and, of course, it poured rain, and the din was deafening—and a freight engine just outside screeched and panted. Nobody could hear a word even though I yelled myself hoarse.

[*On the train to Worcester, Massachusetts—April 23, 1936.*] I'm back in New England again. It's springlike and sunny, and my spirits are fairly high. I've had tremendous audiences lately. The season is rushing to a close.

Bad news about the cartoon strip. They say it's not violent and lurid enough. I'm prepared for it to be a bust. So cheer up, Dad, your wish likely will come true.

My summer plans are still vague. Events will decide me.

[*On the train headed west—April 26, 1936.*] When I got back to New York I had lunch with the *Cosmopolitan* editors. They are keener than ever over my *In America* series, and I hope to get a definite offer from them. Bell is just as ready for another series.

[*St. Francis Hotel, San Francisco—May 1, 1936.*] My plans are quite as blank as ever. I've about decided to stay on the coast for early June in any case. Chambers insists our juvenile book will be a good seller. I'm terribly eager to be in New York for June twenty-fourth when you sail for Europe. I just don't see now how I can make it, but something may *yet* pop up and let me wave to you as you sail away.

I've been on the usual grind since Omaha. Rod Crane and his *very* charming bride drove me to Fremont, Nebraska, to speak. I caught the train there and went on to Colorado; had an enormous audience, 3000 in a gymnasium, with a loudspeaker to help my hoarse voice. Then to Logan, Utah. Such a lovely flowering country, the lake on one side, snow mountains behind, and orchards in bloom everywhere. The Mormons are certainly good farmers. I lectured in the Mormon Tabernacle, to 2000, and came on to San Francisco yesterday.

I've spoken to no one all day—just rested my throat.

He had a complete check-up at the hospital, for, beside the trouble with his voice, he had felt some symptoms of the old exhaustion toward the end of the season. The report was reassuring but he was told to take it easy.

[*Roosevelt Hotel, Hollywood—May 20, 1936.*] See where I am, and I feel quite at home, too. In fact, I've my old room, with new carpets and paper. But I won't live here long. I may go to Laguna or back to San Francisco.

I'm all in favor of your dropping Cook's, and following your own noses. This business of sticking to a fixed, hurried schedule is certainly not my idea of happy traveling. In Cairo, Jerusalem, Constantinople, Athens, you'll find Amexco and Cook's, and you can be taken care of there, locally. It isn't as if you were amateur travelers. You're sure to find places along the way where you'll want to tarry. This way you can.

I had two fine days of sunbathing in San Francisco. It *is* the most wonderful and beautiful city in America. I came on south night before last. Now I must go to the beach and rid myself of all the winter's poisons.

Richard's father, who had steadily advised against the newspaper strip idea, was now informed that it had been definitely abandoned. "The editors felt I was stepping out of character"—which was precisely his father's view. Take it easy? He began at once to formulate plans. "I may try to write the Brooke book—start it at least—and the juvenile both this summer. I have three months and a half from now to lecturing time. I want Dad to collect carefully all the Brooke books in our library. I may have you send them to me in California, and take them to Tahiti for the summer. But I still am not sure. There's no chance now that I can be in New York to wave you goodbye, worse luck."

[*San Francisco—Sunday, June 7, 1936.*] Now that I have an address, Dad can send the Brooke material. It's Apt. 6, 1407 Montgomery Street. I want to write a lot this summer, and must be near a library. Tahiti or Hawaii would be lovely for a vacation, but I've promised to get the children's book done, and won't be able to write in any place so distracting as Tahiti.

You'd love my apartment. It's high over the harbor, so I can see the new bridge and watch the ships. I feel I can write here. I'll buy a re-conditioned Ford, ride horseback in the park, swim and sunbathe a lot, and get ready for next fall.

At Sacramento, June first, I had a fine audience of 500 women at a luncheon club. My suspenders came down and hung around and swung to and fro with each gesture. I didn't know it till people behind me laughed so hard I realized something was wrong.

Friday I was taken across the new eight-mile Oakland bridge. It is marvelous. It's not nearly completed, so my guide and I had to walk on catwalks, and sometimes on hands and knees atop girders—scary, but not really dangerous. I'm going to do a chapter about the bridges for my America kid book. Tomorrow the chief engineer is taking me over the cables of the Golden Gate bridge. This is more spectacular than the Oakland bridge—just the steel towers and the cables—no roadway—but the cables are topped by a side walk, so it's easy and safe.

[*San Francisco—June 10, 1936.*] Yesterday I bought a swell little second-hand Dodge coupé. So I've a house and a car and a job (my child book), and suspect I'll stay right here till October when I'll come home for a visit before the lectures begin.

I'm getting very brown. I can sit on my balcony in my shorts in full sunshine, and look at the harbor, and read.

[*San Francisco—June 18, 1936.*] This is the last letter I can address to you at Memphis. It's to wish you a bon voyage to New York. I'll have another letter for you on the boat. So happy Ammudder is going, too.

The maid who comes twice a week has just left, so the apartment is spotless. I'll hate to leave it next Monday when I start off to the Yosemite. Beginning today I'm going to ride horseback for an hour every morning. So you must think of me as leading (for once) a quiet, relaxed life, while you two are doing the traveling.

A letter to his Princeton classmate and roommate, James Penfield Seiberling:

June 23, 1936

Dear Shorty:—

Your swell triplicate letter made me positively weep with nostalgia for Princeton and '21. How grand and generous of you to take the trouble. Reunions usually discomfort and bewilder me, but, judging from your report, I'd have been entirely at ease at this one. I do envy you and Heinie having been there. It will be one of the bright-remembered days of your life. And I'm overjoyed to hear about Heinie's cup. Was ever such a gesture more royally deserved?

Heinie's note came, too, signed by some twenty of the class—you among them. Patton still stands! For me that is almost holy ground. I'll try to be back there with you in 1941.

Devotedly (and this goes for Harriet and Mary Margaret and the angel-on-the-way),

DICK

[*1407 Montgomery Street—July 1, 1936.*] Your letters and one from Haff telling about your happy sailing cheered me greatly.

I did not get away on the motor trip till last Saturday. The Yosemite was glorious. The waterfalls were at their maximum. One day I climbed the famous Half-Dome mountain, 9000 feet high. It was exhausting but fun.

[*1407 Montgomery Street—July 14, 1936.*] It does seem strange and grand for me to be writing you in Athens, and not you me. And I only wish I could be there to show you around. I do love that town so! Stay several days to climb to the Acropolis twice, and don't you dare miss Delphi.

Today, you're still in Egypt—in Cairo, I believe. If it's hot near the site of ancient Memphis, remember Memphis, Tennessee, is hotter. I know how marvelous you found the Pyramids and Karnak and am eagerly awaiting your letters.

I've still not got down to work. I have no urge, and feel a horseback ride or a sunbath is more important, with next winter's heavy schedule ahead of me. I'm seeing very few people—just lie in the sun and read. The whole summer may go like this; it could be worse spent.

I've a new inspiration. As you know there's to be a World's Fair here in 1939 to celebrate the bridges. The Fair promoters want me to hire a fancy Chinese junk in Shanghai and sail it with Chinese crew and cargo to the Fair. It would make part of a book.

I send my love to you all along the line—you'll pick it up somewhere.

[*1407 Montgomery Street—July 28, 1936.*] After long idleness and uncertainty, I've gone to work on my children's book. It's going to be beautiful, and I'm terribly enthusiastic about it. I've written the introduction and the first two chapters. I've chosen fifty world-marvels and must write a thousand words about each of them. It's easy, but takes time. The first chapter is about the San Francisco bridges.

Each morning I sunbathe for two hours, and then I work all afternoon. I still keep clear of society. But I did go to Carmel over the week end to hear Noel sing in the Bach festival. Carmel is full of interesting poets and artists. On Thursday night Noel is taking me to the famous Bohemian Grove, a glorified camp where prominent San Franciscans go for two weeks each summer, in the big trees. After two days of that I'll cut myself off from everything except exercise and sun and work. My first lecture is October twenty-fifth. The engagements are coming in very nicely. I'll make as much as last year on half the effort.

You should see me cooking my own breakfast! For other meals I go out.

I pray all is well with you, and that every place is as beautiful and exciting to you as it was to me.

He tried to work steadily, but it was only on a fifty-per-cent efficiency, as he was more and more subjected to interruptions in a city where he had many acquaintances. So, early in August, he moved to Laguna Beach. In a letter of the thirtieth welcoming his parents home, he says, "I've a quiet little shack right by the sea. No one knows I'm here, and I've been able to do a chapter every two days, twelve in all. I must do forty, at least. But I'm in the swing now, and can speed up without effort. I wish I had more time, but when I have lots of time I seem unable to concentrate. I'm calling it *Richard Halliburton's Book of Marvels.*"

For all his urgency, and with all the appreciated assistance given him by the Los Angeles Library, he soon realized that it would be impossible to get the book out by Christmas. "But I'm going to work on just the same, and make it better for the delay. I'll need all winter to play with it, and collect pictures." He stopped in Memphis on the way to New York to report for lectures, delighting to see the family in good health and spirits.

On the train—October 15, 1936

Mother dear:—

This is a letter just for you. Sometimes I want to love you specially and apart from Dad and discuss things that concern only you and me. We're not a very demonstrative family, and so I have to write to you what I sometimes fail to show and say. This last visit home was the nicest we've ever had together, and I was much relieved to find you had returned from your trip so young and high-spirited. Naturally I was apprehensive all the time we were so far apart.

I wanted to tell you when I was home about the rumor of my new house in California. You showed antagonism to the idea before I could tell you about it, and I hesitated to disturb our all-too-few days of happiness together. But on thinking it over I don't see why any unhappiness should come from it. I know that my happiness is yours and you want me to be happy more than you want anything else in the world. What I have done in California is exactly what I want to do above all else.

Despite my constant contacts with people I have almost no friends, friends who really are a vital part of my life. It is my own fault. Just to mix with people for excitement bores me painfully, and from them I shrink further and further each year. It has always been my true nature and only in recent times have I learned that in solitude lies my peace of mind. This in some ways is my reason for wanting my own house. This in part explains why much of the joyous wonder has gone out of my writings. It would have gone out anyway because I am older and less astonished and amused by what I see.

All these things I thought about before deciding to build a house and live in it at least from time to time. The idea goes back as far as 1930. I first saw Laguna then and fell in love with it. Sometime after, during the worst of the depression, I was riding horseback one day two miles south of the town on the beach. I looked up and saw a ridge rising broadside 800 feet from the shore. I rode up it to the summit of the ridge to get the view, and on top, 600 feet above the sea, came abruptly upon the inland side of the ridge, a sheer precipice 400 feet high. At the bottom winds away the most beautiful valley you would want to see, between two mountain walls that finally close together in the distance. And then, rising above everything in the distance, are the snowy summits of the Sierras. It is a sensational vista and stops people in their tracks when they stumble unexpectedly upon it. I went back over and over just to look at the peaceful valley on the one side and the full sweep of the ocean on the other. I finally found out who owned the mountain, and, taking advantage of the panic, made an offer for 300 feet upon the ridge and 300 feet down the mountainside facing the ocean.

The view enchanted me and every time I saw it I had a vision of a house on this spectacular ridge. I talked about it for months and decided, with the state of the world and the stock market so jittery, not to sink all I got from *Boots* into stocks and bonds, but to buy insurance and a house and land. So first of all I bought more life insurance, and then I put aside a sum for a house on this lot.

The designing of the house has been enormous fun—a special house for a special place. I decided on modified modern architecture, concrete and glass, a proper type for California. The ground plan is a perfect rectangle about thirty feet by ninety-five. The long side is built sheer with the precipice, and one end of the living room, thirty feet by twenty, overlooks the precipice. The entire end is glass, one window, twenty by fourteen feet. The opposite end, likewise one mass of glass, overlooks the ocean. The cloister or gallery is sixty long and opens on one side to the precipice. It will be inclosed in glass shutters to the floor, but wide open most of the time. Leading off the gallery with windows facing the ocean are three bedrooms and two baths. The bedrooms are all sixteen by fourteen, and have solid glass on the ocean side. The roof is flat and equipped for a sun porch. The garden runs along the edge of the ridge with the precipice and valley on one side and the ocean on the other.

The house will be finished some time next year. I will not see it until late April when my tour takes me west. I am calling it Hangover House, because it overhangs the precipice.

If I had a million dollars, I wouldn't change one inch of it.

When it's finished I shall prevail upon you and Dad to visit me, and when you see it you, too, will fall in love with it and be happy with me that I own it.

[*An old refrain*—"*On the train*"—*October 18, 1936.*] I'm in the grind again—not minding it too much. Kirksville was entertaining 3000 teachers for a conference. The last afternoon a Jewish Rabbi, Madame Perkins and I were the speakers. Once the old machinery got under way, it was easy. A small boy flattered me greatly. He said, "You know what I did? I sat through two speeches to hear you. But it was worth it." The Rabbi's and Miss Perkins' talks were "speeches"—mine, apparently, was something else.

[*On the train—November 3-4, 1936.*] In Columbus I found Mrs. Pahlow in the hospital, shockingly ill. She had just been operated on. She cannot live more than 60 days. She was as gay and charming as ever. I'll feel the loss deeply. I've been devoted to her for so long. My one happy, beautiful gift from Lawrenceville is the friendship of this family.

I had a monster audience in Columbus, 6000 teachers. I rest lots and work on my book every chance.

[*The Bobbs-Merrill Office, New York—November 27, 1936.*] I've been carrying your "serious" November letter about for a month, trying to answer it. It was a fine letter, Dad, and I read it with all seriousness. But I don't think we need be really alarmed—as alarmed as you seem to be. In the first place there's just no helping my unsociable nature. I've always been wearied by the company and minds and hearts of most human beings, ever since early childhood. But this in no way comes from sourness or misanthropy. I'm not in the least antagonistic—just not interested. One who allows himself to speak to a thousand people every night, shake hands with several hundred, isn't a hermit. It's only that, individually, I'm not interested in talking, at length, to anyone in the thousand. Occasionally I do find a fellow spirit, and then I'm as social as anybody. But just to flock where others go, and to listen to and repeat the fifty phrases that make up the usual conversation, seems to me a terrific waste of time, there are so many books I would rather read—and write. I'm never lonely for a moment, only impatient that time is so short when I have so much to do. Don't think that I plan to imprison myself on my mountain top in Laguna, and turn the dogs on visitors. My life will always be too full of activity and ambition for anything of the sort. But I also know that I shall never have more than a few *friends*. I've *never* had, and I shall always stand apart. This is the inevitable result of the international, wide-experienced life I've led. I can't be interested in John Jones and his local affairs. But "morose" and "cynical" are the last words to apply to me.

Please don't be distressed because I'm the way I am. Just be grateful that I'm so much happier than most people and trying to go on an up-climbing curve, rather than marking time with those who have come from the regulation mould.

[*Benjamin Franklin Hotel, Philadelphia—December 4, 1936.*] I'm doing another hideaway act. I had a lecture in Philadelphia last night, and now have none for five days. So I'm digging in here and working on my book. It's hard to do, with New York so close, and all my friends there. But this book must be finished.

On December twelfth Henri Deering plays at the Waldorf. I'll go up for that. I'm very fond of Henri. He and Noel Sullivan and I were at the Bohemian Grove together.

[*The Bobbs-Merrill Office, New York—December 13, 1936.*] When I'm home Xmas I must work more than play. Now is my chance to finish my book. I am going to spend the week end of the nineteenth with Lowell Thomas. Last week I introduced Hugh Walpole at the Philadelphia Forum.

[*New York—January 10, 1937.*] I've been hard at it every day since I got back. The picture gathering for the *Book of Marvels* is exasperatingly slow. I've only well begun. So many copyrights are held in England, which demand correspondence and make a waste of time. I see nobody and go nowhere, except from picture bureaus to my office desk. Soon I'll be sending home the new chapters for Dad to go over. I'm still enjoying our happy visit together.

[*New York—January 14, 1937.*] I'm making tremendous progress. Of my 49 chapters, 29 are checked off for illustrations. The other 20 are partially done. I've looked at so many photographs I'm dizzy. But they are sensationally beautiful. I don't believe there has ever

Laboriously the hull and frame of
the *Sea Dragon* take shape in the
shipyards at Hongkong.

Captain Welch, as he appeared in
Hongkong during the days of outfitting the *Sea Dragon*.

Rigging the *Sea Dragon*. To a Chinese shipwright Richard explains some
essential points, while a crowd of curious bystanders looks on.

High above the quay at Hongkong looms the carved and painted stern of the *Sea Dragon*.

been *any* book with such gorgeous illustrations. They are being collected from all over the world, and for each there must be a credit line, and permission, except the ones I took myself.

There's one picture at home I overlooked—the one of me on the hilltop in Athens, with the Acropolis in the background. Please rush it to me.*

[*New York—January 21, 1937.*] Chambers got to town yesterday, and we came to a clear decision. He saw my magnificent array of pictures, heard my demands for de-luxe printing, binding, maps, spent several minutes figuring, and reported that the price would be prohibitive for *one* volume. We could take my material and make *two* books, one to be published this spring, one next fall or next spring, the first to cover the Occident, the second the Orient. By making two books I can use *all* my gorgeous pictures, full text, and have 29 chapters in each, 200 pictures, and still sell for $2.50.

This seemed so logical, so *necessary,* that I agreed. So we'll end the first book with Moscow, and start the second with Ephesus. The pictures for No. 1 are nearly all in; those for No. 2 I'll collect next June. The first 29 chapters have been written since November. So! We've a book! I must do some rewriting to fit the new scheme, but it can be done in a month.

[*Columbus, Georgia—March 6, 1937.*] I'm seated in a station waiting for a bus to take me to Macon, where I speak tonight. I canceled my date in West Virginia for last Monday. My voice was hoarse after a strenuous week, and the travel killing. We postponed it till later in the month. This respite gave me a chance to catch up on the book. Now I've only three chapters left undelivered.

I must go to New York for a day, the twelfth—the book demands it. Jacket, frontispiece, etc., need my presence. We're wasting time trying to decide things at long range.

[*Jacksonville, Florida—March 8, 1937.*] I am having a quiet and sunny day, *book*-ing. Only two more chapters to rewrite.

---

* It is reproduced in this book.

[*Washington—March 12, 1937.*] My twenty-four hours in New York were well spent in the publishing office. The things which could not be done by mail are now disposed of. I've seen half the picture proofs. I got my last chapter in from Lynchburg. . . .

I know Haff is in much distress. She will grieve for a long time, and nothing but time will console her. We must be glad Aunt Susie's end came so peacefully.

[*Buffalo—March 17, 1937.*] Of course, you saw the notice of Hobson's death. Everyone thought he was in the best of health. . . .

In Syracuse, night before last, we had a fearful blizzard—four feet of snow. All busses and street cars were snowbound. It wrecked my audience. But in Albany last night, despite the slush, we had a fine house.

The color jacket for the *Book of Marvels* has turned out just right, so that you'll like it now. The publication date is put off till May fifteenth.

[*On the train to Chicago—March 31, 1937.*] It was fine, Mother, that you could be with Haff. I know you hated to leave her, and that she feels lost without you.

Easter Sunday got by me without my knowing it. I worked on the book till 3 A.M. the night before, and all Easter day, and enjoyed that much more than parading.

The book grows nearer completion. But *golly* the work! I can't remember having had to work so hard on the others. But this one is so beautiful I forget to do anything else. The pictures *pour* wonder over the stories.

I had tea yesterday with Mrs. Hobson. The Admiral was in apparently perfect health, was kissing her goodbye just before going to his office—and fell dead. Tragic!

[*On the train near Cincinnati—April 3, 1937.*] I've wrecked the book so completely, simplifying and condensing, it must be set up all over again. It improves with each cut. But the office is going crazy. Publication date has now been postponed to the end of May. I don't care. This book must be *right* if it takes forever.

Here is an amusing letter from the Dallas Richard Halliburton. He's a pleasant young fellow—the one I wrote about for the book of "coincidences."

I'm in constant motion but relaxed to it, and in love with our new book. With book over, and lectures over, and the house over, I'll deserve a vacation.

[*Laguna Beach—April 18, 1937.*] I got to Laguna yesterday afternoon and rushed to the house. I can't say in words how amazing it is. Pictures just don't give a small part of its drama and beauty. It doesn't *sit*—it *flies*. It's caused such a sensation up and down the coast that the workmen are bothered by a procession of visitors who come to explore so commanding a site. When they reach the terrace that overlooks the canyon, they gasp with surprise. The living-room walls are finished. One can sit at one end and look into this heavenly canyon (all brilliant green now after the floods) and yet view the blue ocean on the other side through the plate-glass window. The possibilities for landscaping are limitless. I'm looking forward eagerly to getting back in July and spending the rest of the summer working on Vol. 2 of my *Marvels* and making the house look like home.

[*Laguna Beach—April 27, 1937.*] The last of the book is off my hands. The job of fitting the pictures to the text, and writing suitable, long captions, was colossal. My slowness in completing it has delayed things several weeks, but there was no help for it. I couldn't drop my lecture dates. Publication date now is about June tenth.

The house rushes along. It is *the* most wonderful house in the world. It will be finished and all paid for by the middle of July, and I will not have borrowed one cent on it or sold a single stock or bond. The lectures have paid for everything.

Well, the lectures lately have been only so-so, up and down. The Los Angeles date was a flop, but San Diego a fine success. They lost money in Santa Barbara, and made money in San Bernardino.

[*San Francisco—May 9, 1937.*] I left Laguna last night, most regretfully. The last caption proof has come back, and I'm struggling with that. This book seems to go on forever. Back to work.

Portland, Oregon—May 15, 1937

Mother and Dad and Ammudder and *Haffy:*—

Mother's letter telling me Haff is in Memphis just arrived. I'm delighted. I'm so hopeful her poignant distress has become less sharp, and that she is learning to keep her mind diverted from the ache.

My days in San Francisco were wonderful. My lecture there was my best this year. Henri Deering was having a concert right next door at the same time—friendly rivals.

I had a long and satisfactory conference with the San Francisco Fair people, and I'm definitely into it. They cheered over my Chinese junk plans, and wanted me to stop everything else and develop them. But next summer is time enough.

I've read and reread Dad's letter repeatedly. I agree with him that once I'm on my mountain-top house I'll be able to adjust my life onto a calmer plane and grow in spirit rather than in mileage. If I can't get nearer the Eternal in that house, then it's not in me. I never saw a house so far away from man and so close to God. The peace and serenity of that canyon is enough in itself to make one relax and dream.

[*May 24, 1937.*] I've had a wonderful Sunday. With no lectures today I stopped off to visit the Grand Coulee Dam and the Dry Waterfalls of the Columbia River. The Dam is going to be *three* times as big as Boulder, but it's mostly foundations now. The Dry Waterfalls, dead 100,000 years, were once as big as a *hundred* Niagaras, and nearly 500 feet high. When the Glacial Age was melting, some fifty cubic *miles* of water poured over them every day. I want to do a chapter on this world-wonder for our America book.

[*The Bobbs-Merrill Office, New York—June 23, 1937.*] I'll have a new book in my hand tomorrow. I've been doubly busy, handling promotion on *Occident,* and collecting pictures for *Orient,* but I love it—love watching the book grow.

[*New York—July 12, 1937.*] The collection for the second volume is almost over. Once the pictures are in the hands of the engravers, I'm free to leave. I'm inclosing some new house pictures. Everything is finished, except the decoration. I've had all work stopped until I can get out to supervise this myself. I plan now to reach California about August first.

[*Washington—Monday, July 26, 1937.*] On Friday our friend Jack Hamory showed up in a broken-down Ford. I made him drive me to Washington since I simply *had* to have a car here for my Lincoln story. We went by Princeton and Lawrenceville. Yesterday we stopped by Baltimore to visit Fort McHenry where the *Star-Spangled Banner* was written, and came on here for supper.

Today I'm starting out to get maps and pictures, with a view to following Booth's escape on horseback into Virginia.

[*Washington—July 30, 1937.*] Yesterday Hamery and I left Washington on horseback along Booth's route. We go twenty miles more today and sleep at Dr. Mudd's.

[*Laguna—August 16, 1937.*] I slept in my new house last night for the first time. It's completely empty, but beautiful and satisfying even so. The canyon is more glorious than ever—I never think to look out the ocean window. Yesterday, Sunday, I was unable to read or write, for the visitors. Some forty people called to see the place. This visitors' problem must be handled some way. Mechanically the house works perfectly. I'll have to buy a little furniture. I shall be tremendously happy here for the next six weeks, and working well, I'm sure.

I'm off now to look for a carpenter, and to buy a kitchen table on which to write.

[*Laguna, California—Monday night, August 30, 1937.*] I'm just back from San Francisco. My Chinese junk plans were getting very hot, and I had to see the Fair people *now*. We had several profitable conferences, and have taken practical steps forward.

I've been so busy with *Orient,* I've had no time to work on the house. The important things—water, heat, light, etc.—are all functioning beautifully. Sightseers pour in, but my room is cut off and I escape most of it. I *love* my book work and resent every intrusion.

I'll press forward all I can, since the more I accomplish now the less I'll have to do in the winter.

Curiously enough, all the reports I get on *Occident* are from adults.

[*Laguna—September 4, 1937.*] The sunshine pours down here every day. I've been descending my hill for a swim and climbing back each day for exercise. The view becomes more entrancing. I'll have to close my doors to keep it from diverting me entirely.

Today I'm sending off to the typesetter my first nine chapters of *Orient*.

[*Laguna Beach—September 20, 1937.*] I'm jealously watching these peaceful days slip by—only nine more remain before I go back to the grind. However, I'd miss the grind if it were withheld. I'm more alert and alive on a speaking tour than at any other time.

I've been working with pick and shovel with the laborers, on my drive, for three hours every day. My book has suffered, as I'm so tired and sleepy by night I can't write after dinner. But there'll be no chance for sunshine and exercise after October first, and I must grab them now. I'm carefully spending small sums of money on the house to make it *marketable*—better road, better kitchen, etc.

As always I'm deeply enjoying the work on my book. Only half the chapters are finished. But I believe they improve on *Occident*, and the pictures are certainly better.

[*Laguna—Sunday night, September 26, 1937.*] This is my last week end in Laguna. I drove out to a ranch in the desert for a final blast of sunshine. I took my book with me, but didn't write a word. The house continues to thrill me every time I drive up to it. It's inexhaustibly dramatic. The garden grading is about finished, and the Hanging Gardens of Babylon will have nothing on me. The road, which scared people to death, is smoothing out, and will soon scare nobody. I'm putting in a small forest of two-foot eucalyptus trees on the mountain slopes. They'll be six feet high by next summer.

[*On the train—October 6, 1937.*] Getting clear of Laguna was quite a job. My last morning there was the loveliest of all. The Pacific was Mediterranean blue, and the canyon turning gold. Living there, even in an empty shell, was a daily thrill.

The textbook edition of *Occident* is beginning to reach the schools, and we're getting good reports. This encourages me to hurry on with the sequel.

[*Topeka—October 17, 1937.*] A week in the Kansas sticks. I sent in five more chapters of *Orient* yesterday, making fifteen. Walter Hurley* is getting ready for a second printing of *Occident*.

On November thirteenth, Marshall Field and Company, who had always taken a special interest in Richard's books and given a number of parties for him, quite outdid themselves in launching the *Occident* for the holiday season. Every inch of the reception room outside the book department, and the staircase leading from it, was packed with children who came to hear Richard speak at eleven in the morning and again at half past two in the afternoon. His mother came up from Memphis for the occasion. Early in December, after a brief illness, he was on hand for another notable book party at Jordan Marsh's, in Boston.

He lectured on December thirteenth at the Second Congregational Church in Waterbury, Connecticut, where he had spoken several times before and where he was held in special affection. Two years later this church was to hold a memorial service for Richard Halliburton, at which his friend Lowell Thomas delivered the address.

The sales of his various books in 1937 he reckoned to exceed any previous year.

Still somewhat bothered with a chest cold, he flew to Memphis in time for dinner Christmas evening. After a week's recuperation (and work on the *Second Book of Marvels*) he resumed his lecture jaunts, in the Southeast. He got a great deal of fun out of this tour, and enjoyed especially speaking to "six hundred very pretty girls" at a state teachers' college in Central Virginia; at Alexandria, where all his old acquaintances turned out to welcome him, and at Miami, where so many good friends were on hand he "almost never got to bed."

---

* When H. S. Baker died Mr. Hurley had succeeded him in the Bobbs-Merrill office in New York. He had worked with Richard on several books and been with him through the long battle to make the first *Book of Marvels* "right."

CHAPTER XIX

"I've a lively agent in San Francisco, named Wilfred Crowell," he writes on a rocky day-coach between Jacksonville and Winter Park, January 24, 1938. "He is taking charge of the junk plans. I'll have a conference with him in February. I leave El Paso by plane February fourteenth, and must be back in New Orleans the twenty-second. I'll hate like the devil to lose five or six lecture dates, but it's imperative that I go."

On his way to El Paso, he lectured at Baton Rouge, and mentions what a good time he had at a party of the Huey Long family—"a very pretty and attractive daughter and a nineteen-year-old son who has his father's brains."

[*Laguna—February 21, 1938.*] My flight out was uneventful. I find the house marvelously improved. The kitchen is a dream. All the desks, shelves, closets, baths, for the three bedrooms are new, finished and shining. The canyon is at its greenest, the ocean at its bluest, and the sun warm enough to blister me. The work done is superb, in beautiful woods, and in good taste. The little lawn I blasted from the rock last summer is green with grass. The road is stoutly lined with posts and packed hard.

The junk agents met me in San Francisco Thursday and we had a furiously busy two days. I was on the radio three times, had a score of conferences, attended a Chinese dinner the agents gave the Chinese sponsors.

The Fair people named me "official junk-man," agreed on the site where the junk is to anchor, the rent, commission, etc. Lloyd's will insure the investment.

Four Chinese merchants have agreed to finance the expedition. We form a corporation to be called the Richard Halliburton Enterprise. We hope to take in money from ticket sale, souvenirs, radio, stamps, merchandise, letters to school children, and movies.

Back to the platform, in good spirits, and for overflowing audiences.

[*Indianapolis—March 12, 1938.*] I hear that the storms did not harm my house in any way. But, alas, the bottom of my glorious canyon is sanded over, and a great scar will be left across the green floor. This floor was just growing up again after *last* year's floods. I'm having an eight-by-five-foot map made here for the panel in my bedroom. I had found a map three hundred years old, two feet by three, and this is being photographed, enlarged and colored. It will be a stunning decoration.

Chambers and I have had a long conference. He's terribly impatient to get *Orient,* and so am I. I start to work on it again tomorrow. In fact, I'll spend every minute on it. The reception of *Occident* by the schools is gratifying.

[*On the shakiest train—March 26, 1938.*] A furious two weeks— from Indianapolis to New York, to Lancaster, Baltimore, Philadelphia, Akron. Shorty is now president of the Seiberling Rubber Co. His year-old baby boy is a perfect joy.

At Cadillac, Michigan, I was booked for afternoon and evening, but my management forgot to tell me about the afternoon and so I didn't appear for the kids who were waiting. I stayed over to talk to them the next morning.

A snag has come up with my Chinese junk plan—the Chinese backers. I'll know more later.

With an early closing of his lecture season he went back to Indianapolis and for several weeks gave himself up with intense concentration to the *Second Book of Marvels.* He would work every night till dawn broke, sleep till eleven in the morning, go to the office to look over his mail, then after lunch resume writing. He permitted himself no social diversion, no distraction of any sort. In his work on *The Occident,* though he had published five successful books, he had set himself patiently to the task of learning how to write for children— how to move easily within the limitations of a simple vocabulary and of a simple sentence structure, the advantage of using short, familiar

English words, avoidance of crowding his sentences with too many specific statements for the child readily to take in, and restraint in figures of speech. He felt that he had to write, rewrite and rewrite again the chapters of that book. It was partly this conscientiousness that had caused its repeated postponements. With none of his works, as he said, had composition cost him such pains. All this practice stood him in good stead now, but still he was relentless in his self-criticism and ready to tear up and discard whatever did not stand his rigid tests.

[*Indianapolis—April 12, 1938.*] You can imagine how hard I'm trying to get clear. Twenty-seven chapters are almost finished, with only three to go.

News from San Francisco says my Chinese backers have withdrawn completely—not because of percentage, but because they fear the Japs will prevent our sailing. So everything out there is at a standstill again. This doesn't discourage me. All my other projects have stood still several times before they succeeded.

[*Indianapolis—April 25, 1938.*] I'm grinding away on the last chapter. Then I must correct galley proofs, write the illustration captions and prepare the printer's dummy, but I'm speeding toward the end.

The big map for the Laguna house is being shown in a department store window here and stops traffic.

I wish you two would go to Louisville. It's *possible* I might meet you there, and drive to Memphis. Horse racing when I'm alone doesn't excite me much. The Derby with you would.

[*Indianapolis—May 9, 1938.*] I plan now to leave here on the twelfth and arrive in Memphis the next day. I'm still up to my ears in dummy and captions. The worst is over. It's just a manufacturing job now. So I'll see part of the Cotton Carnival.

[*Silver City—May 19, 1938.*] The flight to El Paso was uneventful. I didn't sleep but didn't expect to. The train took me to Deming, and a bus to Silver City. I slept all afternoon, had dinner alone, lectured to a state college, and now I'm ready for bed. I hated to leave home. But my machinery needs exercise and action—or it rusts.

[*Laguna—May 24, 1938.*] I'm safe in Laguna. The house was shining. The rains all spring have made everything intensely green. There are only a few sand spots in the canyon. In fact grass has about taken the yard and slopes, but I've got to imitate Dad and do a lot of weed-pulling.

I'll leave for San Francisco day after tomorrow. A letter from my agent says the junk prospects look black. Yesterday I spent mostly sun-bathing on the sun deck and already feel stimulated.

[*Laguna—June 13, 1938.*] In San Francisco we're forming a corporation and will sell stock to raise the necessary capital for the junk expedition. I have high hopes for it. But even if all goes well, and I get the money, I still can't hope to leave for China till August first. Seeing the Fair Grounds take rapid shape makes me want to press forward.

The Flying Carpet journey, which Richard had hoped to finance from the sale of magazine rights, had proved very expensive for him at the time, though he was later rewarded by the popularity of the book and by the new stories it furnished his lectures. All the spectacular and romantic possibilities of the Chinese junk had taken firm hold on his imagination. He would get the college boys who wanted to go along, and others, to provide most of the capital. He would concern himself, with all his skill at organization, all his notable talent for enlisting public interest, to see that their investment was rewarded. For himself he would have the feeling of security necessary for the wholehearted enjoyment of an extraordinary adventure.

And this adventure would give him a colorful, dramatic opening for the book about his own land, a Royal Road to Romance in the United States which had been suggested to him long before, which had increasingly fired his thought, and which had inspired various activities mentioned from time to time in his letters. The trips to Williamsburg, Yorktown and other historic spots in Virginia, to the haunts of the 'Forty-Niners, to the Grand Coulee Dam and the Dry

Waterfalls, his re-enactment of the flight of John Wilkes Booth, and so on, all pointed to his preparation. At Laguna he had collected a hundred books on exciting episodes in American history which he had been absorbing. He would begin with a pre-Columbian "discovery" of America by sailing a junk from China. Then he would arrange his other incidents chronologically down to the present.

[*Laguna—June 17, 1938.*] My junk has become so well organized I've taken a week end off and come back to Laguna, but I'll return to San Francisco day after tomorrow. I'll be kept busy there working on a prospectus with maps and facts and figures, which we need to spread before the investor.

[*Chancellor Hotel, San Francisco—June 25, 1938.*] My campaign moves along.

I wonder if any other author *ever* worked so hard on a book as I have on the *Marvels*. But I never want to be without a book-in-the-making the rest of my life. The next one must definitely be on America, and the junk trip will be a grand springboard for it. All my creative thoughts for the next two years will be toward this America book. We'll have it out in the fall of 1940.

His mother and father were about to sail for Europe again. He writes:

[*San Francisco—July 6, 1938.*] I can't be there in person but I'll be at the dock in spirit, with all my love and all my wishes for a happy, happy journey.

Ponta Delgada, in the Azores, was my first sight of foreign land, back in 1919, and I'll always remember the thrill. In Lisbon be sure to take the excursion to Cintra. You'll never forget it. In Gibraltar you'll have to accept what they show you. I didn't! In Palermo, don't fail to go to Monreale. And be sure to take a *day*-boat from Patras to Athens.

Vida Halliburton says she is going to take a block of my stock. Three others are promised. I'm more hopeful than ever that my plan is going to succeed. I've never *really* thought otherwise.

Life will be anything but dull between now and next March for our family. You two must put aside all anxiety over my voyage. It's going to be a wonderful adventure, properly safeguarded, and will pitch me out into motion again and on toward another book.

Letters, stock, lawyers, conferences over radio, engines, captain, engineer, crew, stamps, prices, all these keep me rushing around day and night. I get discouraged at the slowness of progress, but try to remember that I went through all this with the Flying Carpet, and realize delays are a part of the game. It's quite likely I'll not sail from San Francisco till September first, just before you get back.

[*San Francisco—August 1, 1938.*] My junk progress continues to be slow, despite the vast amount of pressure I put into it. I've raised $16,000. Most of it has come from Dartmouth lads from Maine who are going along. But I must have $25,000. My crew is all fixed.

I'm as keen as ever for the idea. It's going to be great fun. It's the one thing I most want to do, and I'm going to do it, and make a big success of it. Word came today from the Navy that I could use all the American islands across the Pacific as my own bases. There's never more than a 1200-mile hop between them.

[*San Francisco—August 31, 1938.*] You're safe home, and this is to greet you with wide open arms. I never knew just where you were, and you didn't know whether I was in America or China. Well, you're in New York, safe and sound, and I am still in San Francisco just where you left me.

My summer has been full of struggle, struggle. I had hoped to have the project settled long before this. To date I have $21,000, practically all I need. With my goal so near, I've reserved passage on the *President Coolidge* sailing September 23. And with success in sight, how rapidly the struggle sinks into the background.

Yesterday I went to Treasure Island to examine my anchorage. It's *lovely*. Once safe in the bay, I'm going to have the most exciting concession at the Fair.

Orient has been delayed over and over again. Publication date is now September ninth. The hot weather in New York has kept the ink from drying on sheets printed by the offset process.

[*San Francisco—September 10, 1938.*] Everything is moving rapidly and splendidly forward. My corporation is being closed. With the Barstow check I have more than enough money.

Bertha's wire came this morning—dear old Bertha! It's just what I needed when I needed it most. It will be fine to have her son George with us.

All today I've been thinking about Mother's coming here to see me. She *must* come. She can leave Memphis Wednesday and arrive in Los Angeles early Saturday morning. I'll meet her at the Biltmore, and we'll drive to Laguna for the night and take the train to San Francisco Sunday evening.

Sunday afternoon I'm having a party to say goodbye to my friends. Mother will be here for that, and then we'll have five days together, and she can meet my captain and engineer and see me sail.

I have Dad's magnificent letter written on the boat coming home, surely the finest letter any father ever wrote to any son. Naturally I read with special interest his description of the Hellespont, but every line was fascinating.

Dad, if I could talk to you about the junk trip, I'm sure you would lose all your hesitation over it. Never was any expedition so carefully worked out for safety measures. I've a wonderful captain and engine and engineer. I'll have two months to choose my junk with the best possible help.

I arrive at Yokohama October seventh, and will be in Japan a few days seeing the Jap Navy.

[*S. S. President Coolidge—September 28, 1938.*] I'm still dizzy and bewildered from the last ten days. I don't believe they *could* have been any busier or happier. Mother's visit was a great success. I know she got on the train at Oakland more content about me and my new adventure than she would have been had we not been together.

We did the best we could with the fleeting moments we had together. They were very sweet. Seeing what a mature, experienced captain and engineer I have, she can feel at ease. Both these men think no more of this new sailing job than they thought of any one of the dozens behind them.

We will have ten hours in Honolulu tomorrow. I have a few

friends to see, a swim at Waikiki to take. . . . I don't feel very strenuous. I'm already dreaming of the story I'll do about my *Sea Dragon*.

I'll write every few days. Keep your globe dusted off. Give my sweet Laura my special love. I'll wish for her when I'm living on salt beef and hard tack cooked by a Chinaman. The voyage has been perfect—hot sun and calm seas. I'm *very* happy over my project— and over the calm way you are accepting it.

This was the first of his Bell stories—as before, he thought of all his Sunday stories as letters to his family:

It was seeing a schooner—years ago—with its great wings spread, sailing out through the Golden Gate at San Francisco, that first made me want to go to sea. My heart went straight aboard her, and, until this day, it's never come back—for long.

I spent several years in wandering by sea and land, visiting all the nice warm countries on the map. These travels at last brought me to China. And in the harbor of Foochow I found my first true love again—ships with sails. Not just one or a dozen, but scores and hundreds. The harbor was alive with sails.

These ships, this time, were not schooners—something far more wonderful and exciting than that. Nor were they yachts or yawls, sloops or luggers, barks or barkentines. They were *junks*. And they had, for me, an immediate and tremendous appeal. No ship I'd ever seen before had such glorious bright-colored sails as these Chinese craft, or such carved, up-soaring castles on the poops, or such gay and gaudy dragon-pictures on the sterns.

The moment I set eyes on a Foochow junk I forgot all about my chaste and clean-lined schooners with the white wings, and cast covetous glances at the bedizened, painted galleons from the Orient.

A Chinese junk! Always, in my mind, this meant a ramshackle, unwieldy, unseaworthy scow, slogging along, and manned by laundrymen. Such dismal ignorance! Junks have beauty, grace and glamour. In Foochow they were all adorned with banners, and gleamed with oil and paint. They bristled with cast-iron cannon. On their mast-tops sparkled gilded good-luck charms. Their three bat-wing sails, made of shining yellow mats, drove them over the water with the ease of a flying seagull. Despite their distinctive Oriental rigging I had suspicions, on first seeing their up-climbing poops and half-moon hulls, that Columbus' caravels had reached Asia after all, been seized by the Chinese, given a new paint job, and kept in service under the name of junks.

Then and there I resolved to buy one at the first opportunity, and sail it up and down the Seven Seas.

And now the opportunity has come. As I write, I'm on my way back to China with a group of American comrades, to buy a junk just like the gaudy graceful ships I saw in Foochow.

The name? I chose that long ago—the *Sea Dragon*. On the day of launching, the prettiest Chinese girl whom I can find will break a bottle of rice wine on the *Sea Dragon's* nose. And as the junk slides down the ways we'll all beat gongs and shoot off firecrackers, in proper Chinese fashion, to drive away the demons of storm and shipwreck.

Our *Sea Dragon's* first voyage has already been charted—across the Pacific to San Francisco in order to participate in the Golden Gate International Exposition. We'll leave China early in January and reach Treasure Island—God willing—the middle of March. We would like to go the sunny, southern way—via Manila, Guam, Wake, to Midway and Honolulu. This was my original plan. But I have learned that for a sailing vessel, this southern route, in midwinter, is impossible. The wind blows with such constant violence toward China that sailing toward America consists mostly in being blown backward.

Instead, to get a favorable wind, we will chart our course up the eastern coast of Formosa, and then across 4000 miles of open ocean to Midway.

The torpedo season may be at its height. Since the Japanese launched their attack on China, the invading Navy has sunk hundreds of junks in Chinese waters. The *Sea Dragon,* with its red and white hull and shining yellow sails, would make a splendid target for torpedo boats.

I've just learned one reason why the Japanese wage such a merciless campaign against the apparently harmless fisher-junks. In the early days of the war the Chinese civilians were allowed to sail their junks rather much where they chose. Then one day a Japanese airplane carrier—an object of special hatred in China—appeared off the coast and began to discharge its death-laden planes. The crew was so occupied that it scarcely noticed a group of small junks, busily fishing, which drifted slowly out from shore toward the gray steel monster. Then, when the junks and battleships were only 200 yards apart, a Chinese mosquito boat, hitherto concealed, suddenly dashed from the midst of the junk fleet—full speed at the carrier. Point-blank it loosed a torpedo, and struck the Japanese vessel squarely amidships. The great carrier was so badly damaged that it had to go into drydock for three months.

At once the Japanese swore vengeance on all junks—honest and otherwise. They shelled every junk they could find, set fire to the wreckage, and disposed of the crews (which in China means whole families) by pushing them into the sea without boats or lifebelts. Even at anchor in the harbors of the coastal cities the helpless native craft were systematically bombed—as they still are today. Knowing all this, I plan to go first to Tokyo and formally ask the Japanese Navy to grant a safe-conduct for the *Sea Dragon's* journey through the war zone.

Many people, ignoring the serious dangers resulting from the war, ask me: Isn't midwinter a foolish time to attempt the Pacific in a junk? Perhaps it is. However, this risk is less great than it seems. I can explain why:

First of all, contrary to general belief, junks are among the most seaworthy of ships. For 4000 years China has been building these strange craft, and after forty centuries of trial and error has learned to build them so that they handle remarkably well in all kinds of weather. Far from being a race of landlubbers, the Chinese are very much at home afloat. That they possess the knowledge of good ship design is not surprising. *There are more boats in China than in all other countries put together.* Hundreds of thousands of Chinese live their entire lives on boats—are born on boats, grow up on boats, grow old on boats, and die on boats. To them dry land is a foreign world. Moreover, the coast of China offers every possible danger and difficulty that ever confronted a sailor—sudden storms, treacherous currents, rocky shores, hidden reefs, typhoons. To keep sailing, and trading, and fishing, in such perilous seas the Chinese have *had* to build staunch, safe boats, and to be masterful sailors.

Their seafaring tradition goes back to the beginning of history. Long before the founding of the Roman Empire the Chinese were trading, in their wonderful junks, with India and Arabia, and controlled the Eastern world with their war fleets.

And while the early Mediterranean sailors were hugging the coasts, and using the stars for guidance, the Chinese were sailing up and down the high seas, steering by the compass—one of the many great inventions China has given the world.

Several centuries ago, to make their junks more seaworthy, the Chinese shipwrights divided the hulls with water-tight bulkheads—a safety device which now is used by every ship-building nation.

China's junks were possibly trading with the west coast of Mexico well before Columbus "discovered" America. Apparent evidence of this is especially strong in Yucatan. At Chichen-Itza, the magnificent carved stone capital of the Maya Indians, there is a deep sacrificial pool. Into this pool the Mayan priests flung young maidens and gifts of treasure as sacrifices to Yum-Chac, the god of rain. A few years ago this tragic well was carefully dredged. Bones of the sacrifices were found. Also, sunk deep in the accumulated silt, were found many sacred offerings of carved jade. And since no deposits of jade are known to exist in the Americas, it seems a possible explanation that these treasures were junk-borne from China, 9000 miles away.

In modern times we have incontestable evidence that Chinese junks have sailed in every sea. About a hundred years ago the people of London were astonished by the visit of an extraordinary vessel that came unheralded up the Thames. It had lug sails made of mats, big wooden eyes on the bow, fantastic pictures on the stern. This ship turned out to be the *Keyling,* an eighty-foot Foochow junk that had come to England by way of the southern cape of Africa. It carried a cargo of silk and ivory, and bizarre presents for Queen Victoria.

In 1875 a whole fleet of war junks came to California. In that year news reached the Emperor of China, reigning in Peking, that thousands of Chinese who had gone to California to work on the new railroads were being cruelly mistreated. Outraged at this report, the Emperor resolved to teach the United States a lesson it wouldn't soon forget. He outfitted seven war junks, armed them with brass cannon, and sent them off to attack the coast of California. He would force the offenders to repent their evil deeds!

Somebody told the admiral of this armada that Monterey was the city that must first be subdued. So, eastward-bound across the Pacific to Monterey, the seven junks sailed. Not having realized that the Pacific Ocean was so big, the Emperor had not sufficiently provisioned the fleet. Fresh water gave out before the voyage was half over. The sailors faced death from thirst—when a rainstorm came. Quickly the sails were lowered and used as troughs to funnel rain into the empty tanks.

At last this doughty fleet reached Monterey. Fifty gunners stood by their brass cannon ready to blast the city to pieces if it put up a fight. But far from resisting, the people of Monterey were so astonished, and so delighted, by this unexpected visit of seven Chinese war junks, that the whole town came down to the shore to welcome the invaders. There was a parade. The pig-tailed sailors found themselves overwhelmed with hospitality. They liked California so much they refused to go home. The older members of the crews got jobs on the railroads, but the younger members stayed on in Monterey as fishermen. The seven junks were ultimately broken up and burned. In 1924, several of the crew, who still lived in Monterey, were interviewed by a Chinese magazine editor from San Francisco and to him they gave the details of the story I've told here.

In 1922, another junk, the *Amoy,* sailed by a Dutch captain and his Chinese wife, with three Chinese seamen, left the port of Amoy, and followed the "great circle" route across the Pacific. For stores and repairs they put in at Dutch Harbor in the Aleutian Islands. Later, having visited Vancouver and San Francisco, this brave little ship sailed into the Atlantic via the Canal, and is now tied up for display near New York City.

One of the most amazing of all junk voyages came to a sad end, a few years ago, in Puget Sound. A Japanese junk—less curious in design and decoration than the Chinese models—drifted with the currents, in quest of fish, a thousand miles to the eastward of Yokohama. When food and water began to run low, the master decided to turn back with the catch. But a violent wind arose and drove the ship farther east—east—east. The crew were helpless before the unceasing hurricane. Their water gave out, and there was no rain. Their food came to an end; they could not eat their fish, for the entire catch had rotted. Their sails were ripped to shreds—the masts swept overboard. Weeks of torment passed. One by one the crew died and were pushed into the sea.

And then one morning a ship from the American coast guard, out of Seattle, caught sight of a derelict, obviously from some Oriental port, drifting without guidance into the entrance of Puget Sound. The coast-guardsmen boarded this ghostly visitor. Several men lay dead on the deck, dead from starvation. There was not one living soul aboard. The log was found intact. On every page appeared, over and over, the word *hunger*. This log showed that the junk had started on its helpless, headlong course the end of December. The coast-guardsmen found it in Puget Sound the following April—blown by the storm across the wide expanse of the Pacific, sailing on even after the last man had perished.

The story of Dr. Petersen's 36-foot junk, the *Hummel-Hummel,* whose incredible voyage from Shanghai to San Pedro succeeded so recently, is too well known to need retelling. The first report of his very genuine hardships gave me—as one says—pause (especially as his crossing was in midsummer, and ours must be in winter). However, a communication from Dr. Petersen's two young Russian sailors changed this picture. It seems they have not had their fill of reeling decks, cold beans for supper, and sea-drenched turns at the tiller. For, since their return to Shanghai, they have written me saying they enjoyed their voyage on the *Hummel-Hummel* so much they would like to make the crossing all over again aboard my *Sea Dragon.*

In reply I reminded them of a Japanese proverb which goes like this: "You are a fool not to climb Fujiyama once in your lifetime. But you are a worse fool to climb it twice!"

The time may come when I shall regret having refused the offer of these veteran junkmen. For we are not altogether an expert crew. Three of our sailors—George Barstow, a student from the Juilliard School of Music, Robert Chase, a senior at Dartmouth, and Paul Mooney, a journalist—have never, so far, even helped to set a sail.

John Potter and Gordon Torrey, just out of Dartmouth, are somewhat saltier, having spent their summers aboard their racing yacht at Bar Harbor. Henry von Fehren, in charge of radio and lights and things mechanical, has been aboard an ocean-going yacht for several years, and is thoroughly sea-wise. Fortunately our captain, John Welch, also a veteran seaman, has been master of all manner of sailing ships. He vows, with proper salty language, to make sailors of all of us before we've been at sea many days.

Being for the most part amateurs, we are all quite prepared, in the January weather, to be deathly seasick until we get our sea-legs. And we know that there will be other sorts of hardships, too—scanty space, meals scrambled up by ourselves in a gyrating galley, the damp chill of a winter sea, too little fresh water and too much salt. But these things we must accept as a matter of course. They are part of the adventure. We have chosen to cross the Pacific the hardest but the most exciting way.

As for myself, I have one fervent hope, one prayer: that wind and circumstance will not blow the *Sea Dragon* into Puget Sound or down to Mexico. I want to steer her straight into the Golden Gate, where, a long time ago, I first saw a white-sailed schooner, and first heard the call of the sea.

CHAPTER XX

A GALLEON FROM CHINA

[*Nearing Yokohama—October 7, 1938.*] We'll be landing in another hour. I'm glad to get ashore. Fifteen days on this boat is overlong. I'll 'phone Ambassador Grew at once and try to get an appointment for tomorrow morning with the Jap Navy officials. If this business is rushed through, I may get out of Kobe next day, and on my way.

It's murky, so we can't see Fuji—dammit. I'm terribly sorry my stay in Japan must be so hurried, having come so far. But, with all the complications, I must push, push ahead and get home as soon as possible. I'll try to get a first-story for the newspapers out of Japan and Shanghai.

Richard gave to the syndicate his account of what happened in Japan and Shanghai and down the coast to Hongkong:

The Japanese Foreign Office gave me every courtesy. Its officials loaded me with documents and assurances. I hope all this means something—I hope so despite my strong suspicion that the assurances and documents give me no actual protection. Japan's forces in the field have already proved to be irresponsible. I fear that the *Sea Dragon's* shining new sails will make a target too alluring for the Japanese Navy to resist—"Let's see if we can hit that red junk at five miles!" Our American flag may be taken as some Chinaman's artful dodge. And then when we're sunk the Japanese will apologize as only the Japanese can. However, I have the safe-passage documents in my pocket and will carry them with me—even to the bottom of the China Sea. . . .

I traveled south down the coast. I visited many ports and inspected many junks. Around Shanghai all the junks had fled before the Japanese. I went to Wenchow. Wenchow junks, with their white

408

and scarlet hulls, are famous both for beauty and for speed. I looked at dozens. Every one appeared to be at least ten years old, and some a hundred, and I was distrustful of their seaworthiness.

The fleets at Ningpo, Amoy, Foochow, were inspected. For three centuries Ningpo has built the finest junks in China. But due to the war, Ningpo is a dead port today. Its ships, certain to meet destruction at the hands of the Japanese Navy the moment they put out to sea, are quietly foundering at their anchorages.

In Amoy a shipbuilder offered to build a first-class Amoy junk—in ninety days. I wanted one *now*.

In Foochow, home of the carved and painted junks, there was such a lack (again due to the war) of tools, timbers, gear, canvas, paint, provisions—all vitally necessary for a long sailing trip—that I dared not embark from there.

Hongkong, a British colony still free from Japan's strangling blockade, was my last hope.

Even as our passenger ship approached Hongkong, I knew I was coming to the right place. Protected by the guns on the towering peaks above the harbor, the junks from this port, thumbing their noses at the Japanese, were fishing merrily along the shore. There must have been five hundred in one fleet, their foremasts leaning rakishly forward, their mainsails a vast brown web of matting formed like the wing of a bat, their perky little fan-shaped mizzensails stuck high on the up-swelling poop. To me, who had seen scarcely a junk sail spread all the way down from Shanghai, this glimpse of hundreds together, scudding along before the early morning breeze, was a glorious sight.

Perhaps it was the morning light on the waves and on the gold-brown sails, perhaps it was the gorgeous tropical scenery in the background, perhaps it was the cheery way the fishermen shouted at us as we wound our way through the fishing fleet, that made the Chinese junks seem strikingly beautiful and appealing, all over again. I rejoiced, anew, that I had resolved to possess myself of one, and live aboard it, and sail it out across the biggest ocean in the world.

Within an hour after landing, I was back again among the junks, looking for one which would serve my purpose.

We found a magnificent junk anchored in a cove called—lovely name—Gin Drinker's Bay. The hull, ninety feet long, was built like a battleship; the deck made of polished teak; the mat sails, dyed scarlet, heavy enough to withstand almost any wind. The cabins, occupied by thirty people, were lacquered red. The carved joss shrine, filled with gilded gods, was a work of art. Each of the ship's wooden "eyes" measured a yard across. This junk, with its graceful crescent hull and its scolloped sails, would have won the admiration of sailors in *any* country. It could easily have crossed the broad Pacific in fine style.

But the price was three times what we could afford to pay.

In Joss House Bay we had better luck (or so it seemed at first). We found another junk almost as beautiful as the one described above. Its castled poop swept up thirty feet above the water. And five beautiful iron cannon gave protection from pirates. The price was right. We were on the point of buying it when we found that the hull planking was only an inch thick. We knew better than to tackle the Pacific in *that*.

And so it went, ship after ship. Inevitably, in the face of all these disappointments, we soon reached the only possible conclusion—we must build a new junk suitable to our needs, regardless of the time it took.

Promptly we located a native shipyard, explained to the owner what we wanted—a ship seventy-five feet long, with a twenty-foot beam, extra sturdy, and adorned with every possible flourish.

We made a deal. In twenty-four hours the *Sea Dragon's* keel was laid.

[*Hongkong—November 2, 1938.*] All's well. Our junk will be finished in forty-five days. Fifteen days more to rig and train our crew. Then we plan to set out about January first. The *new* junk is going to be splendid—beautiful and sturdy, *very* strongly and heavily built. We'll do everything right here in Hongkong.

The war is hardly noticed here, except for the many refugees. Canton will be open in a few more days. Life seems normal in every way. We are living in a boarding house, and get along beautifully. The German engineer, Henry von Fehren, is a real gentleman. Captain Welch is dictatorial, but he's a good sailor, so I don't care.

Afloat at last the *Sea Dragon* tests her motor in a trial run on the Bay of Hongkong.

Romance and utility salute each other in Chinese waters: the glamourous *Sea Dragon*, under full sail, passes a cargo vessel steaming into the harbor.

Before the wind, Stars and Stripes aflutter, the *Sea Dragon* surges off on the last great adventure.

Hongkong is a beautiful and interesting town—in fact, I have no troubles of any sort.

I loved my few days in Japan. It seemed busy and prosperous and unconcerned with war. Shanghai was a wasteland.

The four boys are en route. George Barstow gets here first with Torrey; Chase and Potter come later, arriving about December fifteenth, in good time.

I know you will be happy to know that my grand adventure is moving in high gear without a hitch.

[*Hongkong—November 10, 1938.*] I've bought a beautiful Mah Jongg set, in a lacquer box, with tray and cigarette box and brackets to match. I'm having it packed now, ready to ship home on tomorrow's boat.

Two of my boys, Torrey and Barstow, landed in Japan on November third. I cabled them to *stay* in Japan till the first of December. They would be another responsibility if they got here too soon. The other two arrive December fifteenth. A long letter from Crowell says the four of them had a great time in San Francisco.

Our junk is growing fast. We have every hope now of getting clear on New Year's. I spend each morning at the shipyard, and all afternoon with construction details. No battleship was ever built as strong as our junk, and no Chinese emperor ever had a bark as beautiful as ours will be.

Of course, as always I'm perfectly healthy. We have good food and clean water and clean rooms at this small hotel.

The war refugees are sickening.

[*Hongkong—November 11, 1938.*] By this same boat I'm sending Xmas presents to everybody. I've had such fun shopping. Happy days! I'll be thinking of you on Xmas morning.

[*Hongkong—November 21, 1938.*] Rapidly the days roll by, occupied with new and exciting interests. Boats are a new world for me. I've much to learn. Chinese do everything backward and everything slowly. Even so, local people say our progress is astonishing. The entire skeleton of the junk is almost finished. The outside planking starts soon. Today I gave the order for sails. The 65-foot masts are being smoothed off. Unless we have some major setback I still plan to leave Hongkong January first. I'll be sending you pictures of the *Sea Dragon* soon. I'm planning my own quarters alone, on the boat. The four boys and the Captain will stand regular watch—wheel and sails. I'll have no fixed watch, but supervise everything.

I had a chance to buy a baby giant-panda (see inclosed picture) as a mascot. But we all agreed he would suffer too terribly with sea-sickness.

[*Hongkong—December 12, 1938.*] This letter should reach you about Xmas day. So it carries a big embrace to everybody, and the good news that by the time you're reading these lines, I'll be about ready to sail. We are still rushing forward: the masts go up tomorrow, the engine and water tanks by the end of the week. A lifeboat *with sails* is provided. It's a great thrill watching the ship grow in beauty. Everybody is working hard, and eager to set sail. I have complete faith in the captain and the engineer, and feel certain that we'll arrive without the slightest mishap—except a lot of seasickness. Potter and Chase are jewels. All my news is just ship news—rope and bolts, and cabins, and fuel. I'll never want to build another ship. But it's fun building this *one*.

Everything is smooth as can be—so don't you worry about anything.

[*Hongkong—January 1, 1939.*] Happy New Year! I'd hoped to be gone by today, but the usual delays will keep me here till about January tenth. Our ship still goes forward—look at the color negatives I'm sending. The picture was taken a week ago. Since then we've added dragons, etc., to the stern, and improved it vastly.

Yes, Dad, our *Sea Dragon* is new, but we will take a good shakedown cruise first, before really going to sea. Our good captain will take no chances. Our engine is a beauty and perfectly installed. There have been hundreds of ships smaller than ours to cross oceans, and few as staunchly built. All Hongkong is coming out to look at her—there was never such a beautiful ship in China. I've lost none of my enthusiasm, and none of my confidence.

I've hired a fine cook and cook's boy, American, and one more sailor. I've still another unused bunk, and will add a movieman in Honolulu. Our radio is going to be wonderful. We can radio you messages every day or so, and you can wireless me. We've outfitted our kitchen, and we've food and water for ninety days, heavy clothes, some rum, four guns against pirates.

Don't worry about my nerves wearing out. I do work hard, and have plenty to worry about, but I love it, and have never worried about anything so exciting as this. The crew quarrel, of course; it was never otherwise on such an expedition. I'm a better than average mediator and know we'll get along well enough.

I've written four stories for the newspapers. I go to Canton tomorrow to get my souvenir envelopes stamped.

The full story of Hongkong adventures and misadventures appeared in his Sunday articles, light-hearted in tone—but how serious must have been the perplexities:

If any one of my readers wishes to be driven rapidly and violently insane, and doesn't know how to go about it, let me make a suggestion: Try building a Chinese junk in a Chinese shipyard, during a war with Japan. From personal experience I know this to be a most effective method. In fact I don't see how it can fail.

From the hour I signed a contract, here in Hongkong, with Mr. Fat Kau, to build me a beautiful junk—"big, but not *too* big; colorful, but not garish"—until today, when my *Sea Dragon* is ready to sail, I've been through so many ship-building battles, and been so plagued by the superlative perversity of Chinese carpenters, that I'm a mental wreck. Nothing that can happen on our voyage to San Francisco can possibly upset me now. In near-by waters, pirates are a very real and constant menace—wintry storms may play us cruel tricks—most of our crew are green hands, who are amiably planning to mutiny if the work bores them. But whatever dramatics may come, they will be anticlimactic, compared to the state of perpetual crisis which we have endured while building our Chinese junk with Chinese labor.

We wished our junk to be designed, constructed, and decorated in strict accordance with native custom—and the work must be done by natives. One shipbuilder, the worthy Mr. Fat Kau, was recommended above all others. So we picked an interpreter and went to interview him.

The tram carried us along the mountain-framed shore, away from downtown Hongkong, past the British barracks, farther and farther into the squalid Chinese waterfront slums. Opposite a high-smelling soy-sauce factory, and between the Peachy Garage and a Gentleman's Parlor for Beauty, was the place where junks are born.

Mr. Fat Kau welcomed us graciously. We were clearly a group of foreign idiots . . . wanting to build a junk and name it the *Sea Dragon* and sail it to San Francisco, 9000 miles away. But we were cash customers, so the generous man agreed, finally, to accept only twice what we offered. When we departed, we had a contract, beautifully sealed in red with Kau's private *chop,* and the *Sea Dragon*—we imagined—was as good as built.

From that day to this, the cramped little shipyard has been a sort of hired private madhouse for John Welch, our captain; for Henry von Fehren, our engineer; and for me. The *Sea Dragon* is now ready to sail, and I have no doubt it is a sound, seaworthy ship; but I have no doubt, either, that its construction violated every accepted rule of ship-building known to man.

First there was the keel, a magnificent log of jacal-wood, sixty feet long. A sawmill could have squared it off in twenty minutes. I soon realized that, with Chinese methods, this same job would take a week. The carpenters hacked at it with little axes, and sawed it by hand. When I was ready to tear up the contract because of the lack of progress, the workmen smiled blandly and reminded me that the Chinese have been hand-cutting their keels for four thousand years. And what would I do, they asked, with the six days saved by the mill; and how would I pay the carpenters for the six days' work which a machine-saw would cause them to lose? I must remember their wages were paid by the day; if I rushed things, American fashion, they would starve.

I saw myself spending ten months in Hongkong—the while the *Sea Dragon* was expected at San Francisco's Treasure Island in ten weeks.

I went to Mr. Fat Kau to complain, to threaten, to curse—as well as one can curse through an interpreter. He was perfectly calm, invited me to lunch in his living quarters over the shipyard office. Here he hoped I would be more reasonable.

Still fulminating, I followed him.

Mr. Fat Kau looked like a middle-aged, good-natured Buddha. He was very fat, very bald, and very rich. He lived in domestic bliss with four wives. (He had married five, but the youngest, aged sixteen, the day after the wedding had run away with one of his shipwrights. He confessed to me his shame and humiliation. The other four wives, each with a baby to care for, agreed that the errant bride was a minx and a hussy.)

The oldest wife, who bossed the other three, took charge of the meal. We pitched rice, with chopsticks, into our mouths, and flung shrimp-shells and duck bones over our shoulders into the corners. As soon as I was besodden and subdued with food, Mr. Fat Kau suggested that I could have my keel mill-sawn, but I must pay the bill, and pay wages to all his carpenters who would be deprived of their labor.

And in my desperate haste to get on with the job, I agreed.

The thousand bolt holes that had to be drilled were my next problem. Wooden pegs are generally used to hold Chinese junks together. But with nine thousand miles of raging winter sea to face, we needed iron bolts. For drilling, the Chinese intended to use their customary archaic drill—a gadget like an Indian bow, with the string wrapped a couple of times around the shaft of a sharp-tipped arrow which, when rotated, digs the hole. With this primitive tool, the Chinese manage, in the course of an hour or so, to scrape through a plank which an ordinary American brace-and-bit could punch in a few seconds. We thought of the countless holes—and bought an electric drill.

From the first, the Chinese carpenters were too dumfounded by such a marvelous machine to object. Von Fehren operated it. Every time he attacked a teakwood plank, the workmen dropped their jobs to gather round and watch the magical instrument perform. Brrrrr! the drill bit into the wood . . . and when the steel showed through, the entire gallery broke into shouts of amazement. Though it happened about five times every five minutes, they were still amazed. And yet when I suggested that the Chinese themselves use the drill, they threatened to declare war . . . it would ruin their livelihood even quicker than the sawmill.

Once the keel was laid, one might suppose the ribs would follow, and then they would be covered by planks to make the hull. In any sensible shipyard this would be the sequence. But not in Fat Kau's! He put on the planks *without* any ribs, suspending them from bamboo ropes, propping them up with bamboo poles. "How can you tell where the ribs should go, unless you have the planking up first?" he asked. In other words, "How do you know where to put the frame of a house until you have the walls up and the roof on?"

I groaned at this demented idea—but again got the "four thousand years" argument.

Next morning as I approached the shipyard I saw a cloud of flame and smoke pouring out of it. *There,* I felt sure, went my expensive mill-sawn keel, and all the laboriously gathered timbers for our junk. In the greatest alarm I dashed through the gate. The smoke all but choked me, but nobody except me seemed in any way concerned by the conflagration. Through the murk I presently saw that it was my three-inch teak hull-planking (worth its weight in radium at such times as these) going up in flames. Such criminal, stupid carelessness! Such indifference to my burning planks . . . and the wartime blockade! . . . *How* would I get more? . . . Why were the Chinese such infuriating fools!

In another moment I realized that the fires had a purpose. Each teak plank—twenty feet long—was stretched across two wooden saw-horses six feet apart. A heavy cast-iron cannon weighed down each end. Between the saw-horses a bonfire had been built, which heated the wood to combustion point. Whenever it actually burst into flames, a Chinese boy spat a mouthful of water on the burning spot. The heat charred the plank an inch deep, but (with the aid of the weights on the ends) bent the thick plank into a crescent. When the timber cooled off, it retained its shape, and thus fitted the curved lines of the hull. Indeed, exclaimed Mr. Fat Kau, how else would you do it?

Soon after this crisis had passed we had another one to face. I came to the yard to find all the carpenters on a sit-down strike. Their wages had been paid; so far as I knew they had absolutely no grievance.

But apparently I didn't know much. They were striking because I had failed to give them a party. Every self-respecting workman in China expects the employer to give two big parties per job—one at the beginning, one when the work is finished. And we had given no party at all. We were guilty of the worst possible manners. So perhaps a sit-down strike would teach us the customs of the country.

There were something like fifty men on the job at the time. Our interpreter estimated it would cost thirty Hongkong dollars—about nine dollars American—to give them all a whopping big blowout. "But don't give the money to Number One Wife," he cautioned. "She will give only twenty-dollar party and keep the difference." So we turned the money over to Number Four Wife who was supposed to be less grasping. And when she had finished cajoling, intimidating and generally wearing down the shopkeepers, she proudly spread a feast that would have cost anyone else in Hongkong a cool hundred. There were barrels and baskets of Chinese food. The rice wine would almost have floated our *Sea Dragon*. There were girls and music. In no time at all everybody was tipsy. And then—the climax of the evening—they all helped themselves to opium. Without the opium, so I was told, no party was worth being invited to.

I watched each of the fifty guests smoke his fill of the drug. Then, toward dawn, they climbed up onto the unfinished ribs and scaffolding of the *Sea Dragon* and went to sleep.

Next day the men returned to work with redoubled energy, and the pounding, sawing and nailing could be heard from afar.

When not occupied with strikes, parties, and building problems, I sometimes found time to enjoy the pageant of the shipyard. It was wholly, hopelessly Chinese. It sprawled along the waterfront in a wild confusion of timbers, bamboo poles, babies, old cannon, cooking fires, carpenters, and wives. Hens roosted on the big two-man saws. Tailless cats prowled, slant-eyed, among the logs of teak and camphor wood. Cached in every cranny were the workmen's bed-rolls— for all the workmen sleep at the job at night. "Job" and "home" are synonymous in the Chinese laborer's lexicon.

Our ship grew by spurts and whims. Our carefully drawn paper plans made not the slightest impression on Mr. Fat Kau, so we abandoned them and added or subtracted to our hearts' content—as far, that is, as we could without altering the ship's authentic junk lines. Cabins, storerooms and lockers were torn out and rearranged three times. The rest of the ship went through much the same evolution.

We held several earnest conferences on the subject of the wooden "eyes." How wide should they be, and how near the bow should they be placed? We finally ordered ours thirty inches in diameter. With 9000 miles of ocean between Hongkong and San Francisco, I felt we had best give our ship the finest and biggest eyes possible. It took a carver two days to shape them from camphor-tree logs, and four men to lift them into place.

These eyes were nailed to the hull only temporarily. One learns their proper position by trial and error. We are informed that if—on our first shake-down cruise—we run into storms and misadventures, we can be sure that the eyes are not properly set, have seen badly, and taken the wrong course. The eyes must then be moved slightly forward, or aft, until they are placed just right, and can see clearly the safe way to go.

These eyes have a curious history. Scholars say that the idea of painting eyes on a ship came from ancient Egypt, where it was the custom to paint the single eye of Osiris on the ship's prow. Arabs brought the idea to the Far East two thousand years ago.

But Mr. Fat Kau has a different story. He says the idea of eyes came from Tai Toa Fat (no relation), the god of sailors and fishermen. This joss, often seen reproduced in wood or porcelain, is always given a bald head, great rolls of flesh, and a contagious smile. His image is found on every junk.

Years ago when Tai Toa Fat actually lived in China, he wanted to make a long and hazardous voyage up the Yangtse River to Chungking. So he went to a junk owner and asked to be taken there as a passenger. But the junk owner said this could not be; he was getting old and losing his eyesight, and could no longer guide his ship safely.

Tai Toa Fat would not accept this excuse. He just painted big, clear-seeing eyes on the bows of the junk—eyes that could see their way through any weather, even at night.

The voyage was made, and sure enough, the junk arrived at Chungking without mishap.

News of this extraordinary aid to navigation spread far and wide, and thousands of junk owners asked Tai Toa Fat to paint eyes on *their* junks. He taught the Chinese sailors the eye art, and his disciples, down the centuries, have continued to specialize in it. To this day the junk owners still make a religious ceremony out of the eye-placing.

In keeping with this custom I dutifully went, on the day of launching, to a temple near the shipyard, and invited the priest to come down and open the new eyes.

He appeared, dressed in white and yellow robes, and wearing a curious square hat. In one hand he carried a tom-tom. Walking about the unfinished deck he beat his drum loudly and fixed paper prayers to the mast. Then he bathed the eyes in Chinese samchu (rice wine), strung up a string of firecrackers three feet long, and instructed us to "let her go."

With the great eyes dripping wine, and the firecrackers popping, we slid into the bay.

Needless to say we have in our cabin-shrine the finest and jolliest and fattest statue of Tai Toa Fat that could be found anywhere in Hongkong.

Our party of junkmen left America divided on one very important point—an auxiliary engine. Should we install one or not? Captain Welch vowed he'd have no engine aboard—he'd *sail* the blankety-blank junk across. And had we not been limited in time, and had our sailing season not been midwinter, I would have agreed.

But I knew we had a schedule to meet—we were expected in San Francisco on a certain date. And we would be sailing across the lonely, un-Pacific Ocean in January and February. So we brought along a small engine despite the captain's complaints.

For days, after we arrived in Hongkong, Welch had his way—and the engine was ignored. Then came a sign from heaven that made us decide otherwise.

Out from Wenchow another junk—likewise San Francisco bound—put to sea. Three days later she was wrecked on a rocky island near Formosa. Her captain later wrote us saying that if he had possessed an engine, however small, he could have escaped the rocks.

Soon after, a second junk—also headed for America—sailed from Shanghai. Another gale drove the ship backward, snapped the main-mast. Her crew struggled back to port to get an engine before con-tinuing their voyage.

So warned, we tore up our junk's interior for a fourth time, and placed the engine where the main cabin had been. It may or may not work ... and I doubt if Tai Toa Fat will have any influence on the behavior of a motor groaning and coughing in the hold. In this department, we put our whole trust in Henry von Fehren.

However, after providing quarters for a crew of twelve and storage-space for a ten weeks' food supply, we had so little room left for fuel tanks that the engine can be used only in the worst emergen-cies. If we can manage to get home without using it at all, so much the better.

A junk lends itself magnificently to color. And we have tried to take full advantage of this opportunity. We emptied the rainbow on hull, stern, and sails. The hull is a brilliant Chinese red, edged at the rail with bands of white and gold. The "glance" of the eyes is black. On either side of the poop a Chinese artist has painted a ferocious red and yellow dragon twenty feet long, not counting the curves!

Our foresail has been dyed yellow; the mizzensail, vermilion. As an extraordinary gesture toward simplicity, we've left the mainsail white—although, here in China, it would ordinarily be colored a rich russet.

The *Sea Dragon's* stern is my special pride and joy. Surely it is the most gorgeous stern ever seen on a ship since the Chinese began to abandon their ancient art of hand-decorating their junks. (Formerly every type of junk had its distinctive style and color of paint-work; but good specimens of the traditional decoration are becoming rarer every year.) On the *Sea Dragon's* stern, the central section is brilliant with a huge painting of a phoenix—the Chinese good-luck bird. The brightness of his feathers makes up, perhaps, for the fact that the native painter gave him only one leg. Above the phoenix is the ship's name and port—*Sea Dragon, Hongkong*—in great gold Chinese characters. Below the bird is a scene from Chinese mythology, with Oriental angels riding through the clouds on peacocks.

If all this sounds like a circus wagon, blame not me, but the last hundred generations of Chinese junk-builders—for the most careful research proved that this style, and none other, is proper for the Ningpo type of junk which we have built for our voyage. And far from fearing to appear super-gaudy, we only hope that some of the paint will stick until we reach San Francisco.

However, the paint job isn't our greatest worry. Nor, paradoxically, are the long weeks we must spend out of sight of land. The most perilous part of our cruise will probably come on the first two or three days. With the Chinese coast-guard driven to cover by the war, pirates swarm in the waters around Hongkong and all through the China Seas. Not a day has passed, during recent months, but the local papers have reported at least one pirate attack on a junk—with an uncomfortable amount of gunfire, robbery and death. In Hongkong's courts, piracy trials are as frequent as cases of opium-smuggling, child-slave holding, and overtime parking. With our two tons of food aboard, our radio, engine, sails, gear, and possibilities of being ransomed, we would be a rich prize for the sea bandits—and we take it for granted that they will know the hour we set sail.

In anticipation of attack, we have armed the junk with plenty of rifles and shotguns. However, if we find we can't outfight them (for they frequently attack a hundred-strong) we can turn on the engine—and run ingloriously to safety.

We'll be twelve aboard, all American: the captain, engineer, radioman, seven seamen including myself, a cook and a cabinboy.

And because one solitary mascot would make the total thirteen, which superstitious seamen regard with horror, we're taking along *two* mascots—a pair of white Chinese kittens. This means that the *Sea Dragon* will be responsible for twelve souls and (counting the cats) thirty lives.

Our first objective will be the wreck of the *S. S. President Hoover,* off the east coast of Formosa; Keelung, the port at Formosa's northern tip, our first port of call.

CHAPTER XXI

THE SEA DRAGON—HAIL AND FAREWELL!

[*Hongkong—January 23, 1939.*] I know how concerned you've been, not knowing what was happening to me. But, in not hearing, you were sure I was just being delayed, not in trouble. The delays *have* been exasperating, but justified. We have a perfectly gorgeous ship. You can't tell how beautiful it is from a black and white picture. The colors are everything. We've had our shake-down cruise, and found defects that had to be corrected. The *Sea Dragon* sails slowly, we're so deep in the water, but the motor runs like a dream. We were all very clumsy with the sails and tiller on the cruise, and *very* seasick, but these things were to be expected. Our ship rides the waves perfectly, and we've lost the last vestige of uneasiness we may have had about her seaworthiness.

We have her alongside the main dock now, for final touches, and we have to have guards to stand by to control the mobs of people who want to come aboard. The ship has tremendous box-office appeal. I predict we'll have thousands of people aboard in San Francisco.

So be happy, and proud of the expedition, and don't worry one minute about any danger. We have a splendid radio (as you'll soon learn), and a fine crew, and a big medicine case, and lots of food, and 2000 gallons of oil and 2000 of water. The storms will probably be unpleasant, but will only delay our arrival. We hope now to get in the end of April, though it may be sooner.

This last-minute strain is pretty fierce, but I'm so excited and absorbed I don't mind. We're having our clashes and quarrels, but they, too, will pass.

His newspaper article supplied further details:

Our trial trip took place a week ago. We decided, before heading for San Francisco, to give our ship a taste of the rough weather which is ahead of us, most of the way home. We needed to test our auxiliary engine, along with the crew and the sails. We knew that an engine (however small) in a junk was something of an experiment which might or might not work.

So we were all rather surprised and pleased when it started, and chugged merrily away.

Using the engine only, we moved out of Hongkong's spectacular, mountain-bound harbor. As soon as we reached the open sea, Captain Welch's big moment came. Our brilliant orange foresail was raised, the engine killed. Then the huge white mainsail was lifted by five men at the capstan; and finally the little scarlet mizzen was stretched aloft. The rainbow canvas caught the wind. The *Sea Dragon,* shining with its fresh red and white paint, responded. Slanting in the breeze, tilting over the waves, with her dragon flags flying against the blue sky, she was proving herself at last.

The wind was brisk that day, as we had hoped it would be. The waves, compared with our little ship, were mountainous. Gayly the debutante *Sea Dragon* climbed up and down the water, leaning before the wind until her rails were almost buried. The deck slanted and heaved. And our guests, the Chinese, very soon began to regret their excursion. Building a junk was grief enough, said Mr. Fat Kau afterward, but sailing in one . . . never again!

His third wife, who accompanied him, succumbed soonest. Wrapping her head in her shawl, she moaned and groaned. Then the painters and the carpenters and the Chinese pilot's son followed suit. This youngster, a child of twelve, baffled us all by being acutely seasick without once varying his cheerful grin. Our cabinboy went below to die in his bunk, after thirty minutes on the bounding main. And I—the world's worst sailor—lay prone on the deck, praying for a wreck, a pirate attack, or for Doomsday, for anything, in fact, that would end this oscillation. During this crescendo of distress, George Barstow, our accordionist, went around with his movie camera, taking movies of the rest of us as we hung over the rail. We could gladly have killed him, only we didn't have the strength.

Meanwhile the ship was being subjected to every possible strain. Captain Welch put her through her paces violently. The rigging creaked, the timbers groaned. But the ship responded sensitively to the rudder, and though she was slower than we hoped, she sailed well. Our greenest hands managed to hold her to her course. The deck wasn't even wetted with spray, so well she rode the swells.

As we pitched and rolled, Captain Welch and Engineer von Fehren noted every weak point in the junk. On our return they estimated it would take at least seven days to recalk some of the seams, and refit some of the equipment. Minor details, but they might prove of vital importance when we were well at sea.

Now the *Sea Dragon* is ready for her voyage.

Ready, indeed, she seemed. But nature and human nature intervened.

February 4, 1939

RADIO

JUNK SEA DRAGON VIA SAN FRANCISCO

HAVE SAILED NEXT PORT KEELUNG FORMOSA ALLS WELL HIGH SPIRITS LOVE

February 9, 1939

RADIO

JUNK SEA DRAGON VIA SAN FRANCISCO

POTTER VERY ILL THREE DAYS OUT FORCED RETURN HONGKONG JUNK OKAY SAILING AGAIN SOON

[*Hongkong—February 10, 1939.*] The inclosed clipping tells the story. After my two radios to you, we found our way safely back to Hongkong, and went into drydock to add a fin-keel to keep us from rolling and rocking in heavy seas. The six days at sea were tough but good sport. We had storms five out of the six days. The ship held together, the engine works perfectly, and we'll be starting again in a week. Potter is in the hospital with a rupture, and cannot continue. Torrey had appendicitis and is out. Mooney fell down the hatch and broke his ankle. So I am gathering professionals to replace them, and when I start again we'll have two or three real seamen who know what to do. I stood watch with the others through rain and storm, and think I'm going to enjoy the big trip. These delays will put us in San Francisco the end of *May,* now. But by then the winter storms will be over, and our passage easier. The delay has been exasperating, but I'm sure will add to our security, and to our ultimate success. I'm tired and impatient, of course, but in no way downhearted. Don't you be.

His last Bell article "tells the story" much better than the clipping he inclosed from a Hongkong paper:

Hongkong in its hundred years of history has seen many a ship come and go. But few ships in this great port have ever caused as much commotion as the departure for America, on Saturday last, of the Chinese junk *Sea Dragon.* As a member of the crew I was too busy at the tiller to realize what a farewell we were getting. Half the town, it seems, crowded onto the docks to wave goodbye.

After weeks of discouraging delays and false starts, our junk was ready, definitely and at last, for its great adventure. Two thousand gallons of fresh water were aboard, enough oil to fuel our auxiliary engine for ten days, and a three months' supply of food for twelve men.

We had three new men. Ben Flagg, a recent graduate of Bowdoin College, had been a crew-member aboard the *President Pierce.* When he missed his ship in Hongkong, and we found him on the beach, we practically shanghaied him aboard our junk.

Richard Davis, a young American engineer employed here, offered us his services if we would give him a ride as far as Honolulu. We agreed.

Shortly before we left, a seventeen-year-old youth, obviously part Portuguese, applied for the job of messboy. I asked this dark-skinned Latin whether his name was Miguel or Manuel. He said it was Patrick Kelly. The boy had been born in Canton of an American father and a Portuguese mother. He had an American passport, but had never seen America. Now was his chance.

Warning him of the terrors ahead, we invited Pat to join us. When we sailed, the entire Portuguese colony, several hundred strong, came to the dock to bid the messboy bon voyage.

Captain Welch, Engineer von Fehren, Seamen Chase, Potter, and Barstow, Radioman Petrich, Cook Sligh, two Siamese kittens, two Chow puppies, and I, completed the crew.

Occupying the other half of the wharf, on the day we sailed, towered the *President Coolidge,* the biggest American liner on the Pacific. She was sailing too, and her crew and passengers joined in the chorus of goodbyes. Two airplanes flew overhead. Firecrackers popped from our masthead. The sun shone with unusual ardor on our lacquered hull and painted stern. Our new American flag stood out handsomely in the breeze. We could not have asked for a more glorious—or noisier—departure.

Down toward the harbor entrance we went, our orange foresail set, engine chugging. This was the day I had waited for and worked for, these many months. The discouragements, the quarrels, the despair that had hung over us for the long period of ship-building and outfitting vanished. In the battle with bills and Chinese procrastination, the words romance and adventure had faded from our vocabularies. But now, in one exhilarating moment, these words came back again.

We turned up the coast of China, as the Peak above Hongkong faded behind us, as a warm twilight came, as a huge moon rose out of the sea. The northeast monsoon, which, on nine days out of ten at this season would have been blowing a gale against us, had faded to a pleasant starboard breeze. This breeze our foresail caught and it drove us steadily up the channel between China and Formosa.

Midnight came; the watch changed. But nobody, not even the Siamese kittens, would go to bed—not in this tropical night—not on this still and shining ocean.

The *Sea Dragon,* as we wanted it to be, as we had labored hard to make it, had turned into a fantasy of a ship, a picture of a dream-junk from some ancient Chinese painting, a poetry-ship devoid of weight and substance, gliding with bright-hued sails across a silver ocean to a magic land.

Where were the Japanese? Where were the pirates? We were ready to meet both. In my brief-case were letters of introduction to any Japanese naval officers who might stop us. Also we had American flags painted on either side of our hull. In our arsenal were enough shotguns to frighten off whole armadas of pirates.

All night long, traveling this main steamship lane between Shanghai and Hongkong, we were in sight of ships. Our radio kept buzzing away greeting liners and battleships and freighters, but no Japanese destroyers chanced by.

All night long, we sailed through fleet after fleet of fishing junks. We were astonished to see them. Three months previously, steaming south aboard a passenger ship, we had not encountered a single junk along the entire coast. Japanese warcraft were then sinking every junk that left the shore. Apparently this murderous campaign had relaxed. . . . The fishing junks were out again, by the score, by the hundred, with their bat-winged sails silhouetted against the shining waves.

Time and again their path crossed ours. Their crews, startled by the bright spectacle of the *Sea Dragon,* seemed unable to believe their eyes—a junk like theirs in shape, but far bigger, and with colored sails, and red hull, and golden dragons crawling up the poop. These fishermen had had no warning—nobody had told them—they just looked up, and there in the moonlight appeared a beautiful vision of a junk.

One entire fleet of fishers crept close to stare, to exclaim, to shout at us and find out if we were real.

Proudly we shouted back—the captain adding a few oaths as he gesticulated to the blankety-blank visitors to get the blankety-blank out of our path.

When dawn came we were a hundred miles from Hongkong, a hundred miles in fourteen hours—an average of better than six knots. I began to calculate our date of arrival in San Francisco . . . 170 miles a day . . . 1190 miles a week . . . 8000 miles in less than seven weeks. . . . We'd be home by the end of March!

This blissful dream-voyage, obviously, could not last. And we were awakened from it by a blast right between the eyes. At noon on the second day, with incredible suddenness, the sun departed, black clouds raced overhead, the wind swept down, the waves rose. We were heading into a storm.

Pitching and rolling, our decks awash, we held to our course. And junks we saw now were hidden, half the time, behind the waves. One wave pitched us forward so violently that the radio aerial, atop the mizzenmast, was torn from its lashings, leaving the wire to thrash about in the wind.

In a bosun's chair Ben Flagg was lifted aloft. Clinging to the gyrating mast he nailed the aerial in place again.

Everything not fastened down began to be flung about the ship. Cook Sligh was having a frantic time with his pots and pans. Patrick Kelly lay in his bunk, half-dead from seasickness. No cooking—no messboy. Seizing the rail with one hand we fed ourselves apples and dry bread with the other.

In this crisis, we turned on our auxiliary engine full force. The engine-room hatch had to be closed because of the weather, and the fumes from the newly painted tanks and bulkheads, escaping into the main cabin, were almost overpowering.

Potter, our first mate and the most experienced sailor aboard, in struggling with the mainsail boom ruptured himself. We put him to bed, and watched anxiously to see if "rest" would cure him. (Rest, at this point, was about as possible as it would have been on a roller-coaster.)

At six o'clock on the second afternoon we caught sight of a lighthouse on the China coast. At six o'clock next morning the same lighthouse was still in the same place. We had not gained an inch.

Captain Welch decided to change his course, head southeast, and try to sail around the southern tip of Formosa instead of the northern.

With the wind now on our beam, we moved forward again, and on the third day made another hundred miles, despite mountainous seas and howling winds.

In this rough weather we soon found that our steering system was not the best. Junks do not have steering wheels, but rather clumsy tillers manipulated by block and tackle. In calm seas, with a steady wind, one man can handle this apparatus; but when the waves run high and subject the ship to violent motion, it takes two men to hold the course.

Our tiller and compass were on the afterdeck, exposed to wind and weather. The steersmen got the full force of spray and rain.

With the storm came such downpours that we had to wear our oil-skins every waking hour. Unfortunately they had been made in China, so that before long the oil washed off and the rain seeped through. At best, with a full crew, these discomforts would have made us miserable enough. But with Potter prostrate in his bunk in the forward cabin, and Mooney able only to act as lookout, we were short two hands at the tiller. Consequently Flagg, Barstow, Chase and I had to stand watch at the tiller, four hours on, four hours off, day and night, in pairs.

However, nothing seemed able, really, to discourage us. We knew what we were in for, when we set out to cross the Pacific in a junk. We also knew that just as our first idyllic day had run its course and passed—so would this cursed storm. Then the sea and wind would calm down, and we'd soon forget how miserable we'd been.

The southern tip of Formosa was now only fifty miles away. (Welch estimated we were 300 miles east of Hongkong.) Once we were around Formosa we'd have a northerly current which would increase our speed two knots. In a few hours more we'd be out of trouble.

All this time Potter had been suffering torments. A high fever had come upon him. For two days and nights he was unable to take food or water. Obviously he was not getting better, but much worse.

Welch and I held a council. The next possible port was Keelung, 300 miles away, at Formosa's northern tip. We might try to take Potter to Keelung, but there was no guarantee we could make it. If not, the next port of call was Midway Island, 4,000 miles beyond.

For half an hour we suffered from an anguish of indecision. Should we push on and hope to make Keelung, or should we take no chances, and retreat to Hongkong?

One more look at Potter's flushed face and fevered eyes, and we voted to turn around. A life—and a very fine life—might be at stake.

So we swung the tiller with a mighty swing, spun the ship about, and set our course back to China.

On the late afternoon of the sixth day, bearded, exhausted and dejected, we caught sight, far in the distance, of the mountains rising behind Hongkong. In the darkness we crept through the treacherous confusion of reefs and islands that surround the harbor, and found our way to the old familiar dock. We were glad it was midnight, and that no one was on hand to see our ignominious return.

Before going ashore I glanced at our good-luck god, still sitting and smiling in his little temple.

I decided it was a fake and a hoax.

An ambulance rushed Potter off to the hospital. The doctors assured him he could be mended without an operation. But they simply would not consider allowing him to sail with the *Sea Dragon* again.

Patrick Kelly has resigned. Five days of seasickness cured the poor fellow of his hunger for adventure. We'll have a Chinese messboy instead.

Our junk, taking advantage of its return to port, is in drydock. We are adding a fin-keel to the bottom of the ship. Few junks have fin-keels, but few junks plan to tempt the Pacific Ocean. This keel will give us needed stability, and allow us to carry more canvas with less rolling.

We need more men in order to assure our ship three watches. If Americans cannot be found by the time we are ready to leave again, we'll take Chinese sailors.

Next time—in about another week—we plan to slip away as quietly as possible, and head east, again around the southern end of Formosa—and straight on to Midway.

When I send my next dispatch, from there, I hope it will contain the story of a few good storms, but no report of further mishaps to ship or crew.

P.S.—I forgot to say that on our shake-down cruise the Siamese kittens were very seasick, and have asked to be left behind. But the black Chow puppies turned out to be excellent sailors, and seemed as distressed at our retreat to Hongkong as we were ourselves.

[*Hongkong—February 23, 1939.*] Your cable, asking for some sign of life from me, came yesterday. I'll answer it in a day or two from the junk radio.

We've had more ghastly delays, but they seem nearly over and in two days more we expect to sail again. We've been here two weeks

See radio for where to write me next.

March 3 – 1939.

Mother & Dad –

One more – one last – good-bye letter. We sail, again, in a few hours – far more sea-worthy than before. The delay has been heart-breaking, but worth it in added safety. Our crew is far more expert now. We have 2 good sail-men – and four Chinese – (one mess boy + 3 Chinese sailors). These four are old hands at junk-sailing, + will be invaluable. I'll ship 2 of them back from Honolulu. All our leaks have been plugged, + the hull tarred. Our fin-keel will keep us from rolling – so we'll be dry, comfortable, + even keeled. I'm sorry we have to leave Potter + Torrey

Richard Halliburton's last letter.

behind in the hospital. We have food & water for 3 months, & oil for 20 days remaining. So we soon are so prepared as its possible to be. My spirits have sprung back again, now that mio getting away from Hong Kong and its troubles. I'm going to enjoy the trip, & be happy the you to such effort to make it. Am in perfect health if somewhat weary. Wilford would writes me there a big barge anchored in the Lowell. ships basin as the Fair & aid a big ship "Reward anchored to Hoehlnton Sea dragon". So we must hurry & get there.

I had your two cables. Each day I planned tve gone in the finder where I cord radio you for 10 of a week instead of #1 a word cable. I am anxious my letter cd be in your hands soon. But your second cable was good news.

Of course, with all this delay, there is bickering & feuds among the crew. But this will soon pass. And there will be no need of our deviating from our course straight to Midway. You must begin to plan now to meet me end of May in San Francisco —

The last month's sail will be in the spring, & will be doubly pleasant had not been pressed for money, though I have used up the reserve I had in the Bank of America in San Francisco. This all goes into capital stock, & will be made back with profit at the Fair.

It's been a good - + bad 4 months here in Hong Kong worried, but intensely busy building something. I still think I have a swell idea, + that everything is coming out as I dreamed. But, oh - will I be glad to get home + unload all these burdens + & quarreling reasons.

So good bye again - des radio you every few days, so you can enjoy + follow the voyage with me. Rick & it as wonderful food, + not so something besides + foolish. I embrace you all - + will give my sweet Prosha an extra hug on her birthday. You know how much I love you —

R.

since our return. The fin-keel was put on. Then came four days of Chinese New Year holiday; everything was closed and not a coolie to be got. Now we are hiring four Chinese sailors. Today is Thursday. On Sunday, surely, we depart again, and there will be no turning back. I've hired a professional mate, an assistant engineer, and two white sailors and four Chinese. This way we're in good, capable hands. Von Fehren has emerged the faithful friend, capable, serene, dependable. The weather is moderating, and now we'll have March, April, May for our crossing—better than January, February, March. Of course, I'm tired and harassed, but not seriously, and even this will pass once we sail again. With our professional crew we may cut down the sailing time two or three weeks. I've delivered four of the seven letters to school children and seven syndicate stories.

Your cable, "all's well," was a great relief. I'll radio you often. Don't worry—the trouble is nearly over.

I'll radio you where
to write me next.

March 3, 1939.

Mother and Dad:—

One more—one last—goodbye letter. We sail, again, in a few hours—far more seaworthy than before. The delay has been heartbreaking, but worth it in added safety. Our crew is far more expert now. We have two good *sail*-men—and four Chinese—(one messboy and three Chinese sailors). Those four are old hands at junk-sailing, and will be invaluable. I'll ship two of them back from Honolulu. All our leaks have been plugged, and the hull tarred. Our fin-keel will keep us from rolling—so we'll be dry, comfortable and even-keeled. I'm sorry we have to leave Potter and Torrey behind in the hospital.

We have food and water for three months, and oil for twenty days' running. So we seem to be as prepared as it's possible to be. My spirits have sprung back again, now that we're getting away from Hongkong and its troubles. I'm going to enjoy the trip, and be happy. I've gone to such effort to make it. I'm in perfect health—if somewhat weary. Wilfred Crowell writes me there's a big barge anchored in the small-ships' basin at the Fair and on it a big sign,

"Reserved anchorage for Halliburton's *Sea Dragon*." So we must hurry and get there. I had your two cables. Each day I planned to be gone on the junk where I could radio you for ten cents a word instead of a dollar a word cable. I also knew my letter would be in your hands soon. But your second cable was good news.

Of course, with all this delay, there are bickering and feuds among the crew. But this will soon pass. And there will be no need of our deviating from our course straight to Midway. You must begin to plan now to meet me the end of May in San Francisco.

The last month's sail will be in the spring, and will be doubly pleasant. I've been pressed for money, though I have used up the reserve I had in the Bank of America in San Francisco. This all goes into capital stock, and will be made back with profit at the Fair.

It's been a good—and bad—four months here in Hongkong—worried, but intensely busy building something. I still think I have a swell idea, and that everything is coming out as I dreamed. But, *oh,* won't I be glad to get home and unload all these burdens and quarreling seamen!

So goodbye again. I'll radio you every few days, so you can enjoy and follow the voyage with me. Think of it as wonderful sport, and not as something hazardous and foolish. I embrace you all and will give my sweet mother an extra hug on her birthday. You know how much I love you.

R.

March 5, 1939

RADIO

JUNK SEA DRAGON VIA SAN FRANCISCO
SAILED AGAIN TODAY SOUNDER SHIP BETTER CREW FINE WEATHER RADIO
SEADRAGON SANFRANCISCO POSTAL TELEGRAPH HURRYING HOME LOVE

March 13, 1939

RADIO

JUNK SEA DRAGON VIA SAN FRANCISCO
1200 MILES AT SEA ALLS WELL

March 19, 1939

RADIO

JUNK SEA DRAGON VIA SAN FRANCISCO
HALFWAY MIDWAY ARRIVING THERE APRIL FIFTH SKIPPING HONOLULU
WRITE CARE PANAMERICAN MIDWAY AIRMAIL LOVE

March 24, 1939

RADIO

CAPTAIN JOHN WELCH OF THE SEADRAGON TO LINER PRESIDENT COOLIDGE
SOUTHERLY GALES RAIN SQUALLS LEE RAIL UNDER WATER WET BUNKS
HARDTACK BULLY BEEF HAVING WONDERFUL TIME WISH YOU WERE HERE
INSTEAD OF ME

The rest is silence.